LANGUAGE AND
SILENCE

GEORGE STEINER

LANGUAGE AND SILENCE

Essays on Language, Literature, and the Inhuman

ATHENEUM NEW YORK

1982

Thanks and acknowledgments are due to the editors and publishers of the following periodicals and books in which parts of this book first appeared: CARMEN, COLOMBA AND SELECTED STORIES by Prosper Mérimée (New American Library, New York, 1963); COMMENTARY; CONFESSIONS OF FELIX KRULL by Thomas Mann, (New American Library, New York, 1963); ENCOUNTER; ERNST BLOCH ZU EHREN (Suhrkamp Verlag, Frankfurt, 1965); FESTSCHRIFT ZUM ACHTZIGSTEN GEBURTSTAG VON GEORG LUKÁCS (Hermann Luchterhand Verlag, Neuwied and Berlin, 1965); HOMER: TWENTIETH-CENTURY VIEWS (Prentice-Hall, Englewood Cliffs, N.J., 1962); THE KENYON REVIEW; THE LISTENER; THE NEW YORK TIMES BOOK REVIEW; PROBLEMS OF COMMUNISM; THE REPORTER; THE TIMES LITERARY SUPPLEMENT; THE YALE REVIEW

For Churchill College, Cambridge,
where much of the work was done

PREFACE

P rimarily, this is a book about language: about language and politics, language and the future of literature, about the pressures on language of totalitarian lies and cultural decay, about language and other codes of meaning (music, translation, mathematics), about language and silence.

The essays and articles in this collection were written at different times. In most cases they are a response to a specific occasion: the publication of a book, the production of a play or opera, a political event. But their underlying theme is the life of language and of some of the complex energies of the word in our society and culture. What are the relations of language to the murderous falsehoods it has been made to articulate and hallow in certain totalitarian regimes? Or to the great load of vulgarity, imprecision, and greed it is charged with in a mass-consumer democracy? How will language, in the traditional sense of a general idiom of effective relations, react to the increasingly urgent, comprehensive claims of more exact speech such as mathematics and symbolic notation? Are we passing out of an historical era of verbal primacy—out of the classic period of literate expression— into a phase of decayed language, of "post-linguistic" forms, and perhaps of partial silence? These are the questions I try to raise, to get into focus.

Behind them lies the belief that literary criticism, particularly in its present cohabitation with the academic, is no longer a very interesting or responsible exercise. Too much of it exhibits the complacencies of academic or journalistic values and habits of statement developed in the nineteenth century. Books about books and that flourishing though more recent *genre*, books about literary criticism (a threefold remove), will no doubt continue to pour out in great numbers. But it is becoming clear that most of them are a kind of initiate sport, that they have very little to say to those who would ask what coexistence and interaction are possible beween humanism, between the idea of literate communication, and the present shapes of history. The gap between the academic, belle-lettristic treatment of literature and the possible meanings or subversions of literature in our actual lives has rarely been wider since Kierkegaard first pointed to its ironic breadth.

The most vital of modern criticism, that of Georg Lukács, of Walter Benjamin, of Edmund Wilson, of F. R. Leavis, knows this to be the case. In his own style of vision each of these critics has made of literary judgment a critique of society, a utopian or empirical comparison of fact and possibility in human action. But even their achievements, and much in the following pages is obviously indebted to them, are beginning to seem dated. They arose from a contract of literacy which is now in doubt.

The novelty or special nature of our present position of consciousness is the second main theme of this book. I realize that historians are right when they say that barbarism and political savagery are endemic in human affairs, that no age has been innocent of disaster. I know that the colonial massacres of the nineteenth and twentieth centuries, and the cynical destruction of natural and animal resources which accompany them (the extermination of fauna being perhaps the logical and symbolic epilogue to that of native populations) are realities of profound evil. But I think there is hypocrisy in the imagination that would claim universal immediacy, that would seek impartial appropriation throughout the provocations of all history and all places. My own consciousness is possessed by the eruption of barbarism in modern Europe; by the mass murder of the Jews and by the destruction under Nazism and Stalinism of what I try to define in some of these essays as the particular genius of "Central European humanism." I do not claim for this hideousness any singular privilege; but this is the crisis of rational, humane expectation which has shaped my own life and with which I am most directly concerned.

The blackness of it did not spring up in the Gobi Desert or the rain forests of the Amazon. It rose from within, and from the core of European civilization. The cry of the murdered sounded in earshot of the universities; the sadism went on a street away from the theaters and museums. In the later eighteenth century Voltaire had looked confidently to the end of torture; ideological massacre was to be a banished shadow. In our own day the high places of literacy, of philosophy, of artistic expression, became the setting for Belsen.

I cannot accept the facile comfort that this catastrophe was a purely German phenomenon or some calamitous mishap rooted in the persona of one or another totalitarian ruler. Ten years after the Gestapo quit Paris, the countrymen of Voltaire were torturing Algerians and each other in some of the same police cellars. The house of classic humanism, the dream of reason which animated Western society, have largely broken down. Ideas of cultural development, of inherent rationality held since ancient Greece and still intensely valid in the utopian historicism of Marx and stoic authoritarianism of Freud (both of them late outriders of Greco-Roman civilization) can no longer be asserted with much confidence. The reach of technological man, as a being susceptible to the controls of political hatred and sadistic suggestion, has lengthened formidably toward destruction.

To think of literature, of education, of language, as if nothing very important had happened to challenge our very concept of these activities seems to me unrealistic. To read Aeschylus or Shakespeare —let alone to "teach" them—as if the texts, as if the authority of the texts in our own lives, were immune from recent history, is subtle but corrosive illiteracy. This does not mean any indiscriminate or journalistic test of "present relevance"; it means that one tries to take seriously the complex miracle of the survivance of great art, of what answer we can give to it from our own being.

We come after. We know now that a man can read Goethe or Rilke in the evening, that he can play Bach and Schubert, and go to his day's work at Auschwitz in the morning. To say that he has read them without understanding or that his ear is gross, is cant. In what way does this knowledge bear on literature and society, on the hope, grown almost axiomatic from the time of Plato to that of Matthew Arnold, that culture is a humanizing force, that the energies of spirit are transferable to those of conduct? Moreover, it is not only the case that the established media of civilization—the universities, the arts, the book world—failed to offer adequate resistance to political bestiality; they often rose to welcome it and to give it ceremony and apologia. Why? What are the links, as yet scarcely understood, between the mental, psychological habits of high literacy and the temptations of the inhuman? Does some great boredom and surfeit of abstraction grow up inside literate civilization preparing it for the release of barbarism? Many of these notes and essays try to find ways of asking the question more fully and precisely.

In method and scope I am aiming at something different from literary criticism. Knowing well where these essays fall short, I nevertheless want them to suggest the goal of a "philosophy of language." To arrive at such a philosophy should be the next step if we wish to come nearer an understanding of the particular inheritance and partial desolation of our culture, of that which has undermined and that which may restore the resources of insight in modern society. A philosophy of language, as Leibniz and Herder understood the term, will turn to the study of literature with especial intensity; but it will think of literature as inevitably implicated in the larger structures of semantic, formal, symbolic communication. It will think of philosophy, as Wittgenstein has taught it to do, as language in a condition of supreme scruple, the word refusing to take itself for granted. It will look to anthropology for sustaining or correcting evidence of other literacies and structures of significance (how else are we to "step back" from the illusory obviousness of our own particular focus?). A philosophy of language will respond with wary fascination to the suppositions of modern linguistics. It is in linguistics that much of the intelligence once active in literary criticism and history is now concentrated. That literature and linguistics are close-bound has long been known to the poets. As Roman Jakobson says: "The poetic resources concealed in the morphological and syntactic structure of language, briefly the poetry of grammar, and its literary product, the grammar of poetry, have been seldom known to critics and mostly disregarded by linguists but skillfully mastered by creative writers." A philosophy of language would seek to get the relations right.

In short, it would return with that radical wonder habitually absent from literary criticism and the academic study of literature, to the fact that language is the defining mystery of man, that in it his identity and historical presence are uniquely explicit. It is language that severs man from the deterministic signal codes, from the inarticulacies, from the silences that inhabit the greater part of being. If silence were to come again to a ruined civilization, it would be a twofold silence, loud and desperate with the remembrance of the Word.

It is as provisional markers toward a philosophy of language that several of the main essays in this book are intended.

Present in this collection, though not dealt with specifically, are the work and example of Hermann Broch. Broch is one of the principal novelists and masters of feeling of our age. Where I ask about the continued validity of language, about the authority of silence in the face of the inhuman, where I try to understand how poetics border on music and mathematics, I am often developing hints from Broch's fictions and philosophic writings. Broch's life and works are of themselves an exemplary form of civilization, a refusal of cheapness and chaos.

Details of expression have been altered in pieces which first appeared in periodicals or as prefaces. I have tried to correct errors and make references more comprehensive. But in only one case (the close of the article on Lawrence Durrell) is there a substantive change. Twice-baked opinions taste stale. I have added a number of footnotes to qualify or update the original argument; they are set in brackets.

My warm thanks go to Peter du Sautoy of Faber and Faber and to Michael Bessie of Atheneum; their criticism and encouragement have been invaluable in giving this book its present shape.

G.S.

New York
September, 1966

CONTENTS

HUMANE LITERACY

LANGUAGE OUT OF DARKNESS

CLASSICS

MASTERS

FICTIONS AND THE PRESENT

MARXISM AND LITERATURE

HUMANE LITERACY

HUMANE LITERACY

When he looks back, the critic sees a eunuch's shadow. Who would be a critic if he could be a writer? Who would hammer out the subtlest insight into Dostoevsky if he could weld an inch of the Karamazovs, or argue the poise of Lawrence if he could shape the free gust of life in *The Rainbow*? All great writing springs from *le dur désir de durer*, the harsh contrivance of spirit against death, the hope to overreach time by force of creation. "Brightness falls from the air": five words and a trick of darkening sound. But they have outworn three centuries. Who would choose to be a literary critic if he could set verse to sing, or compose, out of his own mortal being, a vital fiction, a character that will endure? Most men have their dusty survivance in old telephone directories (it is a mercy that these are kept at the British Museum); there is in the literal fact of their existence less of life's truth and harvest than in Falstaff or Madame de Guermantes. To have imagined these.

The critic lives at second hand. He writes *about*. The poem, the novel, or the play must be given to him; criticism exists by the grace of other men's genius. By virtue of style, criticism can itself become literature. But usually this occurs only when the writer is acting as critic of his own work or as outrider to his own poetics, when the criticism of Coleridge is work in progress or that of T. S. Eliot propaganda. Is there anyone but Sainte-Beuve who belongs to literature purely as a critic? It is not criticism that makes the language live.

These are simple truths (and the honest critic says them to himself in the gray of morning). But we are in danger of forgetting them, because the present time is peculiarly charged with autonomous critical energy and prestige. Critical journals pour out a deluge of commentary or exegesis; in America there are schools of criticism. The critic exists as a persona in his own right; his persuasions and quarrels have a public role. Critics write about critics, and the bright young man, instead of regarding criticism as defeat, as a gradual, bleak coming to terms with the ash and grit of one's limited talent, thinks of it as a career of high note. This would merely be funny; but it has a corrosive effect. As never before, the student and the person interested in the current of literature reads reviews and critiques of books rather than the books themselves, or before he has made the effort of personal judgment. Dr. Leavis' statement of the maturity and intelligence of George Eliot is part of the common coin of present feeling. How many of those who can echo it have actually read *Felix Holt* or *Daniel Deronda?* Mr. Eliot's essay on Dante is a commonplace in literary education; the *Commedia* is known, if at all, in a few brief excerpts (*Inferno* XXVI or Ugolino famished). The true critic is servant to the poet; today he is acting as master, or being taken as such. He omits Zarathustra's last, most vital lesson: "now, do without me."

Precisely one hundred years ago, Matthew Arnold saw a similar breadth and salience of critical impulse. He recognized that this impulse was secondary to that of the writer, that the joy and importance of creation were of a radically higher order. But he regarded the period of critical bustle as a necessary prelude to a new poetic age. We come *after*, and that is the nerve of our condition. After the unprecedented ruin of humane values and hopes by the political bestiality of our age.

That ruin is the starting point of any serious thought about literature and the place of literature in society. Literature deals essentially and continually with the image of man, with the shape and motive of human conduct. We cannot act now, be it as critics or merely as rational beings, as if nothing of vital relevance had happened to our sense of the human possibility, as if the extermination by hunger or violence of some seventy million men, women, and children in Europe and Russia between 1914 and 1945 had not altered, profoundly, the quality of our awareness. We cannot pretend that Belsen is irrelevant to the responsible life of the imagination. What man has inflicted on man, in very recent time, has affected the writer's primary material—the sum and potential of human behavior —and it presses on the brain with a new darkness.

Moreover, it puts in question the primary concepts of a literary,

4

humanistic culture. The ultimate of political barbarism grew from the core of Europe. Two centuries after Voltaire had proclaimed its end, torture again became a normal process of political action. Not only did the general dissemination of literary, cultural values prove no barrier to totalitarianism; but in notable instances the high places of humanistic learning and art actually welcomed and aided the new terror. Barbarism prevailed on the very ground of Christian humanism, of Renaissance culture and classic rationalism. We know that some of the men who devised and administered Auschwitz had been taught to read Shakespeare or Goethe, and continued to do so.

This is of obvious and appalling relevance to the study or teaching of literature. It compels us to ask whether knowledge of the best that has been thought and said does, as Matthew Arnold asserted, broaden and refine the resources of the human spirit. It forces us to wonder whether what Dr. Leavis has called "the central humanity" does, in fact, educate toward humane action, or whether there is not between the tenor of moral intelligence developed in the study of literature and that required in social and political choice a wide gap or contrariety. The latter possibility is particularly disturbing. There is some evidence that a trained, persistent commitment to the life of the printed word, a capacity to identify deeply and critically with imaginary personages or sentiments, diminishes the immediacy, the hard edge of actual circumstance. We come to respond more acutely to the literary sorrow than to the misery next door. Here also recent times give harsh evidence. Men who wept at *Werther* or Chopin moved, unrealizing, through literal hell.

This means that whoever teaches or interprets literature—and both are exercises seeking to build for the writer a body of living, discerning response—must ask of himself what he is about (to tutor, to guide someone through *Lear* or the *Oresteia* is to take into one's hand the springs of his being). Assumptions regarding the value of literate culture to the moral perception of the individual and society were self-evident to Johnson, Coleridge, and Arnold. They are now in doubt. We must countenance the possibility that the study and transmission of literature may be of only marginal significance, a passionate luxury like the preservation of the antique. Or, at worst, that it may detract from more urgent and responsible uses of time and energy of spirit. I do not believe either to be true. But the question must be asked and explored without cant. Nothing is more worrying regarding the present state of English studies in the universities than the fact that such inquiry should be deemed bizarre or subversive. It is of the essence.

This is where the claim of the natural sciences derives its force. Pointing to their criteria of empirical verification and to their tradition of collaborative achievement (in contrast to the apparent idiosyncrasy and egotism of literary argument), scientists have been tempted to assert that their own methods and vision are now at the center of civilization, that the ancient primacy of poetic statement and metaphysical image is over. And though the evidence is uncertain, it does seem likely that of the aggregate of available talent, many, and many of the best, have turned to the sciences. In the *quattrocento* one would have wished to know the painters; today, the sense of inspired joy, of the mind in free, unshadowed play, is with the physicists, the biochemists, and the mathematicians.

But we must not be deceived. The sciences will enrich language and the resources of feeling (as Thomas Mann showed in *Felix Krull*, it is from astrophysics and microbiology that we may reap our future myths, the terms of our metaphors). The sciences will recast our surroundings and the context of leisure or subsistence in which culture is viable. But though they are of inexhaustible fascination and frequent beauty, the natural and mathematical sciences are only rarely of ultimate interest. I mean that they have added little to our knowledge or governance of human possibility, that there is demonstrably more of insight into the matter of man in Homer, Shakespeare, or Dostoevsky than in the entirety of neurology or statistics. No discovery of genetics impairs or surpasses what Proust knew of the spell or burden of lineage; each time Othello reminds us of the rust of dew on the bright blade we experience more of the sensual, transient reality in which our lives must pass than it is the business or ambition of physics to impart. No sociometry of political motive or tactics outweighs Stendhal.

And it is precisely the "objectivity," the moral neutrality in which the sciences rejoice and attain their brilliant community of effort, that bar them from final relevance. Science may have given tools and insane pretenses of rationality to those who devised mass murder. It tells us scarcely anything of their motives, a topic on which Aeschylus or Dante would be worth hearing. Nor, to judge by the naïve political statements put forward by our present alchemists, can it do much to make the future less vulnerable to the inhuman.

6

Much of the light we possess on our essential, inward condition is still gathered by the poet.

But, undeniably, many parts of the mirror are today cracked or blurred. The dominant characteristic of the present literary scene is the excellence of "nonfiction"—of reportage, history, philosophic argument, biography, the critical essay—over traditional imaginative forms. Most of the novels, poems, and plays produced in the past two decades are simply not as well written, not as strongly felt, as are modes of writing in which the imagination obeys the impulse of fact. Madame de Beauvoir's memoirs are what her novels should have been, marvels of physical and psychological immediacy; Edmund Wilson writes the best prose in America; none of the numerous novels or poems that have taken on the dread theme of the concentration camps rivals the truth, the controlled poetic mercy of Bruno Bettelheim's factual analysis, *The Informed Heart*. It is as if the complication, pace, and political enormity of our age had bewildered and driven back the confident master-builder's imagination of classic literature and the nineteenth-century novel. A novel by Butor and *Naked Lunch* are both escapes. The avoidance of the major human note, or the derision of that note through erotic and sadistic fantasy, points to the same failure of creation. Monsieur Beckett is moving, with unflinching Irish logic, toward a form of drama in which a character, his feet trapped in concrete and his mouth gagged, will stare at the audience and say nothing. The imagination has supped its fill of horrors and of the unceremonious trivia through which modern horror is often expressed. As rarely before, poetry is tempted by silence.

It is in this context of privation and uncertitude that criticism has its modest yet vital place. Its function is, I believe, threefold.

First, it may show us what to reread, and how. The sum of literature is obviously immense, and the pressure of the new constant. One must choose, and in that choice criticism has its use. This does not mean that it should play the role of destiny and single out a handful of authors or works as the only valid tradition, excluding others (the mark of good criticism is that it opens more books than it closes). It means that from the vast, entangled legacy of the past, criticism will bring to light and sustain that which speaks to the present with particular directness or exaction.

This is the proper distinction between the critic and the historian of literature or philologist. To the latter the value of a text is intrinsic; it has a linguistic or chronological fascination independent of larger relevance. The critic, while availing himself of the scholar's authority on the primary meaning and integrity of the work, must choose. And his bias will be toward that which enters into dialogue with the living.

Each generation makes its choice. There is permanent poetry but hardly any permanent criticism. Tennyson shall have his day, and Donne his eclipse. Or to give an instance less dependent on the play of fashion: before the war, it was commonplace in the French lycées in which I was educated to consider Virgil as a fussy, nerveless imitator of Homer. Any boy would tell you so with cool assurance. With disaster, and the routine of flight and exile, this view changed radically. Virgil now seemed the more mature, the more necessary witness. Simone Weil's perverse reading of the *Iliad*, and Hermann Broch's *Death of Virgil* are both part of this revaluation. Time, both historically and on the scale of personal life, alters our view of a work or body of art. There is, notoriously, a poetry of the young and a prose of the aged. Because their trumpetings of a golden future contrast ironically with our actual experience, the romantics have moved out of focus. The sixteenth and early seventeenth centuries, though their language is often remote and intricate, seem nearer to our speech. Criticism can make these changes of need fruitful and discriminating. It can summon from the past what the genius of the present draws upon (the best of French prose at the moment has behind it the sinew of Diderot). And it can remind us that our alternances of judgment are neither axiomatic nor of lasting validity. The great critic will "feel ahead"; he will lean over the horizon and prepare the context of future recognition. At times he hears the echo when the voice is forgotten, or before it is known. There were those who sensed, in the 1920's, that the time of Blake and Kierkegaard was at hand, or who discerned, ten years later, the general truth in the private nightmare of Kafka. This does not mean choosing winners; it means knowing that the work of art stands in a complex, provisional relation to time.

Secondly, criticism can connect. In an age in which rapidity of technical communication in fact conceals obstinate ideological and political barriers, the critic can act as intermediary and custodian. It is part of his job to see that a political regime cannot visit oblivion or distortion on the work of a writer, that of books burned the ash is gathered and deciphered.

Even as he seeks to establish the dialogue between past and present, so the critic will try to keep open the lines of contact between languages. Criticism widens and complicates the map of sensibility. It insists that literatures do not live in isolation, but in a manifold of linguistic and national encounters. Criticism delights in affinity and the far leap of example. It knows that the incitements of a major talent or poetic form spread outward in intricate patterns of diffusion. It works *à l'ensigne de Saint-Jérôme*, knowing that there are no exact equivalences between languages, only betrayals, but that the attempt to translate is a constant need if the poem is to achieve its full life. Both critic and translator strive to communicate discovery.

In practice, this means that literature should be taught and interpreted in a comparative way. To have no direct acquaintance with the Italian epic when judging Spenser, to value Pope without a sure grasp of Boileau, to consider the performance of the Victorian novel and of James without a close awareness of Balzac, Stendhal, Flaubert, is to read thinly or falsely. It is academic feudalism that draws sharp lines between the study of English and of Modern Languages. Is English not a modern language, vulnerable and resilient, at all points in its history, to the pressure of European vernaculars and of the European tradition of rhetoric and genre? But the question cuts deeper than academic discipline. The critic who declares that a man can know only one language well, that the national inheritance of poetry or the national tradition of the novel is alone valid or supreme, is closing doors where they should be opened, is narrowing the mind where it should be brought to the sense of a large and equal achievement. Chauvinism has cried havoc in politics; it has no place in literature. The critic—and here again he differs from the writer—is not a man to stay in his own garden.

The third function of criticism is the most important. It concerns the judgment of contemporary literature. There is a distinction between contemporary and immediate. The immediate hounds the reviewer. But, plainly, the critic has special responsibilities toward the art of his own age. He must ask of it not only whether it represents a technical 'advance or refinement, whether it adds a twist of style or plays adroitly on the nerve of the moment, but what it contributes to or detracts from the dwindled reserves of moral intelligence. What is the measure of man this work proposes? It is not a question which is easily formulated, or which can be put with unfailing tact. But our time is not of the ordinary. It labors under the stress of inhumanity, experienced on a scale of singular magnitude and horror; and the possibility of ruin is not far off. There are luxuries of detachment one should like to afford, but cannot.

This would, for example, lead one to ask whether the talent of Tennessee Williams is being used to purvey a mawkish sadism, whether the rococo virtuosity of Salinger is arguing an absurdly diminished and enervating view of human existence. It would lead one to ask whether the banality of Camus' plays, and of all but the first of his novels, does not connote the persistent vagueness, the statuesque but airy motion of his thought. To *ask;* not to mock or censor. The distinction is immensely important. The asking can only be fruitful where access to the work is wholly free, where the critic genuinely hopes for disagreement and counterstatement. Moreover, while the policeman or the censor asks of the writer, the critic asks only of the book.

What I have been aiming at, throughout, is the notion of *humane literacy.* In that great discourse with the living dead which we call reading, our role is not a passive one. Where it is more than reverie or an indifferent appetite sprung of boredom, reading is a mode of action. We engage the presence, the voice of the book. We allow it entry, though not unguarded, into our inmost. A great poem, a classic novel, press in upon us; they assail and occupy the strong places of our consciousness. They exercise upon our imagination and desires, upon our ambitions and most covert dreams, a strange, bruising mastery. Men who burn books know what they are doing. The artist is the uncontrollable force: no Western eye, since Van Gogh, looks on a cypress without observing in it the start of flame.

So, and in supreme measure, it is with literature. A man who has read Book XXIV of the *Iliad*—the night meeting of Priam and Achilles—or the chapter in which Alyosha Karamazov kneels to the stars, who has read Montaigne's chapter XX (*Que philosopher c'est apprendre l'art de mourir*) and Hamlet's use of it, and who is not altered, whose apprehension of his own life is unchanged, who does not, in some subtle yet radical manner, look on the room in which he moves, on those that knock at the door, differently, has read only with the blindness of physical sight. Can one read *Anna Karenina* or Proust without experiencing a new infirmity or occasion in the very core of one's sexual feelings?

To read well is to take great risks. It is to make vulnerable our identity, our self-possession. In the early stages of epilepsy there occurs a characteristic dream; Dostoevsky tells of it. One is somehow lifted free of one's own body; looking back, one sees oneself and feels a sudden, maddening fear; another presence is entering into one's own person, and there is no avenue of return. Feeling this fear, the mind gropes to a sharp awakening. So it should be when we take in hand a major work of literature or philosophy, of imagination or doctrine. It may come to possess us so completely that we go, for a spell, in fear of ourselves and in imperfect recognition. He who has read Kafka's *Metamorphosis* and can look into his mirror unflinching may technically be able to read print, but is illiterate in the only sense that matters.

Because the community of traditional values is splintered, because words themselves have been twisted and cheapened, because the classic forms of statement and metaphor are yielding to complex, transitional modes, the art of reading, of true literacy, must be reconstituted. It is the task of literary criticism to help us read as total human beings, by example of precision, fear, and delight. Compared to the act of creation, that task is secondary. But it has never counted more. Without it, creation itself may fall upon silence.

THE RETREAT
FROM THE WORD

The Apostle tells us that in the beginning was the Word. He gives us no assurance as to the end.

It is appropriate that he should have used the Greek language to express the Hellenistic conception of the *Logos*, for it is to the fact of its Greek-Judaic inheritance that Western civilization owes its essentially verbal character. We take this character for granted. It is the root and bark of our experience and we cannot readily transpose our imaginings outside it. We live inside the act of discourse. But we should not assume that a verbal matrix is the only one in which the articulations and conduct of the mind are conceivable. There are modes of intellectual and sensuous reality founded not on language, but on other communicative energies such as the icon or the musical note. And there are actions of the spirit rooted in silence. It is difficult to *speak* of these, for how should speech justly convey the shape and vitality of silence? But I can cite examples of what I mean.

In certain Oriental metaphysics, in Buddhism and Taoism, the soul is envisioned as ascending from the gross impediments of the material, through domains of insight that can be rendered by lofty and precise language, toward ever deepening silence. The highest, purest reach of the contemplative act is that which has learned to leave language behind it. The ineffable lies beyond the frontiers of the word. It is only by breaking through the walls of language that visionary observance can enter the world of total and immediate understanding. Where such understanding is attained, the truth need no longer suffer the impurities and fragmentation that speech necessarily entails. It need not conform to the naïve logic and linear conception of time implicit in syntax. In ultimate truth, past, present, and future are simultaneously comprised. It is the temporal structure of language that keeps them artificially distinct. That is the crucial point.

The holy man, the initiate, withdraws not only from the temptations of worldly action; he withdraws from speech. His retreat into the mountain cave or monastic cell is the outward gesture of his silence. Even those who are only novices on this arduous road are taught to distrust the veil of language, to break through it to the more real. The Zen *koan*—we know the sound of two hands clapping, what is the sound of one?—is a beginner's exercise in the retreat from the word.

The Western tradition also knows transcendences of language toward silence. The Trappist ideal goes back to abandonments of speech as ancient as those of the Stylites and Desert Fathers. St. John of the Cross expresses the austere exaltation of the contemplative soul as it breaks loose from the moorings of common verbal understanding:

> *Entréme donde no supe,*
> *Y quedéme no sabiendo,*
> *Toda sciencia trascendiendo.*

But to the Western point of view, this order of experience inevitably carries a flavor of mysticism. And, whatever our lip service (itself a revealing term) to the sanctity of the mystic vocation, the commanding Western attitude is that of Cardinal Newman's quip, that mysticism begins in mist and ends in schism. Very few Western poets— perhaps only Dante—have persuaded the imagination of the authority of transrational experience. We accept, at the lambent close of the *Paradiso*, the blindness of eye and understanding before the totality of vision. But Pascal is nearer the mainstream of classic Western feeling when he says that the silence of cosmic space strikes terror. To the Taoist that selfsame silence conveys tranquillity and the intimation of God.

The primacy of the word, of that which can be spoken and communicated in discourse, is characteristic of the Greek and Judaic genius and carried over into Christianity. The classic and the Christian sense of the world strive to order reality within the governance of language. Literature, philosophy, theology, law, the arts of history, are endeavors to enclose within the bounds of rational discourse the sum of human experience, its recorded past, its present condition and future expectations. The code of Justinian, the *Summa* of Aquinas, the world chronicles and compendia of medieval literature, the *Divina Commedia*, are attempts at total containment. They bear solemn witness to the belief that all truth and realness—with the exception of a small, queer margin at the very top—can be housed inside the walls of language.

This belief is no longer universal. Confidence in it declines after the age of Milton. The cause and history of that decline throw sharp light on the circumstances of modern literature and language.

It is during the seventeenth century that significant areas of truth, reality, and action recede from the sphere of verbal statement. It is, on the whole, true to say that until the seventeenth century the predominant bias and content of the natural sciences were descriptive. Mathematics had its long, brilliant history of symbolic notation; but even mathematics was a shorthand for verbal propositions applicable to, and meaningful within, the framework of linguistic description. Mathematical thought, with certain notable exceptions, was anchored to the material conditions of experience. These, in turn, were ordered and ruled by language. During the seventeenth century, this ceased to be the general case, and there began a revolution that has transformed forever man's relationship to reality and radically altered the shapes of thought.

With the formulation of analytical geometry and the theory of algebraic functions, with the development by Newton and Leibniz of calculus, mathematics ceases to be a dependent notation, an instrument of the empirical. It becomes a fantastically rich, complex, and dynamic language. *And the history of that language is one of progressive untranslatability.* It is still possible to translate back into verbal equivalents, or at least close approximations, the proceedings of classical geometry and classical functional analysis. Once mathematics turns modern, however, and begins exhibiting its enormous powers of autonomous conception, such translation becomes less and less possible. The great architectures of form and meaning conceived by Gauss, Cauchy, Abel, Cantor, and Weierstrass recede from language at an ever accelerated pace. Or rather, they require and develop languages of their own as articulate and elaborate as those of verbal discourse. And between these languages and that of common usage, between the mathematical symbol and the word, the bridges grow more and more tenuous, until at last they are down.

Between verbal languages, however remote in setting and habits of syntax, there is always the possibility of equivalence, even if actual translation can only attain rough and approximate results. The Chinese ideogram can be transposed into English by paraphrase or lexical definition. But there are no dictionaries to relate the vocabulary and grammar of higher mathematics to those of verbal speech. One cannot "translate" the conventions and notations governing the operations of Lie groups or the properties of n-dimensional manifolds into any words or grammar outside mathematics. One cannot even paraphrase. A paraphrase of a good poem may turn out to be bad prose; but there is a discernible continuity between shadow and substance. The paraphrase of a complex theorem in topology can only be a grossly inadequate approximation or a transposal into another branch or "dialect" of the particular mathematical language. Many of the spaces, relations, and events that advanced mathematics deals with have no necessary correlation with sense-data; they are "realities" occurring within closed axiomatic systems. You can speak about them meaningfully and normatively only in the speech of mathematics. And that speech, beyond a fairly rudimentary plane, is not and cannot be verbal. I have watched topologists, knowing no syllable of each other's language, working effectively together at a blackboard in the silent speech common to their craft.

This is a fact of tremendous implication. It has divided the experience and perception of reality into separate domains. The most decisive change in the tenor of Western intellectual life since the seventeenth century is the submission of successively larger areas of knowledge to the modes and proceedings of mathematics. As has often been noted, a branch of inquiry passes from pre-science into science when it can be mathematically organized. It is the development within itself of formulaic and statistical means that gives to a science its dynamic possibilities. The tools of mathematical analysis transformed chemistry and physics from alchemy to the predictive sciences that they now are. By virtue of mathematics, the stars move out of mythology into the astronomer's table. And as mathematics settles into the marrow of a science, the concepts of that science, its habits of invention and understanding, become steadily less reducible to those of common language.

It is arrogant, if not irresponsible, to invoke such basic notions in our present model of the universe as quanta, the indeterminacy principle, the relativity constant, or the lack of parity in so-called

15

weak interactions of atomic particles, if one cannot do so in the language appropriate to them—that is to say, in mathematical terms. Without it, such words are phantasms to deck out the pretense of philosophers or journalists. Because physics has had to borrow them from the vulgate, some of these words seem to retain a generalized meaning; they give a semblance of metaphor. But this is an illusion. When a critic seeks to apply the indeterminacy principle to his discussion of action painting or of the use of improvisation in contemporary music, he is not relating two spheres of experience; he is merely talking nonsense.*

We must guard against such deception. Chemistry uses numerous terms derived from its earlier descriptive stage; but the formulas of modern molecular chemistry are, in fact, a shorthand whose vernacular is not that of verbal speech but that of mathematics. A chemical formula does not abbreviate a linguistic statement; it codifies a numerical operation. Biology is in a fascinating intermediary position. Classically, it was a descriptive science, relying on a precise and suggestive use of language. The force of Darwin's biological and zoological proposals was founded, in part, on the persuasion of his style. In post-Darwinian biology, mathematics has played an ever more commanding role. The change of stress is clearly marked in Wentworth Thompson's great work, *Of Growth and Form*, a book in which poet and mathematician are equally engaged. Today, large areas of biology, such as genetics, are mainly mathematical. Where biology turns toward chemistry, and biochemistry is at present the high ground, it tends to relinquish the descriptive for the enumerative. It abandons the word for the figure.

It is this extension of mathematics over great areas of thought and action that broke Western consciousness into what C. P. Snow calls "the two cultures." Until the time of Goethe and Humboldt, it was possible for a man of exceptional ability and retentiveness to feel

[* I am no longer certain that this is so. Obviously most of the analogies drawn between modern art and developments in the exact sciences are "unrealized metaphors," fictions of analogy which do not have in them the authority of real experience. Nevertheless, even the illicit metaphor, the term borrowed though misunderstood, may be an essential part of a process of reunification. It is very probable that the sciences will furnish an increasing part of our mythologies and imaginative reference. The vulgarizations, false analogies, even errors of the poet and critic may be a necessary part of the "translation" of science into the common literacy of feeling. And the bare fact that aleatory principles in the arts coincide historically with "indeterminacy" *may* have a genuine significance. It is the nature of that significance which needs to be felt and shown.]

16

at home in both the humanistic and the mathematical cultures. Leibniz had still been able to make notable contributions to both. This is no longer a real possibility. The chasm between the languages of words and of mathematics grows constantly wider. Standing on either rim are men who, in respect of each other, are illiterate. There is as great a sum of illiteracy in not knowing the basic concepts of calculus or spherical geometry as there is in not knowing grammar. Or to use Snow's famous example: a man who has read no Shakespeare is uncultured; so is one who is ignorant of the second law of thermodynamics. Each is blind to comparable worlds.

Except in moments of bleak clarity, we do not yet act as if this were true. We continue to assume that humanistic authority, the sphere of the word, is predominant. The notion of essential literacy is still rooted in classic values, in a sense of discourse, rhetoric, and poetics. But this is ignorance or sloth of imagination. Calculus, the laws of Carnot, Maxwell's conception of the electromagnetic field, not only comprise areas of reality and action as great as those comprised by classic literacy; they probably give an image of the perceptible world truer to fact than can be derived from any structure of verbal assertion. All evidence suggests that the shapes of matter are mathematical, that integral and differential calculus are the alphabet of just perception. The humanist today is in the position of those tenacious, aggrieved spirits who continued to envision the earth as a flat table after it had been circumnavigated, or who persisted in believing in occult propulsive energies after Newton had formulated the laws of motion and inertia.

Those of us who are compelled by our ignorance of exact science to imagine the universe through a veil of non-mathematical language inhabit an animate fiction. The actual facts of the case—the space-time continuum of relativity, the atomic structure of all matter, the wave-particle state of energy—are no longer accessible through the word. It is no paradox to assert that in cardinal respects reality now begins *outside* verbal language. Mathematicians know this. "By its geometric and later by its purely symbolic construction," says Andreas Speiser, "mathematics shook off the fetters of language . . . and mathematics today is more efficient in its sphere of the intellectual world, than the modern languages in their deplorable state or even music are on their respective fronts."

Few humanists are aware of the scope and nature of this great change (Sartre is a notable exception and has, time and again, drawn attention to *la crise du langage*). Nevertheless, many of the traditional humanistic disciplines have shown a deep *malaise*, a nervous, complex recognition of the exactions and triumphs of mathematics and the natural sciences. There has taken place in history, economics, and what are called, significantly, the "social sciences" what one might term a fallacy of imitative form. In each of these fields, the mode of discourse still relies almost completely on word-language. But historians, economists, and social scientists have tried to graft on to the verbal matrix some of the proceedings of mathematics or total rigor. They have grown defensive about the essentially provisional and aesthetic character of their own pursuits.

Observe how the cult of the positive, the exact, and the predictive has invaded history. The decisive turn occurs in the nineteenth century, in the work of Ranke, Comte, and Taine. Historians began regarding their material as elements in the crucible of controlled experiment. From impartial scrutiny of the past (such impartiality being, in fact, a naïve illusion) should emerge those statistical patterns, those periodicities of national and economic force, which allow the historian to formulate "laws of history." This very notion of historical "law," and the implication of necessity and predictability, which are crucial to Taine, Marx, and Spengler, are a borrowing from the sphere of the exact and mathematical sciences.

The ambitions of scientific rigor and prophecy have seduced much historical writing from its veritable nature, which is art. Much of what passes for history at present is scarcely literate. The disciples of Namier—not he himself—consign Gibbon, Macaulay, or Michelet to the limbo of *belles-lettres*. The illusion of science and the fashions of the academic tend to transform the young historian into a lean ferret gnawing at the minute fact or figure. He dwells in footnotes and writes monographs in as illiterate a style as possible to demonstrate the scientific bias of his craft. One of the few contemporary historians prepared to defend openly the poetic nature of historical imagining is C. V. Wedgwood. She fully concedes that all style brings with it the possibility of distortion: "There is no literary style which may not at some point take away something from the ascertainable outline of truth, which it is the task of scholarship to excavate and re-establish." But where such excavation abandons style altogether, or harbors the illusion of impartial exactitude, it will light only on dust.

Or consider economics: its classic masters, Adam Smith, Ricardo, Malthus, Marshall, were masters of prose style. They relied upon language to explain and persuade. In the late nineteenth century began the development of mathematical economics. Keynes was perhaps the last to span both the humane and the mathematical branches of his science. Discussing the contributions of Ramsey to economic thought, Keynes pointed out that a number of them, though of signal importance, involved mathematics too sophisticated for the layman or the classical economist. Today the gap has widened tremendously; econometrics is gaining on economics. The cardinal terms—theory of values, cycles, productive capacity, liquidity, inflation, input-output— are in a state of transition. They are moving from the linguistic to the mathematical, from rhetoric to equation. The alphabet of modern economics is no longer primarily the word, but rather the chart, the graph, and the number. The most powerful economic thought of the present is using the analytic and predictive instruments forged by the functional analysts of nineteenth-century mathematics.

The temptations of exact science are most flagrant in sociology. Much of present sociology is illiterate, or, more precisely, anti-literate. It is conceived in a jargon of vehement obscurity. Wherever possible, the word and the grammar of literate meaning are replaced by the statistical table, the curve, or the graph. Where it must remain verbal, sociology borrows what it can from the vocabulary of the exact sciences. One could make a fascinating list of these borrowings. Consider only the more prominent: *norms, group, scatter, integration, function, coordinates.* Each has a specific mathematical or technical content. Emptied of this content and forced into an alien setting, these expressions become blurred and pretentious. They do ill service to their new masters. Yet in using the gibberish of "culture coordinates" and "peer-group integrations" the sociologist pays fervent tribute to the mirage that has haunted all rational inquiry since the seventeenth century—the mirage of mathematical exactitude and predictability.

Nowhere, however, is the retreat from the word more pronounced and startling than in philosophy. Classic and medieval philosophy were wholly committed to the dignity and resources of language, to the belief that words, handled with requisite precision and subtlety, could bring the mind into accord with reality. Plato, Aristotle, Duns Scotus, and Aquinas are master-builders of words, constructing around reality great edifices of statement, definition, and discrimination. They operate with modes of argument that differ

19

from those of the poet; but they share with the poet the assumption that words gather and engender responsible apprehensions of the truth. Again, the turning point occurs in the seventeenth century, with Descartes' implicit identification of truth and mathematical proof, and, above all, with Spinoza.

The *Ethics* represents the formidable impact on a philosophic temper of the new mathematics. In mathematics, Spinoza perceived that rigor of statement, that consistency and majestic certitude of result, which are the hope of all metaphysics. Not even the severest of scholastic arguments, with its array of syllogisms and lemmas, could rival that progress from axiom to demonstration and new concept which is to be found in Euclidean and analytic geometry. With superb naïveté, therefore, Spinoza sought to make of the language of philosophy a verbal mathematics. Hence the organization of the *Ethics* into axioms, definitions, demonstrations, and corollaries. Hence the proud *q.e.d.* at the close of each set of propositions. It is a queer, entrancing book, as pellucid as the lenses Spinoza ground for a living. But it yields nothing except a further image of itself. It is an elaborate tautology. Unlike numbers, words do not contain within themselves functional operations. Added or divided, they give only other words or approximations of their own meaning. Spinoza's demonstrations merely affirm; they cannot give proof. Yet the attempt was prophetic. It confronts all subsequent metaphysics with a dilemma; after Spinoza, philosophers know that they are using language to clarify language, like cutters using diamonds to shape other diamonds. Language is seen no longer as a road to demonstrable truth, but as a spiral or gallery of mirrors bringing the intellect back to its point of departure. With Spinoza, metaphysics loses its innocence.

Symbolic logic, a glimpse of which may already be found in Leibniz, is an attempt to break out of the circle. At first, in the work of Boole, Frege, and Hilbert, it was intended as a specialized tool designed to test the internal consistency of mathematical reasoning. But it soon assumed a much larger relevance. The symbolic logician constructs a radically simplified but entirely rigorous and self-consistent model. He invents or postulates a syntax freed from the ambiguities and imprecisions which history and usage have brought into common language. He borrows the conventions of mathematical inference and deduction and applies them to other modes of thought in order to determine whether such modes have validity. In short, he seeks to objectify crucial areas of philosophic inquiry by stepping outside language. The non-verbal instrument of mathematical symbolism is now being applied to morals and even to aesthetics. The old notion of a calculus of moral impulse, of an algebra of pleasure and pain, has had its revival. A number of contemporary logicians have sought to devise a calculable theoretic basis for the act of aesthetic choice. There is scarcely a branch of modern philosophy in which we do not find the numerals, italicized letters, radicals, and arrows with which the symbolic logician seeks to replace the shopworn and rebellious host of words.

The greatest of modern philosophers was also the one most profoundly intent on escaping from the spiral of language. Wittgenstein's entire work starts out by asking whether there is any verifiable relation between the word and the fact. That which we call fact may well be a veil spun by language to shroud the mind from reality. Wittgenstein compels us to wonder whether reality can be *spoken of*, when speech is merely a kind of infinite regression, words being spoken of other words. Wittgenstein pursued this dilemma with passionate austerity. The famous closing proposition of the *Tractatus* is not a claim for the potentiality of philosophic statement such as Descartes advanced. On the contrary; it is a drastic retreat from the confident authority of traditional metaphysics. It leads to the equally famous conclusion: "It is clear that Ethics cannot be expressed." Wittgenstein would include in the class of inexpressibles (what he calls the mystical) most of the traditional areas of philosophic speculation. Language can only deal meaningfully with a special, restricted segment of reality. The rest, and it is presumably the much larger part, is silence.

Later on, Wittgenstein departed from the restrictive position of the *Tractatus*. The *Philosophic Investigations* take a more optimistic view of the inherent capacities of language to describe the world and to articulate certain modes of conduct. But it is an open question whether the *Tractatus* is not the more powerful and consistent statement. It is certainly deeply felt. For the silence, which at every point surrounds the naked discourse, seems, by virtue of Wittgenstein's force of insight, less a wall than a window. With Wittgenstein, as with certain poets, we look out of language not into darkness but light. Anyone who reads the *Tractatus* will be sensible of its odd, mute radiance.

Though I can only touch on the matter briefly, it seems clear to me that the retreat from the authority and range of verbal language plays a tremendous role in the history and character of modern art. In painting and sculpture, realism in the broadest sense—the representation of that which we apprehend as an imitation of existent reality—corresponds to that period in which language is at the center of intellectual and emotive life. A landscape, a still life, a portrait, an allegory, a depiction of some event out of history or legend are renditions in color, volume, and texture of realities which can be expressed in words. We can give a linguistic account of the subject of the work of art. The canvas and the statue have a title that relates them to the verbal concept. We say: this is a portrait of a man with a golden helmet; or, this is the Grand Canal at sunrise; or, this is a portrayal of Daphne turning into a laurel. In each case, even before we have seen the work, the words elicit in the mind a specific graphic equivalent. No doubt this equivalent is less vivid or revealing than the painting by Rembrandt or Canaletto, or the statue by Canova. But there is a substantive relation. The artist and the viewer are talking about the same world, though the artist says things more profound and inclusive.

It is precisely against such verbal equivalence or concordance that modern art has rebelled. It is because so much eighteenth- and nineteenth-century painting seemed merely to be an illustration of verbal concepts—a picture in the book of language—that post-impressionism broke away from the word. Van Gogh declared that the painter paints not what he sees but what he feels. What is seen can be transposed into words; what is felt may occur at some level anterior to language or outside it. It will find expression solely in the specific idiom of color and spatial organization. Non-objective and abstract art rejects the mere possibility of a linguistic equivalent. The canvas or the sculpture refuses to be entitled; it is labeled "Black and White No. 5" or "White Forms" or "Composition 85." When there is a title, as in many of De Kooning's canvases, the title is often an ironic mystification; it is not meant to mean but to decorate or bewilder. And the work itself has no subject of which one can render a verbal account. The fact that Lassaw calls his twists of welded bronze "Clouds of Magellan" provides no exterior reference; Franz Kline's "Chief" (1950) is merely a whorl of paint. Nothing that can be *said* about it will be pertinent to the habits of linguistic sense. The patches of color, the skein of wire, or the aggregates of cast iron seek to establish reference only to themselves, only inwards.

Where they succeed, their assertion of immediate sensuous energy provokes in the viewer a kinetic response. There are shapes by Brancusi and Arp that draw us after them into a counterpart of their own motion. De Kooning's "Leaves in Weehawken" by-passes language and seems to play directly on our nerve ends. But more often, the abstract design conveys only the rudimentary pleasures of decoration. Much of Jackson Pollock is vivid wallpaper. And in the majority of cases, abstract expressionism and non-objective art communicate nothing whatever. The work stands mute or attempts to shout at us in a kind of inhuman gibberish. I wonder whether future artists and critics will not look back with puzzled contempt upon the mass of pretentious trivia that now fills our galleries.

The problem of atonal, concrete, or electronic music is, obviously, a very different one. Music is explicitly related to language only where it sets a text, where it is music of a specific formal occasion, or where it is program music seeking to articulate in sound a deliberate scene or situation. Music has always had its own syntax, its own vocabulary and symbolic means. Indeed, it is with mathematics the principal language of the mind when the mind is in a condition of non-verbal feeling. Yet, even within music, there has been a distinct movement away from the reaches of the word.

A classical sonata or symphony is not in any way a verbal statement. Except in very simplified instances ("storm-music"), there is no unilateral equivalent between the tonal event and a particular verbal meaning or emotion. *Nevertheless*, there is in classical forms of musical organization a certain grammar or articulation in time which does have analogies with the processes of language. Language cannot translate into itself the binary structure of a sonata, but the statement of successive subjects, the fact of variation on them, and the closing recapitulation do convey an ordering of experience to which language has valid parallels. Modern music shows no such relationships. In order to achieve a kind of total integrity and self-containment, it departs violently from the domain of intelligible "exterior" meaning. It denies to the listener any recognition of content, or, more accurately, it denies him the possibility of relating the purely auditive impression to any verbalized form of experience. Like the non-objective canvas, the piece of "new" music will often dispense with a title lest that title offer a false bridge back to the world of pictorial and verbal imaginings. It calls itself "Variation 42" or "Composition."

In its flight from the neighborhood of language, moreover,

23

music has been drawn inevitably to the chimera of mathematics. Glancing at a recent issue of *The Musical Quarterly*, one finds a discussion of "Twelve-Tone Invariants":

> The initial pitch class of S is denoted by the couple (O,O), and is taken as the origin of the co-ordinate system for both order and pitch numbers, both of which range over the integers O-11 inclusive, each integer appearing once and only once as an order number and a pitch number. In the case of order numbers, this represents the fact that twelve and only twelve pitch classes are involved: in the case of pitch numbers, this is the arithmetical analogue of octave equivalence (congruent mod. 12).

Describing his own method of composition, a contemporary composer, by no means among the most radical, observes:

> The point is that the notion of invariancy inherent by definition to the concept of the series, if applied to all parameters, leads to a uniformity of configurations that eliminates the last traces of unpredictability, or surprise.

The music that is produced by this kind of approach may be of considerable fascination and technical interest. But the vision behind it is clearly related to the great crisis of humane literacy. And only those committed by profession or affectation to the ultra-modern would deny that much of what passes for music at the present time is brutal noise.

II

What I have argued so far is this: until the seventeenth century, the sphere of language encompassed nearly the whole of experience and reality; today, it comprises a narrower domain. It no longer articulates, or is relevant to, all major modes of action, thought, and sensibility. Large areas of meaning and praxis now belong to such non-verbal languages as mathematics, symbolic logic, and formulas of chemical or electronic relation. Other areas belong to the sub-languages or anti-languages of non-objective art and *musique concrète*. The world of words has shrunk. One *cannot* talk of transfinite numbers except mathematically; one *should not*, suggests Wittgenstein, talk of ethics or aesthetics within the presently available categories of discourse. And it is, I think, exceedingly difficult to speak meaningfully of a Jackson Pollock painting or a composition by Stockhausen. The circle has narrowed tremendously, for was there anything under heaven, be it science, metaphysics, art, or music, of which a Shakespeare, a Donne, and a Milton could not speak naturally, to which their words did not have natural access?

Does this signify that fewer words are in actual use today? That is a very intricate and, as yet, unresolved question. Not including taxonomic lists (the names of all species of beetles, for example), it is estimated that the English language at present contains some 600,000 words. Elizabethan English is thought to have had only 150,000. But these rough figures are deceptive. Shakespeare's working vocabulary exceeds that of any later author, and the King James Bible, although it requires only 6000 words, suggests that the conception of literacy prevailing at the time was far more comprehensive than ours. The real point lies not in the number of words potentially available, but in the degree to which the resources of the language are in actual current use. If McKnight's estimate is reliable (*English Words and Their Background*, 1923), fifty percent of modern colloquial speech in England and America comprises only thirty-four basic words; and to make themselves widely understood, contemporary media of mass communication have had to reduce English to a semi-literate condition. The language of Shakespeare and Milton belongs to a stage of history in which words were in natural control of experienced life. The writer of today tends to use far fewer and simpler words, both because mass culture has watered down the concept of literacy and because the sum of realities of which words can give a necessary and sufficient account has sharply diminished.

This diminution—the fact that the image of the world is receding from the communicative grasp of the word—has had its impact on the quality of language. As Western consciousness has become less dependent on the resources of language to order experience and conduct the business of the mind, the words themselves seem to have lost some of their precision and vitality. This is, I know, a controversial notion. It assumes that language has a "life" of its own in a sense that goes beyond metaphor. It implies that such concepts as tiredness and corruption are relevant to language itself, not only to men's use of it. It is a view held by De Maistre and Orwell, and it gives force to Pound's definition of the poet's job: "We are governed

25

by words, the laws are graven in words, and literature is the sole means of keeping these words living and accurate." Most linguists would regard implications of internal, independent vitality in language as suspect. But let me indicate briefly what I mean.

There is in the handling of the English language in the Tudor, Elizabethan, and Jacobean periods a sense of discovery, of exuberant acquisition, which has never been wholly recaptured. Marlowe, Bacon, Shakespeare use words as if they were new, as if no previous touch had clouded their shimmer or muted their resonance. Erasmus tells of how he bent down in a muddy lane ecstatically when his eye lit upon a scrap of print, so new was the miracle of the printed page. This is how the sixteenth and seventeenth centuries seem to look upon language itself. The great treasure of it lies before them, suddenly unlocked, and they ransack it with a sense of infinite resource. The instrument now in our hands, on the contrary, is worn by long usage. And the demands of mass culture and mass communication have made it perform tasks of ever increasing tawdriness.

What save half-truths, gross simplifications, or trivia can, in fact, be communicated to that semi-literate mass audience which popular democracy has summoned into the market place? Only in a diminished or corrupted language can most such communication be made effective. Compare the vitality of language implicit in Shakespeare, in the Book of Common Prayer, or in the style of a country gentleman such as Cavendish, with our present vulgate. "Motivation researchers," those gravediggers of literate speech, tell us that the perfect advertisement should neither contain words of more than two syllables nor sentences with dependent clauses. In the United States, millions of copies have been printed of "Shakespeare" and the "Bible" in the form of comic strips with captions in basic English. Surely there can be no doubt that the access to economic and political power of the semi-educated has brought with it a drastic reduction in the wealth and dignity of speech.

I have tried to show elsewhere, in reference to the condition of German speech under Nazism, what political bestiality and falsehood can make of a language when the latter has been severed from the roots of moral and emotional life, when it has become ossified with clichés, unexamined definitions, and leftover words. What has happened to German is, however, happening less dramatically elsewhere. The language of the mass media and of advertisement in England and the United States, what passes for literacy in the average American high school or the style of present political debate, are manifest proofs of a retreat from vitality and precision. The English spoken by Mr. Eisenhower during his press conferences, like that used to sell a new detergent, was intended neither to communicate the critical truths of national life nor to quicken the mind of the hearer. It was designed to evade or gloss over the demands of meaning. The language of a community has reached a perilous state when a study of radioactive fall-out can be entitled "Operation Sunshine."

Whether it is a decline in the life-force of the language itself that helps bring on the cheapening and dissolution of moral and political values, or whether it is a decline in the vitality of the body politic that undermines the language, one thing is clear. The instrument available to the modern writer is threatened by restriction from without and decay from within. In the world of what R. P. Blackmur calls "the new illiteracy," the man to whom the highest literacy is of the essence, the writer, finds himself in a precarious situation.

What I want to examine next is the effect on the actual practice of literature of the retreat from the word and the concomitant divisions and diminutions of our culture. Not, of course, on all Western literature, nor even on a significant fraction. But only on certain literary movements and individual writers who seem exemplary of the larger withdrawal.

III

The crisis of poetic means, as we now know it, began in the later nineteenth century. It arose from awareness of the gap between the new sense of psychological reality and the old modes of rhetorical and poetic statement. In order to articulate the wealth of consciousness opened to the modern sensibility, a number of poets sought to break out of the traditional confines of syntax and definition. Rimbaud, Lautréamont, and Mallarmé strove to restore to language a fluid, provisional character; they hoped to give back to the word the power of incantation—of conjuring up the unprecedented—which it possesses when it is still a form of magic. They realized that traditional syntax organizes our perceptions into linear and monistic patterns. Such patterns distort or stifle the play of subconscious energies, the multitudinous life of the interior of the mind, as it was revealed by Blake, Dostoevsky, Nietzsche, and Freud. In his prose poems, Rim-

27

baud seeks to liberate language from the innate bond of causal sequence; effects seem to come before causes and events unfold in inconsequent simultaneity. That became a characteristic conceit of surrealism. Mallarmé made of words acts not primarily of *communication* but of *initiation* into a private mystery. Mallarmé uses current words in occult and riddling senses; we recognize them but they turn their back on us.

Although they yield superb poetry, these conceptions are fraught with danger. To work at all, the new private language must have behind it the pressure of genius; mere talent, a far more available commodity, will not do. Only genius can elaborate a vision so intense and specific that it will come across the intervening barrier of broken syntax or private meaning. The modern poet uses words as a private notation, access to which is rendered increasingly difficult for the common reader. Where a master is at work, where privacy of means is an instrument of heightened perception and no mere artifice, the reader will be led toward the necessary effort. Even before one has grasped Rimbaud's vision or the eccentric structure of argument in the *Duino Elegies*, one is aware that Rimbaud and Rilke are using language in new ways in order to pass from the real to the more real. But in the hands of lesser men or impostors, the attempt to make language new is diminished to barrenness and obscurity. Dylan Thomas is a case in point. He realized, with the flair of a showman, that a wide, largely unqualified audience could be flattered by being given access to a poetry of seeming depth. He combined a froth of Swinburnean rhetoric with cabalistic devices of syntax and imagery. He showed that one could have one's Orphic cake and eat it too. But barring certain eloquent exceptions, there is in his poems less than meets the dazzled eye.

Where poetry seeks to dissociate itself from the exactions of clear meaning and from the common usages of syntax, it will tend toward an ideal of musical form. This tendency plays a fascinating role in modern literature. The thought of giving to words and prosody values equivalent to music is an ancient one. But with French Symbolist poetry, it assumes specific force. Implicit in Verlaine's doctrine—*De la musique avant toute chose*—is the attractive but confused notion that a poem should communicate most immediately through its sonorities. This pursuit of the tonal rather than the conceptual mode produced series of poetic works which yield their full implications only when they are actually set to music. Debussy was able to use Maeterlinck's *Pelléas et Mélisande* nearly intact; the same is true of Richard Strauss and Wilde's *Salomé*. In either case, the poetic work is a libretto in search of a composer. The musical values and proceedings are already explicit in the language.

More recently, the submission of literary forms to musical examples and ideals has been carried even further. In Romain Rolland and Thomas Mann, we find the belief that the musician is the artist in essence (he is *more* an artist than, say, the painter or writer). This is because only music can achieve that total fusion of form and content, of means and meaning, which all art strives for. Two of the foremost poetic designs of our time, T. S. Eliot's *Four Quartets* and Hermann Broch's *Death of Virgil*, embody an idea that can be traced back to Mallarmé and *L'Après-midi d'un faune:* they attempt to suggest in language corresponding organizations of musical form.

The Death of Virgil is a novel built in four sections, each of which is figurative of one of the four movements of a quartet. Indeed, there are hints that Broch had before him the structure of a particular late quartet of Beethoven. In each "movement," the cadence of the prose is meant to reflect a corresponding musical tempo: there is a swift "scherzo" in which plot, dialogue, and narrative move at a sharp pace; in the "andante," Broch's style slows down to long, sinuous phrases. The last section, which renders Virgil's actual passage into death, is an astounding performance. It goes beyond Joyce in loosening the traditional bonds of narrative. The words literally flow in sustained polyphony. Strands of argument interweave exactly as in a string quartet; there are fugal developments in which images are repeated at governed intervals; and, at the last, language gathers to a dim, sensuous rush as remembrance, present awareness, and prophetic intimation join in a single great chord. The entire novel, in fact, is an attempt to transcend language toward more delicate and precise conveyances of meaning. In the last sentence, the poet crosses into death, realizing that that which is wholly outside language is outside life.

There is a sociological footnote relevant to these turnings of literature toward music. In the United States, and to a growing extent in Europe, the new literacy is musical rather than verbal. The long-playing record has revolutionized the art of leisure. The new middle class in the affluent society reads little, but listens to music with knowing delight. Where the library shelves once stood, there are proud, esoteric rows of record albums and high-fidelity components.

Compared to the long-playing record, the paperback book is an ephemeral, lightly discarded thing. It does not lead to the collecting of a real library. Music is today the central fact of lay culture. Few adults read aloud to each other; fewer yet spend a regular part of their spare time in a public library or athenaeum as did the generation of the 1880's. Many gather before the hi-fi set or join in musical performance.

There are complex social and psychological reasons for this. The tempo of urban and industrial life leaves one exhausted at nightfall. When one is tired, music, even difficult music, is easier to enjoy than serious literature. It stirs feeling without perplexing the brain. It allows even those who have little previous training access to classic masterpieces. It does not separate human beings into islands of privacy and silence as does the reading of a book, but conjoins them in that illusion of community which our society strives for. Where Victorian wooers sent garlands of verse to their intended, the modern swain will choose a record explicitly meant as background to reverie or seduction. As one looks at recent album-covers, one realizes that music has become the substitute for the candlelight and dark velvets which our style of life no longer provides.

In short, the musical sound, and to a lesser degree the work of art and its reproduction, are beginning to hold a place in literate society once firmly held by the word.

What is, perhaps, the dominant school in contemporary literature has made a virtue of necessity. The style of Hemingway and of his myriad imitators is a brilliant response to the diminution of linguistic possibility. Sparse, laconic, highly artificial in its conventions of brevity and understatement, that style sought to reduce the ideal of Flaubert—*le mot juste*—to a scale of basic language. One may admire it or not. But, undeniably, it is based on a most narrow conception of the resources of literacy. Moreover, the technical mastery of a Hemingway tends to blur a crucial distinction: simple words can be used to express complex ideas and feelings, as in Tacitus, the Book of Common Prayer, or Swift's *Tale of a Tub;* or they can be used to express states of consciousness that are themselves rudimentary. By retrenching language to a kind of powerful, lyric shorthand, Hemingway narrows the compass of observed and rendered life. He is often charged with his monotonous adherence to hunters, fishermen, bullfighters, or alcoholic soldiers. But this constancy is a necessary result of the available medium. How could Hemingway's language

30

convey the inward life of more manifold or articulate characters? Imagine trying to translate the consciousness of Raskolnikov into the vocabulary of "The Killers." Which is not to deny the perfection of this grim snapshot. But *Crime and Punishment* gathers into itself a sum of life entirely beyond Hemingway's thin medium.

The thinning out of language has condemned much of recent literature to mediocrity. There are various reasons why *Death of a Salesman* falls short of the discernible reach of Arthur Miller's talent. But an obvious one is the paucity of its language. The brute snobbish fact is that men who die speaking as does Macbeth are more tragic than those who sputter platitudes in the style of Willy Loman. Miller has learned much from Ibsen; but he has failed to hear behind Ibsen's realistic conventions the constant beat of poetry.

Language seeks vengeance on those who cripple it. A striking example occurs in O'Neill, a dramatist committed, in a somber and rather moving way, to the practice of bad writing. Interspersed in the sodden morass of *A Long Day's Journey into Night*, there are passages from Swinburne. The lines are flamboyant, romantic verbiage. They are meant to show up the adolescent inadequacies of those who recite them. But, in fact, when the play is performed, the contrary occurs. The energy and glitter of Swinburne's language burn a hole in the surrounding fabric. They elevate the action above its paltry level and instead of showing up the character show up the playwright. Modern authors rarely quote their betters with impunity.

But amid the general retreat or flight from the word in literature, there have been a number of brilliant rearguard actions. I shall cite only a few instances, limiting myself to English.

No doubt the most exuberant counterattack any modern writer has launched against the diminution of language is that of James Joyce. After Shakespeare and Burton, literature has known no greater gourmand of words. As if aware of the fact that science had torn from language many of its former possessions and outer provinces, Joyce chose to annex a new kingdom below ground. *Ulysses* caught in its bright net the live tangle of subconscious life; *Finnegans Wake* mines the bastions of sleep. Joyce's work, more than any since Milton, recalls to the English ear the wide magnificence of its legacy. It marshals great battalions of words, calling back to the ranks words long asleep or rusted, and recruiting new ones by stress of imaginative need.

Yet when we look back on the battle so decisively won, we

can attribute to it little positive consequence, and scarcely any wider richening. There have been no genuine successors to Joyce in English; perhaps there can be none to a talent so exhaustive of its own potential. What counts more: the treasures which Joyce brought back to language from his wide-ranging forays remain piled glitteringly around his own labors. They have not passed into currency. They have caused none of that general quickening of the spirit of speech which follows on Spenser and Marlowe. I do not know why. Perhaps the action was fought too late; or perhaps the privacies and parts of incoherence in *Finnegans Wake* have proved too obtrusive. As it stands, Joyce's performance is a monument rather than a living force.

Another rear-guard action, or raid behind enemy lines, has been that of Faulkner. The means of Faulkner's style are primarily those of Gothic and Victorian rhetoric. Within a syntax whose convolutions are themselves expressive of Faulkner's landscape, ornate, regional language makes a constant assault upon our feelings. Often the words seem to grow cancerous, engendering other words in ungoverned foison. At times, the sense is diluted as in a swamp-mist. But nearly always, this idiosyncratic, Victorian night-parlance *is* a style. Faulkner is not afraid of words even where they submerge him. And where he is in control of them, Faulkner's language has a thrust and vital sensuousness that carry all before them. Much in Faulkner is overwritten or even badly written. But the novel is always *written* through and through. The act of eloquence, which is the very definition of a writer, is not let go by default.

The case of Wallace Stevens is particularly instructive. Here is a poet who was by nature a rhetorician, who saw language as ceremonious and dramatic gesture. He was a lover of the savor and shimmer of words, passing them over his tongue like a taster of rare vintage. Yet the inventions or habits of style most characteristic of his work come from a narrow and brittle source. Consider some of his best-known finds: "bright nouveautés," "foyer," "funeste," "peristyle," "little arrondissements," "peignoir," "fictive," "port" (in the sense of posture). Most are Latinizations or naked borrowings from the French. They are conceits superimposed on language, not, as in Shakespeare or Joyce, growths from within the natural soil. Where the intent is one of exotic ornament, as in the "tambourines" and "simpering Byzantines" of "Peter Quince," the effect is memorable. Elsewhere, it is merely florid or rococo. And behind Wallace Stevens' linguistic acquisitiveness, there is a queer streak of provincialism. He borrows French words with obtrusive excitement, rather like a traveler acquiring French bonnets or perfumes. He once declared that English and French are closely related languages. Not only is the proposition shallow, but it betokens a view of his own idiom which a poet should guard against.

Looking at the present scene, I wonder whether the best hope for a renascence of the word, in the purely literary domain, does not lie with an English novelist of Irish descent and Anglo-Indian background:

> Frankly Scobie looks anybody's age; older than the birth of tragedy, younger than the Athenian death. Spawned in the Ark by a chance meeting and mating of the bear and the ostrich; delivered before term by the sickening grunt of the keel on Ararat. Scobie came forth from the womb in a wheel chair with rubber tyres, dressed in a deer-stalker and a red flannel binder. On his prehensile toes the glossiest pair of elastic-sided boots. In his hand a ravaged family Bible whose fly-leaf bore the words "Joshua Samuel Scobie 1870. Honour thy father and thy mother." To these possessions were added eyes like dead moons, a distinct curvature of the pirate's spinal column, and a taste for quinqueremes. It was not blood which flowed in Scobie's veins but green salt water, deep-sea stuff. His walk is the slow rolling grinding trudge of a saint walking on Galilee. His talk is a green-water jargon swept up in five oceans—an antique shop of polite fable bristling with sextants, astrolabes, propentines and isobars. . . . Now the retreating tide has left him high and dry above the speeding currents of time, Joshua the insolvent weather-man, the islander, the anchorite.

I know the objections to Lawrence Durrell. His style beats against the present wind. Anyone trained on Hemingway will sicken and cloy at it. But perhaps it is we who are at fault, having been long kept on thin gruel. Durrell's masters are Burton, Sir Thomas Browne, De Quincey, Conrad. He stands in the old tradition of the fullness of prose. He is attempting to make language once again commensurate with the manifold truths of the experienced world. His attempt has entailed excesses; Durrell is often precious, and his vision of conduct is more flimsy and shallow than are the technical resources

33

at his command. But what he is trying to do is of importance: it is no less than an effort to keep literature literate.

But literature represents, as we have seen, only a small part of the universal crisis. The writer is the guardian and shaper of speech, but he cannot do the job alone. Today, this is truer than ever before. The role of the poet in our society and in the life of words has greatly diminished. Most of the sciences are wholly out of his grasp and he can impose on only a narrow range of the humanities his ideals of clear and inventive discourse. Does this mean that we must abandon to illiterate jargon or pseudo-science those crucial domains of historical, moral, and social inquiry in which the word should still be master? Does this mean that we have no grounds for appeal against the strident muteness of the arts?

There are those who hold out small hope. J. Robert Oppenheimer has pointed out that the breakdown of communication is as grave within the sciences as it is between sciences and humanities. The physicist and mathematician proceed in a growing measure of mutual incomprehension. The biologist and the astronomer look on each other's work across a gap of silence. Everywhere, knowledge is splintering into intense specialization, guarded by technical languages fewer and fewer of which can be mastered by any individual mind. Our awareness of the complication of reality is such that those unifications or syntheses of understanding which made common speech possible no longer work. Or they work only at the rudimentary level of daily need. Oppenheimer goes further: he indicates that the very attempt to find bridges between languages is misleading. There is no use trying to explain to the layman the reality-concepts of modern mathematics or physics. It cannot be done in any honest, truthful way. To do it by approximate metaphor is to spread falsehood and to foster an illusion of understanding. What is needed, suggests Oppenheimer, is a harsh modesty, an affirmation that common men cannot, in fact, understand most things and that the realities of which even a highly trained intellect has cognizance are few and far between.

With respect to the sciences, this somber view seems unassailable. And perhaps it dooms most knowledge to fragmentation. But we should not readily accede to it in history, ethics, economics, or the analysis and formulation of social and political conduct. Here literacy must reaffirm its authority against jargon. I do not know whether this can be done; but the stakes are high. In our time, the language of politics has become infected with obscurity and madness. No lie is too gross for strenuous expression, no cruelty too abject to find apologia in the verbiage of historicism. Unless we can restore to the words in our newspapers, laws, and political acts some measure of clarity and stringency of meaning, our lives will draw yet nearer to chaos. There will then come to pass a new Dark Ages. The prospect is not remote: "Who knows," says R. P. Blackmur, "it may be the next age will not express itself in words . . . at all, for the next age may not be literate in any sense we understand or the last three thousand years understood."

The poet of the *Pervigilium Veneris* wrote in a darkening time, amid the breakdown of classic literacy. He knew that the Muses can fall silent:

> *perdidi musam tacendo, nec me Apollo respicit:*
> *sic Amyclas, cum tacerent, perdidit silentium.*

"To perish by silence": that civilization on which Apollo looks no more will not long endure.

SILENCE AND THE POET

Both Hebraic and Classical mythology have in them the traces of an ancient fear. The tower broken in Babel and Orpheus torn, the prophet blinded so that sight is yielded for insight, Tamyris killed, Marsyas flayed, his voice turning to the cry of blood in the wind—these tell of a sense, deeper rooted than historical memory, of the miraculous outrage of human speech.

That articulate speech should be the line dividing man from the myriad forms of animate being, that speech should define man's singular eminence above the silence of the plant and the grunt of the beast—stronger, more cunning, longer of life than he—is classic doctrine well before Aristotle. We find it in Hesiod's *Theogony* (584). Man is, to Aristotle, a being of the word (ζῷον λόγον ἔχον). How the word came to him is, as Socrates admonishes in the *Cratylus*, a riddle, a question worth asking so as to goad the mind into play, so as to wake it to the wonder of its communicative genius, but it is not a question to which a certain answer lies in human reach.

Possessed of speech, possessed by it, the word having chosen the grossness and infirmity of man's condition for its own compelling life, the human person has broken free from the great silence of matter. Or, to use Ibsen's image: struck with the hammer, the insensate ore has begun to sing.

But this breaking free, the human voice harvesting echo where there was silence before, is both miracle and outrage, sacrament and blasphemy. It is a sharp severance from the world of the animal, man's begetter and sometime neighbor, the animal who, if we rightly grasp the myths of centaur, satyr, and sphinx, has been inwoven with the very substance of man, and whose instinctive immediacies and shapes of physical being have receded only partially from our own form. This harsh weaning, of which antique mythology is so uneasily conscious, has left its scars. Our own new mythologies take up the theme: in Freud's grim intimation of man's backward longing, of his covert wish for re-immersion in an earlier, inarticulate state of organic existence; in Claude Lévi-Strauss's speculations on man's self-banishment, by his Promethean theft of fire (the choice of cooked over raw food), and by his mastery of speech, from the natural rhythms and anonymities of the animal world.

If speaking man has made of the animal his mute servant or enemy—the beasts of the field and forest no longer understand our words when we cry for help—man's control of the word has also hammered at the door of the gods. More than fire, whose power to illumine or to consume, to spread and to draw inward, it so strangely resembles, speech is the core of man's mutinous relations to the gods. Through it he apes or challenges their prerogatives. Nimrud's tower was built of words; Tantalus gossiped, bringing to earth in a vessel of words the secrets of the gods. According to the Neo-Platonic and Johannine metaphor, in the beginning was the Word; but if this *Logos*, this act and essence of God is, in the last analysis, total communication, the word that creates its own content and truth of being—then what of *zoon phonanta*, man the speaking animal? He too creates words and creates with words. Can there be a coexistence other than charged with mutual torment and rebellion between the totality of the *Logos* and the living, world-creating fragments of our own speech? Does the act of speech, which defines man, not also go beyond him in rivalry to God?

In the poet this ambiguity is most pronounced. It is he who guards and multiplies the vital force of speech. In him the old words are kept resonant, and the new are lifted to the common light out of the active dark of individual consciousness. The poet makes in dangerous similitude to the gods. His song is builder of cities; his words have that power which, above all others, the gods would deny to man, the power to bestow enduring life. As Montaigne recognizes of Homer:

> *Et, à la vérité, je m'estonne souvent que luy, qui a produit et mis en credit au monde plusieurs deitez par son auctorité, n'a gaigné rang de Dieu luy mesme. . . .*

37

The poet is maker of new gods and preserver of men: thus Achilles and Agamemnon live, Ajax's great shade is burning still, because the poet has made of speech a dam against oblivion, and death blunts its sharp teeth upon his word. And because our languages have a future tense, which fact is of itself a radiant scandal, a subversion of mortality, the seer, the prophet, men in whom language is in a condition of extreme vitality, are able to look beyond, to make of the word a reaching out past death. For which presumption—to presume means to *anticipate* but also to *usurp*—they are grimly taxed.

Homer, the master-builder and rebel against time, in whom the conviction that the "winged word" shall outlast death speaks out in constant jubilation, goes blind. Orpheus is torn to bleeding shreds. Yet the word will not be quenched; it sings in the dead mouth:

> *membra iacent diversa locis, caput, Hebre, lyramque*
> *excipis: et (mirum!) medio dum labitur amne,*
> *flebile nescio quid queritur lyra, flebile lingua*
> *murmurat exanimis, respondent flebile ripae.*

Mirum! says Ovid: a marvel, a wonder, but also a scandal and defiance to the gods. Out of the gates of death man pours the living stream of words. And how may we read the torment of Marsyas, Apollo's challenger, that cruel fable of lyre against pipe which haunts the Renaissance to the time of Spenser, if not as a warning of the bitter intimacies and necessary vengeances between God and the poet? Poets are not, as officious mythology would have it, sons of Apollo, but of Marsyas. In his death cry they hear their own name:

> this is already beyond the endurance
> of the god with nerves of artificial fiber
>
> along a gravel path
> between box espaliers
> the victor departs
> wondering
> whether out of Marsyas' howling
> there will some day arise
> a new brand
> of art—let us say—concrete
>
> suddenly
> at his feet
> falls a petrified nightingale

he looks back
and sees
that the tree to which Marsyas was fastened
has gone white-haired

completely
>   (from the Polish of Zbigniew Herbert,
>   translated by Czesław Miłosz)

To speak, to assume the privileged singularity and solitude of
man in the silence of creation, is dangerous. To speak with the utmost
strength of the word, which is the poet's, supremely so. Thus even to
the writer, perhaps to him more than to others, silence is a temptation, a refuge when Apollo is near.

Gradually this ambivalence in the genius of language, this notion of the god-rivaling, therefore potentially sacrilegious character of
the act of the poet, becomes one of the recurrent tropes in Western
literature. From Medieval Latin poetry to Mallarmé and Russian
Symbolist verse, the motif of the necessary limitations of the human
word is a frequent one. It carries with it a crucial intimation of that
which lies outside language, of what it is that awaits the poet if he
were to transgress the bounds of human discourse. Being, in the
nature of his craft, a reacher, the poet must guard against becoming,
in the Faustian term, an overreacher. The daemonic creativity of his
instrument probes the outworks of the City of God; he must know
when to draw back lest he be consumed, Icarus-like, by the terrible
nearness of a greater making, of a *Logos* incommensurable with his
own (in the garden of fallen pleasures, Hieronymus Bosch's poet is
racked on his own harp).

But it is decisively the fact that language does have its frontiers,
that it borders on three other modes of statement—light, music, and
silence—which gives proof of a transcendent presence in the fabric of
the world. It is just because we can go no further, because speech so
marvelously fails us, that we experience the certitude of a divine
meaning surpassing and enfolding ours. What lies beyond man's
word is eloquent of God. That is the joyously defeated recognition
expressed in the poems of St. John of the Cross and of the mystic
tradition.

Where the word of the poet ceases, a great light begins. This
topos, with its historical antecedents in neo-Platonic and Gnostic

doctrine, gives to Dante's *Paradiso* its principal motion of spirit. We may understand the *Paradiso* as an exercise, supremely controlled yet full of extreme moral and poetic risk, in the calculus of linguistic possibility. Language is deliberately extended to the limit case. With each act of ascent, from sphere to radiant sphere, Dante's language is submitted to more intense and exact pressure of vision; divine revelation stretches the human idiom more and more out of the bounds of daily, indiscriminate usage. By exhaustive metaphor, by the use of similes increasingly audacious and precise—we hear the prayer in the syntax—Dante is able to make verbally intelligible the forms and meanings of his transcendent experience.

The characteristic rhetorical movement is one of initial retreat from the luminous, hermetic challenge, followed by an ingathering of utmost concentration, and a thrust forward into language unprecedented, into analogies and turns of statement which the poet himself discovers, which he had not known previously to lie within his grasp. First there is defeat. Words cannot convey what the pilgrim sees:

> *Perch' io lo ingegno, l'arte e l'uso chiami*
> *sì nol direi che mai s'imaginasse. . . .*
>
> (x)
>
> *e il canto di quei lumi era di quelle;*
> *chi non s'impenna sìche lassù voli,*
> *dal muto aspetti quindi le novelle.*
>
> (x)

The poet seeks refuge in muteness. Whereupon the upward surge, the verbalization of the hitherto incommunicable occurs through some miracle of simplicity, by way of a simile invoking a ball-game, hot wax flowing from the impress of a seal-ring, the shoemaker hammering at his nails. As if the grace of divine meaning were such that it can, under the poet's persuasion, enter the most natural, straightforward of our imaginings.

But as the poet draws near the Divine presence, the heart of the rose of fire, the labor of translation into speech grows ever more exacting. Words grow less and less adequate to the task of translating immediate revelation. Light passes to a diminishing degree into speech; instead of making syntax translucent with meaning, it seems to spill over in unrecapturable splendor or burn the word to ash. This is the drama of the final Cantos. As the poet moves upward his words fall behind. Until, in verse 55 of Canto xxxiii *il parlar nostro*, our human discourse, fails utterly:

> *Da quinci innanzi il mio veder fu maggio*
> *che il parlar nostro ch' a tal vista cede,*
> *e cede la memoria a tanto oltraggio.*

Words failing, memory, which is their confine, breaks also. This is an outrage (*oltraggio*); but it is a sacred, affirmative outrage, a manifest proof of being of that which surpasses all human speech. From that literally unspeakable light and glory, the tongue of the poet strives to bring back to us one single spark:

> *e fa la lingua mia tanto possente*
> *ch'une favilla sol della tua gloria*
> *possa lasciare alla futura gente* . . . .

After which speech yields entirely to the inexpressible language of light, and the poet, at the absolute summit of his powers, compares his art unfavorably with the inarticulate babblings of an unweaned child:

> *Omai sarà più corta mia favella,*
> *pure a quel ch' io ricordo, che di un fante*
> *che bagni ancor la lingua alla mammella.*

The circle is complete: at its furthest reach, where it borders on light, the language of men becomes inarticulate as is that of the infant before he masters words. Those who would press language beyond its divinely ordained sphere, who would contract the *Logos* into the word, mistake both the genius of speech and the untranslatable immediacy of revelation. They thrust their hands into fire instead of gathering light. That directed light beams (lasers) would one day become carriers of the word might have seemed to Dante a wondrous but not irrational adjunct to his vision.

One tradition finds light at the limits of language. Another, no less ancient or active in our poetry and poetics, finds music.

The interpenetration of poetry and music is so close that their origin is indivisible and usually rooted in a common myth. Still today the vocabulary of prosody and poetic form, of linguistic tonality and

41

cadence, overlaps deliberately with that of music. From Arion and Orpheus to Ezra Pound and John Berryman, the poet is maker of songs and singer of words. There are many and intricate strains (itself a musical term) in the concept of the musical character of poetic speech. The fortunes of Orpheus, as we follow them in Pindar and Ovid, in Spenser, Rilke, and Cocteau, are almost synonymous with the nature and functions of poetry. Because he is part Orpheus, the poet in Western literature is architect of myth, magician over savagery, and pilgrim toward death. The notion that the structure of the universe is ordered by harmony, that there is a music whose modes are the elements, the concord of the planetary orbits, the chime of water and blood, is ancient as Pythagoras and has never lost its metaphoric life. Until the seventeenth century and the "untuning of the sky," a belief in the music of the spheres, in Pythagorean or Keplerian accords and temperance between star and planet, between harmonious functions in mathematics and the vibrant lute string, underlies much of the poet's realization of his own action. The music of the spheres is guarantor and counterpoint to his own use of ordering, harmonious "numbers" (the terminology of rhetoric is consistently musical).

Hearkening to this music, as does Lorenzo in the garden at Belmont, he receives not only echo but that assurance of a transcendent presence, of a convention of statement and communication reaching beyond and concentric to his own which Dante receives from exceeding light:

> Look how the floor of heaven
> Is thick inlaid with patens of bright gold.
> There's not the smallest orb which thou behold'st
> But in his motion like an angel sings,
> Still quiring to the young-eyed cherubins;
> Such harmony is in immortal souls!

Patens are the small flat dishes used in Holy Communion—by which choice of word Shakespeare would have us note that communion and communication through transcendent harmony are vitally akin.

From this vast topic of the interactions of music with language, I want to abstract only one theme: the notion that poetry leads *toward* music, that it passes into music when it attains the maximal intensity of its being. This idea has the evident, powerful

42

implication that music is, in the final analysis, superior to language, that it says more or more immediately. The thought of rivalry between poet and musician is antithetical to the origins and full realization of both; it rends Orpheus more decisively than did the women of Thrace. Yet it too has its long, though often subterranean history. We find evidence of it in Plato's arguments on the respective functions of poetry and music in education, and in Patristic beliefs, which are at once related to Platonism but different in stress and conclusion, on the irrational, perhaps daemonic powers of music as contrasted with the rationality and verifiability of the word. In the Johannine beginning is the Word; in the Pythagorean, the accord. The rival claims of singer and speaker, moreover, are a Renaissance *topos* long before they find comic echo in Molière's *Bourgeois Gentilhomme* and in Richard Strauss's uses of Molière and of the music-language quarrel in *Ariadne*. The possible blackness of that quarrel, the way in which it may search out and articulate the soul's relationship to God, is at the heart of Mann's *Doctor Faustus*.

But it is not the contest I want to draw attention to: it is the recurrent acknowledgment by poets, by masters of language, that music *is* the deeper, more numinous code, that language, when truly apprehended, aspires to the condition of music and is brought, by the genius of the poet, to the threshold of that condition. By a gradual loosening or transcendence of its own forms, the poem strives to escape from the linear, denotative, logically determined bonds of linguistic syntax into what the poet takes to be the simultaneities, immediacies, and free play of musical form. It is in music that the poet hopes to find the paradox resolved of an act of creation singular to the creator, bearing the shape of his own spirit, yet infinitely renewed in each listener.

The fullest statement of this hope, of this submission of the word to the musical ideal, can be found in German Romanticism. It is in the writings and indeed personal lives of Tieck, Novalis, Wackenroder, E. T. A. Hoffmann, that the theory of music as the supreme, quintessential art, and of the word as its prelude and servant, is carried to the highest pitch of technical and philosophic implication. Novalis' *Hymns to the Night* turn on a metaphor of cosmic musicality; they image the spirit of man as a lyre played upon by elemental harmonies, and seek to exalt language to that state of rhapsodic obscurity, of nocturnal dissolution from which it may most naturally

43

pass into song. From Hoffmann to Mann's Adrian Leverkühn, the artist is, archetypally, a musician; for it is in music, far more than in speech or the plastic arts, that aesthetic conventions are brought near to the source of pure creative energy, that their roots in the subconscious and in the Faustian core of life itself are most nearly touched.

These writers were not necessarily of the first rank; but it would be difficult to exaggerate their influence on the European sensibility. Through them the idea of "correspondence"—all sensory stimuli are interchangeable and interwoven dialects in a universal language of perception—the belief in the uniquely generative character of musical composition, in its "privileged daemonism," and the key idea that verbal language is in some manner a lesser thing than music but a road toward it, pass into the repertoire of romantic, symbolist, and modern feeling. These writers prepared Wagner, and their premonitions found in him, and partially in Nietzsche, an extraordinary fulfillment.

Wagner pertains to language and the history of ideas as richly as he does to music (in the very long run perhaps more so). He made of the relationships between language and music the crux of his vision. In the *Gesamtkunstwerk* the upward aspiration of word toward musical tone and the latent antagonism between the two modes of statement were to be conjoined in a synthesis of total expression. In the love-duet of Act II of *Tristan* the words dim to outcry, to a stutter of swooning consciousness (deliberately infantile as is the stutter of the poet at the summit of the *Paradiso*), and pass through virtuosity of sonorous appropriation into something that is no longer speech. Music reaches out into this twilight zone to enclose the word in its own more comprehensive syntax. What is not entirely manifest in Wagner's theory becomes so in fact: music is master of the bargain. Aspiring to synthesis, or more exactly to organic coexistence, language loses the authority of rational statement, of designation through governed structure, which are its proper genius.

The Wagnerian influence on literary aesthetics from Baudelaire to Proust, and on the philosophy of language from Nietzsche to the early Valéry was immense. It brings with it two distinct yet related motifs: the exultation of the poet at being *almost* musician (a vision of self at work no less in Mallarmé than in Auden); but also a sad condescension to the verbal medium, a despair at being restricted to a form of expression thinner, narrower, much nearer the surface of the creative mind than is music. Thus Valéry to Gide in April 1891:

Je suis dans Lohengrin *jusqu' aux yeux. . . . Cette musi-*
que m'amènera, cela se prépare, à ne plus écrire. Déjà trop
de difficultés m'arrêtent. Narcisse a *parlé dans le dé-*
sert . . . être si loin de son rêve. . . . Et puis quelle page
écrite arrive à la hauteur des quelques notes qui sont le
motif du Graal?

Something of this haughty exasperation certainly survives in Valéry's later view of poetry as a mere "exercise" or "game" akin to
mathematics and by no means superior to it.

"What written page can attain the heights of the few notes of
the Grail motif?" The question and the implicit ordering of linguistic
and musical means is current in the whole Symbolist movement. It is
most carefully worked out in the poetry of Rilke, in Rilke's determination to guard both the genius of language and its rights of kinship
to music. Rilke celebrates the power of language to rise toward
music; the poet is the chosen instrument of that upward transmuta-
tion. But the metamorphosis can be achieved only if language preserves the identity of its striving, if it remains itself in the very act of
change. In the *Sonnets to Orpheus* language meditates with delicate
precision on its own limits; the word is poised for the transforming
rush of music. Yet Rilke, who always works on the frontier between
both, recognizes that something is dissolved, perhaps lost, in the
crowning change:

Gesang, wie du ihn lehrst, ist nicht Begehr,
nicht Werbung um ein endlich noch Erreichtes;
Gesang ist Dasein. Für den Gott ein Leichtes.
Wann aber sind wir? Und wann wendet er
an unser Sein die Erde und die Sterne?
Dies ists nicht, Jüngling, dass du liebst, wenn auch
die Stimme dann den Mund dir aufstösst,—lerne
vergessen, dass du aufsangst. Das verrinnt.
In Wahrheit singen, ist ein andrer Hauch.
Ein Hauch um nichts. Ein Wehn im Gott. Ein Wind.

The principal moods and energies of Symbolism and of the
Wagnerian dialectic of musical totality now lie behind us. But the
idea that music *is* deeper, more comprehensive than language, that it
rises with immediacy from the sources of our being, has not lost its
relevance and fascination. As has often been observed, the attempt to

45

deepen or reinforce a literary structure by means of musical analogy is frequent in modern poetry and fiction (in the *Four Quartets*, in Proust, in Broch's *Death of Virgil*). But the impulse toward a musical ideal is more far-reaching.

There is a widespread intimation, though as yet only vaguely defined, of a certain exhaustion of verbal resources in modern civilization, of a brutalization and devaluation of the word in the mass-cultures and mass-politics of the age. What more is there to say? How can that which is novel and discriminating enough to be worth saying get a hearing amid the clamor of verbal inflation? The word, especially in its sequential, typographic forms, may have been an imperfect, perhaps transitory code. Music alone can fulfill the two requirements of a truly rigorous communicative or semiological system: to be unique to itself (untranslatable) yet immediately comprehensible. Thus (in defiance, I think, of the specialized conventions of different musical "languages") argues Lévi-Strauss. He characterizes the composer, the inventor of melody, as *un être pareil aux dieux* even as Homer was characterized by Montaigne. Lévi-Strauss sees in music *le suprême mystère des sciences de l'homme, celui contre lequel elles butent, et qui garde la clé de leur progrès.* In music our deafened lives may regain a sense of the inward motion and temperance of individual being, and our societies something of a lost vision of human accord. Through music the arts and exact sciences may reach a common syntax.

We are back with Pythagoras or, more humbly, we live in rooms in which the record-cabinet has replaced the bookshelf.

Although they go beyond language, leaving verbal communication behind, both the translation into light and the metamorphosis into music are positive spiritual acts. Where it ceases or suffers radical mutation, the word bears witness to an inexpressible reality or to a syntax more supple, more penetrating than its own.

But there is a third mode of transcendence: in it language simply ceases, and the motion of spirit gives no further outward manifestation of its being. The poet enters into silence. Here the word borders not on radiance or music, but on night.

This election of silence by the most articulate is, I believe, historically recent. The strategic myth of the philosopher who chooses silence because of the ineffable purity of his vision or because of the unreadiness of his audience has antique precedent. It contributes to the motif of Empedocles on Aetna and to the gnomic aloofness of Heraclitus. But the poet's choice of silence, the writer relinquishing his articulate enactment of identity in mid-course, is something new. It occurs, as an experience obviously singular but formidable in general implication, in two of the principal masters, shapers, heraldic presences if you will, of the modern spirit: in Hölderlin and Rimbaud.

Each is among the foremost poets of his language. Each carried the written word to the far places of syntactic and perceptual possibility. In Hölderlin German verse attains an unsurpassed concentration, purity, and wholeness of realized form. There is no European poetry more mature, more inevitable in the sense of excluding from itself any looser, more prosaic order. A poem by Hölderlin fills a gap in the idiom of human experience with abrupt, complete necessity, though we had not previously known such a gap to exist. With Rimbaud poetry demands and is accorded the freedom of the modern city— those privileges of indirection, of technical autonomy, of inward reference and sub-surface rhetoric which almost define the twentieth-century style. Rimbaud left his thumbprint on language, on the name and nature of the modern poet, as Cézanne did on apples.

Yet as important as the work itself is the intense after-life of Hölderlin and Rimbaud in the mythology, in the active metaphors of the modern literary condition. Beyond the poems, almost stronger than they, is the fact of renunciation, the chosen silence.

By the age of thirty Hölderlin had accomplished nearly his whole work; a few years later he entered on a quiet madness which lasted thirty-six years, but during which there were a few sparks of the old lucid power (the famous quatrain written down, apparently impromptu, in April 1812). At eighteen Rimbaud completed the *Saison en enfer*, and embarked on the other hell of Sudanese commerce and Ethiopian gun-running. From it he poured out a deluge of exasperated letters; they bear the marks of his temper and harsh concision, but contain no line of poetry or reference to the work of genius left behind. In both cases, the precise motives and genesis of silence remain obscure. But the myths of language and poetic function that spring from the silence are clear and constitute a shaping legacy.

Hölderlin's silence has been read not as a negation of his poetry but as, in some sense, its unfolding and its sovereign logic. The gathering strength of stillness within and between the lines of the poems have been felt as a primary element of their genius. As empty space is so expressly a part of modern painting and sculpture, as the silent intervals are so integral to a composition by Webern, so the void places in Hölderlin's poems, particularly in the late fragments, seem indispensable to the completion of the poetic act. His posthumous life in a shell of quiet, similar to that of Nietzsche, stands for the word's surpassing of itself, for its realization not in another medium but in that which is its echoing antithesis and defining negation, silence.

Rimbaud's abdication is seen to have a very different sense. It signifies the elevation of action over word. "Speech that leads not to action," wrote Carlyle, "still more that hinders it, is a nuisance on the Earth." Having mastered and exhausted the resources of language as only a supreme poet can, Rimbaud turns to that nobler language which is the deed. The child dreams and babbles; the man does.

Both gestures of sensibility, both theoretic models, have exercised tremendous influence. This revaluation of silence—in the epistemology of Wittgenstein, in the aesthetics of Webern and Cage, in the poetics of Beckett—is one of the most original, characteristic acts of the modern spirit. The conceit of the word unspoken, of the music unheard and *therefore* richer is, in Keats, a local paradox, a neo-Platonic ornament. In much modern poetry silence represents the claims of the ideal; to speak is to say less. To Rilke the temptations of silence were inseparable from the hazard of the poetic act:

> *Was spielst du, Knabe? Durch die Gärten gings*
> *wie viele Schritte, flüsternde Befehle.*
> *Was spielst du, Knabe? Siehe deine Seele*
> *verfing sich in den Stäben der Syrinx.*

> *Was lockst du sie? Der Klang ist wie ein Kerker,*
> *darin sie sich versaümt und sich versehnt;*
> *stark ist dein Leben, doch dein Lied ist stärker,*
> *an deine Sehnsucht schluchzend angelehnt.*

> *Gieb ihr ein Schweigen, dass die Seele leise*
> *heimkehre in das Flutende und Viele,*
> *darin sie lebte, wachsend, weit und weise,*
> *eh du sie zwangst in deine zarten Spiele.*

> *Wie sie schon matter mit den Flügeln schlägt:*
> *so wirst du, Traümer, ihren Flug vergeuden,*

dass ihre Schwinge, vom Gesang zersägt,
sie nicht mehr über meine Mauern trägt,
wenn ich sie rufen werde zu den Freuden.

This sense of the work of art as entrapped, diminished when it is given articulate form and thus enters into a condition where it is both static and public, is not mystical, though it borrows some of the traditional tones of mysticism. It is grounded in historical circumstance, in a late stage of linguistic and formal civilization in which the expressive achievements of the past seem to weigh exhaustively on the possibilities of the present, in which word and genre seem tarnished, flattened to the touch, like coin too long in circulation. It is also part of a recognition, developed during the Romantic movement and given new metaphors of rationality by Freud, that art, so far as it is public communication, must share in a common code of surface meaning, that it necessarily impoverishes and generalizes the unique, individual life-force of unconscious creation. Ideally each poet should have his own language, singular to his expressive need; given the social, conventionalized nature of human speech, such language can only be silence.

But neither the paradox of silence as the final logic of poetic speech nor the exaltation of action over verbal statement, which is so strong a current in romantic existentialism, accounts for what is probably the most honest temptation to silence in contemporary feeling. There is a third and more powerful impulse, dating from circa 1914. As Mrs. Bickle expresses it in the closing sentence of that black comedy of novelist and recalcitrant subject, James Purdy's *Cabot Wright Begins*, "I won't be a writer in a place and time like the present."

The possibility that the political inhumanity of the twentieth century and certain elements in the technological mass-society which has followed on the erosion of European bourgeois values have done injury to language is the underlying theme of this book. In different essays I have discussed specific aspects of linguistic devaluation and dehumanization.

To a writer who feels that the condition of language is in question, that the word may be losing something of its humane genius, two essential courses are available: he may seek to render his own idiom representative of the general crisis, to convey through it the precariousness and vulnerability of the communicative act; or he may choose the suicidal rhetoric of silence. The sources and development of both attitudes can be seen most clearly in modern German literature, written as it is in the language which has most fully embodied and undergone the grammar of the inhuman.

To Kafka—and this is the core of his representative role in modern letters—the act of writing was a miraculous scandal. The live nakedness of his style takes no syllable for granted. Kafka names all things anew in a second Garden full of ash and doubt. Hence the tormented scruple of his every linguistic proposal. The *Letters to Milena* (they are the finest of modern love letters, the least dispensable) come back and back to the impossibility of adequate statement, to the hopelessness of the writer's task which is to find language as yet unsullied, worn to cliché, made empty by unmeditated waste. Arrested, in his own life and background, between conflicting idioms (Czech, German, Hebrew), Kafka was able to approach the very act of speech from outside. Listening to the mystery of language with more acute humility than ordinary men, he heard the jargon of death growing loud inside the European vulgate. Not in any vague, allegoric sense, but with exact prophecy. From the literal nightmare of *The Metamorphosis* came the knowledge that *Ungeziefer* ("vermin") was to be the designation of millions of men. The bureaucratic parlance of *The Trial* and *The Castle* have become commonplace in our herded lives. The instrument of torture in "In the Penal Colony" is also a printing press. In short, Kafka heard the name Buchenwald in the word *birchwood*. He understood, as if the bush had burned for him again, that a great inhumanity was lying in wait for European man, and that parts of language would serve it and be made base in the process (one thinks of the modulations from "central intelligence" in the fiction of Henry James to Central Intelligence in Washington). In such a time the act of writing might be either frivolous—the cry in the poem smothering or beautifying the cry in the street—or altogether impossible. Kafka found metaphoric expression for both alternatives.

So did Hofmannsthal in the most mature, elusive of his comedies, *Der Schwierige*. Momentarily buried alive in the trenches, Hans Karl Bühl returns from the wars profoundly distrustful of language. To use words as if they could truly convey the pulse and bewilderments of human feeling, to entrust the quick of the human spirit to the inflated currency of social conversation, is to commit self-deception and "indecency" (the key word in the play). "I understand

myself much less well when I speak than when I am silent," says
Bühl. Asked to orate in the Upper House on the high theme of the
"reconciliation of nations," Kari draws back with fastidious, pessi-
mistic insight. To open one's mouth on such a topic is to "wreak
unholy confusion." The very fact that one sees to *say* certain things
"is an indecency." The close contemporaneity between Wittgenstein's *Tractatus* and the parables of silence in Hofmannsthal and
other German and Austrian writers of the 1920's needs study. An
estrangement from language was, presumably, a part of a more
general abandonment of confidence in the stabilities and expressive
authority of central European civilization.

Nine years after Kafka's death, on the eve of actual barbarism,
Schoenberg concluded *Moses und Aron* with the cry "O word, thou
word that I lack." At almost the same time, the incompatibility
between eloquence, the poet's primary delight in speech, and the
inhuman nature of political reality, became the theme of the art of
Hermann Broch.

Because their language had served at Belsen, because words
could be found for all those things and men were not struck dumb for
using them, a number of German writers who had gone into exile or
survived Nazism, despaired of their instrument. In his *Song of Exile*,
Karl Wolfskehl proclaimed that the true word, the tongue of the
living spirit, was dead:

> *Und ob ihr tausend Worte habt:*
> *Das Wort, das Wort ist tot.*

Elisabeth Borcher said: "I break open stars and find nothing, and
again nothing, and then a word in a foreign tongue." A conclusion to
an exercise in linguistic-logical analysis, which Wittgenstein carefully stripped of all emotive reference, though he stated it in a mode
strangely poetic, strangely reminiscent of the atmosphere of Hölderlin's notes on Sophocles, of Lichtenberg's aphorisms, had turned to a
grim truth, to a precept of self-destructive humanity for the poet.
"Whereof one cannot speak, thereof one must be silent."

But this sense of a death in language, of the failure of the word
in the face of the inhuman, is by no means limited to German.

During the political crisis of 1938, Adamov asked himself
whether the thought of being a writer was not an untimely joke,
whether the writer would ever again, in European civilization, have a
living, humane idiom with which to work:

51

Le nom de Dieu ne devrait plus jaillir de la bouche de l'homme. Ce mot dégradé par l'usage, depuis si longtemps, ne signifie plus rien. Il est vidé de tout sens, de tout sang. . . . Les mots, ces gardiens du sens ne sont pas immortels, invulnérables. . . . Comme les hommes, les mots souffrent. . . . Certains peuvent survivre, d'autres sont incurables. . . . Dans la nuit tout se confond, il n'y a plus de noms, plus de formes.

When war came, he wrote: "Worn, threadbare, filed down, words have become the carcass of words, phantom words; everyone drearily chews and regurgitates the sound of them between their jaws."

More recently, Ionesco has published the following from his *Journal:*

> It is as if, through becoming involved in literature, I had used up all possible symbols without really penetrating their meaning. They no longer have any vital significance for me. Words have killed images or are concealing them. A civilization of words is a civilization distraught. Words create confusion. Words are not the word [*les mots ne sont pas la parole*]. . . . The fact is that words say nothing, if I may put it that way. . . . There are no words for the deepest experience. The more I try to explain myself, the less I understand myself. Of course, not everything is unsayable in words, only the living truth.

These two last sentences echo, almost exactly, Hofmannsthal's Kari Bühl. The writer, who is by definition master and servant of language, states that the living truth is no longer sayable. The theater of Beckett is haunted by this insight. Developing Chekhov's notion of the near-impossibility of effective verbal interchange, it strains toward silence, toward an *Act Without Words.* Soon there will be plays in which absolutely nothing is said, in which each personage will struggle to achieve the outrage or futility of speech only to have the sound turn to gibberish or die in their grimacing mouths. The first articulate word spoken will bring down the curtain.

Under the influence, perhaps, of Heidegger and of Heidegger's gloss on Hölderlin, recent French linguistic philosophy also assigns a special function and prestigious authority to silence. For Brice Parain, "language is the threshold of silence." Henri Lefebvre finds that silence "is at once inside language, and on its near and far sides." Much of his theory of speech depends on the organized patterns of silence in the otherwise continuous and consequently indecipherable linguistic code. Silence has "another speech than ordinary saying" (*un autre Dire que le dire ordinaire*), but it is meaningful speech nevertheless.

These are not macabre fantasies or paradoxes for logicians. The question of whether the poet should speak or be silent, of whether language is in a condition to accord with his needs, is a real one. "No poetry after Auschwitz," said Adorno, and Sylvia Plath enacted the underlying meaning of his statement in a manner both histrionic and profoundly sincere. Has our civilization, by virtue of the inhumanity it has carried out and condoned—we are accomplices to that which leaves us indifferent—forfeited its claims to that indispensable luxury which we call literature? Not for ever, not everywhere, but simply in this time and place, as a city besieged forfeits its claims to the freedom of the winds and the cool of evening outside its walls.

I am not saying that writers should stop writing. This would be fatuous. I am asking whether they are not writing too much, whether the deluge of print in which we seek our deafened way is not itself a subversion of meaning. "A civilization of words is a civilization distraught." It is one in which the constant inflation of verbal counters has so devalued the once numinous act of written communication that there is almost no way for the valid and the genuinely new to make themselves heard. Each month must produce its masterpiece and so the press hounds mediocrity into momentary, fake splendor. The scientists tell us that the acceleration of specialized, monographic publication is such that libraries will soon have to be placed in orbit, circling the earth and subject to electronic scanning as needed. The proliferation of verbiage in humanistic scholarship, the trivia decked out as erudition or critical re-assessment, threatens to obliterate the work of art itself and the exacting freshness of personal encounter on which true criticism depends. We also speak far too much, far too easily, making common what was private, arresting into the clichés of false certitude that which was provisional, personal, and therefore alive on the shadow-side of speech. We live in a culture which is, increasingly, a wind-tunnel of gossip; gossip that reaches from theology and politics to an unprecedented noising of private concerns (the psychoanalytic process is the high rhetoric of gossip). This world will end neither with a bang nor a whimper, but with a headline, a slogan, a pulp novel larger than the cedars of Lebanon. In how much of what is now pouring forth do words become word—and where is the silence needed if we are to hear that metamorphosis?

The second point is one of politics, in the fundamental sense. It is better for the poet to mutilate his own tongue than to dignify the inhuman either with his gift or his uncaring. If totalitarian rule is so effective as to break all chances of denunciation, of satire, then let the poet cease—and let the scholar cease from editing the classics a few miles down the road from the death camp. Precisely because it is the signature of his humanity, because it is that which makes of man a being of striving unrest, the word should have no natural life, no neutral sanctuary, in the places and season of bestiality. Silence *is* an alternative. When the words in the city are full of savagery and lies, nothing speaks louder than the unwritten poem.

"Now the Sirens have a still more fatal weapon than their song," wrote Kafka in his *Parables*, "namely their silence. And though admittedly such a thing has never happened, still it is conceivable that someone might possibly have escaped from their singing; but from their silence certainly never."

How silent must that sea have been; how ready for the wonder of the word.

TO CIVILIZE OUR GENTLEMEN

A man would have to be an outright optimist or gifted with self-deception to argue that all is well in the study and teaching of English literature. There is a distinct malaise in the field, a sense of things going wrong or by default. The quality of students in respect of intellectual rigor and independence of mind is not always very impressive, compared, say, with the man coming up to read economics, or the good historian, let alone the natural scientist. Motives are unclear or faintly hypocritical. A man reads English because he wants time in which to write fiction or verse, to act or produce plays, or simply because English looks like the soft option before he enters business and begins serious life. Reading a number of good books which an educated man should have read anyway is a pleasant enough way of spending three or four years at a university, pleasanter than learning a lot of mathematics needed for economics or irregular verbs in a foreign tongue.

The malaise in research studies is of a different nature, but no less disturbing. The entire notion of research, when applied to literature, is problematic. As there are fewer and fewer really significant texts to edit, and this is what doctoral research in literature originally meant, as the historical or technical problems to be cleared up grow less and less substantial, the whole thesis business grows more tenuous. And already the hunt for genuine subjects is a difficult one. Many dissertations, particularly the safe ones, deal with trivia or with matters so restrictive that the students themselves lose respect for what they are doing.

The contrasting notion that a dissertation should be a piece of literary criticism, that a young man or woman in the very early twenties should have something fresh or profound or decisive to say about Shakespeare or Keats or Dickens is equally perplexing. Few people are ever able to say anything very new about major literature, and the idea that one can do so when one is young is almost paradoxical. Literature takes a great deal of living with and living by. So which is it to be? The combing of increasingly barren ground for some tiny fragments, or the large, uneasy vagueness of premature generality and judgment? Is either a genuine discipline? Indeed is "English Lit." in its academic guise? Exactly what is happening, what is being achieved, when a man reads novels, poems, or plays which he might well have read in the course of ordinary life and certainly ought to have read if he regards himself as a literate member of his society?

English is not the only field in which such questions can be put. The problem of research, of what graduate study means, pertains to the arts as a whole. But the restiveness of many who are engaged in the teaching and study of English literature and the peculiar public acrimony which seems to characterize their professional disagreements suggest that the difficulties have reached a fairly acute stage. All I want is to try to put the question in some kind of historical and moral focus, to try to point to some of the roots of our present dilemmas. In fact these go back almost to the beginning of English literature as an academic pursuit. Much of what needs saying today is already implicit in William Morris' well-known dissent from the establishment of a chair of English Literature at Oxford. It dates to the eighteen-eighties when Morris spoke, and to the late eighteen-sixties when Farrar edited the *Essays on a Liberal Education* and Matthew Arnold produced his *Culture and Anarchy*. We must look there for the assumptions on which faculties of English Literature were founded.

What were these assumptions? Do they still hold good? Are they relevant to our present needs? In method and intellectual organization, the academic study of modern languages and literature reflects the older tradition of classical studies. The critical, textual, historical study of Greek and Latin literature not only gave precedent and justification for a similar study of the European vulgate; they were foundations on which that study was built. Behind the analysis of Spenser or Pope or Milton or Shelley lay an assumed classic literacy, a natural familiarity with Homeric, Virgilian, Horatian, and Platonic models and energies. The classic background and interests of Matthew Arnold, Henry Sidgwick, Saintsbury, are representative. The notion that a man could study modern literature, could study or edit it honestly without having the classical background, would have seemed shocking and implausible.

The second major assumption was nationalism. It is no accident that German philology and Germanic textual criticism coincided with the dynamic rise of the German national consciousness (and let us not forget that it was on the genius of the German scholars that the rest of Europe, England, and America drew so heavily). As Herder, the Grimm brothers, and the whole lineage of German literary teachers and critics were frank to proclaim, the study of one's own literary past played a vital part in affirming national identity. To this point of view Taine and the historical positivists added the theory that one gets to know the unique racial genius of a people, of one's own people, by studying its literature. Everywhere the history of modern literary studies shows the mark of this nationalist ideal of the mid-and late-nineteenth century.

The third major body of assumption is even more vital, but I find it difficult to analyze briefly. Perhaps I could put it this way: behind the formation of modern literary analysis, editorial scholarship, and literary history, lies a kind of rational and moral optimism. In its philological and historical methods the field of literary study reflects a large hope, a great positivism, an ideal of being something like a science, and we find this all the way from Auguste Comte to I. A. Richards. The brilliant work of the classical and semitic philologists and textual analysts in the nineteenth century, which is one of the chapters of intellectual glory in Europe, seemed to give warrant for the use of similar means and standards in studying a modern text. The variorum, the concordance, the rigorous bibliography—all these are a direct inheritance of this positivist tradition. But the optimism lay much deeper. The study of literature was assumed to carry an almost necessary implication of moral force. It was thought self-evident that the teaching and reading of the great poets and prose writers would enrich not only taste and style but moral feeling; that it would cultivate human judgment and act against barbarism.

There is a remark here by Henry Sidgwick which is typical. He wants us to study English literature so that our views and sympathies may be enlarged and expanded, "by apprehending noble, subtle and profound thoughts, refined and lofty feelings," and he sees in literature the "source and essence of a truly humanizing culture." I think

57

that is the key phrase. And this high claim extends from Matthew Arnold's idea of poetry as a vital substitute for religious dogma to Dr. Leavis' definition of the study of English Literature as the "central humanity." Again we should note the carry-over from the Renaissance and eighteenth-century view of the role of the classics.

Do these assumptions—the classic background, the nationalist consciousness, and the rational, moralizing hope—these habits and traditions of feeling still hold today? In regard to the classics our condition has formidably altered. Consider two passages from Shakespeare. The first is the celebrated nocturne of love between Lorenzo and Jessica:

Lorenzo: The moon shines bright. . . . In such a night as this,
When the sweet wind did gently kiss the trees,
And they did make no noise, in such a night
Troilus methinks mounted the Troyan walls,
And sighed his soul toward the Grecian tents,
Where Cressid lay that night.

Jessica: In such a night
Did Thisbe fearfully o'ertrip the dew,
And saw the lion's shadow ere himself,
And ran dismayed away.

Lorenzo: In such a night
Stood Dido with a willow in her hand
Upon the wild sea banks, and waft her love
To come again to Carthage.

Jessica: In such a night
Medea gathered the enchanted herbs
That did renew old Aeson.

The second is a brief passage from Berowne's mockeries in Act IV of *Love's Labour's Lost:*

O me, with what strict patience have I sat
To see a king transformed to a gnat!
To see great Hercules whipping a gig,
And profound Solomon to tune a jig,

And Nestor play at push-pin with the boys,
And critic Timon laugh at idle toys!

The classical references in these two passages, as in countless others in Shakespearean drama, were most probably immediately familiar to a large part of Shakespeare's audience. Troilus, Thisbe, Medea, Dido, Hercules, Nestor would be part of the repertoire of recognition to anyone with a measure of Elizabethan grammar-schooling, having come down as living resonance from Plutarch and Ovid's *Metamorphoses* through Chaucer's *Legend of Good Women*. And these allusions are no mere ornament; they organize the essential focus of Shakespeare's text (the partially comic, partially sinister precedents invoked by Lorenzo and Jessica beautifully articulate the impulsive, somewhat frivolous quality of their infatuation). The worthies cited by Berowne reflect ironically on his own role and image of himself.

These several references would have been eloquent to an Augustan with any serious claim to literacy, to a Victorian public-school boy, to much of the educated European and English bourgeoisie until, say, 1914. But what of today? Hercules, Dido, and Nestor, probably. What of critic Timon and Medea's murderous rejuvenation of Aeson, with its grim hint of Jessica's view of old Shylock? Difficult for those without a classical education.

The point is not trivial. As footnotes lengthen, as glossaries become more elementary (right now it might still be "Troilus: Trojan hero in love with Cressida, daughter of Calchas, and betrayed by her," but in a few years the *Iliad* itself may require identification), the poetry loses immediate impact. It moves out of any direct line of vision into a place of special learning. This fact marks a very large change in the consensus assumed between poet and public. The world of classical mythology, of historical reference, of scriptural allusion, on which a preponderant part of English and European literature is built from Chaucer to Milton and Dryden, from Tennyson to Eliot's *Sweeney Agonistes*, is receding from our natural reach.

Take the second assumption, the glorious, hopeful view of national genius. From being a nineteenth-century dream, nationalism has grown to a present nightmare. In two world wars it has all but ruined Western culture. It may end by driving us like crazed lemmings to destruction. In the case of England's political and psychological position the change has been particularly drastic. The implications of the supremacy of the English language, of the exemplary moral and institutional authority of English life, which we see everywhere in the treatment of English literature before the first world war, are no longer tenable. The center of creative and linguistic gravity has begun to shift. Thinking of Joyce, Yeats, Shaw, O'Casey, T. S. Eliot, Faulkner, Hemingway, Fitzgerald, one makes a commonplace observation. The great energies of the language now enter into play outside England. Only Hardy, John Cowper Powys, and Lawrence can be compared to these major writers. The American language is not only asserting its autonomous power and showing far greater facilities of assimilation, of innovation, than is standard English, but it is more and more pressing on England itself. American words express economic and social realities attractive to the young in England, to the hitherto underprivileged, and these words are becoming part of the dream life and vulgate of the post-war English scene. African English, Australian English, the rich speech of West Indian and Anglo-Indian writers, represent a complicated, polycentric field of linguistic force, in which the language taught and written in England is no longer the inevitable authority or focus.

If these new literacies are to be excluded from our curriculum, will that curriculum become almost wholly historical? Will the student of English literature be taught in a kind of museum? But if we are to include these new literacies, and this is particularly relevant with respect to American literature, what is to be dropped? How are lines of continuity to be drawn? Less Dryden, so we can have more Whitman? Miss Dickinson instead of Mrs. Browning?

To the historian and literary scholar of the late nineteenth century the tremendous advance of the sciences was no threat. He looked on it as a glorious parallel adventure. I think this is no longer the case. I have tried to outline the new situation in "The Retreat from the Word."

The bearing of the multiplication and scattering of literacies on the entire shape, on the integrity of literary studies, seems to me to be profound and far-ranging. Until now it has hardly been understood or brought into rational perspective.

If the relationship of literary studies and literary awareness to the ensemble of knowledge and expressive means in our society has radically altered, so surely has the confident link between literature and civilized values. This, I think, is the key point. The simple yet appalling fact is that we have very little solid evidence that literary studies do very much to enrich or stabilize moral perception, that they *humanize*. We have little proof that a tradition of literary studies in fact makes a man more humane. What is worse—a certain body of evidence points the other way. When barbarism came to twentieth-century Europe, the arts faculties in more than one university offered very little moral resistance, and this is not a trivial or local accident. In a disturbing number of cases the literary imagination gave servile or ecstatic welcome to political bestiality. That bestiality was at times enforced and refined by individuals educated in the culture of traditional humanism. Knowledge of Goethe, a delight in the poetry of Rilke, seemed no bar to personal and institutionalized sadism. Literary values and the utmost of hideous inhumanity could coexist in the same community, in the same individual sensibility; and let us not take the easy way out and say "the man who did these things in a concentration camp just said he was reading Rilke. He was not reading him well." That is an evasion. He may have been reading him very well indeed.

Unlike Matthew Arnold and unlike Dr. Leavis, I find myself unable to assert confidently that the humanities humanize. Indeed, I would go further: it is at least conceivable that the focusing of consciousness on a written text, which is the substance of our training and pursuit, diminishes the sharpness and readiness of our actual moral response. Because we are trained to give psychological and moral credence to the imaginary, to the character in a play or a novel, to the condition of spirit we gather from a poem, we may find it more difficult to identify with the real world, to take the world of actual experience to heart—"to heart" is a suggestive phrase. The capacity for imaginative reflex, for moral risk in any human being is not limitless; on the contrary, it can be rapidly absorbed by fictions, and thus the cry in the poem may come to sound louder, more urgent, more real than the cry in the street outside. The death in the novel may move us more potently than the death in the next room. Thus there may be a covert, betraying link between the cultivation of aesthetic response and the potential of personal inhumanity. What then are we doing when we study and teach literature?

It seems to me that the wide gap between the orthodox academic formulation of "Eng.Lit." as it is still so largely prevalent in universities, and the realities of our intellectual and psychological situation may account for the general malaise in the field. There are questions we must be tactless and undiplomatic enough to raise if we are to stay honest with ourselves and our students. But I have no answers; only suggestions and further queries.

The profusion and stylishness of modern poetic translations from the classics, during the two generations from Pound to Lattimore and Robert Fitzgerald, are comparable to those of the age of Tudor and Elizabethan translation. But this tells not so much of a return to traditional humanism as of the fact that even the better schooled among us can no longer cope with Greek and Latin. These translations are often superb and should be used, but they cannot replace that immediacy of response, that natural background, which Milton, Pope, and even Tennyson assumed in their readers. It is therefore possible that such works as Dryden's *Absalom and Achitophel*, a good deal of *Paradise Lost*, of *The Rape of the Lock*, or Shelley's Aeschylaean and Platonic verse will pass increasingly into the custody and delight of the specialist. Milton's *Lycidas* is perhaps a test case; there is scarcely a passage to which the generally educated modern reader has immediate access.

I am not saying that we must abandon our classic legacy; we cannot. But I wonder whether we must not recognize its limited, difficult survival in our culture, and whether that recognition should not lead us to ask whether there may be other coordinates of cultural reference that touch more urgently on the present contours of our lives, on the way we now think and feel and try to find our way. This is quite simply a plea for modern comparative studies. Monsieur Etiemble in Paris may be right when he says that an acquaintance with a Chinese novel or a Persian lyric is almost indispensable to contemporary literacy. Not to know Melville or Rimbaud, Dostoevsky or Kafka, not to have read Mann's *Doctor Faustus* or Pasternak's *Doctor Zhivago* is a disqualification so severe from the notion of a vital literacy that we must raise, if not answer, the entire question of whether the close study of one literature makes good sense. Is it not as important for the survival of feeling today for a man to know another living language as it was once important for him to be intimate with the classics and Scripture?

Monsieur Etiemble argues that the Anglo-Saxon and western-European sensibility, the way we in the West think and feel and imagine the present world, will remain largely artificial and dangerously obsolete if we do not make the effort of learning one of the major languages outside the park—say Russian or Hindi or Chinese.

62

How many of us have tried to acquire even the most preliminary knowledge of Chinese, of the oldest of all literate cultures—a culture which is borne by the energies of the largest nation on earth and many features of which are certain to dominate the next era of history? Or, less ambitiously, is a man who has spent his last years of school and his university career in the study of English literature to the exclusion of nearly every other language and tradition, an educated man? Many reorientations, many ways of ordering and choosing are available to scholarship and the imagination. English literature can be taught in its European context: an awareness of George Eliot implying a simultaneous response to Balzac; Walter Scott being seen in relation to Victor Hugo, Manzoni, and Pushkin, as part of that great turn of the human imagination toward history which takes place after the French Revolution. English literature can be seen in its increasingly reciprocal relationship to American literature and the American language. An inquiry can be made into the fascinating divisions of meaning and imaginative connotation which the two communities are making today while still preserving largely a common vocabulary.

Why not study the history of English poetry in close comparison with that of another expansionist and colonizing tradition, say Spanish? How have the characteristics of the language in far places developed in relation to the home tradition? Are the problems of form and consciousness met by the Spanish poet in Mexico comparable to those of the Anglo-Indian; are certain languages better media of cultural exchange than others? The directions of vision are manifold. The alternative is parochialism and retrenchment from reality. The almost total lack of comparative studies in English academic circles (and I open parentheses here to acknowledge that in the new universities such comparative studies are being undertaken and to note my fear that what does not originate at the center of England, at the top of the academic establishment, does not always have much chance of life) may in itself be a very small thing. But it may also be a symptom of a more general withdrawal, of the fist closing tight against an altered, uncomfortable world. This would be alarming because in culture, no less than in politics, chauvinism and isolation are suicidal options.

The displacement of traditional linguistic modes from an essentially dominant function in our civilization has consequences so intricate and large that we have not even begun to take stock.

It is naïve to suppose that a little teaching of poetry to the

biophysicist or a little mathematics to the student of English literature will solve the problem. We are in mid-tide of divisive energies
too new, too complicated, to allow of any confident remedy. Ninety
percent of all the scientists in human history are now living. Scientific
publications over the next twenty-five years, if laid next to each other
on an imaginary shelf, would reach to the moon. The shapes of reality
and of our imaginative grasp are exceedingly difficult to foresee. Nevertheless, the student of literature now has access to and responsibility toward a very rich terrain, intermediate between the arts and
sciences, a terrain bordering equally on poetry, on sociology, on
psychology, on logic, and even on mathematics. I mean the domain of
linguistics and of the theory of communication.

Its expansion in the post-war period is one of the most exciting
chapters of modern intellectual history. The entire nature of language
is being re-thought and re-examined as it has not been since Plato and
Leibniz. The questions being asked about the relations between
verbal means and sensory perception, about the way in which syntax
mirrors or controls the reality-concept of a given culture, about the
history of linguistic forms as a record of ethnic consciousness—these
questions go to the very heart of our poetic and critical concern. The
precise analysis of verbal resources and grammatical changes over
any period of history which may soon be feasible by means of computers may have close bearing on literary history and interpretation.
We are within reach of knowing the rate at which new words enter a
language. We can discern graphic contours and statistical patterns
relating linguistic phenomena to economic, sociological changes. Our
whole sense of the medium is being revalued.

Let me give only two examples which are familiar to any student of modern linguistics. There is a Latin-American Indian language, indeed there are a number, in which the future—the notion of
that which is yet to happen—is set at the back of the speaker. The
past which he can see, because it has already happened, lies all before
him. He backs into the future unknown; memory moves forward,
hope backward. This is the exact reversal of the primary coordinates
by which we ourselves organize our feelings in root metaphors. How
does such a reversal affect literature or, in a larger sense, to what
extent is syntax the ever renewed cause of our modes of sensibility
and verbal concept? Or take the well-known instance of the astounding range of terms—I believe it is in the region of one hundred—by
which the gauchos of the Argentine discriminate between the shad-

ings of a horse's hide. Do these terms in some manner precede the perception of the actual nuance of color, or does that perception, sharpened by professional need, cause the invention of new words? Either hypothesis throws a rich light on the processes of poetic invention and on the essential fact that translation means the meshing of two different world images, of two entirely different patterns of human life.

To a contemporary student of literature the latest recension of Dryden or essay on the point of view in *Nostromo* are certainly of interest. But is the work of Jakobson on the structure of speech or of Lévi-Strauss on the relations between myth, syntax, and culture not as important, or dare I say even more so? The theory of communications is a branch of linguistics peculiarly enriched by advances in mathematical logic. The advance since I. A. Richards began his work on the nature of poetic statement, and Wittgenstein inquired into the structure of meaning has been dramatic. I am thinking of the work being done on the relations between visual, auditive, and verbal communications and impulses in Russia, at M.I.T., in the Centre for Culture and Technology at the University of Toronto—particularly at Toronto under Marshall McLuhan. The reception accorded to McLuhan's work by the "Eng.Lit." establishment is one of the most disturbing of recent symptoms of parochialism and laziness of mind. The *Gutenberg Galaxy* is an irritating book, full of wildness and imprecision, full of unnecessary gesture, egotistical, almost at certain points megalomaniac; but so, of course, is Coleridge's *Biographia Literaria* or Blake's *Descriptive Catalogue*. And like Blake, who has greatly influenced his thought, McLuhan has the gift of radical illumination. Even when we cannot follow his leap of argument, we are made to re-think our basic concepts of what literature is, what a book is, and how we read it. Together with Sartre's *Qu'est-que ce la littérature?* the *Gutenberg Galaxy* should stand on the shelf of anyone who calls himself a student or teacher of writing and of English literature. Are these directions not as exciting, as demanding of stringency as the latest edition of yet another minor poet or the fiftieth analysis of Henry James's narrative style?

The last point I want to touch on is the most difficult to put, even in a provisional way. We do not know whether the study of the humanities, of the noblest that has been said and thought, can do very much to humanize. We do not know; and surely there is something rather terrible in our doubt whether the study and delight a man finds in Shakespeare make him any less capable of organizing a concentration camp. Recently one of my colleagues, an eminent scholar, inquired of me, with genuine bafflement, why someone trying to establish himself in an English literature faculty should refer so often to concentration camps; why they were in any way relevant. They are profoundly relevant, and before we can go on teaching we must surely ask ourselves: are the humanities humane and, if so, why did they fail before the night?

It is at least possible that our emotion in the written word, in the detail of the remote text, in the life of the poet long dead, blunts our sense of present realness and need. One recalls Auden's prayer at the grave of Henry James: "Because there is no end to the vanity of our calling: make intercession/ For the treason of all clerks." Because this is so our hopes should be uneasy yet tenacious, and our claims to relevance modest, yet at all times urgently pressed. I believe that great literature *is* charged with what grace secular man has gained in his experience, and with much of the harvest of experienced truth at his disposal. But to those who challenge, who query the pertinence of my calling, I must more than ever before give scrupulous hearing. In short, I must at every point be ready to answer to them and to myself the question: What am I trying to do? Where has it failed? Can it succeed at all?

If we do not make our humanistic studies responsible, that is if we do not discriminate in our allocation of time and interest between that which is primarily of historical or local significance and that which has in it the pressure of sustained life, then the sciences will indeed enforce their claim. Science can be neutral. That is both its splendor and its limitation and it is a limitation which makes science in the final analysis almost "trivial." Science cannot begin to tell us what brought on the barbarism of the modern condition. It cannot tell us how to salvage our affairs though it has made the immediate menace to them more precise. A great discovery in physics or biochemistry can be neutral. A neutral humanism is either a pedantic artifice or a prologue to the inhuman. I cannot put it more exactly or in a succinct formula. It is a matter of seriousness and emotional risk, a recognition that the teaching of literature, if it can be done at all, is an extraordinarily complex and dangerous business, of knowing that one takes in hand the quick of another human being. Negatively, I suppose it means that one should not publish three hundred pages on some sixteenth- or seventeenth-century writer without expressing any opinion on whether he is worth reading today. Or, as Kierkegaard said: "It is not worth while remembering that past which cannot become a present."

To teach literature as if it were some kind of urbane trade, of professional routine, is to do worse than teach badly. To teach it as if the critical text were more important, more profitable than the poem, as if the examination syllabus mattered more than the adventure of private discovery, of passionate digression, is worst of all. Kierkegaard made a cruel distinction, but we could do worse than bear it in mind when we enter a room to give a lecture on Shakespeare or Coleridge, or Yeats: "There are two ways, one is to suffer; the other is to become a professor of the fact that another suffers."

In I. A. Richards' *Practical Criticism* we find the following:

> The question of belief or disbelief, in the intellectual sense, never arises when we are reading well. If unfortunately it does arise, either through the poet's fault or our own, we have for the moment ceased to be reading and have become astronomers, or theologians, or moralists, persons engaged in quite a different type of activity.

To which the answer should be: No, we have become men. To read great literature as if it did not have upon us an urgent design, to be able to move unchanged on the day after reading Pound's LXXXIst *Canto*, is to do little more than to make entries in a librarian's catalogue. When he was twenty, Kafka wrote in a letter:

> If the book we are reading does not wake us, as with a fist hammering on our skull, why then do we read it? So that it shall make us happy? Good God, we would also be happy if we had no books, and such books as make us happy we could, if need be, write ourselves. But what we must have are those books which come upon us like ill-fortune, and distress us deeply, like the death of one we love better than ourselves, like suicide. A book must be an ice-axe to break the sea frozen inside us.

Students of English literature, of any literature, must ask those who teach them, as they must ask themselves, whether they know, and not in their minds alone, what Kafka meant.

NIGHT WORDS

High Pornography & Human Privacy

Is there any science-fiction pornography? I mean something *new*, an invention by the human imagination of new sexual experience? Science fiction alters at will the coordinates of space and time; it can set effect before cause; it works within a logic of total potentiality —"all that can be imagined can happen." But has it added a single item to the repertoire of the erotic? I understand that in a forthcoming novel the terrestrial hero and explorer indulges in mutual masturbation with a bizarre, interplanetary creature. But there is no real novelty in that. Presumably one can use anything from seaweed to accordions, from meteorites to lunar pumice. A galactic monster would make no essential difference to the act. It would not extend in any real sense the range of our sexual being.

The point is crucial. Despite all the lyric or obsessed cant about the boundless varieties and dynamics of sex, the actual sum of pos-

[Controversy over this article continued for many months, and is continuing still. My knowledge of and interest in pornography are, I would suppose, no greater than the middle-class average. What I was trying to get into focus is the notion of the "stripping naked" of language, of the removal from private, intensely privileged or adventurous use, of the erotic vocabulary. It does seem to me that we have scarcely begun to understand the impoverishment of our imaginings, the erosion into generalized banality of our resources of individual erotic representation and expression. This erosion is very directly a part of the general reduction of privacy and individual style in a mass-consumer civilization. Where everything can be said with a shout, less and less can be said in a low voice. I was also trying to raise the question of what relation there *may* be between the dehumanization of the individual in pornography and the making naked and anonymous of the individual in the totalitarian state (the concentration camp being the logical epitome of that state). Both pornography and totalitarianism seem to me to set up power relations which must necessarily violate privacy. Though the discussion which followed on publication has been heated, neither of these two issues has, I feel, been fully understood or engaged.]

sible gestures, consummations, and imaginings is drastically limited. There are probably more foods, more undiscovered eventualities of gastronomic enjoyment or revulsion than there have been sexual inventions since the Empress Theodora resolved "to satisfy all amorous orifices of the human body to the full and at the same time." There just aren't that many orifices. The mechanics of orgasm imply fairly rapid exhaustion and frequent intermission. The nervous system is so organized that responses to simultaneous stimuli at different points of the body tend to yield a single, somewhat blurred sensation. The notion (fundamental to Sade and much pornographic art) that one can double one's ecstasy by engaging in *coitus* while being at the same time deftly sodomized is sheer nonsense. In short: given the physiological and nervous complexion of the human body, the number of ways in which orgasm can be achieved or arrested, the total modes of intercourse, are fundamentally finite. The mathematics of sex stop somewhere in the region of *soixante-neuf;* there are no transcendental series.

This is the logic behind the *120 Days*. With the pedantic frenzy of a man trying to carry *pi* to its final decimal, Sade labored to imagine and present the sum total of erotic combinations and variants. He pictured a small group of human bodies and tried to narrate every mode of sexual pleasure and pain to which they could be subject. The variables are surprisingly few. Once all possible positions of the body have been tried—the law of gravity does interfere—once the maximum number of erogenous zones of the maximum number of participants have been brought into contact, abrasive, frictional, or intrusive, there is not much left to do or imagine. One can whip or be whipped; one can eat excrement or quaff urine; mouth and private part can meet in this or that commerce. After which there is the gray of morning and the sour knowledge that things have remained fairly generally the same since man first met goat and woman.

This is the obvious, necessary reason for the inescapable monotony of pornographic writing, for the fact well known to all haunters of Charing Cross Road or pre-Gaullist bookstalls that dirty books are maddeningly the same. The trappings change. Once it was the Victorian nanny in high-button shoes birching the master, or the vicar peering over the edge of the boys' lavatory. The Spanish Civil War brought a plethora of raped nuns, of buttocks on bayonets. At present, specialized dealers report a steady demand for "WS" (stories of wife-swapping, usually in a suburban or honeymoon-resort setting).

But the fathomless tide of straight trash has never varied much. It operates within highly conventionalized formulas of low-grade sadism, excremental drollery, and banal fantasies of phallic prowess or feminine responsiveness. In its own way the stuff is as predictable as a Boy Scout manual.

Above the pulp line—but the exact boundaries are impossible to draw—lies the world of erotica, of sexual writing with literary pretensions or genuine claims. This world is much larger than is commonly realized. It goes back to Egyptian literary papyri. At certain moments in Western society, the amount of "high pornography" being produced may have equaled, if not surpassed, ordinary *belles-lettres*. I suspect that this was the case in Roman Alexandria, in France during the *Régence*, perhaps in London around the 1890's. Much of this subterranean literature is bound to disappear. But anyone who has been allowed access to the Kinsey library in Bloomington, and has been lucky enough to have Mr. John Gagnon as his guide, is made aware of the profoundly revealing, striking fact that there is hardly a major writer of the nineteenth or twentieth century who has not, at some point in his career, be it in earnest or in the deeper earnest of jest, produced a pornographic work. Likewise there are remarkably few painters, from the eighteenth century to post-Impressionism, who have not produced at least one set of pornographic plates or sketches. (Would one of the definitions of abstract, non-objective art be that it cannot be pornographic?)

Obviously a certain proportion of this vast body of writing has literary power and significance. Where a Diderot, a Crébillon *fils*, a Verlaine, a Swinburne, or an Apollinaire write erotica, the result will have some of the qualities which distinguish their more public works. Figures such as Beardsley and Pierre Louÿs are minor, but their lubricities have a period charm. Nevertheless, with very few exceptions, "high pornography" is not of pre-eminent literary importance. It is simply not true that the locked cabinets of great libraries or private collections contain masterpieces of poetry or fiction which hypocrisy and censorship banish from the light. (Certain eighteenth-century drawings and certain Japanese prints suggest that the case of graphic art may be different; here there seems to be work of the first quality which is not generally available.) What emerges when one reads some of the classics of erotica is the fact that they too are intensely conventionalized, that their repertoire of fantasy is limited, and that it merges, almost imperceptibly, into the dream-trash of straight, mass-produced pornography.

In other words: the line between, say, *Thérèse Philosophe* or *Lesbia Brandon* on the one hand, and *Sweet Lash* or *The Silken Thighs* on the other, is easily blurred. What distinguishes the "forbidden classic" from under-the-counter delights on Frith Street is, essentially, a matter of semantics, of the level of vocabulary and rhetorical device used to provoke erection. It is not fundamental. Take the masturbating housemaid in a very recent example of the Great American Novel, and the housemaid similarly engaged in *They Called Her Dolly* (n.d., price six shillings). From the point of view of erotic stimulus, the difference is one of language, or more exactly—as verbal precisions now appear in high literature as well—the difference is one of narrative sophistication. Neither piece of writing adds anything new to the potential of human emotion; both add to the waste.

Genuine additions are, in fact, very rare. The list of writers who have had the genius to enlarge our actual compass of sexual awareness, who have given the erotic play of the mind a novel focus, an area of recognition previously unknown or fallow, is very small. It would, I think, include Sappho, in whose verse the Western ear caught, perhaps for the first time, the shrill, nerve-rending note of sterile sexuality, of a libido necessarily, deliberately, in excess of any assuagement. Catullus seems to have added something, though it is at this historical distance nearly impossible to identify that which startled in his vision, which caused so real a shock of consciousness. The close, delicately plotted concordance between orgasm and death in Baroque and Metaphysical poetry and art clearly enriched our legacy of excitement, as had the earlier focus on virginity. The development in Dostoevsky, Proust, and Mann of the correlations between nervous infirmity, the psychopathology of the organism, and a special erotic vulnerability, is probably new. Sade and Sacher-Masoch codified, found a dramatic syntax for, areas of arousal previously diffuse or less explicitly realized. In *Lolita* there is a genuine enrichment of our common stock of temptations. It is as if Vladimir Nabokov had brought into our field of vision what lay at the far edge, in Balzac's *La Rabouilleuse*, for instance, or what had been kept carefully implausible through disproportion (*Alice in Wonderland*). But such annexations of insight are rare.

The plain truth is that in literary erotica as well as in the great mass of "dirty books" the same stimuli, the same contortions and fantasies, occur over and over with unutterable monotony. In most

71

erotic writing, as in man's wet dreams, the imagination turns, time and time again, inside the bounded circle of what the body can experience. The actions of the mind when we masturbate are not a dance; they are a treadmill.

Mr. Maurice Girodias would riposte that this is not the issue, that the interminable succession of fornications, flagellations, onanisms, masochistic fantasies, and homosexual punch-ups which fill his *Olympia Reader* are inseparable from its literary excellence, from the artistic originality and integrity of the books he published at the Olympia Press in Paris. He would say that several of the books he championed, and from which he has now selected representative passages, stand in the vanguard of modern sensibility, that they are classics of post-war literature. If they are so largely concerned with sexual experience, the reason is that the modern writer has recognized in sexuality the last open frontier, the terrain on which his talent must, if it is to be pertinent and honest, engage the stress of our culture. The pages of the *Reader* are strewn with four-letter words, with detailed accounts of intimate and specialized sexual acts, precisely because the writer has had to complete the campaign of liberation initiated by Freud, because he has had to overcome the verbal taboos, the hypocrisies of imagination in which former generations labored when alluding to the most vital, complex part of man's being.

> Writing dirty books was a necessary participation in the common fight against the Square World . . . an act of duty.

Mr. Girodias has a case. His reminiscences and polemics make sour reading (he tends to whine); but his actual publishing record shows nerve and brilliance. The writings of Henry Miller matter to the history of American prose and self-definition. Samuel Beckett's *Watt* appeared with Olympia, as did writings of Jean Genet, though not the plays or the best prose. *Fanny Hill* and, to a lesser degree, *Candy*, are mock-epics of orgasm, books in which any sane man will take delight. Lawrence Durrell's *Black Book* seems to me grossly overrated, but it has its serious defenders. Girodias himself would probably regard *Naked Lunch* as his crowning discernment. I don't see it. The book strikes me as a strident bore, illiterate and self-satisfied right to its heart of pulp. Its repute is important only for what it tells us of the currents of homosexuality, camp, and modish brutality which dominate present "sophisticated" literacy. Burroughs indicts his readers, but not in the brave, prophetic sense argued by Girodias. Nevertheless, there can be no doubt of the genuineness of Girodias' commitment or of the risks he took.

Moreover, two novels on his list *are* classics, books whose genius he recognized and with which his own name will remain proudly linked: *Lolita* and *The Ginger Man*. It is a piece of bleak irony— beautifully appropriate to the entire "dirty book" industry—that a subsequent disagreement with Nabokov now prevents Girodias from including anything of *Lolita* in his anthology. To all who first met Humbert Humbert in *The Traveller's Companion Series*, a green cover and the Olympia Press's somewhat mannered typography will remain a part of one of the high moments of contemporary literature. This alone should have spared Mr. Girodias the legal and financial harryings by which Gaullist Victorianism hounded him out of business.

But the best of what Olympia published is now available on every drugstore counter—this being the very mark of Girodias' foresight. The *Olympia Reader* must be judged by what it actually contains. And far too much of it is tawdry stuff, "doing dirt on life," with only the faintest pretensions to literary merit or adult intelligence.

It is almost impossible to get through the book at all. Pick it up at various points and the sense of *déjà-vu* is inescapable ("This is one stag-movie I've seen before"). Whether a naked woman gets tormented in Sade's dungeons (*Justine*), during Spartacus' revolt (Marcus Van Heller: *Roman Orgy*), in a kinky French *château* (*The Story of O*), or in an Arab house (*Kama Houri* by one Ataullah Mordaan) makes damn little difference. *Fellatio* and buggery seem fairly repetitive joys whether enacted between Paris hooligans in Genet's *Thief's Journal*, between small-time hustlers and ex-prize-fighters (*The Gaudy Image*), or between lordly youths by Edwardian gaslight in *Teleny*, a silly piece attributed to Oscar Wilde.

After fifty pages of "hardening nipples," "softly opening thighs," and "hot rivers" flowing in and out of the ecstatic anatomy, the spirit cries out, not in hypocritical outrage, not because I am a poor Square throttling my libido, but in pure, nauseous boredom. Even fornication can't be as dull, as hopelessly predictable, as all that.

Of course there are moments which excite. *Sin for Breakfast* ends on a subtle, comic note of lewdness. *The Woman Thing* uses all the four-letter words and anatomical exactitudes with real force; it exhibits a fine ear for the way in which sexual heat compresses and erodes our uses of language. Those, and I imagine it includes most men, who use the motif of female onanism in their own fantasy life will find a vivid patch. There may be other nuggets. But who can get through the thing? For my money, there is one sublime moment in the *Reader*. It comes in an extract (possibly spurious?) from Frank Harris' *Life and Loves*. Coiling and uncoiling in diverse postures with two naked Oriental nymphets and their British procuress, Harris is suddenly struck with the revelation that "there indeed is evidence to prove the weakness of so much of the thought of Karl Marx. It is only the bohemian who can be free, not the proletarian." The image of Frank Harris, all limbs and propensities ecstatically engaged, suddenly disproving *Das Kapital* is worth the price of admission.

But not really. For that price is much higher than Mr. Girodias, Miss Mary McCarthy, Mr. Wayland Young, and other advocates of total frankness seem to realize. It is a price which cuts deep not only into the true liberty of the writer, but into the diminishing reserves of feeling and imaginative response in our society.

The preface to the *Olympia Reader* ends in triumph:

> Moral censorship was an inheritance from the past, deriving from centuries of domination by the Christian clergy. Now that it is practically over, we may expect literature to be transformed by the advent of freedom. Not freedom in its negative aspects, but as the means of exploring all the positive aspects of the human mind, which are all more or less related to, or generated by, sex.

This last proposition is almost unbelievably silly. What needs a serious inquiry is the assertion about freedom, about a new and transforming liberation of literature through the abolition of verbal and imaginative taboos.

Since the *Lady Chatterley* case and the defeat of a number of attempts to suppress books by Henry Miller, the sluice gates stand open. Sade, the homosexual elaborations of Genet and Burroughs, *Candy*, *Sexus*, *L'Histoire d'O* are freely available. No censorship would choose to make itself ridiculous by challenging the sadistic eroticism, the minutiae of sodomy (smell and all) which grace Mailer's *American Dream*. This is an excellent thing. But let us be perfectly clear why. Censorship is stupid and repugnant for two empirical reasons: censors are men no better than ourselves, their judgments are no less fallible or open to dishonesty. Secondly, the thing won't work: those who really want to get hold of a book will do so somehow. This is an entirely different argument from saying that pornography doesn't in fact deprave the mind of the reader, or incite to wasteful or criminal gestures. *It may, or it may not.* We simply do not have enough evidence either way. The question is far more intricate than many of our literary champions of total freedom would allow. But to say that censorship won't work and should not be asked to is *not* to say that there has been a liberation of literature, that the writer is, in any genuine sense, freer.

On the contrary. The sensibility of the writer is free where it is most humane, where it seeks to apprehend and re-enact the marvelous variety, complication, and resilience of life by means of words as scrupulous, as personal, as brimful of the mystery of human communication, as the language can yield. The very opposite of freedom is cliché, and nothing is less free, more inert with convention and hollow brutality, than a row of four-letter words. Literature is a living dialogue between writer and reader only if the writer shows a twofold respect: for the imaginative maturity of his reader, and, in a very complex but central way, for the wholeness, for the independence and core of life, in the personages he creates.

Respect for the reader signifies that the poet or novelist invites the consciousness of the reader to collaborate with his own in the act of presentment. He does not tell all because his work is not a primer for children or the retarded. He does not exhaust the possible responses of his reader's own imaginings, but delights in the fact that we will fill in from our own lives, from resources of memory and desire proper to ourselves, the contours he has drawn. Tolstoy is infinitely freer, infinitely more exciting, than the new eroticists when he arrests his narrative at the door of the Karenins' bedroom, when he merely initiates, through the simile of a dying flame, of ash cooling in the grate, a perception of sexual defeat which each of us can re-live or detail for himself. George Eliot is free, and treats her readers as free, adult human beings, when she conveys, through inflection of style and mood, the truth about the Casaubon honeymoon in *Middlemarch*, when she makes us imagine for ourselves how Dorothea has been violated by some essential obtuseness. These are profoundly exciting scenes, these enrich and complicate our sexual awareness, far beyond the douche-bag idylls of the contemporary "free" novel. There is no real freedom whatever in the compulsive physiological exactitudes of present "high pornography," because there is no respect for the reader, whose imaginative means are set at nil.

And there is none for the sanctity of autonomous life in the characters of the novel, for that tenacious integrity of existence which makes a Stendhal, a Tolstoy, a Henry James tread warily around their own creations. The novels being produced under the new code of total statement shout at their personages: strip, fornicate, perform this or that act of sexual perversion. So did the S.S. guards at rows of living men and women. The total attitudes are not, I think, entirely distinct. There may be deeper affinities than we as yet understand between the "total freedom" of the uncensored erotic imagination and the total freedom of the sadist. That these two freedoms have emerged in close historical proximity may not be coincidence. Both are exercised at the expense of someone else's humanity, of someone else's most precious right—the right to a private life of feeling.

This is the most dangerous aspect of all. Future historians may come to characterize the present era in the West as one of a massive onslaught on human privacy, on the delicate processes by which we seek to become our own singular selves, to hear the echo of our specific being. This onslaught is being pressed by the very conditions of an urban mass-technocracy, by the necessary uniformities of our economic and political choices, by the new electronic media of communication and persuasion, by the ever-increasing exposure of our thoughts and actions to sociological, psychological, and material intrusions and controls. Increasingly, we come to know real privacy, real space in which to experiment with our sensibility, only in extreme guises: nervous breakdown, addiction, economic failure. Hence the appalling monotony and *publicity*—in the full sense of the word —of so many outwardly prosperous lives. Hence also the need for nervous stimuli of an unprecedented brutality and technical authority.

Sexual relations are, or should be, one of the citadels of privacy, the nightplace where we must be allowed to gather the splintered, harried elements of our consciousness to some kind of inviolate order and repose. It is in sexual experience that a human being alone, and two human beings in that attempt at total communication which is also communion, can discover the unique bent of their identity. There we may find for ourselves, through imperfect striving and repeated failure, the words, the gestures, the mental images which set the blood to racing. In that dark and wonder ever renewed both the fumblings and the light must be our own.

The new pornographers subvert this last, vital privacy; they do our imagining for us. They take away the words that were of the night and shout them over the rooftops, making them hollow. The images of our love-making, the stammerings we resort to in intimacy, come pre-packaged. From the rituals of adolescent petting to the recent university experiment in which faculty wives agreed to practise onanism in front of the researchers' cameras, sexual life, particularly in America, is passing more and more into the public domain. This is a profoundly ugly and demeaning thing whose effects on our identity and resources of feeling we understand as little as we do the impact on our nerves of the perpetual "sub-eroticism" and sexual suggestion of modern advertisement. Natural selection tells of limbs and functions which atrophy through lack of use; the power to feel, to experience and realize the precarious uniqueness of each other's being, can also wither in a society. And it is no mere accident (as Orwell knew) that the standardization of sexual life, either through controlled license or compelled puritanism, should accompany totalitarian politics.

Thus the present danger to the freedom of literature and to the inward freedom of our society is not censorship or verbal reticence. The danger lies in the facile contempt which the erotic novelist exhibits for his readers, for his personages, and for the language. Our dreams are marketed wholesale.

Because there were words it did not use, situations it did not represent graphically, because it demanded from the reader not obeisance but live echo, much of Western poetry and fiction has been a school to the imagination, an exercise in making one's awareness more exact, more humane. My true quarrel with the *Olympia Reader* and the *genre* it embodies is not that so much of the stuff is boring and abjectly written. It is that these books leave a man less free, less himself, than they found him; that they leave language poorer, less endowed with a capacity for fresh discrimination and excitement. It is not a new freedom that they bring, but a new servitude. In the name of human privacy, enough!

77

THE PYTHAGOREAN GENRE

A Conjecture in Honor of Ernst Bloch

Old men read few novels. Histories of the Republic of Venice, botanical treatises, memoirs, political tracts, or metaphysics; books in which the content and matter of life are argued direct. But few novels, or only those which are "classics," having entered by force of time or authority of imagination into the corona of truth, of historical record. Novels such as those of Stendhal and Tolstoy which address us in the voice of history rather than through the individual, contingent fiat of fictional invention. Perhaps old men have less time, and have grown to be master taxonomists, seeking the excitement and economy of order, the rich bone-spareness of the documentary statement, the nucleus of the fact. As if novels were, in some important sense, uninteresting and wasteful.

The notion (or, as Ernst Bloch would say, "category") of waste is pertinent. An undermining puritanism nags at the history of fiction: the idea, advanced first by the calvinist rebuke to all license of feeling, then by the bourgeois stress on utility and parsimony of emotional commitment, that fiction was not an adult or serious thing. That the reading of novels was an uneconomic, ultimately insidious use of time. More, perhaps, than any other literary *genre*, the modern prose novel developed in a context of demeaning analogues: the children's tale, the *roman rose*, on the one hand; the immense spate of trash-fiction, erotic, melodramatic, or merely sentimental, on the other. Hence the strenuous plea which Flaubert, Turgenev, and Henry James put forward either in explicit argument or by example of scrupulous virtuosity, that fiction is a mode of supreme seriousness, that it exacts from its readers energies of intelligence and sensibility as full, as mature as are required by any other high literary form. A plea the more urgent as there presses against it in so many novelists—Hawthorne, Tolstoy, Zola, Kafka—the old, unsilenced query: is fiction *really* a serious pursuit? Should a man not use his talent, his resources of language and insight toward a more *open* critique of life (art is, even at its most formal remove, a critique of values, a counter-proposal to life in the name of freer, deeper possibility)?

The cogency of this challenge, the fact that so many novelists registered its discomforts, may account for the realistic format and particular ambitions of fiction between Balzac and Joyce—the brief century of the major novel. As if aware that the act of fiction was, in a literal sense, eccentric to the ruling historicism and positivism of the modern age, the novel sought to make itself master and inventory of the sum of life. Crucial to the secular *commedia* of Balzac, to Dickens' exhaustive mythology of urban and rural England, to Zola's catalogues of the real, to Joyce, is the ideal of the encompassing record, of the organization of the totality of social, psychological data inside a fictional framework. *Nihil humani alienum:* driven by a fierce energy of observation, the realistic novel reached out to absorb every new quality and locus of experience. From Scott and Manzoni to the moderns, historical fiction has tried to make the past an animate present (as did the historical painters, Gothic decorators, and stage designers of the bourgeois realistic age). Science fiction has tried to project rational maps of the future. Jules Verne and H. G. Wells are naturalists who transpose forward. Between past and future lies the zone of present totality each of whose categories—economic, sexual, political, private, technological, ideological, religious—has at some point become the object of fictional representation. Finally, and by logical culmination, the magnitude of available *données*, the crowded weave of fact and event, became itself the subject, the central myth of the novel. This is what takes place in Proust and *Ulysses*, the imagination circling, surfeited and victorious, around the compendium, the *summa* of European civilization.

This surfeit brought a natural reaction. The few novels that matter after Joyce, which explore new possibilities in the *genre* or educate new echoes in the reader, are striking for their reduction of focus, for their implicit resolve to approach reality with wariness. Like Klee, Kafka moves in total ambush, as if nothing could be depended on as solid or within rational call, as if a constant earth tremor were underfoot. William Empson's

79

> Hours before dawn we were woken by the quake.
> My house was on a cliff. The thing could take
> Bookloads off shelves, break bottles in a row

could almost be the motto of the new situation. Broch's *Death of Virgil*, the only fiction to move any distance inward from Joyce, concentrates its fantastic means of realization and expression on a single vanishing point, the instant of the passage into death, of the momentary transition into what cannot be narrated because it lies a breath beyond language. Mann's *Doctor Faustus* is a turning point not only because it argues, by subtle and tragic implication, the pre-eminence of music, with its polyphonic modes and freedom from realistic props, over language and verbal narrative; but because it shows how the classic form and claims of the novel are inseparable from the bias of a middle-class, humanistic culture, how their ruin is a common one. (Thus it is no accident that the critique of the Communist revolution made essentially from the values of the humanistic past should be a novel, *Doctor Zhivago;* whereas the critique in the name of the future, stated from inside a collective idiom, should be the lyric verse of the new young poets.)

All of which amounts to saying, quite simply, that there *is* a crisis of the novel. One knows the denials, the assurance that good novels are being written, that every major literary *genre* has been perennially accused of decay, that neither writers nor readers of fiction are aware of any ominous condition. To which the answer is: yes, but. At either end of the spectrum, whether it be in the monotonous, hysterical authenticities of reportage-fiction, the surrender of the eye to camera-blindness, or in the *nouveau roman* with its fetishistic naturalism and moral neutrality, the sense of disarray is perceptible. It is eloquent also in the lunatic economics of the fiction business. At rough estimate, some ten novels are published each day in Europe and the United States. Of these, the iceberg bulk is ephemeral trash calculated to go under almost immediately. The tip is the presumably serious novels: they enter a lottery, a race for success in which only a minute proportion can survive. Having half a dozen new "serious" works of fiction to review weekly, the critic does an absurdly modish, superficial job. Often success or failure is merest chance. But failure is irremediable. The law of the trade is such that the decried or unnoticed novel vanishes from the publisher's advertisement and the bookseller's table in a fortnight or three weeks.

Thence to be remaindered or pulped. Saturation is obviously near. Significantly, over the last five years statistics of new books published and sold in England (where figures are most reliable) show a distinct decline in fiction, a turn of the literate public to history, biography, science, and argument.

But these are externals.

The novel is doubly undermined. First, by the change in the nature, in the availability to imaginative order, of that social and psychological reality in which novelists found their principal matter. *Ulysses* is probably the last coherent attempt at a *summa mundi*. Already Faulkner's saga is deliberately parochial, cunningly eccentric to the main locale and fabric of contemporary affairs. The pace and complication of human experience in urban, technological society have increased exponentially over the last forty years. What Goethe foresaw in the Prologue to *Faust*, what Wordsworth feared in the Preface to the *Lyrical Ballads* and the 1846 sonnet on "Illustrated Books and Newspapers" has become commonplace: the dramatic, "totalizing" function of modern political and economic happenings, the graphic authority and speed with which they are thrust home to our nerves and brains by means of instantaneous reproduction, the nerve-consuming "journalism" of our existence, have sharply reduced the freshness, the discriminations of our imaginative response. In its endeavor to excite and hold our interest, the novel now has to compete with media of dramatic presentation far more "authentic," far easier to assimilate into our increasingly lazy, inert sensibilities. To compete at all with the strident alternatives of television and film, of the photograph and the tape recording, the novel has had to find new areas of emotional shock—or, more exactly, the serious novel has had to choose topics formerly exploited by trash-fiction. Hence the compulsive sadism and eroticism of so many current novels.

More essentially, instead of mastering the documentary background, of selecting and reorganizing to his own artistic and critical purpose the multitudinous material of our lives, the novelist has become a harried witness. He is not master but servant of his observations; the transition can be located in Zola. The great mass of current fiction is reportage—less convincing, less acute, less impressive on the memory, than are current works of history, of biography, of social and political narrative. By absurd but unassailable logic, the mass-circulation magazines which purvey sentimental romances or tales of contrived terror now call themselves "True Fiction."

The change in the flavor of life, the power of the media which control and communicate that flavor—for to most men in an urban, mass-media culture the world now looks and feels as newspaper or television chooses to present it—affect the novel in a second major way.

Literary *genres* have their specific economic and social context. We can no more separate the heroic epic from the particular character of an aristocratic, clannish pre-feudalism than we can the theater of Racine and Molière from the complicated poise of absolutism and rising middle class in seventeenth-century France. As is well known, the rise and primacy of the prose novel are closely inwoven with that of the post-revolutionary bourgeoisie. In its moral and psychological focus, in the technology of its production and distribution, in the domestic privacy, leisure, and reading habits which it required from its audience, the novel matches precisely the great age of the industrial, mercantile bourgeoisie. *Floruit* 1830–1930, Balzac to Proust and Joyce. That age is obviously over, gutted by two world wars and the decline of Europe from economic preponderance. The new shapes of history—collective, racially mixed yet antagonistic, highly mobile, scientifically oriented—are now discernible, though their full quality and weight are as yet difficult to assess. The literate middle-class figure, reading a novel which he owns and for which he has a library, in a quiet room in his own house or apartment (silence being a function of size), embodies a complex of economic privileges, stabilities, psychological safeguards, and deliberately nurtured tastes of which Thomas Mann was the last full representative and ironic valedictorian.

This is why the paperback book in its present format is a significant transitional phenomenon. It realizes both triumphs and illusions of the new, post-bourgeois literacy. It brings to a very large audience, often of limited means, the potential of high literature. But its physical shape is inherently ephemeral; it does not make for a library privately collected; its low cost, visual attractiveness, and ease of acquisition may have created a situation in which far more books are purchased than read. Above all, the literary experience is "prepackaged" as so much else in our technological lives. Paperbacks do not impel a man to make his own discoveries, to enter into that personal dialogue with a writer which arises where a set of complete works is involved, where the neglected or less accomplished takes its qualifying place next to the classic. A certain dust and difficulty of search are part of genuine literacy, of that which we have discovered with our own nerve ends. (I recently paid £3 for twelve volumes of George Eliot in mint condition. The bookseller remarked that they had lain unnoticed while a fairly expensive paperback of one particular novel, fashionably prefaced and got up, had sold rapidly. But to be read? Or to be part of the lively wallpaper and status objects in the rabbit warrens in which so many of us pass our falsely bright lives?)

After the novel, what then? I have tried to suggest elsewhere that in an era of electronic and primarily visual means of statement, and among the new collective societies now emerging, drama—and specially the kind of drama open to audience participation and critique —has an immense future. More than any other *genre* the theater can organize, explore, and symbolize the consciousness of a developing community. And it can, very precisely, stimulate the transition of its audience from pre-literate to literate habits of representation, combining within its flexible ensemble every idiom, from dance, mime, and music to highly stylized verbal codes.

But in Western culture, with its urban and technological character, the representative transitional *genre* seems to be a kind of documentary poetic or "post-fiction."

When a major literary form declines, its energies and instigations are not wholly or rapidly dispersed. They animate the new modes. Thus the achievements of the heroic epic (and even the *Iliad* and *Odyssey* were late, summarizing cases) carried over strongly into the language, uses of myth, and heroic stance of Greek tragedy. In the growing confidence of the novel, in its articulation of mood, milieu, and tone, we note the legacy of the decayed drama. Congreve and Sheridan had no adequate successors on the English stage; but their control of dialogue and private crisis is vital in the art of Jane Austen. Though it is itself no longer a very interesting medium, the novel has developed and made available to other literary modes a large range of ideals and technical resources. We can now see these at work throughout the varieties of nonfiction.

In modern biographies and historical writing there is a wide measure of collaboration, one might almost say collusion, between factual material and a particular rhetoric of vivid presentation. Colorful setting, dramatic psychology, imaginary dialogue—devices derived from the novel—are put at the service of the archive. The problem is not one of stylistic liveliness, but of the inevitable manipulations which the idiom and psychology of the novel bring to the historical evidence. Sociology, especially in its more popular, influential versions, draws heavily on the dramatic concreteness and personifications of fiction. The latent strength of the fictional ideal can be seen even in the most "objective," neutral arrangements of sociological data. Oscar Lewis' *The Children of Sanchez* is, no doubt, an honest selection of tape recordings; but as grouped and, in a real sense, "heard" by the particular listener, the rawness of life takes on the cumulative order of a novel.

In that characteristic contemporary *genre* which might be called "high journalism," techniques inherited from the novel play a decisive role. The eye of the political and social reporter is direct heir to that of the novelist. Hence the obvious stylization, the deceptive dramatic or sentimental gloss on so much that passes itself off as scrupulous witness. Much of the interpretation and record offered us of the causes of political actions, of the behavior of great persons, comes in the dramatic conventions of the realistic novel, conventions now worn to cliché.

The novel's promise of vivacity, organized emotion, and direct address is also honored in a good deal of current writing about the sciences. Ours is a brilliant period of didacticism, of books that teach us about the deeps of the sea, about radio-stars, microbiology, or archaeology. They do so in an unencumbered, stylish prose and with an attitude of feeling which can be related to the dramatic or poetic uses of learning and documentation in fiction. Here again, Thomas Mann is the master of transition: the musicology in *Doctor Faustus*, the morphology, botany, and cosmology so handsomely conveyed in *Felix Krull*, go beyond the incorporation of technical and "abstract" matter into the body of the classic novel. They are preliminary models of a new virtuosity in the exposition of specialized and scientific information to the layman.

In short: there is at this point in Western culture a mass of nonfiction whose particular qualities of vividness, dramatic pace, and psychological appeal derive from the fact that it has behind it the major epoch of the novel. In De Quincey's terms, the distinction between the "literature of knowledge" and the "literature of power" is no longer a sharp or obvious one; wherever possible, and often in disregard of its theoretic or moral commitments, the knowledge draws on the power. Thinking on the period of *haute vulgarisation* which preceded the French Revolution, one wonders whether such periods—a society making total inventory of its skills—are logical forerunners to political and social crisis. Do societies harvest before a storm?

But although the "lyric documentary" is at present the dominant mode in that it concentrates much of the best general prose and usurps yearly on the actual readership of serious fiction, it is not a very significant genre. It cannot go much beyond itself except by embroidery, or by pressing the fact to yield more than it is worth. Moreover, precisely where it is honest with the current state of politics or science or historical scholarship, this "literature of knowledge" has a built-in obsolescence, the facts changing almost as soon as they are presented. One values the eloquent welcome shown to the general reader by science, history, sociology, and all the techniques of which we have to know the contour if we are to get on. But the essential life of literary form has more subterranean, obstinate channels.

Our culture has seen the rise and decay of the verse epic and of "high" drama; it has seen the retreat of poetry from a central mnemonic or argumentative function in society; it is at present witnessing the decline of the novel from essential purpose. But there are other possibilities of form, other shapes of expression dimly at work. In the disorder of our affairs—a disorder made worse by the seeming coherence of *kitsch*—new modes of statement, new grammars or poetics for insight, are becoming visible. They are tentative and isolated. But they exist like those packets of radiant energy around which matter is said to gather in turbulent space. They exist, if only in a number of rather solitary, little understood books.

It is not the actual list that matters. Anyone can add to it or take away under the impulse of his own recognitions. It is the common factor in these works—the reaching out of language toward new relations (what we call logic), and in a wider sense toward a new syntax by which to tempt reality into the momentary but living order of words. There are books, though not many, in which the old divisions between prose and verse, between dramatic and narrative voice, between imaginary and documentary, are beautifully irrelevant or false. Just as criteria of conventional verisimilitude and common perspective were beginning to be irrelevant to the new focus of Impressionism. Starting in late eighteenth and early nineteenth centuries, books have appeared which allow no ready answer to the question: what species of literature am I, to what *genre* do I belong? Works so organized—we tend to forget the imperative of life in that word—that their expressive form is integral only to themselves, that they modify, by the very fact of their existence, our sense of how meaning may be communicated.

Blake would be relevant: because of his anger at set forms, because of his redisposal of statement in all manner of personal and complex spaces, part aphorism, part sung prose, part epic verse so hurtling and uncertainly stressed that the paragraphs achieve an effect of prose-poetry or *prose libre*. Also because of his uses of art not to illustrate or comment from the margin but as an active partner to language inside a total statement. Blake's drawings are in harness with the poem or strike out at the obstinate radiance of the unspoken vision. Their incompleteness, the fluidity of the line beyond the frame is like the incompleteness in many of Blake's visionary texts. When picture and word come together, they re-group each other in a dynamic suggestion of new meanings and new relations. It has been said that Blake's failure, the lapse of fresh authority into singularity and chaos, derives from the lack of a responsible echo, from the absence in his society of adequate "social collaboration." Thus "he very early gave up publishing in any serious sense." But part of the reason may be more radical. Like Mallarmé, but with greater honesty of need, Blake was striving toward a new form of book altogether, toward new interactions of typography and syntax, of language and space, of graphic means and verbal codes. This is apparent in the *Descriptive Catalogue* of 1809 and in the *Laocoon Group* (engraved ca. 1820), with its use of Hebrew, Greek, and English, its disposal of aphoristic clusters at various points in the composition, its bordure of lapidary statements. I realize that there are eighteenth-century precedents and contemporary analogues to this kind of pictorial-poetic device; but Blake lives.

Kierkegaard is obviously important here. Each of the fragments he detached from the marvelously unflagging discourse of his mind, what Donne would call "this dialogue of one," carries the mark of a central design, secret but coherent, of a logic and architecture of literary form so appropriate and resilient that it could contain and express the great forces of doubt and renewal in Kierkegaard's meditation. He did not achieve or publish (make public) this design; perhaps he only saw it fitfully himself. But *Either/Or*, the dramatic spiral of the parables in *Fear and Trembling*, the synthesis of intimate lyricism and philosophic dialectic, of pain and logic, in Kierkegaard's books communicate, as do the incompletions, the different possible alignments of Pascal's *Pensées*, the impact of a new form. After Kierkegaard the conventions of philosophic argument are as "open," as subject to revision, as are the shapes of trees after Van Gogh.

A need to make all expression unprecedented, so acute that it ended in inevitable silence, governs the forms of Nietzsche. In Nietzsche's style, in the experimental guise of his successive works, the pressure of new feelings and philosophic demands on traditional modes of presentation is constant. If one tries to rearrange the aphoristic segments of *Morgenröte* or *Beyond Good and Evil*, a force of necessary location asserts itself. The discontinuities, which keep the reader alert and vulnerable, mesh into an implicit logic, like iron filings above a hidden magnet. *Zarathustra* is, in one sense, almost old-fashioned: rhapsodic, orientalizing cadences, the bardic stance, can be found throughout the century, from Ossian to Whitman and Renan. But in another sense the work is profoundly original. It proclaims, as does Ungaretti's famous distich, *M'illumino d'immenso*. It renders philosophic argument musical. It has a polyphonic texture in which different styles and literary modes proceed together, almost simultaneously. There are great fugues of thought which lead to the particular effect of musical resolution—unreconciled energy inside repose. This use of music, not for outward sonority or tricks of rhythm, but as a model for the actions of the mind within language—as an attendant major language to make the writer's consciousness in some root sense bilingual—is vital to both Kierkegaard and Nietzsche (the latter being, in fact, a musician). Precisely as line and color are vital to the poetic syntax of Blake.

In short: wherever literary structure strives toward new potentialities, wherever the old categories are challenged by genuine compulsion, the writer will reach out to one of the other principal grammars of human perception—art, music, or more recently, mathematics.

There are other examples of nascent form, of anarchic style moving toward new discipline, which one would want to look at. Péguy is a minor figure, and a bully of language. But his attempt to slow down the natural pace of French, to give the prose of *Nôtre Jeunesse* and *Victor-Marie, Comte Hugo* a ponderous, erosive drive, as of lava, is more than rhetoric. Péguy wanted to make the logic of

87

persuasion visceral and incantatory as it had not been since before Descartes. Proof arises out of the vehemence of reassertion, each insistence spiraling back on its premise. His essays and books are like no others; slow beasts that tread the mind.

Karl Kraus was, like Péguy, a pamphleteer, a man who made eloquence of journalistic occasion. But *Die letzten Tage der Menschheit* is more than that. Part mammoth drama, part philosophic dialogue, part lyric *feuilleton*, it declares a crisis of disequilibrium between traditional literary genres and the voice and quality of the historical epoch. It says, in its own exorbitant way, that neither poetic nor realistic drama, neither the essay nor the novel, can cope. That their settled forms are given the lie by the shapeless ferocity of social and political realities. There is in Kraus an attempt toward a "total form," a *Gesamtsprachwerk*, though he lacked the invention and "negative capability" needed to sustain it.

These might have been in Walter Benjamin, had he not died early, after a life too much harrassed by foresight. Benjamin's essays with their resolve to make of literary criticism a form almost lyric, a mirror creating images, belong to our theme. As do the *Vexierbilder und Miniaturen*, and the essay on Paris, instigated by Baudelaire's *Tableaux de Paris*, whose shape is a mimesis of the city, district following district with sudden avenues or winding alleys between them. In an early essay, Benjamin spoke of the necessary opaqueness of language, of the difficulty that confronts the writer because each language communicates only itself, only its own essence. Thus the writer who has something new to feel and say must hammer out his own speech against the grain or just to one side of the conventional ensemble of words, signs, grammars. Otherwise, how shall *he* be heard?

This refusal to accept the sufficiency of established literary forms, this desire to make of each book a free yet necessary *genre* and to bring the pressure of musical and mathematical "speech" to bear on literary style, underlies the work of Broch. It is so rich and unequal an achievement that one cannot deal with it summarily. Already in *The Sleepwalkers* we find a conjunction of fiction and philosophic essay. In the *Schuldlosen* we find not only a corroboration of verse and novella, but a fictional design built around a musical axis (Mozart's *Don Giovanni* is meant to give the narrative its implicit shape). The *Death of Virgil* is composed in the form of a string quartet, the prose of the different sections being imitative of the mood and rhythms of corresponding musical movements. In Broch, technical experiment sprang, as it must if it is not to be frivolous, from moral need, from the need to find symbols or shapes adequate to the pain or anger or prophetic shock of the exploring intellect. Toward the end of his life, Broch inclined more and more to mathematics and silence (mathematics being, in one way, the language of silence).

This is no accident. The entire radical, experimental tradition which I have been referring to carries inside it a potential of silence, the recognized possibility that literature may be insufficient. Perhaps our culture has grown wasteful of its words. Perhaps it has cheapened or spent what assurance of perception and numinous value they once contained. This thought is hinted at in the distinction between loquacious and laconic cultures drawn by Lévi-Strauss in his *Anthropologie structurale*. The point is made even more impressively in *Le Cru et le cuit*, a book which affirms that music is superior to language, being both intelligible and untranslatable, and which is itself organized in musical patterns—overture, themes and variations, cantata, symphonic interlude.

Wherever it reaches out toward the limits of expressive form, literature comes to the shore of silence. There is nothing mystical in this. Only the realization that the poet and philosopher, by investing language with the utmost precision and illumination, are made aware, and make the reader aware, of other dimensions which cannot be circumscribed in words. For Broch this is one way of saying that death has another language. Reached by way of linguistic philosophy and formal logic (logic is one of the prosodies of the mind, one of the ways in which it scans the world), the borderline is Wittgenstein's: what we cannot speak about we must consign to silence.

The *Tractatus* is a graphic example of the kind of book, of the forms and motions of spirit, which I am trying to define. It is built of aphorisms and numbers, as if borrowing from another kind of certitude. It makes its own syntax and idiom and object of doubt and rigorous appraisal. Wittgenstein has a poet's capacity to make every word seem new and full of untapped, possibly destructive vitality. At several points the *Tractatus*, with its economy of image and its typographical effects, reads almost like a poem. And like the *Sonnets to Orpheus*, of which it is close contemporary, it commends us to silence.

If we take all these elements together—the determination to make style and *genre* unique to the particular occasion, the proximity of music and mathematics to the writer's sense of his own medium, an implication, arising directly out of the language, that we are near silence (call it a core of magic) —a name may suggest itself, a metaphor by which to keep these different books in focus. Relations between things are fully grasped only when the class to which they belong has been recognized. Thus we may come to see this apparently discontinuous, idiosyncratic series, which begins in the region of Blake and Kierkegaard and has continued to Wittgenstein, as part of a new form. I would call it the "Pythagorean *genre*."

Not only for its music and numbers, its metaphysical poetics and frequent meditation on silence and death, but because pre-Socratic philosophy—or what we gather from the ever dubious, therefore vital order of the fragments—recalls a time in which literary form was an act of magic, an exorcism of ancient chaos. A time when metaphysics and mineralogy spoke verse, and words had the driven force of the dance. The books I have cited are like sparks from Heraclitus' fire.

Pythagoras and Heraclitus appear often in *Das Prinzip Hoffnung*. And what I have said can be seen as a footnote to one of the aspects of the work of Ernst Bloch. I have wanted to suggest that he is perhaps the foremost living writer in the Pythagorean genre.

The importance of Ernst Bloch to the historian of utopian Marxism, to the epistemologist and student of natural law, to the *Kulturphilosoph* and historian of the German-Jewish mind in the twentieth century, is obvious. But a rich share of his achievement concerns the literary critic and student of language. As early as the essays of 1912–1917 and *Thomas Münzer*, Bloch makes of the act of writing a peculiarly individual and urgent deed. Though strongly influenced by Expressionism, Bloch's earlier prose has its own abrupt lyric insistence. In Bloch's mature style, there are pages we can set beside Hölderlin and Nietzsche for their subtle brightness. Like few other masters of German, he has broken the generically ponderous, clotted norms of German syntax.

Das Prinzip Hoffnung is like no other book. There is no ready designation for its shape and tone, for its fantastic range and metaphoric logic. On its first page, we find number and space (the typographical equivalent to silence), headings full of abrupt mystery, and three prose paragraphs, each longer than the one before as in a stanzaic pattern. The page asserts an unprecedented need and the determination to give it unique voice. The first sentence is set in large letters as an aubade to the mind starting on its great voyage: "We begin empty." That is the watchword of the Pythagorean form. The book we begin tomorrow must be as if there had been none before; new and outrageous as the morning sun.

LANGUAGE OUT OF DARKNESS

THE HOLLOW MIRACLE

Agreed: post-war Germany is a miracle. But it is a very queer miracle. There is a superb frenzy of life on the surface; but at the heart, there is a queer stillness. Go there: look away for a moment from the marvel of the production lines; close your ears momentarily to the rush of the motors.

[Understandably, this essay, written in 1959, caused much hurt and anger. Discussion and misquotation of it have continued in Germany to the present time. The journal *Sprache im technischen Zeitalter* devoted a special number to the debate, and controversy arose anew at the meeting in the United States in the spring of 1966 of the German writers known as the *Gruppe 47.* The academic profession, to which I somewhat uneasily belong, took a particularly adverse view of the case.

If I republish "The Hollow Miracle" in this book, it is because I believe that the matter of the relations between language and political inhumanity is a crucial one; and because I believe that it can be seen with specific and tragic urgency in respect of the uses of German in the Nazi period and in the acrobatics of oblivion which followed on the fall of Nazism. De Maistre and George Orwell have written of the politics of language, of how the word may lose its humane meanings under the pressure of political bestiality and falsehood. We have scarcely begun, as yet, to apply their insights to the actual history of language and feeling. Here almost everything remains to be done.

I republish this essay also because I believe that its general line of argument is valid. When I wrote it, I did not know of Victor Klemperer's remarkable book *Aus dem Notizbuch eines Philologen*, published in East Berlin in 1946 (now reissued by Joseph Melzer Verlag, Darmstadt, under the title *Die unbewältigte Sprache*). In far more detail than I was able to give, Klemperer, a trained linguist, traces the collapse of German into Nazi jargon and the linguistic-historical background to that collapse. In 1957, there appeared a small, preliminary lexicon of Nazi German: *Aus dem Wörterbuch des Unmenschen*, compiled by Sternberger, Storz, and Süskind. In 1964, suggestions I had made for more detailed study were taken up in Cornelia Berning's *Vom "Abstammungsnachweis" zum "Zuchtwart."* Dolf Sternberger has come back to the whole question in his essay on *"Mass/stäbe der Sprachkritik"* in *Kriterien* (Frankfurt, 1965). In Hochhuth's *The Deputy*, particularly in the scenes involving Eichmann and his business cronies, Nazi German is given precise, nauseating expression. The same is true in Peter Weiss's *Investigation* and, as

The thing that has gone dead is the German language. Open the daily papers, the magazines, the flood of popular and learned books pouring off the new printing presses; go to hear a new German play, listen to the language as it is spoken over the radio or in the Bundestag. It is no longer the language of Goethe, Heine, and Nietzsche. It is not even that of Thomas Mann. Something immensely destructive has happened to it. It makes noise. It even communicates, but it creates no sense of communion.

Languages are living organisms. Infinitely complex, but organisms nevertheless. They have in them a certain life-force, and certain powers of absorption and growth. But they can decay and they can die.

A language shows that it has in it the germ of dissolution in several ways. Actions of the mind that were once spontaneous become mechanical, frozen habits (dead metaphors, stock similes, slogans). Words grow longer and more ambiguous. Instead of style, there is rhetoric. Instead of precise common usage, there is jargon. Foreign roots and borrowings are no longer absorbed into the blood stream of the native tongue. They are merely swallowed and remain an alien intrusion. All these technical failures accumulate to the essential failure: the language no longer sharpens thought but blurs it. Instead of charging every expression with the greatest available energy and directness, it loosens and disperses the intensity of feeling. The language is no longer adventure (and a live language is the highest adventure of which the human brain is capable). In short, the language is no longer lived; it is merely spoken.

That condition can last for a very long time; observe how Latin remained in use long after the springs of life in Roman civilization had run dry. But where it has happened, something essential in a civilization will not recover. And it has happened in Germany. That is why there is at the center of the miracle of Germany's material resurrection such a profound deadness of spirit, such an inescapable sense of triviality and dissimulation.

I try to show in the "Note on Günter Grass" which follows this essay, in *Hundejahre*.

In these past ten years, moreover, a new chapter has begun in the complex history of the German language and of its articulations of political reality. East German is once again developing much of that grammar of lies, of totalitarian simplifications, which was brought to such a high degree of efficiency in the Nazi era. Walls can be built between two halves of a city, but also between words and humane content.]

What brought death to the German language? That is a fascinating and complicated piece of history. It begins with the paradoxical fact that German was most alive before there was a unified German state. The poetic genius of Luther, Goethe, Schiller, Kleist, Heine, and in part that of Nietzsche, pre-dates the establishment of the German nation. The masters of German prose and poetry were men not caught up in the dynamism of Prussian-Germanic national consciousness as it developed after the foundation of modern Germany in 1870. They were, like Goethe, citizens of Europe, living in princely states too petty to solicit the emotions of nationalism. Or, like Heine and Nietzsche, they wrote from outside Germany. And this has remained true of the finest of German literature even in recent times. Kafka wrote in Prague, Rilke in Prague, Paris, and Duino.

The official language and literature of Bismarck's Germany already had in them the elements of dissolution. It is the golden age of the militant historians, of the philologists and the incomprehensible metaphysicians. These mandarins of the new Prussian empire produced that fearful composite of grammatical ingenuity and humorlessness which made the word "Germanic" an equivalent for dead weight. Those who escaped the Prussianizing of the language were the mutineers and the exiles, like those Jews who founded a brilliant journalistic tradition, or Nietzsche, who wrote from abroad.

For to the academicism and ponderousness of German as it was written by the pillars of learning and society between 1870 and the First World War, the imperial regime added its own gifts of pomp and mystification. The "Potsdam style" practiced in the chancelleries and bureaucracy of the new empire was a mixture of grossness ("the honest speech of soldiers") and high flights of romantic grandeur (the Wagnerian note). Thus university, officialdom, army, and court combined to drill into the German language habits no less dangerous than those they drilled into the German people: a terrible weakness for slogans and pompous clichés (*Lebensraum*, "the yellow peril," "the Nordic virtues"); an automatic reverence before the long word or the loud voice; a fatal taste for saccharine pathos (*Gemütlichkeit*) beneath which to conceal any amount of rawness or deception. In this drill, the justly renowned school of German philology played a curious and complex role. Philology places words in a context of older or related words, not in that of moral purpose and conduct. It gives to language formality, not form. It cannot be a mere accident that the essentially philological structure of German education yielded such loyal servants to Prussia and the Nazi Reich. The finest record of how the drill call of the classroom led to that of the barracks is contained in the novels of Heinrich Mann, particularly in *Der Untertan.*

When the soldiers marched off to the 1914 war, so did the words. The surviving soldiers came back, four years later, harrowed and beaten. In a real sense, the words did not. They remained at the front and built between the German mind and the facts a wall of myth. They launched the first of those big lies on which so much of modern Germany has been nurtured: the lie of "the stab in the back." The heroic German armies had not been defeated; they had been stabbed in the back by "traitors, degenerates, and Bolsheviks." The Treaty of Versailles was not an awkward attempt by a ravaged Europe to pick up some of the pieces but a scheme of cruel vengeance imposed on Germany by its greedy foes. The responsibility for unleashing war lay with Russia or Austria or the colonial machinations of "perfidious England," not with Prussian Germany.

There were many Germans who knew that these were myths and who knew something of the part that German militarism and race arrogance had played in bringing on the holocaust. They said so in the political cabarets of the 1920's, in the experimental theater of Brecht, in the writings of the Mann brothers, in the graphic art of Käthe Kollwitz and George Grosz. The German language leapt to life as it had not done since the Junkers and the philologists had taken command of it. It was a brilliant, mutinous period. Brecht gave back to German prose its Lutheran simplicity and Thomas Mann brought into his style the supple, luminous elegance of the classic and Mediterranean tradition. These years, 1920–1930, were the *anni mirabiles* of the modern German spirit. Rilke composed the *Duino Elegies* and the *Sonnets to Orpheus* in 1922, giving to German verse a wing-stroke and music it had not known since Hölderlin. *The Magic Mountain* appeared in 1924, Kafka's *Castle* in 1926. *The Three-Penny Opera* had its premiere in 1928, and in 1930 the German cinema produced *The Blue Angel.* The same year appeared the first volume of Robert Musil's strange and vast meditation on the decline of Western values, *The Man Without Qualities.* During this glorious decade, German literature and art shared in that great surge of the Western imagination which encompassed Faulkner, Hemingway, Joyce, Eliot, Proust, D. H. Lawrence, Picasso, Schoenberg, and Stravinsky.

But it was a brief noontime. The obscurantism and hatreds built

98

into the German temper since 1870 were too deep-rooted. In an uncannily prophetic "Letter from Germany," Lawrence noted how "the old, bristling, savage spirit has set in." He saw the country turning away "from contact with western Europe, ebbing to the deserts of the east." Brecht, Kafka, and Thomas Mann did not succeed in mastering their own culture, in imposing on it the humane sobriety of their talent. They found themselves first the eccentrics, then the hunted. New linguists were at hand to make of the German language a political weapon more total and effective than any history had known, and to degrade the dignity of human speech to the level of baying wolves.

For let us keep one fact clearly in mind: the German language was not innocent of the horrors of Nazism. It is not merely that a Hitler, a Goebbels, and a Himmler happened to speak German. Nazism found in the language precisely what it needed to give voice to its savagery. Hitler heard inside his native tongue the latent hysteria, the confusion, the quality of hypnotic trance. He plunged unerringly into the undergrowth of language, into those zones of darkness and outcry which are the infancy of articulate speech, and which come before words have grown mellow and provisional to the touch of the mind. He sensed in German another music than that of Goethe, Heine, and Mann; a rasping cadence, half nebulous jargon, half obscenity. And instead of turning away in nauseated disbelief, the German people gave massive echo to the man's bellowing. It bellowed back out of a million throats and smashed-down boots. A Hitler would have found reservoirs of venom and moral illiteracy in any language. But by virtue of recent history, they were nowhere else so ready and so near the very surface of common speech. A language in which one can write a "Horst Wessel Lied" is ready to give hell a native tongue. (How should the word *"spritzen"* recover a sane meaning after having signified to millions the "spurting" of Jewish blood from knife points?)

And that is what happened under the Reich. Not silence or evasion, but an immense outpouring of precise, serviceable words. It was one of the peculiar horrors of the Nazi era that all that happened was recorded, catalogued, chronicled, set down; that words were committed to saying things no human mouth should ever have said and no paper made by man should ever have been inscribed with. It is nauseating and nearly unbearable to recall what was done and spoken, but one must. In the Gestapo cellars, stenographers (usually women) took down carefully the noises of fear and agony wrenched, burned, or beaten out of the human voice. The tortures and experiments carried out on live beings at Belsen and Matthausen were exactly recorded. The regulations governing the number of blows to be meted out on the flogging blocks at Dachau were set down in writing. When Polish rabbis were compelled to shovel out open latrines with their hands and mouths, there were German officers there to record the fact, to photograph it, and to label the photographs. When the SS elite guards separated mothers from children at the entrance to the death camps, they did not proceed in silence. They proclaimed the imminent horrors in loud jeers: *"Heida, heida, juchheisassa, Scheissjuden in den Schornstein!"*

The unspeakable being said, over and over, for twelve years. The unthinkable being written down, indexed, filed for reference. The men who poured quicklime down the openings of the sewers in Warsaw to kill the living and stifle the stink of the dead wrote home about it. They spoke of having to "liquidate vermin." In letters asking for family snapshots or sending season's greetings. Silent night, holy night, *Gemütlichkeit.* A language being used to run hell, getting the habits of hell into its syntax. Being used to destroy what there is in man of man and to restore to governance what there is of beast. Gradually, words lost their original meaning and acquired nightmarish definitions. *Jude, Pole, Russe* came to mean two-legged lice, putrid vermin which good Aryans must squash, as a party manual said, "like roaches on a dirty wall." "Final solution," *endgültige Lösung*, came to signify the death of six million human beings in gas ovens.

The language was infected not only with these great bestialities. It was called upon to enforce innumerable falsehoods, to persuade the Germans that the war was just and everywhere victorious. As defeat began closing in on the thousand-year Reich, the lies thickened to a constant snowdrift. The language was turned upside down to say "light" where there was blackness and "victory" where there was disaster. Gottfried Benn, one of the few decent writers to stay inside Nazi Germany, noted some of the new definitions from the dictionary of Hitler German:

In December 1943, that is to say at a time when the Russians had driven us before them for 1,500 kilometers, and had pierced our front in a dozen places, a first lieutenant, small as a hummingbird and gentle as a puppy, re-marked: "The main thing is that the swine are not break-ing through." "Break through," "roll back," "clean up," "flexible, fluid lines of combat"—what positive and nega-tive power such words have; they can bluff or they can conceal. Stalingrad—tragic accident. The defeat of the U-boats—a small, accidental technical discovery by the British. Montgomery chasing Rommel 4,000 kilometers from El Alamein to Naples—treason of the Badoglio clique.

And as the circle of vengeance closed in on Germany, this snowdrift of lies thickened to a frantic blizzard. Over the radio, between the interruptions caused by air-raid warnings, Goebbels' voice assured the German people that "titanic secret weapons" were about to be launched. On one of the very last days of Götterdämme-rung, Hitler came out of his bunker to inspect a row of ashen-faced fifteen-year-old boys recruited for a last-ditch defense of Berlin. The order of the day spoke of "volunteers" and elite units gathered invincibly around the Führer. The nightmare fizzled out on a shame-less lie. The *Herrenvolk* was solemnly told that Hitler was in the front-line trenches, defending the heart of his capital against the Red beasts. Actually, the buffoon lay dead with his mistress, deep in the safety of his concrete lair.

Languages have great reserves of life. They can absorb masses of hysteria, illiteracy, and cheapness (George Orwell showed how English is doing so today). But there comes a breaking point. Use a language to conceive, organize, and justify Belsen; use it to make out specifications for gas ovens; use it to dehumanize man during twelve years of calculated bestiality. Something will happen to it. Make of words what Hitler and Goebbels and the hundred thousand *Untersturmführer* made: conveyors of terror and falsehood. Some-thing will happen to the words. Something of the lies and sadism will settle in the marrow of the language. Imperceptibly at first, like the poisons of radiation sifting silently into the bone. But the cancer will begin, and the deep-set destruction. The language will no longer grow and freshen. It will no longer perform, quite as well as it used to, its two principal functions: the conveyance of humane order which we call law, and the communication of the quick of the human spirit which we call grace. In an anguished note in his diary for 1940,

Klaus Mann observed that he could no longer read new German books: "Can it be that Hitler has polluted the language of Nietzsche and Hölderlin?" It can.

But what happened to those who are the guardians of a language, the keepers of its conscience? What happened to the German writers? A number were killed in the concentration camps; others, such as Walter Benjamin, killed themselves before the Gestapo could get at them to obliterate what little there is in a man of God's image. But the major writers went into exile. The best playwrights: Brecht and Zuckmayer. The most important novelists: Thomas Mann, Werfel, Feuchtwanger, Heinrich Mann, Stefan Zweig, Hermann Broch.

This exodus is of the first importance if we are to understand what has happened to the German language and to the soul of which it is the voice. Some of these writers fled for their lives, being Jews or Marxists or otherwise "undesirable vermin." But many could have stayed as honored Aryan guests of the régime. The Nazis were only too anxious to secure the luster of Thomas Mann's presence and the prestige that mere presence would have given to the cultural life of the Reich. But Mann would not stay. And the reason was that he knew exactly what was being done to the German language and that he felt that only in exile might that language be kept from final ruin. When he emigrated, the sycophantic academics of the University of Bonn deprived him of his honorary doctorate. In his famous open letter to the dean, Mann explained how a man using German to communicate truth or humane values could not remain in Hitler's Reich:

> The mystery of language is a great one; the responsibility for a language and for its purity is of a symbolic and spiritual kind; this responsibility does not have merely an aesthetic sense. The responsibility for language is, in essence, human responsibility. . . . Should a German writer, made responsible through his habitual use of language, remain silent, quite silent, in the face of all the irreparable evil which has been committed daily, and is being committed in my country, against body, soul and spirit, against justice and truth, against men and man?

Mann was right, of course. But the cost of such integrity is immense for a writer.

The German writers suffered different degrees of deprivation and reacted in different ways. A very few were fortunate enough to find asylum in Switzerland, where they could remain inside the living stream of their own tongue. Others, like Werfel, Feuchtwanger, and Heinrich Mann, settled near each other to form islands of native speech in their new homeland. Stefan Zweig, safely arrived in Latin America, tried to resume his craft. But despair overcame him. He was convinced that the Nazis would turn German into inhuman gibberish. He saw no future for a man dedicated to the integrity of German letters and killed himself. Others stopped writing altogether. Only the very tough or most richly gifted were able to transform their cruel condition into art.

Pursued by the Nazis from refuge to refuge, Brecht made of each of his new plays a brilliant rear-guard action. *Mother Courage* was first produced in Zurich in the dark spring of 1941. The further he was hounded, the clearer and stronger became Brecht's German. The language seemed to be that of a primer spelling out the ABC of truth. Doubtless, Brecht was helped by his politics. Being a Marxist, he felt himself a citizen of a community larger than Germany and a participant in the forward march of history. He was prepared to accept the desecration and ruin of the German heritage as a necessary tragic prelude to the foundation of a new society. In his tract "Five Difficulties Encountered When Writing the Truth," Brecht envisioned a new German language, capable of matching the word to the fact and the fact to the dignity of man.

Another writer who made of exile an enrichment was Hermann Broch. *The Death of Virgil* is not only one of the most important novels European literature has produced since Joyce and Proust; it is a specific treatment of the tragic condition of a man of words in an age of brute power. The novel turns on Virgil's decision, at the hour of his death, to destroy the manuscript of the *Aeneid*. He now realizes that the beauty and truth of language are inadequate to cope with human suffering and the advance of barbarism. Man must find a poetry more immediate and helpful to man than that of words: a poetry of action. Broch, moreover, carried grammar and speech beyond their traditional confines, as if these had become too small to contain the weight of grief and insight forced upon a writer by the inhumanity of our times. Toward the close of his rather solitary life (he died in New Haven, nearly unknown), he felt increasingly that communication might lie in modes other than language, perhaps in mathematics, that other face of silence.

103

Of all the exiles, Thomas Mann fared best. He had always been a citizen of the world, receptive to the genius of other languages and cultures. In the last part of the *Joseph* cycle, there seemed to enter into Mann's style certain tonalities of English, the language in the midst of which he was now living. The German remains that of the master, but now and again an alien light shines through it. In *Doctor Faustus*, Mann addressed himself directly to the ruin of the German spirit. The novel is shaped by the contrast between the language of the narrator and the events which he recounts. The language is that of a classical humanist, a touch laborious and old-fashioned, but always open to the voices of reason, skepticism, and tolerance. The story of Leverkühn's life, on the other hand, is a parable of unreason and disaster. Leverkühn's personal tragedy prefigures the greater madness of the German people. Even as the narrator sets down his pedantic but humane testimony to the wild destruction of a man of genius, the Reich is shown plunging to bloody chaos. In *Doctor Faustus* there is also a direct consideration of the roles of language and music in the German soul. Mann seems to be saying that the deepest energies of the German soul were always expressed in music rather than in words. And the history of Adrian Leverkühn suggests that this is a fact fraught with danger. For there are in music possibilities of complete irrationalism and hypnosis. Unaccustomed to finding in language any ultimate standard of meaning, the Germans were ready for the sub-human jargon of Nazism. And behind the jargon sounded the great dark chords of Wagnerian ecstasy. In *The Holy Sinner*, one of his last works, Mann returned to the problem of the German language by way of parody and pastiche. The tale is written in elaborate imitation of medieval German, as if to remove it as far as possible from the German of the present.

But for all their accomplishment, the German writers in exile could not safeguard their heritage from self-destruction. By leaving Germany, they could protect their own integrity. They witnessed the beginnings of the catastrophe, not its full unfolding. As one who stayed behind wrote: "You did not pay with the price of your own dignity. How, then, can you communicate with those who did?" The books that Mann, Hesse, and Broch wrote in Switzerland or California or Princeton are read in Germany today, but mainly as valuable proof that a privileged world had lived on "somewhere else," outside Hitler's reach.

What, then, of those writers who did stay behind? Some became lackeys in the official whorehouse of "Aryan culture," the *Reichssch-rifttumskammer*. Others equivocated till they had lost the faculty of saying anything clear or meaningful even to themselves. Klaus Mann gives a brief sketch of how Gerhart Hauptmann, the old lion of realism, came to terms with the new realities:

> "Hitler . . . after all, . . . My dear friends! . . . no hard feelings! . . . Let's try to be . . . No, if you please, allow me . . . objective . . . May I refill my glass? This champagne . . . very remarkable, indeed—the man Hitler, I mean . . . The champagne too, for that matter . . . Most extraordinary development . . . German youth . . . About seven million votes . . . As I often said to my Jewish friends . . . Those Germans . . . incalculable nation . . . very mysterious indeed . . . cosmic impulses . . . Goethe . . . Nibelungen Saga . . . Hitler, in a sense, expresses . . . As I tried to explain to my Jewish friends . . . dynamic tendencies . . . elementary, irresistible. . . ."

Some, like Gottfried Benn and Ernst Jünger, took refuge in what Benn called "the aristocratic form of emigration." They entered the German Army, thinking they might escape the tide of pollution and serve their country in the "old, honorable ways" of the officer corps. Jünger wrote an account of the victorious campaign in France. It is a lyric, elegant little book, entitled *Gärten und Strassen*. Not a rude note in it. An old-style officer taking fatherly care of his French prisoners and entertaining "correct" and even gracious relations with his new subjects. Behind his staff car come the trucks of the Gestapo and the elite guards fresh from Warsaw. Jünger does not mention any such unpleasantness. He writes of gardens.

Benn saw more clearly, and withdrew first into obscurity of style, then into silence. But the sheer fact of his presence in Nazi Germany seemed to destroy his hold on reality. After the war, he set down some of his recollections of the time of night. Among them, we find an incredible sentence. Speaking of pressures put on him by the régime, Benn says: "I describe the foregoing not out of resentment against National Socialism. The latter is now overthrown, and I am not one to drag Hector's body in the dust." One's imagination dizzies at the amount of confusion it must have taken to make a decent writer write that. Using an old academic cliché, he makes Nazism the

105

equivalent of the noblest of Homeric heroes. Being dead, the language turns to lies.

A handful of writers stayed in Germany to wage a covert resistance. One of these very few was Ernst Wiechert. He spent some time in Buchenwald and remained in partial seclusion throughout the war. What he wrote he buried in his garden. He stayed on in constant peril, for he felt that Germany should not be allowed to perish in voiceless suffering. He remained so that an honest man should record for those who had fled and for those who might survive what it had been like. In *The Forest of the Dead* he gave a brief, tranquil account of what he saw in the concentration camp. Tranquil, because he wished the horror of the facts to cry out in the nakedness of truth. He saw Jews being tortured to death under vast loads of stone or wood (they were flogged each time they stopped to breathe until they fell dead). When Wiechert's arm developed running sores, he was given a bandage and survived. The camp medical officer would not touch Jews or Gypsies even with his glove "lest the odor of their flesh infect him." So they died, screaming with gangrene or hunted by the police dogs. Wiechert saw and remembered. At the end of the war he dug the manuscript out of his garden, and in 1948 published it. But it was already too late.

In the three years immediately following the end of the war, many Germans tried to arrive at a realistic insight into the events of the Hitler era. Under the shadow of the ruins and of economic misery, they considered the monstrous evil Nazism had loosed on them and on the world. Long rows of men and women filed past the bone heaps in the death camps. Returned soldiers admitted to something of what the occupation of Norway or Poland or France or Yugoslavia had been like—the mass shootings of hostages, the torture, the looting. The churches raised their voice. It was a period of moral scrutiny and grief. Words were spoken that had not been pronounced in twelve years. But the moment of truth was rather short.

The turning point seems to have come in 1948. With the establishment of the new Deutschmark, Germany began a miraculous ascent to renewed economic power. The country literally drugged itself with hard work. Those were the years in which men spent half the night in their rebuilt factories because their homes were not yet viable. And with this upward leap of material energy came a new myth. Millions of Germans began saying to themselves and to any foreigner gullible enough to listen that the past had somehow not happened, that the horrors had been grossly exaggerated by Allied propaganda and sensation-mongering journalists. Yes, there were some concentration camps, and *reportedly* a number of Jews and other unfortunates were exterminated. "But not six million, *lieber Freund*, nowhere near that many. That's just propaganda, you know." Doubtless, there had been some regrettable brutalities carried out on foreign territory by units of the S.S. and S.A. "But those fellows were *Lumpenhunde*, lower-class ruffians. The regular army did nothing of the kind. Not our honorable German Army. And, really, on the Eastern Front our boys were not up against normal human beings. The Russians are mad dogs, *lieber Freund*, mad dogs! And what of the bombing of Dresden?" Wherever one traveled in Germany, one heard such arguments. The Germans themselves began believing them with fervor. But there was worse to come.

Germans in every walk of life began declaring that they had not known about the atrocities of the Nazi régime. "We did not know what was going on. No one told us about Dachau, Belsen, or Auschwitz. How should we have found out? Don't blame us." It is obviously difficult to disprove such a claim to ignorance. There *were* numerous Germans who had only a dim notion of what might be happening outside their own backyard. Rural districts and the smaller, more remote communities were made aware of reality only in the last months of the war, when battle actually drew near them. But an immense number *did* know. Wiechert describes his long journey to Buchenwald in the comparatively idyllic days of 1938. He tells how crowds gathered at various stops to jeer and spit at the Jews and political prisoners chained inside the Gestapo van. When the death trains started rolling across Germany during the war, the air grew thick with the sound and stench of agony. The trains waited on sidings at Munich before heading for Dachau, a short distance away. Inside the sealed cars, men, women, and children were going mad with fear and thirst. They screamed for air and water. They screamed all night. People in Munich heard them and told others. On the way to Belsen, a train was halted somewhere in southern Germany. The prisoners were made to run up and down the platform and a Gestapo man loosed his dog on them with the cry: "Man, get those dogs!" A crowd of Germans stood by watching the sport. Countless such cases are on record.

Most Germans probably did not know the actual details of liquidation. They may not have known about the mechanics of the gas ovens (one official Nazi historian called them "the anus of the world"). But when the house next door was emptied overnight of its tenants, or when Jews, with their yellow star sewn on their coats, were barred from the air-raid shelters and made to cower in the open, burning streets, only a blind cretin could not have known.

Yet the myth did its work. True, German audiences were moved not long ago by the dramatization of *The Diary of Anne Frank*. But even the terror of the *Diary* has been an exceptional reminder. And it does not show what happened to Anne *inside* the camp. There is little market for such things in Germany. Forget the past. Work. Get prosperous. The new Germany belongs to the future. When recently asked what the name Hitler meant to them, a large number of German schoolchildren replied that he was a man who had built the *Autobahnen* and had done away with unemployment. Had they heard that he was a bad man? Yes, but they did not really know why. Teachers who tried to tell them about the history of the Nazi period had been told from official quarters that such matters were not suitable for children. Some few who persisted had been removed or put under strong pressure by parents and colleagues. Why rake up the past?

Here and there, in fact, the old faces are back. On the court benches sit some of the judges who meted out Hitler's blood laws. On many professorial chairs sit scholars who were first promoted when their Jewish or Socialist teachers had been done to death. In a number of German and Austrian universities, the bullies swagger again with their caps, ribbons, dueling scars, and "pure Germanic" ideals. "Let us forget" is the litany of the new German age. Even those who cannot, urge others to do so. One of the very few pieces of high literature to concern itself with the full horror of the past is Albrecht Goes's *The Burnt Offering*. Told by a Gestapo official that there will be no time to have her baby where *she* is going, a Jewish woman leaves her baby carriage to a decent Aryan shopkeeper's wife. The next day she is deported to the ovens. The empty carriage brings home to the narrator the full sum of what is being committed. She resolves to give up her own life as a burnt offering to God. It is a superb story. But at the outset, Goes hesitates whether it should be told: "One has forgotten. And there must be forgetting, for how could a man live who had not forgotten?" Better, perhaps.

Everything forgets. But not a language. When it has been injected with falsehood, only the most drastic truth can cleanse it.

Instead, the post-war history of the German language has been one of dissimulation and deliberate forgetting. The remembrance of horrors past has been largely uprooted. But at a high cost. And German literature is paying it right now. There are gifted younger writers and a number of minor poets of some distinction. But the major part of what is published as serious literature is flat and shoddy. It has in it no flame of life.* Compare the best of current journalism with an average number of the *Frankfurter Zeitung* of pre-Hitler days; it is at times difficult to believe that both are written in German.

This does not mean that the German genius is mute. There is a brilliant musical life, and nowhere is modern experimental music assured of a fairer hearing. There is, once again, a surge of activity in mathematics and the natural sciences. But music and mathematics are "languages" other than language. Purer, perhaps; less sullied with past implications; abler, possibly, to deal with the new age of automation and electronic control. But not language. And so far, in history, it is language that has been the vessel of human grace and the prime carrier of civilization.

[* This statement was valid in 1959; not today. It is precisely by turning to face the past that German drama and fiction have resumed a violent, often journalistic, but undeniable force of life.]

A NOTE ON GÜNTER GRASS

Günter Grass is an industry: 300,000 copies of *The Tin Drum* sold in Germany; more than 60,000 in France; the American edition passed 90,000 in hardcover, well over 100,000 in paperback. In England, the vignette of the little man with the daemonic drum has become a publisher's symbol. Now there is hardly a bookstore window in Europe from which the black dog of Grass's second major novel, *Hundejahre*, does not stick out his red, phallic tongue. But it is not Grass's enormous success that matters most, nor the fact that he has put German literature back on the market. It is the power of that bawling voice to drown the siren-song of smooth oblivion, to make the Germans—as no writer did before—face up to their monstrous past.

A grim fantasy lurks at the heart of *Hundejahre*. The fable turns on the love-hate and blood brotherhood of Nazi and Jew. Walter Matern, the S.A. man—Eduard Amsel, the Jew; brothers under skin and soul, twin shadows in a weird, ferocious parable of how Germany turned to night.

The neurotic conjecture of some secret, foredoomed relationship between Nazi and Jew, of a hidden fraternity or mutual fascination deeper than the outward show of loathing and destruction, crops up tenaciously. We find it in the suspicion, argued with varying degrees of historical finesse, that Nazism derived from Judaism its own dogma of a "chosen race" and of a millennial, messianic nationalism. It emerges in Hannah Arendt's macabre reading of Eichmann's "Zionism," and in the persistent belief or allegation that certain eminent Nazis—Heydrich, Rosenberg, Hitler himself—had traces of Jewish descent.

This intimation feeds on two deep-buried sources. Jewish maso-

110

chism at times inclines to the notion that there was an occult rationale for the catastrophe, a savage yet somehow natural rebuke to the proud hopes fostered by Jewish assimilation into German culture. The German or the outsider, on the other hand, yields to the obscure imagining that German Jewry in some way brought the whirlwind on itself, that the temptations it offered to bestiality were too subtle, too intimate to be resisted. So utter a process of recognition and extermination must have involved some hidden complicity between torturer and victim. For all men kill the Jew they love.

Two boys play and dream by the sedge and mud-banks of the Vistula, in the flat marshes on the Polish frontier and around Danzig which Grass has made uniquely his own. Matern, the teeth-gnasher and miller's son; Amsel, the half-Jew (or is it more, who knows?). The schoolboy pack yelps at Amsel; he is a butterball with a jackdaw tongue, and their fists hammer at him. Matern becomes his strong shield. When he's about, no one clobbers Amsel or screams *kike!* Butterball gives Matern a penknife. But the river has a strange drag, and one day, finding no stone at hand, Matern throws in the knife. So what? It was only a dime-store penknife, and Edi Amsel is a smart kid. Give him a bundle of rags, a few wood-shavings and scraps of wire. Before you know it, there's a scarecrow (in German, *Vogelscheuche* has lewd undertones). These are no ordinary scarecrows. They look like people in the neighborhood, and the birds spin above them in affrighted swarms. Put a few gears in their straw gut, and they start moving.

Matern isn't so dumb either. He tries the Communists and finds the beer thin. Down at the club, all the boys are turning brown. And they're nice about it: "We'd rather have one repentant Red than a dozen farting bourgeois." Matern joins. What the hell. And there's that screwball Amsel begging for all the cast-off S.A. uniforms Matern can scrounge, for the greasy caps and brown shirts torn in the latest street brawl. He drapes them on his scarecrows, and the hollow men, the stuffed men, start strutting. Goose-strutting, eyes right, arms outflung. As if they were legion.

There's snow in Amsel's yard. One day something queer happens. A covey of S.A. boys, their faces masked, comes soft over the fence. The kike is pounded to bloody shreds. Then they roll him in the snow; Amsel the snowman with no teeth left in his mouth. Not one. Who were the hooligans? Jochen Sawatzki, Paul Hoppe, Willy Eggers . . . Names that stretch from Pomerania to the Rhineland and

Bavaria. Alfons Bublitz, Otto Warnke ... Keep counting. Eight names. But there were nine men. It's all so complicated and long ago. Like in a foul dream or attack of nausea. You can't expect a man to remember everything. The snow lay deep and there were thirty-two teeth in it. And eighteen fists pounding Amsel into a bloody pulp. Eight fine German names. There's one missing. Still.

So Matern decides to find out. War is over and the thousand-year Reich lies in a stinking heap. But amid the graffiti in the men's urinal at the Cologne railway station, Matern sees the name and address of friend Sawatzki. He finds other names. Roaming north and south through the moon landscape of rubble and defeat, he tracks them down one by one. He asks for truth and justice. Where were you when the mad carpet-eater led us into the great brown sea? Where were you when they rolled my friend Edi Amsel into a bloody snowball and cleaned their boots on his face?

Matern is not alone. He travels with a large German shepherd. Prinz is Hitler's dog. He has escaped from the Führer's last redoubt, in the Berlin death-bunker. Straying westward, he meets Matern coming out of a P.O.W. camp. Now they're inseparable. While Matern infects the wives and daughters of his old cronies with venereal disease—it's odd how little things get into the German bloodstream and make it all hot and wild—Prinz fattens. But he's now called Pluto. *Nice* dog; have a biscuit; be a Disney dog.

Matern becomes a radio idol. One day he consents to be interviewed by a chorus of eager, well-scrubbed young folk. But some lunatic firm has been selling them glasses. Put them on and you see mom and dad in a queer brown light. You see them doing all sorts of surprising things—smashing shopwindows, yelling like apes in heat, making old, frightened men wipe latrines with their beards. Is that you, dad? So the bright young things ask Matern: who are those nine masked thugs climbing over the garden fence? Herr Walter Matern, friend of the Jews, anti-Nazi first class, will broadcast their names to the repentant nation. Eight names.

Then he starts running. Eastward. To the other Germany beyond the silent wall. He leaves Pluto safely tied up at the Cologne station. The train is smooth and swift. The Germans are expert at making trains race across Europe. But there's a dog bounding along the track, quicker than a diesel. And just at the border, a shadow steps out of the shadows. An old friend. He has a pen-knife. And when Matern throws it into the Berlin canal, he doesn't even mind.

Canals can be dredged. But certain things can never be lost, never thrown away. Knives, for instance.

The tale ends in a grotesque *Walpurgisnacht*, a descent into a potash mine which is also the forecourt of damnation. Now we know what we have known all along. That Walter Matern loved Eduard Amsel so well that he had to get his hands on the very heart of him, and see his thirty-two teeth in the snow. That when the right man whistles, German shepherds are the hounds of hell.

Such a summary is not only inadequate (there are half a dozen novels crowded into this one baggy monster), but it makes the book sound tighter, more persuasive than it is. Before reaching the *Materniade*—the mock-epic of Matern's vengeful wanderings—the reader has to slog through a morass of allegory and digression. The middle section, some three hundred pages, is cast in the form of letters (at moments a parody of Goethe's *Wahlverwandschaften*). Through them, we glimpse the chaotic destinies of Matern, of Amsel, who survives the Nazi period under a false name, and numerous minor characters.

There are various welds. Prinz-Pluto is descended from a long pedigree beginning with Perkum the wolfhound. The story of his forebears interweaves with that of the Materns. The two boys played with the dog Senta on the low banks of the river. The birch copse in which the children moiled and listened for owls seems to melt and darken into other groves (*Birken-Buchen*—put an extra syllable on a German tree and what do you have?). But although Grass plots and ravels with crazy gusto, the book tends to fall apart. What sticks in one's mind is the general statement of chaos and the brilliance of discrete episodes.

The early chapters of boyhood and river, with their meandering, heavy cadence, are an extraordinary feat. Grass wraps himself inside the visceral totality of children. He sees as they do, in slow wakings and abrupt flashes. Like *The Tin Drum*, *Hundejahre* conveys the impression that there is in Grass's power a deliberate streak of infantilism, a child's uninhibited, brutal directness of feeling.

The narrative of an S.A. gang-up in a beer hall is unforgettable. Grass brings to light the banal roots of Nazi bestiality. We see the steamy, cozy vulgarity of German lower-middle-class manners, the wet cigar ash, and the slap on the buttocks, twist, by a sudden jerk of hysteria, into the sweating fury of the killers. One comes to understand how the sheer grossness of German pleasures—the bursting

113

sausages and the flowered chamber-pots, the beer-warmers and the fat men in tight leather shorts—was the ideal terrain for the sadistic-sentimental brew of Nazism. Again, one feels that Grass has allowed a certain freedom of vulgarity in himself, in his own talent. That is what gives his plunge into the mind and voice of Sawatzki and his boys its nauseating truth. Only in Rudolf Nassauer's neglected novel, *The Hooligan*, is there anything that cuts as deep.

Grass is merciless on post-war Germany, on the miracle of amnesia and cunning whereby the West Germans shuffled off the past and drove their Volkswagens into the new dawn. He reproduces, with murderous exactitude, the turns of phrase and gesture, the private silences and the public clichés, through which Adenauer Germany persuaded itself, its children, and much of the outside world, that all those frightful things hadn't really happened, that "figures are grossly exaggerated," or that no one in red-roofed Bad Pumpleheim really knew *anything* of what was going on in the woods three miles away. Quite a few fine houses and villas *did* come on the market in those years (Lieschen and I and little Wolfram are living in one right now, as a matter of fact). But you know how Jews are—always off to Sorrento or South America. The Führer? Now that you mention it, I never saw him. But I did see his dog once. *Nice* dog. Biscuit, please.

Grass singles out the moment of untruth. In the three years of desolation from 1945 to 1948, there was a real chance that the Germans might come to grips with what they had wrought. "Germany had never been as beautiful. Never as healthy. There had never been more expressive human faces in Germany than in the time of the thousand and thirty-two calories. But as the little Mulheim ferry accosted, Inge Sawatzki said: 'Now we'll soon be getting our new money.' "

With the currency reform of 1948, and the brilliant recovery of German economic strength (in the very combines and steel mills where slave labor had been ground to death only a little while earlier), the past was declared irrelevant. Prosperity is an irresistible detergent: it scours the old darkness and the old smells out of the house. Grass has captured the whole ambience: the evasions and the outright lies, the cynicism of the little men grown fat on the manure of the dead, and the nervous queries of the young. The shadow of Amsel (or is it the man himself?) is full of genuine admiration for the German genius. Look at all these good folk "cooking their little pea-soup over a blue gas-flame and thinking nothing of it." Why should

114

they? What's wrong with gas ovens?

On May 8, 1945, Prinz comes to the banks of the Elbe. Should he head east or west? After mature sniffing, Hitler's dog decides that the West is the right place for him. In that central fable, Adenauer Germany has its mocking epitaph.

Hundejahre confirms what was already apparent in *The Tin Drum* and *Cat and Mouse*. Grass is the strongest, most inventive writer to have emerged in Germany since 1945. He stomps like a boisterous giant through a literature often marked by slim volumes of whispered lyricism. The energy of his devices, the scale on which he works, are fantastic. He suggests an action painter wrestling, dancing across a huge canvas, then rolling himself in the paint in a final logic of design.

The specific source of energy lies in the language. *Hundejahre* will prove formidably difficult to translate (even the title has no just equivalent). In these seven hundred pages, Grass plays on a verbal instrument of uncanny virtuosity. Long stretches of Baltic dialect alternate with parodies of Hitlerite jargon. Grass piles words into solemn gibberish or splinters them into unsuspected innuendo and obscenity. He has a compulsive taste for word-lists, for catalogues of rare or technical terms (it is here that he most resembles Rabelais). There are whole pages out of dictionaries of geology, agriculture, mechanical engineering, ballet. The language itself, with its powers of hysteria and secrecy, with its private parts and official countenance, becomes the main presence, the living core of this black fairy tale.

I asked in the previous essay whether the German language had survived the Hitler era, whether words poisoned by Goebbels and used to regulate and justify Belsen, could ever again serve the needs of moral truth and poetic perception. *The Tin Drum* appeared in 1959, and there are many to proclaim that German literature has risen from the ashes, that the language is intact. I am not so sure.

Grass has understood that no German writer after the holocaust could take the language at face value. It had been the parlance of hell. So he began tearing and melting; he poured words, dialects, phrases, clichés, slogans, puns, quotations, into the crucible. They came out in a hot lava. Grass's prose has a torrential, viscous energy; it is full of rubble and acrid shards. It scars and bruises the landscape into bizarre, eloquent forms. Often the language itself is the subject of his abrasive fantasy.

115

Thus one of the most astounding sections in *Hundejahre* is a deadly pastiche of the metaphysical jargon of Heidegger. Grass knows how much damage the arrogant obscurities of German philosophic speech have done to the German mind, to its ability to think or speak clearly. It is as if Grass had taken the German dictionary by the throat and was trying to throttle the falsehood and cant out of the old words, trying to cleanse them with laughter and impropriety so as to make them new. Often, therefore, his uncontrolled prolixity, his leviathan sentences and word inventories, do not convey confidence in the medium; they speak of anger and disgust, of a mason hewing stone that is treacherous or veined with grit. In the end, moreover, his obsessed exuberance undermines the shape and reality of the work. Grass is nearly always too long; nearly always too loud. The raucous brutalities which he satirizes infect his own art.

That art is, itself, curiously old-fashioned. The formal design of the book, its constant reliance on *montage*, on fade-outs, and on simultaneities of public and private events, are closely modeled on *U.S.A.* The case of Grass is one of many to suggest that it is not Hemingway, but Dos Passos who has been the principal American literary influence of the twentieth century. *Hundejahre* is also Joycean. One can hardly imagine the continuous interior monologue and the use of verbal association to keep the narrative moving, without the pattern of *Ulysses*. Finally, there is the near voice of Thomas Wolfe. Grass's novels have Wolfe's bulk and disordered vehemence. *Of Time and the River* prefigures, by its title and resort to the flow of lyric remembrance, the whole opening section of *Hundejahre*.

Where Grass knits on to the tradition of German fiction, it is not the modernism and originality of Broch and Musil that count, but the "Dos Passos-expressionism" of the late 1920's. Technically, *Hundejahre* and *The Tin Drum* take up where Döblin's *Berlin Alexanderplatz* (1929) left off.

This is, in part, because Grass is resolutely "non-literary," because he handles literary conventions with the unworried naïveté of an artisan. He came to language from painting and sculpture. He is indifferent to the fine-spun arguments and expectations of modern literary theory. His whole approach is essentially manual. But there is a second reason. Totalitarianism makes provincial. The Nazis cut the German sensibility off from nearly all that was alive and radical in modern art. Grass takes up where German literature fell silent in the 1930's (even as young Soviet poets are now "discovering" surrealism or Cocteau). His ponderous gait, the outmoded flavor of his audacities, are part of the price German literature has to pay for its years in isolation.

But no matter. In his two major novels Grass has had the nerve, the indispensable tactlessness to evoke the past. By force of his macabre, often obscene wit, he has rubbed the noses of his readers in the great filth, in the vomit of their time. Like no other writer, he has mocked and subverted the bland oblivion, the self-acquittal which underlie Germany's material resurgence. Much of what is active conscience in the Germany of Krupp and the Munich beer halls lies in this man's ribald keeping.

K

Franz Kafka died in 1924, having published a few stories and fragments. To a circle of friends—Max Brod, Franz Werfel, Felix Weltsch, Gustav Janouch—his remembrance was deep-etched. His shy, riddling irony, the probing innocence of his speech and manner, had cast a spell. But at large the word *kavka* meant no more than jackdaw. Less than twenty years later, when Kafka himself would have been in his late fifties, Auden could write, without seeking to provoke paradox or shock:

> Had one to name the author who comes nearest to bearing
> the same kind of relation to our age as Dante, Shakespeare
> and Goethe bore to theirs, Kafka is the first one would
> think of.

And from the vantage of his dogmatic certitude and prodigious labor, Claudel could say: "Besides Racine, who is for me the greatest writer, there is one other—Franz Kafka."

Around a man who, in his own lifetime, published half a dozen stories and sketches there has grown up an immense literature. To Rudolf Hemmerle's *Franz Kafka: Eine Bibliographie* (Munich, 1958), which already included some 1,300 works of criticism and exegesis, one must add the valuable check-list of "Biography and Criticism" in *Franz Kafka Today* (Madison: University of Wisconsin Press, 1959), Harry Järv's *Die Kafka-Literatur*, and the listing of most recent articles and studies in Heinz Politzer's *Franz Kafka: Parable and Paradox*. Mr. Järv's catalogue fills close to 400 pages, and shows that from Brazil to Japan there is hardly a major language or literary culture without its Kafka translations and commentaries. The Soviet Union offers a significant exception. Returning home from western Europe, Victor Nekrasov, one of the most mature voices among the younger Russian writers, declared that nothing had shamed him more, or been more revealing of Soviet parochialism, than the fact that he had not previously heard of Kafka. The very name has become a password to the house of literacy.

To some of Kafka's early admirers there is something distasteful in this tumult of critical voices. They scorn the dispersal through renown of a recognition and treasure once shared by a passionate few. In his haughty essay on "The Fame of Franz Kafka" Walter Muschg, himself a master of withdrawal, mourns that "even so solitary a poet as Kafka cannot avoid being distorted to a fantastic shadow on the wall of time." Through the posthumous publication by Max Brod of the three novels (two of them clearly incomplete), a publication carried out against Kafka's professed intent, the cabalistic values and intimacies of Kafka's art have been made common ground. To those who remember the man's strange, secretive radiance, the present image is both exaggerated and dimmed. Glory brings its darkness.

Kafka himself gave support to those who see in his work an essentially private, fragmentary achievement:

> Max Brod, Felix Weltsch, all my friends, seize upon something I have written, and then surprise me with a signed and sealed publisher's agreement. I don't want to create awkwardness for them, and so, in the end, things get published which were, in fact, no more than private sketches or diversions. Private vestiges of my human weakness are printed and even sold, because my friends, Max Brod in the lead, have set their minds on making literature of them, and because I am not strong enough to destroy these testimonials (*Zeugnisse*) of my solitude.

But at once, in characteristic subversion and qualification of his meaning, Kafka added: "What I said here is, of course, exaggerated."

We cannot act today as if the weight of Kafka lay with the early stories and shards of expressionistic prose. *The Trial* (1925), *The Castle* (1926), *Amerika* (1927), and the tales published in 1931 have given to the modern imagination some of its principal shapes of perception and identity. In the terms of Kafka's parable, we must make certain that the Chinese walls of criticism do not imprison the work, that the messenger can pass through the gates of commentary. The former privacies, the sense of initiate possession, are unrecapturable. Nor should one obscure the crucial fact: Kafka throws so large a shadow, he is the object of so serried a critical enterprise, because, and only because, the labyrinth of his meanings open out, at its secret, difficult exits, to the high roads of modern sensibility, to what is most urgent and relevant in our condition. It would be absurd to deny the deeply personal quality of Kafka's maze; but being marvelously at the center, it compels many approaches, many trials of insight. That is the force of Auden's claim. The contrast between the generality of statement and classic form in Dante or Goethe and the covert, idiosyncratic mode of Kafka denotes the tenor of the age. We hear a shaping echo to our speech in a code full of silence and despairing paradox.

Political glosses on Kafka are often naïve; they fail to discriminate between the partisan and the prophetic. Yet, with time, it has become obvious that much of Kafka's "transrealism," his edging of reality out of focus so as to produce the economy and logic of hallucination, is derived from a precise, ironic observance of local historical circumstance. Behind the nightmare exactitudes of Kafka's setting lies the topography of Prague and of the Austro-Hungarian empire in its decline. Prague, with its legacy of cabalistic and astrological practices, its compactness of shadow and spire, is inseparable from the landscape of the parables and fictions. Kafka had a keen sense of the symbolic resources gathered in reach; during the winter of 1916–17 he lived in the Zlatá ulička, the Golden lane of the Emperor's alchemists, and there is no need to deny the associations between the castle on Hradčany Hill and that in the novel. Kafka's phantoms had their solid local roots.

Moreover, as Georg Lukács has argued, there are in Kafka's inventions specific strains of social criticism. His vision of radical hope was somber; behind the march of proletarian revolution he saw the inevitable profit of the tyrant and demagogue. But Kafka's training in law, and his professional concern with industrial accidents and compensation, gave him a sharp view of class relations and economic realities. Central to *The Trial* is the portrayal of a malevolent yet ultimately powerless bureaucracy. With its foreshadowings in *Bleak*

House, the novel is a daemonic myth of red tape. *The Castle* is more than a bitter allegory of Austro-Hungarian bureaucratic feudalism; but that allegory is implicit. And as Mr. Politzer shows, the sense of the industrial machine as a destructive, abstractly evil force haunted Kafka and found terrible realization in "In the Penal Colony." Kafka was heir not only to Dickens' mastery of emblematic distortion, but also to his anger against the sadistic anonymities of bureau and assembly line.

Kafka's true politics, however, and his passage from the real to the more real, lie deeper. He was, in a literal sense, a prophet. The case is one to which the vocabulary of modern criticism, with its wariness and secular presumptions, has imperfect access. But the key fact about Kafka is that he was possessed of a fearful premonition, that he saw, to the point of exact detail, the horror gathering. *The Trial* exhibits the classic model of the terror state. It prefigures the furtive sadism, the hysteria which totalitarianism insinuates into private and sexual life, the faceless boredom of the killers. Since Kafka wrote, the night knock has come on innumerable doors, and the name of those dragged off to die "like a dog!" is legion. Kafka prophesied the actual forms of that disaster of Western humanism which Nietzsche and Kierkegaard had seen like an uncertain blackness on the horizon.

Seizing on a hint in Dostoevsky's *Notes from the Underground*, Kafka portrayed the reduction of man to tormented vermin. Gregor Samsa's metamorphosis, which was understood by those who first heard the tale to be a monstrous dream, was to be the literal fate of millions of human beings. The very word for vermin, *Ungeziefer*, is a stroke of tragic clairvoyance; so the Nazis were to designate the gassed. "In the Penal Colony" foreshadows not only the technology of the death-factories, but that special paradox of the modern totalitarian regime—the subtle, obscene collaboration between victim and torturer. Nothing written about the inward roots of Nazism is comparable, in exact perception, to Kafka's image of the tormentor plunging, suicidally, into the cogs of the torture-engine.

Kafka's nightmare-vision may well have derived from private hurt and neurosis. But that does not diminish its uncanny relevance, the proof it gives of the great artist's possession of antennae which reach beyond the rim of the present and make darkness visible. The fantasy turned to concrete fact. Members of Kafka's immediate family perished in the gas ovens; Milena and Miss Grete B. (who may have borne Kafka's child) died in concentration camps. The world of east and central European Judaism, in which Kafka's genius is so deeply at home, was scattered to ash.

No less than the Prophets, who cried out against the burden of revelation, Kafka was haunted by specific intimations of the inhuman. He observed in man the renascence of the bestial. The walls of the old city of order had grown ominous with the shadow of near ruin. Cryptically he remarked to Gustav Janouch that "the Marquis de Sade is the veritable patron of our age." Kafka came on Buchenwald in the beech wood. And beyond it, he discerned no necessary promise of grace. Mr. Politzer concludes of "In the Penal Colony":

> The real hero of the story, the "peculiar piece of apparatus," survives in spite of its ruin, unconquered and unconquerable. Kafka did not find an end to the visions of horror which haunted him.

Or as Kafka put it, in an aphorism written down in 1920: "Some deny misery by pointing to the sun, he denies the sun by pointing to misery."

This denial of the sun is implicit in Kafka's ambiguous view of literature and his own writing. His diffidence evokes the Old Testament motif of the stammerers afflicted with God's message, of the seers seeking to hide from the presence and exactions of the Word. In 1921 he spoke to Brod of

> the impossibility of not writing, the impossibility of writing in German, the impossibility of writing differently. One could almost add a fourth impossibility: the impossibility of writing.

That fourth impossibility proved the supreme temptation. Mr. Politzer analyzes, with masterly tact, the intricate game Kafka played with his legacy. "All these things without exception are to be burned, and I beg you to do this as soon as possible." Brod countered: "Let me tell you here and now that I shall not carry out your wishes." Kafka retained Brod as executor of his will, yet reiterated the plea that all but his few published writings should be destroyed. Even the printed works were ambiguously damned:

122

should they disappear altogether, this would correspond to my real wishes. Only, since they do exist, I do not wish to hinder anyone who so desires from keeping them.

Mr. Politzer argues that Kafka's ideal of formal and stylistic perfection was so rigorous that it allowed for no compromise. The incomplete novels and stories were imperfect, and should therefore perish. Yet, at the same time, the act of writing had been to Kafka the only avenue of escape from the sterility and enclosedness which he suffered in his personal life. He sought, in irreconcilable paradox, "a freedom beyond all words, a freedom *from* words," which could be achieved only through literature. "There is a goal, but no way," wrote Kafka; "what we call the way is hesitation." In the most illuminating reading yet proposed of "Josephine the Singer, or the Mouse Folk" (one of Kafka's deeply veiled legends), Mr. Politzer shows Kafka's equivocation on the artist's necessary silence. The narrator is uncertain: "Is it her singing that enchants us, or is it not rather the solemn stillness enclosing her frail little voice?"

But we may go farther. Kafka knew Kierkegaard's warning: "An individual cannot assist or save a time, he can only express that it is lost." He saw the coming of the age of the inhuman and drew its intolerable visage. But the temptation of silence, the belief that in the presence of certain realities art is trivial or impertinent, was near to hand. The world of Auschwitz lies outside speech as it lies outside reason. To speak of the *unspeakable* is to risk the survivance of language as creator and bearer of humane, rational truth. Words that are saturated with lies or atrocity do not easily resume life. This apprehension was not Kafka's alone. The fear of the erosion of the *Logos*, of the gain of letter on spirit, is strong in Hofmannsthal's *Letter of Lord Chandos* and the polemics of Karl Kraus. Wittgenstein's *Tractatus* and Broch's *Death of Virgil* (which may, in part, be read as a gloss on Kafka's dilemma) are pervaded by the authority of silence.

In Kafka the question of silence is posed most radically. It is this which gives him his exemplary place in modern literature. Should the poet cease? In a time when men are made to pipe or squeak their sufferings like beetles and mice, is literate speech, of all things the most human, still possible? Kafka knew that in the beginning was the

Word; he asks us: what of the end?

It is here that Kafka's Judaism is of immediate relevance. Many aspects of that Judaism have been explored by critics and biographers. Little more need be said of Kafka's indebtedness to the Gnostic and Chassidic traditions, of his vivid, though fitful, interest in Zionism, of the uneasy nostalgia for the emotional cohesion of the eastern Jewish community which made him say to Janouch:

> I should like to run to the poor Jews of the Ghetto, kiss the hem of their garment, and say nothing. I should be totally happy if they would silently suffer my nearness.

Kafka's proud, prophetic statement that those who "strike at the Jew kill Man" (*Man schlägt den Juden und erschlägt den Menschen*) is well known. But the more difficult task remains to be done: the placing of Kafka's achievement and silences in the context of the relationship of the Jewish sensibility to European languages and literature.

Mr. Politzer's study is an indispensable preliminary. Though it is thin in its treatment of the vexed problem of the sources of Kafka's manner (Robert Walser is referred to only once), it goes further than any previous inquiry in showing Kafka's scrupulous craftsmanship and technical means. No responsible reading of Kafka can ignore what its author argues of the arrangement of the novels, of the successive stages of composition, and of Kafka's habits of work. This ingenious, patient study has brought into just prominence Kafka's *métier*.

But Mr. Politzer's judgment lacks critical and philosophic insistence; it does not press to the core. Kafka's linguistic situation was precarious. The condition of the German-speaking Jewish minority in Prague enforced a characteristic sense of isolation and labyrinthine complexity. Kafka's German grated on Czech ears; often he felt guilty because he was not using his talent toward the renascence of Czech literature and national consciousness, and that guilt is poignant in the encounter with Milena. Yet at the same time his Jewishness affronted the rising pressure of German nationalism. Kafka noted wryly that the German spoken by students and businessmen who came to Prague from Germany was alien to his own, that it was, inevitably, "the language of enemies." By abdicating from the Czech milieu and speaking German, the Jewish middle class was hoping to assert its emancipation, its partnership in liberal European values.

Kafka sensed that such hope was vain.

Beyond the local circumstance lay the more general crux. The European Jew had come late to secular literature, to the realm of "truthful lies" which is poetry and fiction. Everywhere he found languages which had sprung from historical realities and habits of vision alien to his own. The very words belonged to the heritage of Slavonic or Latin Christianity, as did the high places of power and esteem. Where it relinquished Hebrew and passed through *Jüdisch-Deutsch* to the use of the European vernaculars, the eastern Jewish sensibility had to slip into the garb and glove of its oppressors. Languages codify immemorial reflexes and twists of feeling, remembrances of action that transcend individual recall, contours of communal experience as subtly decisive as the contours of sky and land in which a civilization ripens. An outsider can master a language as a rider masters his mount; he rarely becomes as one with its undefined, subterranean motion. Schoenberg developed a new syntax, a convention of statement inviolate by alien or previous usage. The Jewish writers of the romantic period and the twentieth century were less radical. They strove to weld the genius of their legacy, the uniqueness of their social and historical condition, to an idiom borrowed.

The relation between the Jewish writer and German was peculiarly tense and problematic, as if it contained forebodings of later catastrophe. As Theodor Adorno says of Heine:

> The fluency and clarity which Heine appropriated from current speech is the very opposite of native "at-homeness" (*Geborgenheit*) in a language. Only he who is not truly at home inside a language uses it as an instrument.

Kafka's diary for October 24, 1911, bears tragic witness to the alienation he felt within his own idiom:

> Yesterday it occurred to me that I did not always love my mother as she deserved and as I could, only because the German language prevented it. The Jewish mother is no "Mutter," to call her "Mutter" makes her a little comic. ... for the Jew, "Mutter" is specifically German, it unconsciously connotes together with Christian splendor Christian coldness also, the Jewish woman who is called "Mutter" therefore becomes not only comic but strange. .... I believe that it is solely the memories of the

Ghetto which preserve the Jewish family, for the word "Vater" does not approximate to the Jewish father either.

We can read Kafka's last story, "The Burrow," as a parable of estrangement, of the artist unhoused in his language. However much he seeks to guard himself within the mastered intimacy of his craft, the haunted builder knows that there is a rift in the wall, the "outside" is waiting to pounce (*geborgen* and *verborgen* express the deep linguistic kinship between being safely at home and safely hidden). Kafka was inside the German language as is a traveler in a hotel— one of his key images. The house of words was not truly his own.

That was the shaping impulse behind his unique style, behind the fantastic nakedness and economy of his writing. Kafka stripped German to the bone of direct meaning, discarding, wherever possible, the enveloping context of historical, regional, or metaphoric resonance. He drew from the fund of the language, from its deposits of accumulated verbal overtones, only what he could appropriate strictly to his own use. He set puns in strategic places, because a pun, unlike a metaphor, echoes only inward, only to the accidental structure of the language itself.

The idiom of "In the Penal Colony" or "The Hunger Artist" is miraculously translucent, as if the richness and tint of German historical and literary precedent had been effaced. Kafka polished words as Spinoza polished lenses; an exact light goes through them unblurred. But often there is a cold and thinness in the air. Indeed, Kafka may be seen as admonitory to the Jewish genius of the likelihood that it is in Hebrew, not in the borrowed dress of other tongues, that a Jewish literature will strike root.

The extremity of Kafka's literary position together with the shortness and torments of his personal life make the representative stature and centrality of his achievement the more notable. No other voice has borne truer witness to the dark of our time. Kafka remarked, in 1914: "I find the letter K offensive, almost nauseating, and yet I write it down, it must be characteristic of me." In the alphabet of human feeling and perception that letter now belongs unalterably to one man.

SCHOENBERG'S
MOSES AND AARON

It is difficult to conceive of a work in which music and language interact more closely than in Arnold Schoenberg's *Moses und Aron*. (The German title has an advantage of which Schoenberg, half in humor, half in superstition, was aware: its twelve letters are a symbolic counterpart to the twelve tones which form a basic set in serial composition.) It is, therefore, impertinent to write about the opera if one is unable to analyze its powerful, intensely original musical structure. This analysis has been undertaken by several musicologists and students of Schoenberg.[1] One would wish that the intrinsic difficulty of the subject had not been aggravated by the "initiate" technicality of their approach. This is especially true of the account of the music written by Milton Babbit and issued with the only recording so far available of *Moses and Aaron* (Columbia K-31-241).

If I write this program note, it is because the great majority of those in the audience at Covent Garden will be in my position; they do not have the training or knowledge needed to grasp the technical unfolding of the score. The demands made are, in fact, severely beyond those required by a classical composition, or even by the

[1] The most complete discussion of the work is to be found in Karl H. Wörner: *Schoenberg's "Moses and Aaron"* (trans. P. Hamburger, London, 1963). Among the most important technical discussions of the music are those by Hans Keller in *The Score* (No. 21, 1957) and W. Zillig in *Melos, Zeitschrift für Neue Musik* (vol. 3, 1957). A fascinating, though often quirky and unnecessarily obscure survey of the philosophic and historical background of the opera may be found in T. W. Adorno: *"Sakrales Fragment: Ueber Schoenberg's Moses und Aron"* (a lecture delivered in Berlin in April 1963 and reprinted that same year in Adorno's *Quasi una fantasia*).

orchestral density of Mahler. Together we shall have to take comfort in Schoenberg's frequent admonition:

> I cannot often enough warn against the overrating of analysis since it invariably leads to what I have always fought against: the knowledge of how something is *made;* whereas I have always tried to promote the knowledge of what something *is.*

And one recalls Kierkegaard's observation at the outset of his discussion of *Don Giovanni:*

> though I feel that music is an art which to the highest degree requires experience to justify one in having an opinion about it, still I comfort myself . . . with the paradox that, even in ignorance and mere intimations, there is also a kind of experience.

In the case of *Moses and Aaron* I would go further. It belongs to that very small group of operas which embody so radical and comprehensive an act of imagination, of dramatic and philosophic argument articulated by poetic and musical means, that there are aspects of it which go well beyond the normal analysis of an operatic score. It belongs not only to the history of modern music—in a critical way, as it exemplifies the application of Schoenberg's principles on a large, partly conventional scale—but to the history of the modern theater, of modern theology, of the relationship between Judaism and the European crisis. These aspects do not define or in any way exhaust the meaning of the work; that meaning is fundamentally musical. But an account of them may prove helpful to those who approach the work for the first time, and who would place it in its historical and emotional context. Like other very great and difficult works of art, Schoenberg's opera goes decisively outside the confines of its *genre* while giving to that *genre* a new and seemingly obvious fulfillment.

In a letter to Alban Berg of October 16, 1933, when he had just returned formally to Judaism in the face of Nazi anti-Semitism, Schoenberg wrote:

> As you have doubtless realised, my return to the Jewish religion took place long ago and is indeed demonstrated in some of my published work (*"Thou shalt not, thou must"*) as well as in *Moses and Aaron*, of which you

have known since 1928, but which dates from at least five years earlier; but especially in my drama *The Biblical Way* which was also conceived in 1922 or '23 at the latest.[2]

Der Biblische Weg remains unpublished; but what is known about it points clearly to the theme of the opera. It tells of a Zionist visionary, in whose name, Max Arun, there may be a foreshadowing of Moses and Aaron, who fails to achieve his goal through human imperfection. Equally relevant is the other piece referred to by Schoenberg, the second of the *Four Pieces* for mixed chorus, op. 27. Written in 1925, it sets to music the prohibition of Mosaic law against the making of images. "An image asks for names. . . . Thou shalt believe in the Spirit; thou must, chosen one." This injunction, expressed in a cadenced prose which anticipates the "spoken song" of the opera, summarizes the central dramatic idea and conflict of *Moses and Aaron*. But Schoenberg's interest in the musical statement of religious thought and in the dramatic idiom of the Old Testament goes back even further: to *Die Jakobsleiter*, an oratorio left incomplete in 1917.

This concern persisted throughout Schoenberg's later work: in the *Kol Nidre* of 1938, in the brief, harrowing cantata *A Survivor from Warsaw* (1947), in the setting of Psalm 130 (1950), in Schoenberg's final opus, the unfinished *Modern Psalms*. The last words he set to music were: "And yet I pray as all that lives prays." Thus *Moses and Aaron* is thematically and psychologically related to an entire set of works in which Schoenberg sought to express his highly individual, though at the same time profoundly Judaic concept of identity, of the act of spiritual creation, and of the dialogue—so inherent in music—between the song of man and the silences of God. The opera is both Schoenberg's *magnum opus* (what T. W. Adorno calls his "*Hauptwerk quand-même*") and a composition rooted in the logic and development of his entire musical thought.

Schoenberg began writing *Moses and Aaron* in Berlin in May 1930; he completed Act II in Barcelona on March 10, 1932. Roberto Gerhard, in whose Barcelona flat Schoenberg often worked, tells an instructive anecdote. Schoenberg did not mind friends chatting in the room, even when he was engaged on the fantastically complex score; what he could not tolerate were sudden spells of quiet. The dates of

[2] All quotations are from the *Letters*, ed. by Erwin Stein (London, 1964).

composition are, of course, important. On the one hand they mark Schoenberg's hard-fought professional acceptance, as Ferruccio Busoni's successor at the Prussian Academy of Arts. But they also mark bouts of illness which led Schoenberg to seek refuge in a southern climate, and, above all, the rise of the Nazi menace. A year after he had completed Act II, Schoenberg was compelled to leave Berlin and start a life of exile.

He did not live to complete the opera or hear it performed. An extract was given in concert form at Darmstadt on July 2, 1951 (plans for a production at the *Maggio Musicale* in Florence fell through). Schoenberg died less than a fortnight later. The first complete concert program was given at the Musikhalle in Hamburg under the direction of Hans Rosbaud in March 1954. On June 16, 1957, Rosbaud directed the stage *première* of *Moses und Aron* at the Stadttheater in Zurich. This was followed by a Berlin production under Hermann Scherchen in October 1959. Since that time there have been few major opera houses in Europe or the United States which have not expressed the hope of producing the work, and retreated before its formidable demands.

Karl Wörner says that *Moses and Aaron* "is without precedent." This is not so: as opera, it is related to Wagner's *Parsifal*, and there are orchestral anticipations both in Mahler and in Schoenberg's own earlier compositions and in his short operas, *Erwartung* and *Die Glückliche Hand*. But it is technically more demanding than any other major opera, and the quality of the religious-philosophic conflict requires from the performers and producer an unusual range of insight and sympathy. Schoenberg has deliberately used a *genre* saturated with nineteenth-century values of unreality and modish display to express an ultimate seriousness. In so doing he reopened the entire question of opera.

The libretto is organized wholly in terms of musical form and development (if serial music anticipates electronic music it is in the totality of control which the composer aims at in every aspect of the musical experience). As Schoenberg remarked: "It is only while I'm composing that the text becomes definite, sometimes even after composition." Nevertheless, the book of *Moses and Aaron* is itself of great fascination. Schoenberg has a distinctive style which one sees in his paintings and theoretical writings no less than in his music. He worked in large strokes, and achieved an effect of clarity and abstract energy by leaving out syntactical qualifications or half-tones. Like much in Schoenberg's musical texts and literary tastes, the libretto shows traces of German expressionism, and of the sources of expressionism. Characteristically, Strindberg plays a part: Schoenberg knew *Wrestling Jacob* when he planned *Die Jakobsleiter*, and was aware of Strindberg's *Moses* when writing his own very different treatment of the theme.

The idiom used in *Moses and Aaron* is highly personal. It is kept apart from the rhythms and tonality of the Luther Bible. Schoenberg wrote to Berg on August 5, 1930: "I am of the opinion that the language of the Bible is medieval German, which, being obscure to us, should be used at most to give colour; and that is something I don't need." Above all, each German word, whether in *Sprechgesang*, in direct song or choral declaration, is uniquely and precisely fitted to the musical context. The words are no less *durchkomponiert* ("fully composed, musicalised") than are the notes. This is what makes any decision to produce *Moses and Aaron* in English so wrong-headed. To alter the words—their cadence, stress, tonalities—as must be done in translation, is tantamount to altering the key relations or orchestration in a piece of classical music. Moreover, there is no need to subvert Schoenberg in this way: the story of *Exodus* is known to everyone, and Schoenberg's presentation of the plot is utterly lucid. A brief outline would have given an English-speaking audience all the help it wants.

The relationship of language to music in *Moses and Aaron* is unlike that in any other opera. The problem of that relationship, of how to apportion the stress between word and musical tone, of whether the ideal libretto should not be weak precisely in order to mark the distance between music drama and the spoken play, underlies the whole history of opera. As Joseph Kerman has shown, it is the problematic achievement of Wagner, the late Verdi, and twentieth-century operatic composers to have given the libretto a new seriousness. Hence the marked affinity to modern literature and psychological argument in the operas of Janáček, Berg, and Stravinsky. Hence the ironic allegoric treatment of the debate between poet and composer in Richard Strauss's *Capriccio*.

But *Moses and Aaron* goes much deeper. It belongs to that group of works produced in the twentieth century, and crucial to our present aesthetics, which have their own possibility as essential theme. I mean that it asks of itself—as Kafka does of fiction, as Klee asks of visual form—whether the thing can be done at all, whether

131

there are modes of communication adequate. Kierkegaard wrote of Mozart: "The happy characteristic that belongs to every classic, that which makes it classic and immortal, is the absolute harmony of the two forces, form and content." One would say of modern art that what makes it such and unmistakable to our sensibility is the frequent dissonance between moral, psychological content and traditional form. Being a drama of non-communication, of the primal resistance of intuitive or revealed insight to verbal and plastic incarnation (the refusal of the Word to be made flesh), *Moses and Aaron* is, on one vital plane, an opera about opera. It is a demonstration of the impossibility of finding an exhaustive accord between language and music, between sensual embodiment and the enormous urgency and purity of intended meaning. By making the dramatic conflict one between a man who speaks and a man who sings, Schoenberg has argued to the limit the paradoxical convention, the compromise with the unreal, inherent in all opera.

The paradox is resolved in defeat, in a great cry of necessary silence. This alone makes it difficult to think of a serious opera coming after or going beyond *Moses and Aaron*. But that was exactly Schoenberg's own problem as a post-Wagnerian, and as an heir to Mahler in artistic morality even more than in orchestral technique. Like Mahler, he was proposing to aggravate, in the literal sense, the easy coexistence, the *libertinage* between music and public which obtained in the opera house at the turn of the century and which Strauss, for all his musical integrity, never refuted. As Adorno notes, *Moses and Aaron* can be approached in the same spirit as a major cantata of Bach. But unlike Bach, it is a work which at every moment calls to account its own validity and expressive means.

The motif of a sharp conflict between Moses and Aaron is, of course, present in the Pentateuch. It may well be that later priestly editors, with their particular professional association with Aaron's priesthood, smoothed away some of the grimmer evidence, and obscured the full, murderous consequences of the clash. Schoenberg made of this archaic, hidden antagonism a conflict of ultimate moral and personal values, of irreconcilable formulations or metaphors of man's confrontation with God. Working on the principle—discernible at the roots of Greek tragic drama—that fundamental human conflict is internal, that dramatic dialogue is in the final analysis between self and self, Schoenberg gathered the entire force of collision into a single consciousness.

132

This is the drama of Moses. Aaron is one of the possibilities, the most seductive, the most humane, of Moses' self-betrayals. He is Moses' voice when that voice yields to imperfect truth and to the music of compromise. Schoenberg remarked in 1933: "My Moses more resembles—of course only in outward respect—Michelangelo's. He is not human at all." So far as the harsh, larger-than-life stature of the personage goes, this may be so. But the poignancy of the opera, its precise focus of emotion and suffering, comes above all from Moses' humanity, from that in him which is riven and inarticulate. It is not of the fiercely contained eloquence of Michelangelo's statue that one thinks when listening to *Moses and Aaron*, but of Alban Berg's *Wozzeck* (written just before Schoenberg started composing his own opera). Moses and Wozzeck are both brilliant studies in dramatic contradiction, operatic figures unable to articulate with their own voices the fullness of their needs and perceptions. In both cases the music takes over where the human voice is strangled or where it retreats into desperate silence.

Schoenberg admitted to Berg: "Everything I have written has a certain inner likeness to myself." This is obviously true of Moses, and it is here that Michelangelo's figure, which fascinated Freud in a similar way, may be relevant. To any Jew initiating a great movement of spirit or radical doctrine in a profoundly hostile environment, leading a small group of disciples, some of them perhaps recalcitrant or ungrateful, to the promised land of a new metaphysic or aesthetic medium, the archetype of Moses would have a natural significance. By introducing into music, whose classical development and modes seemed to embody the very genius of the Christian and Germanic tradition, a new syntax, an uncompromisingly rational and apparently dissonant ideal, Schoenberg was performing an act of great psychological boldness and complexity. Going far beyond Mahler, he was asserting a revolutionary—to its enemies an alien, Jewish—presence in the world of Bach and Wagner. Thus the twelve-tone system is related, in point of sensibility and psychological context, to the imaginative radicalism, to the "subversiveness" of Cantor's mathematics or Wittgenstein's epistemology.

Like Freud, Schoenberg saw himself as a pioneer and teacher, reviled by the vast majority of his contemporaries, driven into solitude by his own unbending genius, gathering a small band around him and going forward, in exile, to a new world of meaning and vital possibility. In Moses' bitter cry that his lessons are not being understood, that his vision is being distorted even by those nearest him, one hears Schoenberg's own inevitable moments of discouragement and angry loneliness. And there is almost too apt an analogy in the fact that he died on the threshold of acceptance, before his stature had been widely acknowledged, before he could complete *Moses and Aaron* or hear any of it performed.

Except for one moment (I, 2, bars 208–217) —and I have never understood just why it should be at *this* particular point in the opera —Moses does not sing. He speaks in a highly cadenced, formal discourse, his voice loud and bitter against the fluencies of the music and, in particular, against Aaron's soaring tenor. (The parodistic yet profoundly engaged treatment of Aaron's vocal score seems to be full of references to traditional operatic *bel canto* and the ideal of the Wagnerian *Heldentenor*.) The fact that the protagonist of a grand opera should not sing is a powerful theatrical stroke, even more "shocking" than the long silence of Aeschylus' Cassandra or the abrupt, single intervention of the mute Pylades in *The Libation Bearers*. But it is also much more than that.

Moses' incapacity to give expressive form (music) to his vision, to make revelation communicable and thus translate his individual communion with God into a community of belief in Israel, is the tragic subject of the opera. Aaron's contrasting eloquence, his instantaneous translation—hence traduction—of Moses' abstract, hidden meaning into sensuous form (the singing voice), dooms the two men to irreconcilable conflict. Moses cannot do without Aaron; Aaron is the tongue which God has placed into his own inarticulate mouth. But Aaron diminishes or betrays Moses' thought, that in him which is immediate revelation, in the very act of communicating it to other men. As in Wittgenstein's philosophy, there is in *Moses and Aaron* a radical consideration of silence, an inquiry into the ultimately tragic gap between what is apprehended and that which can be said. Words distort; eloquent words distort absolutely.

This is implicit in the first lines of the opera spoken by Moses against the background of the orchestral opening and the murmur of the six solo voices which portray the Burning Bush. The fact that Moses so often speaks simultaneously with Aaron's song, or that we hear his voice in conflict with the orchestra, points to Schoenberg's essential design. Moses' words are internal, they are his thought, clear and integral only before it moves outward into the betrayal of speech.

134

Moses addresses his God as "omnipresent, invisible, and inconceivable." *Unvorstellbar*, that which cannot be imagined, conceived, or represented (*vorstellen* means, precisely, to enact, to mime, to dramatize concretely), is the key word of the opera. God is *because* He is incommensurate to human imagining, because no symbolic representation available to man can realize even the minutest fraction of His inconceivable omnipresence. To know this, to serve a Deity so intangible to human mimesis, is the unique, magnificent destiny which Moses envisions for his people. It is also a fearful destiny. As the Voice out of the Burning Bush proclaims:

> This people is chosen
> before all others,
> to be the people of the only God,
> that it should know Him
> and be wholly His;
> that it undergo all trials
> conceivable to thought
> over the millennia.

The last two lines are eloquently ambiguous: the words can also be read to mean: "all trials to which this thought—of a God invisible and inconceivable—may be exposed."

Aaron enters and the misunderstanding between the two brothers is immediate and fatal. Aaron rejoices in the proud uniqueness of Israel's mission, in the grandeur of a God so much more powerful and demanding than all other gods (these other gods continue to be real to Aaron). He exults in *imagining* such a God, in finding words and poetic symbols by which to make Him present to His people. Yet even as he sings, Moses cries out: "No image can give you an image of the unimaginable." And when Aaron elaborates, with a rich ease of perception mirrored in the music, the notion of a God who will punish and reward His people according to their deserts, Moses proclaims a Kierkegaardian God, infinitely, scandalously transcending any human sense of cause and effect:

> Inconceivable because invisible;
> because immeasurable;
> because everlasting;
> because eternal;
> because omnipresent;
> because omnipotent.

135

To which litany of abstraction, of inexpressible apprehension, Aaron responds with the joyous assurance that God shall bring wonders to pass on behalf of His enslaved people.

He does. Confronted with the rebellious bewilderment of the Jews, with their call for visible signs of the new revelation, Moses retreats into his own inarticulateness. It is Aaron who proclaims himself the word and the deed. It is he who casts Moses' rod to the ground where it turns into a serpent, and shows Moses' hand to be leprous and then miraculously restored. During the entire last part of the Act, Moses is silent. It is Aaron who proclaims the doom of Pharaoh and the covenant of the Promised Land. Fired by his eloquence, the people of Israel march forth and the music is exultant with Aaron's certitude. It is through him that God appears to be speaking.

In one sense, in one possible idiom, He is. Moses' understanding of God is much more authentic, much deeper; but it is essentially mute or accessible only to very few. Without Aaron, God's purpose cannot be accomplished; through Aaron it is perverted. That is the tragic paradox of the drama, the metaphysical scandal which springs from the fact that the categories of God are not parallel or commensurate to those of man.

Act II centers on the Golden Calf. With Moses' long absence on Sinai, the Elders and the people have grown rebellious and afraid. The invisibility of God has become an intolerable anguish. Aaron yields to the voices that cry out for an image, for something that eye and hand can grasp in the act of worship. On the darkening stage the Golden Calf shines forth.

What follows is one of the most astonishing pieces of music written in the twentieth century. As musical analysts point out, it is a symphony in five movements with solo voices and choruses. The orchestration is so intricate yet dramatic in its statements and suggestions that it seems incredible that Schoenberg should have *heard* it all inside him, that he should have known exactly (if he did) how these fantastic instrumental and rhythmic combinations would work without, in fact, ever hearing a note played. The pageant of the Golden Calf makes the utmost demands on orchestras, singers, and dancers. Rearing horses, treasure-laden camels, and Four Naked Virgins are requirements which even the most resourceful of opera houses find difficult to meet.

What Schoenberg had in mind is something very different from an ordinary operatic ballet. It is a total dramatic integration of voice, bodily motion, and orchestral development. Even the most frenzied moments of the idolatrous, sexual orgy are plotted in terms of a rigorous, immensely subtle musical structure. As Schoenberg wrote to Webern:

> I wanted to leave as little as possible to those new despots of the theatrical art, the producers, and even to envisage the choreography as far as I'm able to. . . . You know I'm not at all keen on the dance. . . . Anyway so far I've succeeded in thinking out movements such as at least enter into a different territory of expression from the caperings of common-or-garden ballet.

But these "caperings" are not wholly irrelevant. In Schoenberg's treatment of the Golden Calf, as in so much of *Moses and Aaron*, there is a revaluation—either straightforward or parodistic—of the conventions of opera. Are these conventions applicable to the modern circumstance? How much seriousness can they sustain? Thus the Golden Calf is both the logical culmination of, and a covert satire on, that catalogue of orgiastic ballets and ritual dances which is one of the distinctive traits of grand opera from Massenet's *Hérodiade* to *Tannhäuser*, from *Aïda* and *Samson et Dalila* to *Parsifal* and *Salome*. Schoenberg is fully aware of the dual quality of the scene. It is at the same time supremely serious and ironic in its exhaustive use of the convention:

> In the treatment of this scene, which actually represents the very core of my thought, I went pretty much to the limit, and this too is probably where my piece is most *operatic;* as indeed it must be.

With the return of Moses—his indistinct, terrifying figure looms suddenly on the horizon and is seen by one of the exhausted revelers—the drama moves swiftly to its climax. At a glance from Moses, the Golden Calf vanishes:

> Begone, you that are the image of the fact that what is measureless cannot be bounded in an image.

The two brothers confront each other on the empty stage. And once more it is Aaron who has the better of the argument. He has given the people an image so that Israel may live and not fall into despair. He loves the people and knows that the demands of abstraction and inwardness which Moses makes upon the human spirit are beyond the power of ordinary men. Moses loves an idea, an absolute vision, relentless in its purity. He would make of Israel the hollow, tormented vessel of an inconceivable presence. No people can endure such a task. Even the Tables of the Law which Moses has brought from the mountain are only an image, a palpable symbol of hidden authority.

Baffled, incensed by Aaron's argument, Moses smashes the Tables. Aaron accuses him of faint-heartedness. The tribes of Israel shall continue their march to the Promised Land whether or not they have grasped the full meaning of God's revelation. As if to confirm his words, the Chorus resumes its march across the stage. It is led by a pillar of fire, and Aaron goes forth glorying in the visible wonder of God.

Moses is left alone. Is Aaron right? Must the inconceivable, unimaginable, unrepresentable reality of God diminish to mere symbol, to the tangible artifice of miracle? In that case all he has thought and said (the two are identical to Moses) has been madness. The very attempt to express his vision was a crime. The orchestra falls silent as the unison violins play a retrograde inversion of the basic twelve-tone set. Moses cries out, "O word, thou word that I lack!" and sinks to the ground, broken.

This is one of the most moving, dramatic moments in the history of opera and of the modern theater. With its implicit allusion to the *Logos*, to the Word that is yet to come but which lies beyond speech, it gathers into one action both the claims of music to be the most complete idiom, the carrier of transcendent energies, and all that is felt in twentieth-century art and philosophy about the gap between meaning and communication. But Moses' defeat also has a more specific, historical bearing, which may help us understand why Schoenberg did not complete the opera.

The letters of 1932 and 1933 show that he had every intention of doing so. As late as November 1948, Schoenberg could write: "I should really best like to finish *Die Jakobsleiter* and *Moses and Aaron*." What intervened?

There is evidence that Schoenberg found it difficult to give the third Act a coherent dramatic shape. He wrote to Walter Eidlitz on March 15, 1933, that he had re-cast Aaron's Death for the fourth time "because of some almost incomprehensible contradictions in the Bible." As it stands, the text of Act III is a curious torso, both repetitive and moving. Once more, Moses and Aaron, now in chains, state their opposite conceptions of idea and image. But Moses no longer addresses his brother directly. He is speaking to the Jewish people as it prepares to enter into the mire and compromise of history. He prophesies that Jews will prosper only so long as they dwell in the stern wilderness of the spirit, in the presence of the One and Inconceivable God. If they forget their great act of renunciation and seek an ordinary haven in the world, they will have failed and their suffering shall be the greater. Salvation lies in apartness. The Jew is himself when he is a stranger.

Freed of his chains, Aaron falls dead at Moses' feet. (Is there here, one wonders, a reminiscence of Hunding's death when Wotan glances at him in scorn?) As we have no music to accompany the words, it is difficult to judge their effect. But the third Act is essentially static. There is no dramatic justification for Moses' triumph over a prostrate Aaron. Much is missing.

But the real impediment probably lay deeper. As Adorno remarks, *Moses and Aaron* was "a preventive action against the looming of Nazism." But even as Schoenberg worked on the score, Nazism was moving rapidly to its triumph. The words *Volk* and *Führer* figure prominently in the opera; they designate its supreme historical values, Israel and Moses. Now they were wrested out of Schoenberg's grasp by the million voices bawling them at Nuremberg. How could he continue to set them to music? As he labored on the third Act in March 1933, Schoenberg must have known that the culture in which he had hammered out his vision of a new music, and for whose opera houses he had conceived *Moses and Aaron*, was heading for ruin or exile—as was his own personal life.

It is this which gives the end of Act II its tremendous authority and logic. The events that were now to come to pass in Europe were, quite literally, beyond words, too inhuman for that defining act of humane consciousness which is speech. Moses' despairing cry, his collapse into silence, is a recognition—such as we find also in Kafka, in Broch, in Adamov—that words have failed us, that art can neither stem barbarism nor convey experience when experience grows unspeakable. Thus *Moses and Aaron* is, despite its formal incompletion, a work of marvelous finality. There was no more to be said.[3]

[3] This is why it seems to me that a spoken performance of the third Act, which Schoenberg himself envisioned and regarded as permissible, adds nothing and, in fact, weakens the uncanny force and beauty of the musical close.

A KIND OF SURVIVOR

For Elie Wiesel

Not literally. Due to my father's foresight (he had shown it when leaving Vienna in 1924), I came to America in January 1940, during the phony war. We left France, where I was born and brought up, in safety. So I happened not to be there when the names were called out. I did not stand in the public square with the other children, those I had grown up with. Or see my father and mother disappear when the train doors were torn open. But in another sense I am a survivor, and not intact. If I am often out of touch with my own generation, if that which haunts me and controls my habits of feeling strikes many of those I should be intimate and working with in my present world as remotely sinister and artificial, it is because the black mystery of what happened in Europe is to me indivisible from my own identity. Precisely because I was not there, because an accident of good fortune struck my name from the roll.

Often the children went alone, or held the hands of strangers. Sometimes parents saw them pass and did not dare call out their names. And they went, of course, not for anything they had done or said. But because their parents existed before them. The crime of being one's children. During the Nazi period it knew no absolution, no end. Does it now? Somewhere the determination to kill Jews, to harass them from the earth simply because they *are*, is always alive. Ordinarily, the purpose is muted, or appears in trivial spurts—the obscenity daubed on the front door, the brick through the shop window. But there are, even now, places where the murderous intent might grow heavy: in Russia, in parts of North Africa, in certain countries of Latin America. Where tomorrow? So, at moments, when I see my children in the room, or imagine that I hear them breathing in the still of the house, I grow afraid. Because I have put on their backs a burden of ancient loathing and set savagery at their heels. Because it may be that I will be able to do no more than the parents of the children gone to guard them.

That fear lies near the heart of the way in which I think of myself as a Jew. To have been a European Jew in the first half of the twentieth century was to pass sentence on one's own children, to force upon them a condition almost beyond rational understanding. And which may recur. I have to think that—it is the vital clause—so long as remembrance is real. Perhaps we Jews walk closer to our children than other men; try as they may, they cannot leap out of our shadow.

This is my self-definition. Mine, because I cannot speak for any other Jew. All of us obviously have something in common. We do tend to recognize one another wherever we meet, nearly at a glance, by some common trick of feeling, by the darkness we carry. But each of us must hammer it out for himself. That is the real meaning of the Diaspora, of the wide scattering and thinning of belief.

To the Orthodox my definition must seem desperate and shallow. Entire communities stayed close-knit to the end. There were children who did not cry out but said *Shema Yisroel* and kept their eyes wide open because His kingdom lay just a step over the charnel pit; not as many as is sometimes said, but there *were*. To the strong believer the torture and massacre of six million is one chapter—one only—in the millennial dialogue between God and the people He has so terribly chosen. Though Judaism lacks a dogmatic eschatology (it leaves to the individual the imagining of transcendence), the Orthodox can meditate on the camps as a forecourt of God's house, as an almost intolerable but manifest mystery of His will. When he teaches his children the prayers and rites (my own access to these was that of history, not of present faith), when they sing at his side at the high holidays, the pious Jew looks on them not with fear, not as hostages that bear the doom of his love, but in pride and rejoicing. Through them the bread shall remain blessed and the wine sanctified. They are alive not because of a clerical oversight in a Gestapo office, but because they no less than the dead are part of God's truth. Without them history would stand empty. The Orthodox Jew defines himself (as I cannot) in the rich life of his prayer, of an inheritance both tragic and resplendent. He harvests the living echo of his own being from the voices of his community and the holiness of the word. His children are like the night turned to song.

141

The Orthodox Jew would not only deny me the right to speak for him, pointing to my lack of knowledge and communion; he would say, "You are not like us, you are a Jew outwardly, in name only." Exactly. But the Nazis made of the mere name necessary and sufficient cause. They did not ask whether one had ever been to synagogue, whether one's children knew any Hebrew. The anti-Semite is no theologian; but his definition is inclusive. So we would all have gone together, the Orthodox and I. And the gold teeth would have come out of our dead mouths, song or no song.

Two passages from *Exodus* help the mind grasp enormity. Perhaps they are mistranslations or archaic shards interpolated in the canonic text. But they help me as does poetry and metaphor, by giving imaginative logic to grim possibility. *Exodus* 4.24 tells how God sought to kill Moses: "And it came to pass by the way in the inn, that the Lord met him and sought to kill him." I gloss this to mean that God suffers gusts of murderous exasperation at the Jews, toward a people who have made Him a responsible party to history and to the grit of man's condition. He may not have wished to be involved; the people may have chosen Him, in the oasis at Kadesh, and thrust upon Him the labors of justice and right anger. It may have been the Jew who caught Him by the skirt, insisting on contract and dialogue. Perhaps before either God or living man was ready for proximity. So as in marriage, or the bond between father and child, there are moments when love is changed to something very much like itself, pure hatred.

The second text is *Exodus* 33.22–3. Moses is once more on Sinai, asking for a new set of Tablets (we have always been nagging Him, demanding justice and reason twice over). There follows a strange ceremony of recognition: "And it shall come to pass, while my glory passeth by, that I will put thee in a cleft of the rock, and will cover thee with my hand while I pass by: And I will take away mine hand, and thou shalt see my back parts: but my face shall not be seen." This may be the decisive clue: God can turn His back. There may be minutes or millennia—is our time His?—in which He does not see man, in which He is looking the *other way*. Why? Perhaps because through some minute, hideous error of design the universe is too large for His surveillance, because somewhere there is a millionth of an inch, it need be no more, out of His line of sight. So He must turn to look there also. When God's back parts are toward man, history is Belsen.

If the Orthodox Jew cannot allow my definition, or this use of the holy word as metaphor and paradox, neither can the Zionist and the Israeli. They do not deny the catastrophe, but they know that it bore splendid fruit. Out of the horror came the new chance. The state of Israel is undeniably a part of the legacy of German mass murder. Hope and the will to action spring from the capacity of the human mind to forget, from the instinct of necessary oblivion. The Israeli Jew cannot look back too often; his must be the dreams not of night but of day, the forward dreams. Let the dead bury the mounds of the dead. His history is not theirs; it has just begun. To someone like myself, the Israeli Jew might say: "Why aren't you here? If you fear for the lives of your children, why not send them here and let them grow up amid their own kind? Why burden them with your own perhaps literary, perhaps masochistic, remembrance of disaster? This is their future. They have a right to it. We need all the brains and sinews we can get. We're not working for ourselves alone. There isn't a Jew in the world who doesn't hold his head higher because of what we've done here, because Israel exists."

Which is obviously true. The status of the Jew everywhere has altered a little, the image he carries of himself has a new straightness of back, because Israel has shown that Jews can handle modern weapons, that they can fly jets, and turn desert into orchard. When he is pelted in Argentina or mocked in Kiev, the Jewish child knows that there is a corner of the earth where he is master, where the gun is his. If Israel were to be destroyed, no Jew would escape unscathed. The shock of failure, the need and harrying of those seeking refuge, would reach out to implicate even the most indifferent, the most anti-Zionist.

So why not go? Why not leave the various lands in which we still live, it seems to me, as more or less accepted guests? Many Russian Jews might go if they could. North African Jews are doing so even at the price of destitution. The Jews of South Africa might before too long be forced to the same resolve. So why don't I go, who am at liberty, whose children could grow up far from the spoor of the inhuman past? I don't know if there is a good answer. But there is a reason.

If the way I think of my Jewishness will appear unacceptable or self-defeating to the Orthodox and the Israeli, it will also seem remote and overdramatized to most American Jews. The idea that Jews everywhere have been maimed by the European catastrophe, that the massacre has left all who survived (even if they were nowhere near

143

the actual scene) off balance, as does the tearing of a limb, is one which American Jews can understand in an intellectual sense. But I don't find that it has immediate personal relevance. The relationship of the American Jew to recent history is subtly and radically different from that of the European. By its very finality, the holocaust justified every previous impulse of immigration. All who had left Europe to establish the new Jewish communities in America were proved terribly right. The Jewish soldier who went to the Europe of his fathers came better armed, technologically more efficient than his murderous enemy. The few Jews he found alive were out of a hideous but spectral world, like a nightmare in a foreign tongue. In America, Jewish parents listen at night for their children; but it is to make sure the car is back in the garage, not because there is a mob out. It cannot happen in Scarsdale.

I am not sure, not completely (this is precisely where I am an outsider). Most American Jews are aware of anti-Semitism in specialized areas of life—the club, the holiday resort, the residential district, the professional guild. But in comparative terms, it tends to be mild, perhaps because America, unlike Europe or Russia, has no history of guilt toward the Jew. The size and human wealth of the American Jewish community are such, moreover, that a Jew need hardly go outside his own sphere to enjoy American life at its best and freest. The principal dynamism of American life, however, is a middle- and lower-middle-class conformity, an enforcing consensus of taste and ideal. Nearly by definition, the Jew stands in the way of uniform coherence. Economic, social, or political stress tend to make this latent disparity—the hostile recognition and reciprocal self-awareness of "difference"—more acute. Depression or a drastic increase in unemployment would isolate the status of the Jew, focusing resentment on his prosperity and on the ostentatious forms that prosperity has taken in certain aspects of Jewish life. The struggle over Negro rights, which is coming to overshadow so much of American life, has obvious bearing. Among urban Negroes anti-Semitism is often open and raw. It can be used by the Negro as a basis of temporary alliance with other underprivileged or resentful elements in the white community. Beyond these possibilities lies the larger pattern: the stiffening of consensus, the increasing concentration of American values in a standardized moralistic nationalism.

I agree that American anti-Semitism will stay mild and covert. So long as the economy expands and the racial conflict can be kept in tolerable bounds. So long as Israel is viable and can offer refuge. This is probably the root condition. The support given to Israel by the American Jewish community is both thoroughly generous and thoroughly self-interested. If a new wave of immigration occurred, if the Russian or Tunisian Jew came knocking at America's door, the status of American Jewry would be immediately affected.

These complex safeguards and conditions of acceptance can break down. America is no more immune than any other nationalistic, professedly Christian society from the contagion of anti-Semitism. In a crisis of resentment or exclusion, even the more assimilated would be driven back to our ancient legacy of fear. Though he might have forgotten it and turned Unitarian (a characteristic halfway house), Mr. Harrison's neighbors would remind him that his father was called Horowitz. To deny this is to assert that in America human character and historical forces have undergone some miraculous change—a utopian claim which the actual development of American life in the twentieth century has more than once rebuked.

Nevertheless, the sense I have of the Jew as a man who looks on his children with a dread remembrance of helplessness and an intimation of future, murderous possibility, is a very personal, isolated one. It does not relate to much that is now alive and hopeful. But it is not wholly negative either. I mean to include in it far more than the naked precedent of ruin. That which has been destroyed—the large mass of life so mocked, so hounded to oblivion that even the names are gone and the prayer for the dead can have no exact foothold—embodied a particular genius, a quality of intelligence and feeling which none of the major Jewish communities now surviving has preserved or recaptured. Because I feel that specific inheritance urgent in my own reflexes, in the work I try to do, I am a kind of survivor.

In respect of *secular* thought and achievement, the period of Jewish history which ended at Auschwitz surpassed even the brilliant age of coexistence in Islamic Spain. During roughly a century, from the emancipation of the ghettos by the French Revolution and Napoleon to the time of Hitler, the Jew took part in the moral, intellectual, and artistic noon of bourgeois Europe. The long confinement of the ghetto, the sharpening of wit and nervous insight against the whetstone of persecution, had accumulated large reserves of consciousness. Released into the light, a certain Jewish elite, and the wider middle-class circle which took pride and interest in its accomplishments, quickened and complicated the entire contour of Western thought. To every domain they brought radical imaginings; more specifically, the more gifted Jews repossessed certain crucial elements of classic European civilization in order to make them new and problematic. All this is commonplace; as is the inevitable observation that the tenor of modernity, the shapes of awareness and query by which we order our lives are, in substantial measure, the work of Marx, Freud, and Einstein.

What is far more difficult to show, though it seems to me undeniable, is the extent to which a common heritage of fairly recent emancipation, a particular bias of rational feeling—specialized in origin but broadening out to become the characteristic modern note—informs their distinct, individual genius. In all three, we discern a mastering impulse to visionary logic, to imagination in the abstract, as if the long banishment of the Eastern and European Jew from material action had given to thought a dramatic autonomy. The intimation of an energy of imagination at once sensuous and abstract, the release of the Jewish sensibility into a world dangerously new, unencumbered by reverence, is similarly at work in the subversions of Schoenberg and Kafka, and in the mathematics of Cantor. It relates Wittgenstein's *Tractatus* to that of Spinoza.

Without the contribution made by the Jews between 1830 and 1930, Western culture would be obviously different and diminished. At the same time, of course, it was his collision with established European values, with classic modes of art and argument, which compelled the emancipated Jew to define his range and identity. In this collision, in the attempt to achieve poise in an essentially borrowed milieu, the converted Jew or half-Jew, the Jew whose relation to his own past grew covert or antagonistic—Heine, Bergson, Hofmannsthal, Proust—played a particularly subtle and creative role.

Those who helped define and shared in this *Central European humanism* (each of the three terms carrying its full charge of implication and meaning) showed characteristic traits, characteristic habits of taste and recognition. They had a quick way with languages. Heine is the first, perhaps the only great poet whom it is difficult to locate in any single linguistic sensibility. The habits of reference of this European Jewish generation often point to the Greek and Latin classics; but these were seen through the special focus of Winckelmann, Lessing, and Goethe. An almost axiomatic sense of Goethe's transcendent stature, of the incredible ripeness and humanity of his art, colors the entire European-Jewish enlightenment, and continues to mark its few survivors (Goethe's fragment *On Nature* converted Freud from an early interest in law to the study of the biological sciences). The Central European Jewish bourgeoisie was frequently intimate with the plays of Shakespeare and assumed, rightly, that the performance of Shakespearean drama in Vienna, Munich, or Berlin, often acted and staged by Jews, more than matched what could be found in England. It read Balzac and Stendhal (one recalls Léon Blum's pioneer study of Beyle), Tolstoy, Ibsen, and Zola. But it often read them in a special, almost heightened context. The Jews who welcomed Scandinavian drama and the Russian novel tended to see in the new realism and iconoclasm of literature a part of the general liberation of spirit. Zola was not only the explorer of erotic and economic realities, as were Freud, Weininger, or Marx: he was the champion of Dreyfus.

The relationship of Jewish consciousness to Wagner was passionate, though uneasy. We see late instances of this duality in the musicology of Adorno and the fiction of Werfel. It recognized in Wagner the radicalism and histrionic tactics of a great outsider. It caught in Wagner's anti-Semitism a queer, intimate note, and gave occasional heed to the stubborn myth that Wagner was himself of Jewish descent. Being new to the plastic arts, hence beautifully free and empiric in its responses, Jewish taste, in the guise of dealer, patron, and critic, backed Impressionism and the blaze of the modern. Through Reinhardt and Piscator it renovated the theater; through Gustav Mahler the relations between serious music and society. In its golden period, from 1870 to 1914, then again in the 1920's, the Jewish leaven gave to Prague and Berlin, to Vienna and Paris a specific vitality of feeling and expression, an atmosphere both quintessentially European and "off-center." The nuance of spirit is delicately mocked and made memorable in the unquiet hedonism, in the erudite urbanity of Proust's Swann.

Almost nothing of it survives. This is what makes my own, almost involuntary, identification with it so shadowy a condition. European Jewry and its intelligentsia were caught between two waves of murder, Nazism and Stalinism. The implication of the European and Russian Jew in Marxism had natural causes. As has often been said, the dream of a secular millennium—which is still alive in Georg Lukács and the master historian of hope, Ernst Bloch —relates the social utopia of Communism to the messianic tradition.

For both Jew and Communist, history is a scenario of gradual humanization, an immensely difficult attempt by man to become man. In both modes of feeling there is an obsession with the prophetic authority of moral or historical law, with the right reading of canonic revelations. But from Eduard Bernstein to Trotsky, from Isaac Babel to Pasternak, the involvement of the Jewish personality in Communism and the Russian revolution follows an ironic pattern. Nearly invariably it ends in dissent or heresy—in that heresy which claims to be orthodox because it is seeking to restore the betrayed meaning of Marx (the Polish Marxist Adam Schaff would be a contemporary instance of this "Talmudic revisionism"). As Stalinism turned to nationalism and technocracy—the new Russia of the managerial middle class has its precise origins in the Stalinist period—the revolutionary intelligentsia went to the wall. The Jewish Marxist, the Trotskyite, the socialist fellow-traveler were trapped in the ruins of utopia. The Jew who had joined Communism in order to fight the Nazis, the Jewish Communist who had broken with the party after the purge trials, fell into the net of the Hitler-Stalin pact.

In one of the vilest episodes in modern history, the militia and police of European appeasement and European totalitarianism collaborated in handing over Jews. The French delivered to the Gestapo those who had fled from Spain and Germany. Himmler and the G.P.U. exchanged anti-Stalinist and anti-Nazi Jews for further torture and elimination. One thinks of Walter Benjamin—one of the most brilliant representatives of radical humanism—committing suicide lest the French or Spanish border-guards hand him over to the invading S.S.; of Buber-Neumann whose widow was nearly hounded to death by Stalinist cadres *inside* a Nazi concentration camp; of a score of others trapped between the Nazi and the Stalinist hunter (the memoirs of Victor Serge close with the roll of their several and hideous deaths). Which bestial bargain and exchange at the frontier made eloquent the decision to hound the Jew out of European history. But also the peculiar dignity of his torment. Perhaps we can define ourselves thus: *the Jews are a people whom totalitarian barbarism must choose for its hatred.*

A certain number escaped. It is easily demonstrable that much important work in American scholarship in the period from 1934 to circa 1955, in the arts, in the exact and social sciences, is the afterlife of the Central European renascence and embodied the talent of the refugee. But the particular cast of the American Jewish intelligence on native ground, which I first met at the University of Chicago in the late 1940's, and which now plays so obviously powerful a role in American intellectual and artistic life, is something very different. There is little of Karl Kraus's notion of style and humane literacy in, say, *Partisan Review*. Kraus is very nearly a touchstone. Ask a man if he has heard of him or read his *Literature and Lies*. If so, he is probably one of the survivors.

In Kraus, as in Kafka and Hermann Broch, there is a mortal premonition and finality. Broch, who seems to me the major European novelist after Joyce and Mann, is a defining figure. His *Death of Virgil*, his philosophic essays, are an epilogue to humanism. They focus on the deed which should dominate our rational lives so far as we still conduct them, which should persistently bewilder our sense of self—the turn of civilization to mass murder. Like certain parables of Kafka and the epistemology of the early Wittgenstein, the art of Broch goes near the edge of necessary silence. It asks whether speech, whether the shapes of moral judgment and imagination which the Judaic-Hellenic tradition founds on the authority of the Word, are viable in the face of the inhuman. Is the poet's verse not an insult to the naked cry? Broch died in America in a strange, vital solitude, giving voice to a civilization, to an inheritance of humane striving, already done to death.

The humanism of the European Jew lies in literal ash. In the accent of survivors—Hannah Arendt, Ernst Bloch, T. W. Adorno, Erich Kahler, Lévi-Strauss—whose interests and commitments are, of course, diverse, you will hear a common note as of desolation. Yet it is these voices which seem to me contemporary, whose work and context of reference are indispensable to an understanding of the philosophic, political, aesthetic roots of the inhuman; of the paradox that modern barbarism sprang, in some intimate, perhaps necessary way, from the very core and locale of humanistic civilization. If this is so, why do we try to teach, to write, to contend for literacy? Which question, and I know of none more urgent, or the idiom in which it is put, probably puts the asker thirty years out of date—on either side of the present.

As do certain other questions, increasingly muted and out of focus. Yet which cannot go unasked if we are to argue the values and possibilities of our culture. I mean the general complicity, in the massacre. There were superb exceptions (in Denmark, Norway, Bulgaria), but the tale is sordid and much of it remains an ugly riddle. At a time when nine thousand Jews were being exterminated *each day*, neither the R.A.F. nor the U.S. Air Force bombed the ovens or sought to blow open the camps (as Mosquitoes, flying low, had broken wide a prison in France to liberate agents of the *maquis*). Though the Jewish and Polish underground made desperate pleas, though the German bureaucracy made little secret of the fact that the "final solution" depended on rail transport, the lines to Belsen and Auschwitz were not bombed. Why? The question has been asked of Churchill and Tedder. Has there been an adequate answer? When the *Wehrmacht* and *Waffen-S.S.* poured into Russia, Soviet intelligence quickly noted the mass killing of the Jews. Stalin forbade any public announcement of the fact. Here again, the reasons are obscure. He may not have wanted a rekindling of separate Jewish consciousness; he may have feared implicit reference to his own anti-Semitic policies. Whatever the cause, many Jews who could have fled eastward stayed behind unknowing. Later on, in the Ukraine, local gangs helped the Germans round up those who cowered in cellars and woods.

I wonder what would have happened if Hitler had played the game after Munich, if he had simply said, "I will make no move outside the Reich so long as I am allowed a free hand inside my borders." Dachau, Buchenwald, and Theresienstadt would have operated in the middle of twentieth-century European civilization until the last Jew in reach had been made soap. There would have been brave words on Trafalgar Square and in Carnegie Hall, to audiences diminishing and bored. Society might, on occasion, have boycotted German wines. But no foreign power would have taken action. Tourists would have crowded the *Autobahn* and spas of the Reich, passing near but not too near the death-camps as we now pass Portuguese jails or Greek prison-islands. There would have been numerous pundits and journalists to assure us that rumors were exaggerated, that Dachau had pleasant walks. And the Red Cross would have sent Christmas parcels.

Below his breath, the Jew asks of his gentile neighbor: "If you had known, would you have cried in the face of God and man that this hideousness must stop? Would you have made some attempt to get my children out? Or planned a skiing party to Garmisch?" The Jew is a living reproach.

Men are accomplices to that which leaves them indifferent. It is this fact which must, I think, make the Jew wary inside Western culture, which must lead him to re-examine ideals and historical traditions that, certainly in Europe, had enlisted the best of his hopes and genius. The house of civilization proved no shelter.

But then, I have never been sure about houses. Perforce, the Jew has often been wanderer and guest. He can buy an old manse and plant a garden. An anxious pastoralism is a distinctive part of the attempt of many American middle-class and intellectual Jews to assimilate to the Anglo-Saxon background. But I wonder whether it's quite the same. The dolls in the attic were not ours; the ghosts have a rented air. Characteristically, Marx, Freud, Einstein end their lives far from their native ground, in exile or refuge. The Jew has his anchorage not in place but in time, in his highly developed sense of history as personal context. Six thousand years of self-awareness are a homeland.

I find that the edge of strangeness and temporary habitation carries over into language, though here again my experience is obviously different from that of the native-born American Jew. European Jews learned languages quickly; often they had to as they wandered. But a final "at homeness" may elude us, that unconscious, immemorial intimacy which a man has with his native idiom as he does with the rock, earth, and ash of his acre. Hence the particular strategies of the two greatest European Jewish writers. Heine's German, as Adorno has pointed out, is a brilliantly personal, European idiom on which his fluent knowledge of French exercised a constant pressure. Kafka wrote German as if it were all bone, as if none of the enveloping texture of colloquialism, of historical and regional overtone, had been allowed him. He used each word as if he had borrowed it at high interest. Many great actors are or have been Jews. Language passes *through* them, and they shape it almost too well, like a treasure acquired, not inalienable. This may be pertinent also to the Jewish excellence in music, physics, and mathematics, whose languages are international and codes of pure denotation.

The European Jew did not want to remain a guest. He strove, as he has done in America, to take root. He gave strenuous, even macabre proof of his loyalty. In 1933–4, Jewish veterans of the First World War assured Herr Hitler of their patriotism, of their devotion to the German ideal. Shortly thereafter, even the limbless and the decorated were hauled to the camps. In 1940, when Vichy stripped French Jews of their rights, veterans of Verdun, holders of the *Médaille militaire*, men whose families had lived in France since the early nineteenth century, found themselves harried and stateless. In

151

the Soviet Union a Jew is so designated on his identity card. Is it foolish or hysterical to suppose that, labor as he may, the Jew in a gentile nation-state sits near the door? Where, inevitably, he arouses distrust.

From Dreyfus to Oppenheimer, every burst of nationalism, of patriotic hysteria, has focused suspicion on the Jew. Such statistics probably have no real meaning, but it may well be that the proportion of Jews actually implicated in ideological or scientific disloyalty has been high. Perhaps because they have been vulnerable to blackmail and clandestine menace, because they are natural middle-men with an ancient ease in the export and import of ideas. But more essentially, I imagine, because they are pariahs whose sense of nationality has been made critical and unsteady. To a man who may tomorrow be in desperate flight across his own border, whose graveyard may be ploughed up and strewn with garbage, the nation-state is an ambiguous haven. Citizenship becomes not an inalienable right, a sacrament of *Blut und Boden*, but a contract which he must re-negotiate, warily, with each host.

The rootlessness of the Jew, the "cosmopolitanism" denounced by Hitler, by Stalin, by Mosley, by every right-wing hooligan, is historically an enforced condition. The Jew finds no comfort in "squatting on the window sill" (T. S. Eliot's courteous phrase). He would rather have been *echt Deutsch* or *Français de vieille souche* or Minuteman born than "Chicago Semite Viennese." At most times he has been given no choice. But though uncomfortable in the extreme, this condition is, if we accept it, not without a larger meaning.

Nationalism is the venom of our age. It has brought Europe to the edge of ruin. It drives the new states of Asia and Africa like crazed lemmings. By proclaiming himself a Ghanaean, a Nicaraguan, a Maltese, a man spares himself vexation. He need not ravel out what he is, where his humanity lies. He becomes one of an armed, coherent pack. Every mob impulse in modern politics, every totalitarian design, feeds on nationalism, on the drug of hatred which makes human beings bare their teeth across a wall, across ten yards of waste ground. Even if it be against his harried will, his weariness, the Jew —or some Jews, at least—may have an exemplary role. To show that whereas trees have roots, men have legs and are each other's guests. If the potential of civilization is not to be destroyed, we shall have to develop more complex, more provisional loyalties.   There are, as

Socrates taught, necessary treasons to make the city freer and more open to man. Even a Great Society is a bounded, transient thing compared to the free play of the mind and the anarchic discipline of its dreams.

When a Jew opposes the parochial ferocity into which nationalism so easily (inevitably) degenerates, he is paying an old debt. By one of the cruel, deep ironies of history, the concept of a chosen people, of a nation exalted above others by particular destiny, was born in Israel. In the vocabulary of Nazism there were elements of a vengeful parody on the Judaic claim. The theological motif of a people elected at Sinai is echoed in the pretense of the master race and its chiliastic dominion. Thus there was in the obsessed relation of Nazi to Jew a minute but fearful grain of logic.

But if the poison is, in ancient part, Jewish, so perhaps is the antidote, the radical humanism which sees man on the road to becoming man. This is where Marx is most profoundly a Jew—while at the same time arguing the dissolution of Jewish identity. He believed that class and economic status knew no frontiers, that misery had a common citizenship. He postulated that the revolutionary process would abolish national distinctions and antagonisms as industrial technology had all but eroded regional autonomy. The entire socialist utopia and dialectic of history is based on an international premise.

Marx was wrong; here, as in other respects, he thought too romantically, too well of men. Nationalism has been a major cause and beneficiary of two world wars. The workers of the world did not unite; they tore at each other's throats. Even beggars wrap themselves in flags. It was Russian patriotism, the outrage of national consciousness, not the vision of socialism and class solidarity, which enabled the Soviet Union to survive in 1941. In Eastern Europe, state socialism has left national rivalries fierce and archaic. A thousand miles of empty Siberian steppe may come to matter more to Russia and China than the entire fabric of Communist fraternity.

But though Marx was wrong, though the ideal of a non-national society seems mockingly remote, there is in the last analysis no other alternative to self-destruction. The earth grows too crowded, too harassed by the shadow of famine, to waste soil on barbed wire. Where he can survive as guest, where he can re-examine the relations between conscience and commitment, making his exercise of national loyalty scrupulous but also skeptical and humane, the Jew can act as

153

a valuable irritant. The chauvinist will snarl at his heels. But it is in the nature of a chase that those who are hunted are in advance of the pack.

That is why I have not, until now, been able to accept the notion of going to live in Israel. The State of Israel is, in one sense, a sad miracle. Herzl's Zionist program bore the obvious marks of the rising nationalism of the late nineteenth century. Sprung of inhumanity and the imminence of massacre, Israel has had to make itself a closed fist. No one is more tense with national feeling than an Israeli. He must be if his strip of home is to survive the wolfpack at its doors. Chauvinism is almost the requisite condition of life. But although the strength of Israel reaches deep into the awareness of every Jew, though the survival of the Jewish people may depend on it, the nation-state bristling with arms is a bitter relic, an absurdity in the century of crowded men. And it is alien to some of the most radical, most humane elements in the Jewish spirit.

So a few may want to stay in the cold, outside the sanctuary of nationalism—even though it is, at last, their own. A man need not be buried in Israel. Highgate or Golders Green or the wind will do.

If my children should happen to read this one day, and if luck has held, it may seem as remote to them as it will to a good many of my contemporaries. If things go awry, it may help remind them that somewhere stupidity and barbarism have already chosen them for a target. This is their inheritance. More ancient, more inalienable than any patent of nobility.

POSTSCRIPT

Two passages at random: the first from *Scroll of Agony: The Warsaw Diary of Chaim Kaplan*, the second from Jean-François Steiner's study *Treblinka:*

> A rabbi in Lodz was forced to spit on a Torah scroll that was in the Holy Ark. In fear of his life, he complied and desecrated that which is holy to him and to his people. After a short while he had no more saliva, his mouth was dry. To the Nazi's question, why did he stop spitting, the rabbi replied that his mouth was dry. Then the son of the "superior race" began to spit into the rabbi's mouth, and the rabbi continued to spit on the Torah.

> Despite all the precautions taken by his friends, Professor Mehring was called out of the ranks during roll-call. When the punishment squad, performing its "exercise," began to thin out, Professor Mehring was seized by an extraordinary will to live and started running like a madman. "Lalka" observed this and, when a quarter of the prisoners had fallen, made the "exercise" go on to see how long the old man, running a few yards behind the others, could hold out.
>
> He yelled—If you catch up with them, your life is saved.
>
> And gave the order to whip on the survivors.
>
> The survivors faltered and slowed down in order to help the Professor; but the blows redoubled, making them

155

stumble, shredding their clothes, covering their faces with blood. Blinded with blood, reeling with pain, they again speeded up. The Professor, who had gained a little ground, saw them pull away from him again and threw his arms forward, as if to grasp the other prisoners, as if to plead with them. He stumbled once, then a second time; his tortured body seemed to fall apart; he tried once more to recover his balance, then, all at once, stiffened and collapsed in the dust. When the Germans drew near, they saw a thread of blood flowing from his mouth. Professor Mehring was dead.

Indeed, rather lucky: not hung by his feet and flogged to death like Langner, the lashes being so timed that he would not die until evening. Not thrown alive into the crematoria fire. Not drowned, as were many, by slow immersion in urine and ordure. Principally, perhaps, without having with his own hands hanged his child in the barrack at night, to preserve him from further torture in the morning.

One of the things I cannot grasp, though I have often written about them, trying to get them into some kind of bearable perspective, is the time relation. At a previous point in rational time, Professor Mehring was sitting in his study, speaking to his children, reading books, passing his hand over a white tablecloth on Friday evening. And flayed alive, "blood splashing slowly from his hair," Langner was, in some sense, the same human being who had, a year earlier, perhaps less, walked the daylight street, done business, looked forward to a good meal, read an intellectual monthly. But in what sense? Precisely at the same hour in which Mehring or Langner were being done to death, the overwhelming plurality of human beings, two miles away on the Polish farms, five thousand miles away in New York, were sleeping or eating or going to a film or making love or worrying about the dentist. This is where my imagination balks. The two orders of simultaneous experience are so different, so irreconcilable to any common norm of human values, their coexistence is so hideous a paradox—Treblinka *is* both because some men have built it and almost all other men let it be—that I puzzle over time. Are there, as science fiction and Gnostic speculation imply, different species of time in the same world, "good times" and enveloping folds of inhuman time, in which men fall into the slow hands of living damnation? If we reject some such module, it becomes exceedingly difficult to grasp the continuity between normal existence and the hour at which hell starts, on the city square when the Germans begin the deportations, or in the office of the *Judenrat* or wherever, an hour marking men, women, children off from any precedent of life, from any voice "outside," in that other time of sleep and food and humane speech. On the fake station platform at Treblinka, cheerfully painted and provided with window boxes so as not to alert the new arrivals to the gas ovens half a mile further, the painted clock pointed to three. Always. There is an acute perception in this on the part of Kurt Franz, the commander of the extermination camp.

This notion of different orders of time simultaneous but in no effective analogy or communication may be necessary to the rest of us, who were not there, who lived as if on another planet. That, surely, is the point: to discover the relations between those done to death and those alive then, and the relations of both to us; to locate, as exactly as record and imagination are able, the measure of unknowing, indifference, complicity, commission which relates the contemporary or survivor to the slain. So that, being now instructed as never quite before—and it is here that history *is* different—of the fact that "everything is possible," that starting next Monday morning at, say, 11.20 a.m. time can change for oneself and one's children and drop out of humanity, we may better gauge our own present position, its readiness for or vulnerability to other forms of "total possibility." To make oneself concretely aware that the "solution" was not "final," that it spills over into our present lives, is the only but compelling reason for forcing oneself to continue reading these literally unbearable records, for going back or, perhaps, forward into the non-world of the sealed ghetto and extermination camp.

Moreover, despite the large amount of work done by historians, despite the mountains of documentation amassed during the trials, very important questions of "relation" remain obscure or unanswered. There is, first of all, the matter of the unwillingness of European powers and the United States during the late 1930's to make more than token gestures toward the rescue of Jewish children. There is the appalling evidence of the enthusiasm shown in Poland and western Russia by the local population when it came to helping the Germans kill Jews. Of the six hundred who succeeded in escaping from Treblinka to the forests, only forty survived, the majority being killed by Poles. "Go to Treblinka where you Jews belong," was a not uncommon answer to Jewish women and children seeking refuge among Polish neighbors. In the Ukraine, where many Jews remained in the face of the German advance because Stalinist policy carefully prohibited any warning to them of Nazi intentions, matters were, if conceivable, even worse. Had the people of occupied Europe chosen to help the Jews, to identify themselves even symbolically with the fate of their Jewish fellow-countrymen, the Nazi massacre could not have succeeded. This is shown by the solidarity and courage of Christian communities helping Jews in Norway, Denmark, and parts of Bulgaria.

But what of the outside, what of the powers actually at war with Nazi Germany? Here the evidence is, until now, controversial and full of ugly undertones. Many questions remain almost taboo. There are motives of internal politics, historical prejudice, and personal cruelty which may account for the indifference toward and even participation in the destruction of the Jews by Stalinist Russia. The failure of the R.A.F. and U.S. Air Force to bomb the gas ovens and rail lines leading to the death camps after substantial information about the "final solution" had reached London from Poland and Hungary, and after desperate pleas to that effect had been transmitted by elements in the Polish underground, remains an ugly riddle. The absence of any such raids—even *one day* of interruption in the gas ovens would have meant the life of *ten thousand* human beings—cannot be accounted for merely on technical grounds. Low-flying R.A.F. planes blew open the door of a prison in France rescuing vital members of the Resistance from further torture and execution. Just when did the names Belsen, Auschwitz, Treblinka first turn up in allied intelligence files, and what was done about them?

It has been said that the answer is one of psychological paralysis, of the sheer incapacity of the "normal" mind to imagine and hence give active belief to the enormities of the circumstance and the need. Even those—and they may have been few—who came to believe that the news out of eastern Europe was authentic, that millions of human beings were being methodically tortured and gassed in the middle of the twentieth century, did so at some abstract remove, as we might believe a piece of theological doctrine or an historical occurrence far in the past. The belief did not relate. We are post-Auschwitz *homo sapiens* because the evidence, the photographs of the sea of bones and gold fillings, of children's shoes and hands leaving a black claw-mark on oven walls, have altered our sense of possible enactments. Hearing whisperings out of hell again we would know how to interpret the code; the skin of our hopes has grown thinner.

This is obviously an important argument, particularly when extended to the problem of German awareness of what was going on and to the even more vexed matter of Jewish unreadiness, disbelief, even in some passive or metaphoric sense, acquiescence in the massacre. The earth at Treblinka contained, in one corner of the camp, seven hundred thousand bodies, "weighing approximately thirty-five thousand tons and filling a volume of ninety thousand cubic metres." If the Jews could not, until the closing of the oven door or the stench of the fire-pit believe this to be true, if the intelligence of a people prepared for apocalyptic anguish by two thousand years of harrying could not focus on this new and final possibility, how could that of other men? It is one of the daemonic attributes of Nazism (as of sadistic literature) to taint those who accept its imaginings as literally feasible—even when they reject them with loathing—with an element of self-doubt and unbalance. To *believe* the reports on Auschwitz smuggled out by the underground, to credit the statistical facts before such credence had become irrefutable and generally shared throughout the surviving world, was to yield in some measure to the monstrousness of the German intent. Skepticism ("such things cannot happen now, not at this point in man's history, not in a society that has produced Goethe") had its part of humane dignity and self-respect. And tragically so among east European Jews, with their complex involvement in German culture and Western enlightenment.

This is clearly shown both in the fictionalized account of Vilna at the start of Steiner's *Treblinka*, and in the opening pages of Kaplan's diary. Jewish reactions fluctuated wildly between hope that German occupation would bring some rational order to suffering—imprisonment in a ghetto could signify protection from the ever recurrent if random brutalities of gentile neighbors—and the hope that Hitler would soon allow the departure of the Jews from Europe. What wisps of information did leak through about Nazi mass exterminations were, for a long time, treated either as the natural fantasies of the affrighted or as dangerous falsehoods disseminated by provocateurs to demoralize the Jews or incite them to some act of rebellion. The latter would provide the Nazis with an "excuse" to act "more harshly." Above all, there was the hope that the world outside would come in aid. On January 24, 1940, Kaplan wrote:

159

A small ray of light has shone forth from between the clouds that are spread across our skies. The information has reached us that the American Quakers will send a rescue mission to Poland. This time the aid will be offered in American fashion, without regard to race or religion, and even the Jews will be able to benefit from the proffered aid. May they be blessed! For us this is the first time that, instead of "except the Jews," the expression "including the Jews" has reached us, and it rings in our ears with a strange sound. Is it really true?

And on June 11, 1940, the Jews of Warsaw took comfort from the firm belief that "the French are fighting like lions with the last of their strength." Hope, the radical property of man to regard himself in some kind of mutual relationship to other men, died inch by inch. The memory of hope cries out in one of the last messages received by the outside world during the rising of the Warsaw ghetto: "The world is silent. The world *knows* (it is inconceivable that it should not) and stays silent. God's vicar in the Vatican is silent; there is silence in London and Washington; the American Jews are silent. This silence is astonishing and horrifying." In fact there was noise just outside the ghetto walls, carefully recorded by German newsreel teams: the frequent laughter and applause of Polish spectators watching men leaping into flames and the houses blowing up.

When did belief darken to certitude? According to J.-F. Steiner (but his account is partially dramatic fiction or rearrangement) it was Langner, dying under the lash, who cried out with his last breath that "you will all be slain. They cannot let you out of here after what you have witnessed." In Kaplan's testimony the process of recognition is gradual. Each spasm of tenacious vitality—a joke made, a child fed, a German sentry cajoled or outwitted—seemed to Kaplan a guarantee of survival: "A nation which can live in such terrible circumstances as these without losing its mind, without committing suicide—and which can still laugh—is sure of survival. Which will disappear first, Nazism or Judaism? I am willing to bet! Nazism will go first!" Thus on August 15, 1940. By June 1942 the possibility of the "final solution" was becoming plain in Kaplan's mind. Though "imprisoned within double walls: a wall of brick for our bodies, and a wall of silence for our spirits," Kaplan could state, on June 25, that Polish Jewry was being totally slaughtered. He even refers to "lethal gas." But it was not until the deportation order in late July 1942 that the recognition of doom closed in. Rumor flew about that it had been Himmler's sadistic jest to promulgate the decree on the eve of the Ninth of Av, "a day of retribution, a day fated for mourning through all generations. But all that is irrelevant. In the last analysis there are accidental, momentary manifestations. They did not cause the decree. The real purpose is deeper and more fundamental—the total destruction of the Jewish nation." That this purpose has survived Nazism in many individuals and certain societies, even societies where there are scarcely any Jews left alive, that it runs close beneath the surface of many aspects of Soviet life, enforces the need to look back. There are elements of anti-Semitism deeper than sociology or economics or even historical superstition. The Jew sticks like a bone in the throat of any other nationalism. "God of Gods!" wrote Kaplan as the end drew near, "shall the sword devour thy sons forever?"

The diary breaks off in the evening hours of August 4, with Jewish police under Nazi supervision scouring block after city block. Taken to the *Umschlagplatz* (whose features and tablet of remembrance the present régime in Warsaw has all but obliterated), Kaplan and his wife were deported. They are thought to have been murdered in Treblinka in December 1942 or January 1943. Kaplan's foresight and the help of a Pole outside the ghetto ensured the survival of these small notebooks. Together with Emmanuel Ringelblum's *Notes from the Warsaw Ghetto*, this diary constitutes the only complete record of Jewish life in Warsaw from the outbreak of war to the time of deportation. Over and over Kaplan writes that this diary is his reason for survival, that the record of atrocity must reach the outside world. The last sentence reads: "If my life ends—what will become of my diary?" He won his desperate, patient gamble; his voice has overcome the ash and the forgetting.

It is the voice of a rare human being. A teacher of Hebrew, an essayist, a scholar of Jewish history and customs, Chaim Aron Kaplan chose to stay in Warsaw in 1941, though his American and Palestinian contacts might have secured him an exit visa. He wrote in Hebrew, but with that erudite, critical background of classical and European humanism characteristic of the modern Jewish intelligentsia. On October 26, 1939, he set down his credo:

161

Even though we are now undergoing terrible tribula-
tions and the sun has grown dark for us at noon, we have
not lost our hope that the era of light will surely come. Our
existence as a people will not be destroyed. Individuals will
be destroyed, but the Jewish community will live on.
Therefore, every entry is more precious than gold, so long
as it is written down as it happens, without exaggerations
and distortions.

This latter clause he fulfilled to an almost miraculous degree. In
midst of hell, Kaplan discriminates between the horror witnessed and
that which is only reported. Through extreme precision he came to a
deep, diagnostic perception. As early as October 28, 1939, Kaplan
had defined the root condition of the relations between Germans and
Jews: "In the eyes of the conquerors we are outside the category of
human beings. This is the Nazi ideology, and its followers, both
common soldiers and officers, are turning it into a living reality." He
knew what not very many, as yet, are prepared to see plainly: that
Nazi anti-Semitism is the logical culmination of the millennial Christian vision and teaching of the Jew as killer of God. Commenting on
the murderous beatings of Jews by German and Polish gangs at
Easter 1940, Kaplan adds: "Christian 'ethics' became conspicuous in
life. And then—woe to us!" He observed the queer mystery of German culture, the coexistence in the same men of bestiality and eager
literacy: "We are dealing with a nation of high culture, with 'a
people of the Book.' . . . The Germans have simply gone crazy for
one thing—books. . . . Where plunder is based on an ideology, on a
world outlook which in essence is spiritual, it cannot be equaled in
strength and durability. . . . The Nazi has both book and sword, and
this is his strength and might." That the book might well be Goethe
or Rilke remains a truth so vital yet outrageous that we try to spit it
out, that we go on mouthing our hopes in culture as if it were not
there to break our teeth. It may do so, if we do not come to understand its meaning with something of Kaplan's calm and precision of
feeling.

That precision extends to Kaplan's observation of moments of
humanity on the part of the Germans. The flush of embarrassment on
the face of a German sentry is gratefully recorded; an officer stopping
to help a child trampled by a German soldier, and adding, "Go and
tell your brethren that their suffering will not last much longer!" is

remembered as if he were a mysterious harbinger of grace (January 31, 1940). At all times there is the effort to understand how "this pathological phenomenon called Nazism," this "disease of the soul" can affect an entire people or class of human beings. In Kaplan the very act of truthful observation becomes an exercise in rational possibility, a counter-statement to the madness and degradation in the street. There is scarcely a touch of hate in this book, only the desire to understand, to test insight against reason. Seeing a German whip an old peddler to death in the open street, Kaplan writes:

> It is hard to comprehend the secret of this sadistic phenomenon. . . . How is it possible to attack a stranger to me, a man of flesh and blood like myself, to wound him and trample upon him, and cover his body with sores, bruises, and welts, without any reason? How is it possible? Yet I swear that I saw all this with my own eyes.

In such labor of understanding lies the only mode of forgiveness. Only those who actually passed through hell, who survived Auschwitz after seeing their parents flogged to death or gassed before their own eyes (like Elie Wiesel), or who found their own kin amid the corpses from which they had to extract gold teeth, a daily encounter at Treblinka, can have the right to forgive. *We* do not have that right. This is an important point, often misunderstood. What the Nazis did in the camps and torture chambers is wholly unforgivable, it is a brand on the image of man and will last; each of us has been diminished by the enactment of a potential sub-humanity latent in all of us. But if one did not undergo the thing, hate or forgiveness are spiritual games—serious games no doubt—but games none the less. The best *now*, after so much has been set forth, is, perhaps, to be silent; not to add the trivia of literary, sociological debate, to the unspeakable. So argues Elie Wiesel, so argued a number of witnesses at the Eichmann trial. The next best is, I believe, to try and understand, to keep faith with what may well be the utopian commitment to reason and historical analysis of a man like Kaplan.

But as I write this, a minute splinter of the enormity drives home. There is no other man precisely like Chaim Aron Kaplan. This is so of every death; metaphysically an absolute uniqueness passes from the store of human resources. But despite its outward democracy death is not wholly equal. The integrity, the fineness of intelligence, the human rationalism exhibited on every page of this indispensable book—representing a specific tradition of feeling, of linguistic practice—are irretrievably lost. The particular type of human possibility realized in central and east European Judaism is extinct. We know next to nothing about genetic reserves, about the raw material of diverse inheritance on which the human species draws for its labored progress. But numerical renewal is only a part of the story. In murdering Chaim Kaplan and those like him, in making certain that their children would be ash, the Germans deprived human history of one of the versions of its future. Genocide is the ultimate crime because it pre-empts on the future, because it tears up one of the roots from which history grows. There can be no meaningful forgiveness because there can be no repair. And this absence from our present needs, from our evolutionary hopes, of the strains of moral, psychological, cerebral quality extinguished at Belsen and Treblinka constitutes both the persistence of the Nazi action and the slow, sad vengeance of the unremembered dead.

A lack of modesty, of the finely shaping ironies which mark the *Warsaw Diary*, has been notable in the debates over *Treblinka*. Born in 1938, of a Jewish father who was deported and killed by the Germans and a Catholic mother, Jean-François Steiner did not experience the actual massacre. It was a trip to Israel and the well-known malaise felt by younger Jews throughout the Eichmann trial—"why did Jews in Europe go like lambs to the slaughter?"—that prompted Steiner to interview the handful of survivors of Treblinka (twenty-two in Israel, five in the United States, one in England) and to write an account of "the revolt in an extermination camp." Hailed by Madame de Beauvoir as a vindication of Jewish courage and as a pioneer work in the sociological, psychological interpretation of a community in hell, *Treblinka* has been bitterly attacked by others (David Rousset and Léon Poliakov among them) for its alleged inaccuracies, racism, and for what comfort its general thesis of Jewish passivity may give to Miss Hannah Arendt. The recriminations have been ugly, as they were in the Arendt case. And this, though humiliating and subversive to intelligence, is proper. For it is by no means certain that rational discourse *can* cope with these questions, lying as they do outside the normative syntax of human communication, in the explicit domain of the bestial; nor is it clear that those who were not themselves fully involved should touch upon these agonies unscathed. Those who were inside—Elie Wiesel in *La Nuit, Les Portes de la forêt, Le Chant des morts*, Koppel Holzmann in *Die Höhlen der Hölle*

—can find right speech, often allegoric, often a close neighbor to silence, for what they choose to say. We who come after are shrill and discomfort each other with claims of anger or impartial perception. Monsieur Poliakov speaks of the successive "scandals" which attend all books on the murder of the Jews from Schwarz-Bart's *The Last of the Just* to Hochhuth's *The Deputy* and now *Treblinka.* Silence during the murder, but scandal over the books.

Steiner has set himself a difficult, somewhat strange task: to reconstruct the life and insurrection in a death camp in the form of a fictionalized documentary, of a piece of closely documented reportage using the imaginary dialogues, character sketches, and dramatized montage of fiction. The fact that almost all the survivors of the rising of August 2, 1943, were later murdered by Polish peasants, by Ukrainian Fascist bands, by right-wing units in the Polish resistance or by the *Wehrmacht,* has meant that Steiner had to rely on the tortured memories of a few individuals for the bulk of his material. His choice of a dramatized *genre,* which is profoundly honest in so far as it represents the effort of a non-witness to imagine backward, to enter hell by act of imaginative talent, entails obvious risks. Repeatedly during the Eichmann trial, witnesses blunted the prosecutor's questions saying "You cannot understand. Who was not *there* cannot imagine." And unable to imagine entirely, to translate document into self, into the indelible mark on one's own skin, Jean-François Steiner resorts, probably unconsciously, to the conventions of violence and suspense current in modern fiction and high journalism.

Consequently *Treblinka* uses the cinematic chronology and stills of a *Time* story. It is full of memorable dialogue and dramatic silences. Actual and imagined personages appear in episodes grouped and cut by an obviously skilled eye (a Truman Capote stretched to fury). The mental life of Kurt Franz ("Lalka") is rendered with Dostoevskyan nuance. Now I have no doubt that all these monstrous and heroic scenes took place: that fathers and sons helped one another commit suicide in the barracks, that naked girls offered themselves to *kapos* in a last striving for life, that Ukrainian guards and doomed Jews danced and played music together on hot summer evenings in the bizarre death-village built by Franz. I know from other evidence that Steiner's account of the Treblinka symphony orchestra is true, that the boxing matches and cabaret he describes did indeed take place, that a small number of Jewish men and women, hunted past endurance, came voluntarily to the gates of Treblinka asking for admission and death. In the great majority of cases, Steiner's narrative and dialogue is firmly grounded in direct and documentary evidence. But because that evidence is mastered by the literary talent of the writer, because a narrative persona full of distinct rage and stylistic force interposes between the insane fact and the profoundly exciting economy, hence order, of the book, a certain unreality obtrudes. Where it is represented with such skill, intricate modulations affect the hideous truth. It becomes more graphic, more terribly defined, but also has more acceptable, conventional lodging in the imagination. We believe; yet do not believe intolerably, for we draw breath at the recognition of a literary device, of a stylistic stroke not finally dissimilar from what we have met in a novel. The aesthetic makes endurable.

But although this is not a book I can unreservedly trust—the pressure it puts on the imagination is not always that which most nearly, most scrupulously relates us to the presence of the dead— many of the charges made against Steiner are unjust.

It is true that insurrection was not as rare as Steiner makes out —witness actions recorded at Bialistok, Grodne, Sobivor, Auschwitz, and, above all, in Warsaw itself. Nevertheless, Treblinka was the only death-camp actually destroyed by a Jewish uprising, and the conditions under which that uprising was planned were indeed fantastic.

Treblinka is not the first or most authoritative attempt at a sociology of the damned. Kogon's *S.S.-Staat* and Bettelheim's *The Informed Heart* are much more reliable. But Bettelheim's observations in particular bear on an earlier, relatively imaginable version of camp life. In Treblinka, with its incessant assembly line of death and technology of mass disposal, with its fake railway station and Teutonic village, with its dogs trained to attack men's private parts and its official Jewish marriages, life had reached a pitch of extreme insanity. Jean-François Steiner conveys this world, extra-territorial to reason, not, I imagine, in its complete, literal truth. How could he? "I who was there still do not understand," writes Elie Wiesel. But what he has translated from the silences, necessary forgettings, partial speech of the survivors often rings true. Principally, he makes one grasp something of the deliberate torture of hope and choice by which the Nazis broke the spring of will in men. In a world in which, as in the cruel myth of Plato's *Gorgias*, men constantly had before their eyes the calendar of their own deaths, the Nazis introduced a mechanism of minimal hope. "You can go on living if you do this or that to our satisfaction." But the doing almost invariably involved a choice so hideous, so degrading that it further diminished the humanity of those who made it. The father had to choose to let his child die; the *kapo* had to flog harder; the informer had to betray; husband had to let wife go unknowing to the ovens lest he himself be immediately selected. To live was to choose to become less human.

Exactly this same process is analyzed by Kaplan. It was the notorious game of yellow or white passes and labor-cards. Which one meant life, which death? Or three cards are issued to a family of four, forcing parents and children to select one of their own number for extermination. Hope mocked can break a human identity more swiftly than hunger. But hunger there was, and continuous physical torment, and the sudden cessation of all human privacy.

Thus the riddle is *not* why the eastern European Jews failed to offer more resistance, why thrust out of humanity, deprived of all weapons, methodically starved, they did not revolt (in essence, Hannah Arendt's thesis suffers from a failure of imagining). In fact, this is a radically indecent question, asked as it so often is by those who remained silent during the massacre. The question is how it was possible for Chaim Kaplan to keep his sanity, and how Galewski and his resistance committee were able to rise from amid the stinking mountains of the dead and lead an attack against S.S. machine-guns. The mystery is that even *one* man should have retained sufficient remembrance of normal life to recognize man in his companions and in his own brutalized image. Only from such recognition can rebellion and that supreme deed of identity which is to give one's life for the survival of others—as the entire Treblinka committee did—arise.

Certain Jewish mystics have said that Belsen and Treblinka embody a momentary eclipse or madness of God; others have spoken of God's especial, and therefore unfathomable, nearness to His chosen in the gas oven and at the whipping block. These are metaphors of reason when reason suffers despair or a hope more grievous than despair. What the documents tell us is that in the dark of God's absence, certain men, buried alive, buried by that silence of Christianity and Western civilization which makes all who were indifferent accomplice to the Nazis, rose and destroyed their parcel of hell. For all its unpleasant stylistic virtuosity, for all its contrivances and, perhaps, inaccuracies, *Treblinka* gives us some understanding of how this came about. The charge that J.-F. Steiner has somehow humiliated the Jews by showing them through the eyes of German and Ukrainian torturers, and that his account of the initial paralysis of Jews at Treblinka contributes to a racist myth of Jewish passivity, seems to me unfounded. It overlooks his primary intent which is to imagine for himself and for us the unimaginable, to speak where only silence or the Kadish for the unnumbered dead have a natural place.

But enough of the debate. These books and the documents that have survived are not for "review." Not unless "review" signifies, as perhaps it should in these instances, a "seeing-again," over and over. As in some Borges fable, the only completely decent "review" of the *Warsaw Diary* or of Elie Wiesel's *Night* would be to re-copy the book, line by line, pausing at the names of the dead and the names of the children as the orthodox scribe pauses, when re-copying the Bible, at the hallowed name of God. Until we know many of the words by *heart* (knowledge deeper than mind) and can repeat a few at the break of morning to remind ourselves that we live *after*, that the end of the day may bring inhuman trial or a remembrance stranger than death.

In the Warsaw ghetto a child wrote in its diary: "I am hungry, I am cold; when I grow up I want to be a German, and then I shall no longer be hungry, and no longer cold." And now I want to write that sentence again: "I am hungry, I am cold; when I grow up I want to be a German, and then I shall no longer be hungry, and no longer cold." And say it many times over, in prayer for the child, in prayer for myself. Because when that sentence was written I was fed, beyond my need, and slept warm, and was silent.

CLASSICS

HOMER AND THE SCHOLARS

W hen a small boy, I was confronted with one of those question-
naires inquiring what personages of history I should most
like to have met. I answered Homer, Christ, and Shakespeare. Not
out of any precocious sublimity, but because I was resolved to discover from each whether he had, in fact, existed and whether he had
spoken the marvelous words attributed to him. Unaware, I had
chanced on the triple theme of what the nineteenth century called the
higher criticism.

On these deep waters scholarship had launched its grand ar-
madas. The discovery of the nature of Homeric composition, the
analytic study of the Gospels and of the historical Jesus, and the
quest for the identity of Shakespeare were the three classic mysteries
toward which scholarship directed its modern weapons: archaeology,
linguistics, bibliographic recension. But in the wake of the great
galleons of erudition there has always swarmed a motley host of
amateurs, mystics, and inspired cranks. The Homeric question, scriptural exegesis, and the problem of the authorship of Shakespeare's
plays have always been regarded by the layman as fair game. Here
everyman has his persuasion, and no decade passes without its new
theory. Of late, we have been assured that the *Odyssey* was written
by a young woman, that Christ survived Calvary and lies buried in
Northern India, and that the manuscripts of Shakespeare are to be
found in Marlowe's tomb.

Professional scholars react to such beliefs with bitter scorn. But
they are haunted by a curious fact: in each of these three pre-eminent
riddles of literary and historical criticism, it is the outsider who has

made some of the most brilliant and decisive discoveries. An obsessed amateur dug up Troy, and a young architect with a passion for cryptography broke the secret of the Minoan script. A literary critic —admittedly, an Edmund Wilson—was among the first to realize the implications of the Dead Sea scrolls. An eighteenth-century civil servant, Maurice Morgann, was the first to bring to bear on a Shakespearean text modern psychological and historical insights.

Homeric scholars, Semitic philologists, and professional students of Shakespeare, moreover, are themselves creatures of passion and fanatic conviction. No areas of humane learning solicit more ferocious controversy. There is something in philology that appeals to the worst in man. A. E. Housman's reviews were founded on the axiom that a false emendation is a far worse crime than murder. But behind the brutality and pontifications in high academic places, we hear a whistling in the dark. No one would deny the extraordinary accomplishments of historians, comparative linguists, and archaeologists. Yet the stubborn truth remains: today the Homeric question is not much nearer solution than it was in 1795, when Wolf published his *Prolegomena ad Homerum*. The historical person of Christ and the composition of the Gospels are matters for conjecture no less than when Renan wrote the *Vie de Jésus* (1863). And there are numerous puzzles regarding Shakespeare's plays and the range of reference in them baffling enough to convert sane men to Baconianism even now.

But, though the problems remain, our methods of approach to them change. And the fascinating aspect is this: in each case— Homer, Christ, Shakespeare—the currents of scholarship and judgment follow the same pattern.

In the late nineteenth century, dismemberment was all the rage. Wilamowitz, a titan among Homeric scholars, declared that the *Iliad* was at some points "wretched patchwork." In a single chapter of Luke, Germanic analysis revealed five distinct levels of authorship and interpolation. The plays attributed to that illiterate actor Shakespeare appeared to have been compiled by a committee which included Bacon, the Earl of Oxford, Marlowe, recusant Catholics, and printers' devils of extraordinary ingenuity. This fine fury of decomposition lasted well into the 1930's. As late as 1934, Gilbert Murray could discover no reputable scholar ready to defend the view that a single poet had written either or both the *Iliad* and the *Odyssey*.

Today, the wheel has come to a full turn. In Homeric, Biblical, and Shakespearean scholarship, unitarianism is the dominant trend. To Professor Whitman of Harvard, the central personal vision and "ineradicable unity" of the *Iliad* are beyond doubt.

There are material and psychological reasons for this reversal of judgment. We have grown increasingly respectful of the tenacity of the written word. The higher criticism assumed that if a text was very ancient or had been often reproduced, it would necessarily be corrupt. We are no longer so sure. Comparisons between the Dead Sea scrolls and the canonic version of the Bible suggest that ancient literature, where it was regarded in a sacred light, was handed down with great fidelity. In reverence, later scribes or scholiasts even reproduced errors or archaic words which they no longer understood.

What is still more important, a post-Freudian age regards the act of literary composition as one of extreme complexity. Where the nineteenth-century editor saw a lacuna or interpolation, we tend to see the indirections or special logic of the poetic imagination. Our entire image of the mind has altered. The higher critics, Wilamowitz or Wellhausen, were anatomists; to get at the heart of a thing they took it to pieces. We, like the men of the sixteenth century, incline to regard mental processes as organic and integral. A modern art historian has written of *la vie des formes*, the implication being that in the life of art, as in that of organic matter, there are complications of design and autonomous energies which cannot be dissected. Whenever possible, we prefer to leave a thing whole.

Moreover, we no longer expect from genius a constant performance. We know that great painters on occasion produce bad pictures. The fact that *Titus Andronicus* is full of shoddy violence is no proof whatever that Shakespeare did not write it; or, more precisely, it is no proof that he wrote only the good lines. This change in perspective is vital with reference to the *Iliad* and *Odyssey*. A hundred years ago, a passage which struck an editor as inferior was confidently bracketed as an interpolation or textual corruption. Today, we simply invoke the fact that poets are not always at their best. Homer can nod.

Finally, there has occurred a deep change in our understanding of myth. We have come to realize that myths are among the subtlest and most direct languages of experience. They re-enact moments of signal truth or crisis in the human condition. But mythology is more than history made memorable; the mythographer—the poet—is the historian of the unconscious. This gives to the great myths their haunting universality. Not since the chiliastic panics of the late tenth century, when men believed that the Second Coming was at hand, moreover, has there been an age more nightmare-ridden by mythical imaginings than our own. Men who have placed the figure of Oedipus at the heart of their psychology, or who have fought for political survival against the myth of the superman and the thousand-year Reich, know that fables are deadly serious. More than our predecessors, therefore, we approach Homer on his own terms.

At the core of the Homeric poems lies the remembrance of one of the greatest disasters that can befall man: the destruction of a city. A city is the outward sum of man's nobility; in it, his condition is most thoroughly humanized. When a city is destroyed, man is compelled to wander the earth or dwell in the open fields in partial return to the manner of a beast. That is the central realization of the *Iliad*. Resounding through the epic, now in stifled allusion, now in strident lament, is the dread fact that an ancient and splendid city has perished by the edge of the sea.

Homer does not narrate the fiery death of Troy. Perhaps there is in this reticence an element of poetic tact (Dante's blindness at the climax of vision); perhaps a shrewd hunch that if the *Iliad* had shown Troy burning, the feelings of the audience would have shifted wholly to the Trojan side. Cunningly, Homer suggests the final catastrophe by depicting it on a miniature scale; we are shown Hector assailing the ramparts of the Greek encampment and threatening to fire the ships.

Lacking the close of the story, we do not know over precisely which city the wooden horse cast its murderous shadow. The topography of the *Iliad* would fit what archaeologists designate as Troy VI. But signs of violent ruin are strongest in that level of the mound designated as Troy VII A. Some scholars have even argued that the setting of the poem should be transposed from Asia Minor to the Greek mainland, where a fierce, protracted siege appears to have taken place in the early Mycenaean age.

Most probably, the *Iliad* reflects not only a single episode but a great catalogue of ruin. The fabled Knossos fell circa 1400 B.C. The cause of its overthrow is not known, but legendary recollections of the event reappear in the Greek imagination for centuries thereafter. The next two hundred years are a period of extreme obscurity. Part of the problem lies in the identification of the mysterious Peoples of the Sea, whose attacks seem to have carried as far as Egypt. One thing is certain: on both sides of the Aegean, the Mycenaean world, with its great palaces and complex dynastic and commercial relations, met with violent disaster. The citadels of Pylos and Iolkos were burned around 1200, and golden Mycenae itself was destroyed within the century. It was during this dark, confused period, circa 1180, that Troy VII A was sacked.

The remembrance of these ancient terrors, of city gates broken and towers burned, beats loud in the *Iliad*. The *Odyssey* speaks of the aftermath. It is the epic of the displaced person. The cities are down, and survivors wander the face of the earth as pirates or beggars. This, in fact, is what seems to have taken place during the period from 1100 to 900. The Dorian invasions drove before them groups of Helladic refugees. These fugitives carried with them shattered yet rich fragments of their own culture. The main stream of migration seems to have passed through Attica between the early eleventh and late ninth centuries. Shortly after the year 1000 B.C., the uprooted peoples began colonizing Asia Minor and the islands. Some appear to have settled in and around Athens.

But even if we assume a continuity of civilization on the Greek mainland, a most difficult question arises. In the form in which we know them, the *Iliad* and the *Odyssey* were set down between circa 750 and 700 B.C. The siege of Troy, however, falls in the early part of the twelfth century, in the closing phase of the Mycenaean age. The manner of life dramatized in the *Iliad* is strongly Mycenaean; nearly all of the fighting embodies the weapons and tactics of the Bronze Age. The world of Agamemnon, as Sir John L. Myres said, is one of which later Greeks "knew little and understood less." How, then, were memories and traditions out of the archaic past transmitted over a gap of at least four hundred years?

The discovery made in 1952 by Michael Ventris (again an amateur of genius, an outsider), gives a lead toward a possible answer. He showed that the inscriptions on tablets found at various Mycenaean sites are written in a very ancient but recognizable form of Greek. A bridge of language spans the Dark Ages. But, despite the enthusiasm of certain scholars, such as Professor Webster of London, it is a tenuous bridge. The Greek in Linear B is half a millennium older than anything to compare it with. The tablets yield inventories of goods and weapons, lists of names, some of which reappear in Homer, and fragmentary invocations to the gods. There is no evidence, so far, of Mycenaean literature in any real sense. The script is ill suited to the writing of poetry, and the next written Greek, which belongs to the second half of the eighth century, is, of course, in our own kind of alphabet (as derived from the Phoenicians). What came between is still a mystery. A Mycenaean *Iliad* may have existed in some linear script, and the art of writing did survive in Cyprus. But what little evidence we have suggests that the Mycenaean inheritance of the *Iliad* came down to the eighth century by word of mouth. What we now know is that the word was Greek.

Does this mean that the *Iliad* and *Odyssey*—as distinct from the archaic material in them—were composed orally? Since the great work of Milman Parry, it is an established fact that much of Homeric verse is formulaic. It consists of set phrases which fill the natural metrical units of the lines. Thus, for example, there are forty-six noun epithets to describe Achilles. Each has a different metrical value, and the poet chooses the one most appropriate to the prosody of the line. He creates his epic as he chants it, using a vast stock of traditional motifs and formulas to sustain his invention or his variations on a given epic theme. Such heroic recitation still exists, notably in Yugoslavia and among the Berbers of North Africa. Narrations of the fall of Troy and the wanderings of Odysseus must have been recited on numerous occasions, each time in a different version. In this light, Homer emerges as one of many itinerant singers improvising on traditional motifs for an illiterate audience: "fortunately, some master of the new art of writing had the wit to set down on papyrus this outstanding singer's renderings of a couple of themes from the repertoire." This, in essence, is the thesis argued most recently by Albert B. Lord in *The Singer of Tales*.

No doubt the Homeric epics contain much that is of an archaic and mnemonic character. And it is true that Yugoslav shepherds, sitting in front of tape recorders, have improvised lays of prodigious length. But what does this tell us of the composition of the *Iliad*? Next to nothing. The work of Homer, as we know it, is art of dazzling and intricate unity. Its design is tight and deliberate. Set it beside the finest of recorded folk poetry, and the difference leaps to the eye. We are dealing in the *Iliad* with a commanding vision of man, articulate in every detail, not with a tale of adventure automatically or discursively carried forward. The entrance into action via the oblique theme of Achilles' anger is art of high sophistication. The entire design, with its inner echoes and alternance of stress and repose, follows on the particular drama of the opening. Only Book X seems to stand apart as an intrusion or late addition.

It is the merit of Professor Whitman's *Homer and the Heroic Tradition* to have insisted on this essential truth. He contends that the *Iliad* is a counterpart, in language, of the famous geometric symmetry distinctive of Greek vases in the period 850 to 700. He argues that "the poem as a whole forms one large concentric pattern." Whitman's scheme is too neat, and it overlooks the fact that the division of the poem into twenty-four books is a late editorial convenience. But the main point is surely valid: the *Iliad* is a design of extreme complexity and formal control. That there should be embedded in it large fragments of traditional, oral poetry is certain; but that the epic as a whole should have been composed and preserved without writing is most unlikely.

But in what writing? This, again, is an intricate problem on which scholars disagree. The Ionic script, in which the *Iliad* and *Odyssey* were handed down, came into official use only in the fifth century B.C. We know scarcely anything of its previous history. This leads Whitman to conclude that the Homeric epics were initially set down in what is known as the Old Attic alphabet and later transliterated (this could account for certain oddities in our present text). The first manuscript might date from the second half of the eighth century, "from the time, if not the hand, of Homer himself." Only thirty years ago, such a theory would have made scholars howl with derision!

We have no evidence to show that a written text of such length and elaboration could have been produced at so early a date. But the alphabet was available, and trade with Phoenicia could have provided the necessary papyrus. Moreover, if such a manuscript did not exist, how could we explain the startling fact that the *Iliad* and *Odyssey* have in them no material, either linguistic or narrative, that can be dated as later than 700 B.C.? The theory that the two epics were memorized and transmitted perfectly by word of mouth until they could be written down in the fifth century simply won't hold.

Let me speculate here, not as a qualified classicist but as a reader seeking to apprehend the genius of the poem. I venture to guess that Homer was the first great poet in Western literature because he was the first to have understood the infinite resources of the written word. In the zest of the Homeric narrative, in its superb intricacy, flashes the delight of a mind which has discovered that it need not deliver its creation into the fragile trust of memory. The harsh gaiety of the *Iliad* and its constant equivocation between shortness of life and eternity of fame mirror the poet's new and proud sense of his own survival. In the beginning of poetry is the word, but very near the beginning of poetry on the scale of the *Iliad* is writing.

It is entirely possible that the original "Homer manuscript" was something unique and that it was kept in the jealous possession of a bardic guild (the Homeridae). The newly established Panhellenic festivals of the eighth century created an audience for the "sons of Homer." These singers may well have preserved the *Iliad* and *Odyssey* in a small number of canonic texts until their wider publication in sixth-century Athens (what scholars call the Pisistratean Recension).

Nor need we assume that Homer himself was literate. He may have dictated to a scribe. Indeed, I would guess that the ancient and persistent tradition of his blindness is connected to this very point. Wishing to conceal from a later, more critical age the fact of the master's technical illiteracy, the Homeridae described him as blind. Above all else, the *Iliad* and *Odyssey* proclaim that men's lives go to forgotten dust unless they are given immortality by the song of a poet. Is not that the faith of a supreme artist who, for the first time in Western literature, had at his command, if not within his own resource, the full glory of the written word?

By far the greater part of recent Homeric scholarship deals with the *Iliad*. Excavation and decipherment seem to lead to Troy rather than to Ithaca. The *Odyssey* accords neither with the search for a Mycenaean tradition nor with the theory of a geometric style. This is revealing. It points to a conviction which many readers have held from the start. The two epics are profoundly different; different in tone, in formal structure, and, most important, in their vision of life. The Homeric question, therefore, goes beyond problems of authorship and text. It must deal with the literary and psychological relations between the *Iliad* and the *Odyssey*. What happens when we read the *Iliad* through the eyes of Odysseus?

Archaeologists differ on the way in which the world image of the *Iliad* was put together. Some assert that the narratives of battle are realistic and that efforts have been made to bring archaic details up to date (the classic instance being Homer's awkward treatment of Ajax's body shield, a piece of equipment which went out of use in the tenth century). Others regard the world of Homeric Troy as a "visionary structure" in which elements ranging from the Bronze Age to the eighth century are woven together by the set formulas and conventions of the heroic style. But one thing is clear: the *Iliad* expresses a specific view of the human condition. In no other work of world literature, with the possible exception of *War and Peace*, do we find the same image of man. And certainly not in the *Odyssey*.

The poet of the *Iliad* looks on life with those blank, unswerving eyes which stare out of the helmet slits on early Greek vases. His vision is terrifying in its sobriety, cold as the winter sun:

"So, friend, you die also. Why all this clamour about it?
Patroklus also is dead, who was better by far than you are.
Do you not see what a man I am, how huge, how splendid
and born of a great father, and the mother who bore me immortal?
Yet even I have also my death and my strong destiny,
and there shall be a dawn or an afternoon or a noontime
when some man in the fighting will take the life from me also
either with a spearcast or an arrow flown from the bowstring."
So he spoke, and in the other the knees and the inward
heart went slack. He let go of the spear and sat back, spreading
wide both hands; but Achilleus drawing his sharp sword struck him
beside the neck at the collar-bone, and the double-edged sword
plunged full length inside. He dropped to the ground face downward,
and lay at length, and the black blood flowed, and the ground was
    soaked with it.
                        —*Iliad*, XXI; Richmond Lattimore's translation

The narration proceeds with inhuman calm. The sharp directness of the poet's vision is never sacrificed to the demands of pathos. In the *Iliad* the truth of life, however harsh or ironic, prevails over the occasions of feeling. This is strikingly illustrated in the crowning moment of the epic: the night encounter of Priam and Achilles. There is a stillness in the midst of hell. Looking upon each other, the bereft king and the slayer of men give voice to their great griefs. Their sorrows are immeasurable. Yet, when they have spoken they feel hungry and sit down to an ample meal. For as Achilles says of Niobe, "She remembered to eat when she was worn out with weeping." No other poet, not even Shakespeare, would have run the risk of so humble a truth at such an instant of tragic solemnity.

But this magnificent clearheadedness derives not from bitter resignation. The *Iliad* is no lament over man's estate. There is joy in it, the joy that burns in the "ancient glittering eyes" of the sages in Yeats's "Lapis Lazuli." The poet revels in the gusto of physical

179

action and in the stylish ferocity of personal combat. He sees life lit by the fires of some central, ineradicable energy. The air seems to vibrate around the heroic personages, and the force of their being electrifies nature. Achilles' horses weep at his impending fall. Even insensate objects are kindled by this excess of life. Nestor's drinking bowl is so palpably real that archaeologists claim to have dug it up three thousand years after the event.

Pure energy of being pervades the *Iliad* like the surge of the wine-dark sea, and Homer rejoices at it. Even in the midst of carnage, life is in full tide and beats forward with a wild gaiety. Homer knows and proclaims that there is that in men which loves war, which is less afraid of the terrors of combat than of the long boredom of the hearth.

In the sphere of Agamemnon, Hector, and Achilles, war is the measure of man. It is the only pursuit he has been trained for (in the shadow of death, Hector worries who will teach his son how to throw a spear). Beyond the shadow, moreover, gleams the light of returning dawn. Around the ashes of Patroclus, the Greek chieftains wrestle, race, and throw the javelin in celebration of their strength and aliveness. Achilles knows he is foredoomed, but "bright-cheeked" Briseis lies with him each night. War and mortality cry havoc, yet the center holds. That center is the affirmation that actions of body and heroic spirit are in themselves a thing of beauty, that renown shall outweigh the passing terrors of death, and that no catastrophe, not even the fall of Troy, is final. For beyond the charred towers and brute chaos of battle rolls the tranquil sea. Elsewhere dolphins leap and shepherds drowse in the peace of the mountains. Homer's famous similes, in which he compares some moment of battle to an episode from pastoral or domestic life, act as an assurance of ultimate stability. They tell us that the waves will race to the shore when the location of Troy is a disputed memory.

It is a specific and unique portrayal of man. Truer, says John Cowper Powys, than that given by any other poet: "it is more like what has happened, is happening, and will happen to us all, from the very beginning, in our history in this world until the end of human life upon this earth." This may well be; but the truth of the *Iliad* is not that of the *Odyssey*.

To the "ancient glittering eyes" of the *Iliad*, Odysseus opposes a roving and ironic glance. The war epic is hewn of great solid blocks; the story of the long voyage home is a cunning weave. Like the sea water which laps its every page, the vision of the poem is swift, changing, exploratory, prone to odd shallows and sudden depths. "This novel," said T. E. Lawrence. A marvel of design and variousness, but difficult to get into focus. The old fires of the heroic are banked, and the muscular simplicity of life around Troy has yielded to all manner of irony and complication. The work was revered by its ancient readers, but it put them ill at ease. Papyrus fragments of the *Iliad* far outnumber those of the *Odyssey*.

The geography of the tale is a riddle. It appears to include Greece and Ionia, Crete, Lycia, Western Sicily, Egypt, and even a hint of Mesopotamia. At times, it is clearly a geography of the imagination, bristling like medieval maps with fabled beasts and wind daemons blowing out of every quarter. Certain elements in the *Odyssey* correspond to the period of the decline of Mycenaean feudalism (the fact that the societies shown are illiterate, the vague status of kingship in Ithaca, the queer economics of Penelope's marriage settlement). But other aspects of the poem seem to reflect the values of the new city-states as they began to emerge in the very late eighth century. What there is in the *Odyssey* of Mycenaean culture, moreover, appears to derive from those outposts and colonies of Mycenae which long survived in Asia Minor. For what is inescapable in the *Odyssey* is a sense of the Oriental.

That the poet knew the Babylonian *Gilgamesh* epic is probable. That very ancient Asiatic and African myths are echoed in the Wanderer's saga is almost certain. Consider one of the most haunting touches in the entire *Odyssey*. Speaking out of death, Tiresias prophesies to Odysseus that another voyage awaits him beyond Ithaca:

> go forth under your shapely oar till you come to a people who know not the sea and eat their victuals unsavoured with its salt: a people ignorant of purple-prowed ships and of the smoothed and shaven oars which are the wings of a ship's flying. I give you this token of them, a sign so plain that you cannot miss it: you have arrived when another wayfarer shall cross you and say that on your doughty shoulder you bear the scatterer of haulms, a winnowing-fan.

> —*Odyssey*, XI; T. E. Lawrence's translation

Where is that saltless land, and what does the confusion between oar and winnowing-fan signify? We do not know. But in his remarkable

181

study *Genèse de l'Odyssée*, the French anthropologist Gabriel Germain has shown that the tenor of the myth is profoundly un-Greek. To find the motif of a landlocked kingdom in which men know neither salt nor ships, we must look to the legend world of pre-Islamic North Africa.

Dante learned of Tiresias' prophecy through Seneca (he had no direct knowledge of the Homeric *Odyssey*). He gave it a grim Christian reading. Making of Odysseus a Faustian man, too grasping of life and hidden science, he launched him on a last fatal voyage past Gibraltar (*Inferno*, XXVI). The mariner's ghost, however, would not stay put. It rose from damnation to assume countless shapes in Western art and literature. Most of these shapes—even those given it in our time by Joyce and Kazantzakis—are already implicit in the first Odysseus. The characters of the *Iliad* are of a rich simplicity and move in a clear light. The hero of the *Odyssey* is elusive as fire. He has enjoyed an afterlife even more various and fascinating than that accorded to an Achilles or a Hector precisely because his initial adventures comprise areas of thought and experience undreamed of by the bronze warriors before Troy.

Twice, at least, the winds that drive Odysseus blow out of Araby. He seems to come to Nausicaä straight from *A Thousand and One Nights*. The entire episode is an Oriental fairy tale. The afflicted beggar is washed up by the sea. Invisible powers guide him to the royal palace, and there he reveals his true splendor. He departs laden with riches and falls into a magic sleep. Woven into this romance of beggar and caliph is the theme of a young girl's nascent love for a much older man. Again, there is in the thing a flavor which has little in common with the classic Greek sensibility. It foreshadows the romances of Alexandrine Hellenism.

Or take the only fully explored relationship in the *Odyssey*, the friendship of Athene and Odysseus. The goddess and the Wanderer delight in virtuosities of deception. They lie to each other in a gay rivalry of falsehood. They bargain like street merchants of Damascus, seeking to outwit one another with affectionate larceny. More than two thousand years before Shakespeare's Beatrice and Benedick, Homer knew that there can be between men and women affairs of the brain as well as of the heart. At one point, the goddess nearly admits herself beaten. Her loving mockery could come straight out of Shaw:

Any man, or even any God, who could keep pace with your all-round craftiness must needs be a canny dealer and sharp-practised. O plausible, various, cozening wretch, can you not even in your native place let be these crooked and shifty words which so delight the recesses of your mind? Enough of such speaking in character between us two past-masters of these tricks of trade—you, the cunningest mortal to wheedle or blandish, and me, famed above other Gods for knavish wiles.

—*Odyssey*, XIII

Once more, we are at a great distance from the tone and vision of the *Iliad*. The quarrels and lusts of the Olympians are, at times, satirized in the *Iliad*. But more often, the deities are seen as random and malignant forces destroying or favoring men at their caprice. Nowhere do we find the crafty, amused, deeply feminine amity which binds Athene to Odysseus. The flavor is Oriental.

The thought that the *Odyssey* is somehow anchored in the world of the Eastern Mediterranean is not new. In 1658 an Oxford scholar, Zachary Bogan, published a book entitled *Homerus Hebraizon*, and somewhat later another Greek scholar declared that both epics were written by King Solomon. Modern erudition is more cautious; but Victor Bérard has argued for a Phoenician *Odyssey*, and Joyce, with a characteristic leap of insight, made of his Ulysses a Jew.

But if the *Iliad* and *Odyssey* differ so notably in tone and in their view of human conduct, what is the relation between them?

Whitman contends that the "vast and obvious" change occurring between the composition of the two epics corresponds to a change in the style of Greek ceramics. In contrast to the geometric, the proto-Attic style is "breezy, open and slightly orientalizing." The proto-Attic vase painter handles his subjects as a series of fluid episodes, as does the *Odyssey*. We are no longer in the rigid, concentric world of the *Iliad*. Many scholars have rejected Whitman's entire thesis, arguing that poetry and ceramics cannot be compared. But Whitman has made one arresting observation. The physical appearance of personages in the *Iliad* is stylized. The descriptive epithet is a stock formula; thus, women are almost invariably "white-armed." In the *Odyssey*, flesh tones appear; Odysseus is darkly tanned and Penelope's skin is like cut ivory. The same change occurs in vase painting.

The two works may not only have been written at different times but in different places. Professor Denys Page insists that their vocabularies are so different that one cannot assign them to the same locality. The *Iliad* might have been composed in Attica; the *Odyssey* in Ionia, or even Sicily (as Robert Graves argues). This thesis has come under fire. Critics point out that an epic which deals with land warfare must necessarily use a different vocabulary from one mainly concerned with navigation. Nevertheless, it is hard to believe that the same ground was native to both. The Homer of the *Odyssey* seems to have verified with his own eyes certain settings and activities which the poet of the *Iliad* had only imagined.

Readers of Homer who are themselves writers or men of war nearly always reject the idea of a single authorship. Samuel Butler and Robert Graves discern in the *Odyssey* a woman's hand unraveling the ancient web of heroic action. John Cowper Powys states that the two poems "had different authors or originals" and that there is "an historic gap of three or four hundred years between them." T. E. Lawrence characterized the poet of the *Odyssey* as a "great if uncritical reader of the *Iliad*" and guessed that he was not much of a practical soldier. We seem to be dealing with contrasting qualities of mind.

Consider the image we get of the *Iliad* when looking at it through the *Odyssey*. It is exceedingly complex. We get nearest to it in Book VIII, when Demodocus, the minstrel, sings of the fall of Priam's towers in the hidden presence of Odysseus. This is one of the great moments of divided focus in all literature (it reminds one of the performance of an air from *The Marriage of Figaro* in the last scene of *Don Giovanni*). To the audience of the blind singer, the quarrels of Agamemnon and Achilles are remote. They have the muted radiance of legend. To Odysseus they are unbearably close. He draws his purple cloak around him and weeps. His position is ambiguous, for he is both within and outside the saga of Troy. Hearing himself sung about, he knows that he has entered the realm of the legendary dead. But he is also a living man seeking return to Ithaca. Thus, he looks upon the Trojan War both in tragic remembrance and refutation. This is the crucial point. There is in the *Odyssey* a critique of the archaic values of the *Iliad* in the light of new energies and perceptions.

This critique is made dramatically explicit in the brief dialogue between Odysseus and the shade of Achilles:

"How I envy your lot, Achilles, happiest of men who have been or will be! In your day all we Argives adored you with a God's honours: and now here I find you a Prince among the dead. To you, Achilles, death can be no grief at all." He took me up and said, "Do not make light of Death before me, O shining Odysseus. Would that I were on earth a menial, bound to some insubstantial man who must pinch and scrape to keep alive! Life so were better than King of Kings among these dead who have had their day and died.

—*Odyssey*, XI

The Achilles of the *Iliad* would not have said quite this, even in death. He has his moods of harsh gloom, and carps at the predestined imminence of his fall. But he never rejects the excellence or necessity of the heroic ideal. Had he done so, there would have been peace before Troy. That Achilles should prefer to be alive as a poor man's slave rather than king of the immortal dead is to query the very impulse of the *Iliad*.

Though it is conceivable, it seems unlikely that the same poet should have articulated both conceptions of life. I find no other example in literature of a writer producing two masterpieces that look to each other with that mixture of awe and ironic doubt which the *Odyssey* displays toward the *Iliad*. And yet, time and again, a single voice seems to resound through the differences of narrative technique and world view. Certain glories of the *Iliad* are fully visible only in the mirror of the *Odyssey*. When Achilles laments over Patroclus, he is compared to a father mourning the death of his newly married son. The exact converse of this simile expresses Odysseus' joy at seeing land after the destruction of his raft. Both similes, in turn, are hinted at in Penelope's recognition of the Wanderer. Subtle but tenacious strands relate the two poems. How can we reconcile the sense of contrast to that of unity?

I believe that the Homer whom we know, the poet who continues to shape many of the principal forms of the Western imagination, was the compiler of the *Iliad* and the inventor of the *Odyssey*. He assembled and ordered the fragmentary battle sagas of the Mycenaean tradition. He had the insight to group them around the dramatic and unifying motif of the rage of Achilles. He treated the ancient material and folk legends with profound respect. At times, he misun-

185

derstood the language and technical circumstances of the remote action. But he chose to retain what was obscure rather than improve upon it. He grasped the austere symmetries inherent in the archaic mode of narrative and saw life through the harsh, glittering eyes of battle. To the brief intensities of oral poetry, he made available the new amplitude and elaboration of the written form. The compiler of the *Iliad*, like the men who wove together the sagas of the Pentateuch, was an editor of genius; but the gold and the bronze lay ready in the crucible.

I imagine that he completed his task in the first powers of maturity. The *Iliad* has the ruthlessness of the young. But as he richened in experience and sensibility, the vision of the *Iliad* may have struck Homer as incomplete. One can readily conceive of him as a constant and observant voyager. "He had sailed upon and watched the seas," says T. E. Lawrence. In particular, I would suppose that he grew familiar with the complex, Orientalized civilizations of the Eastern Mediterranean. The part of the Orient in the *Iliad* has the stiffness of ancient legend. It is traditional material dating back to the commerce of the Bronze Age. The Orient of the *Odyssey* is more modern, more immediately observed.

In the afternoon of his life, this much-traveled man may have turned back to the world of the *Iliad* in order to compare its vision of human conduct with that of his own experience. From that comparison, with its delicate poise of reverence and criticism, grew the *Odyssey*. With marvelous acumen, Homer chose for his protagonist the one figure out of the Trojan saga nearest to the "modern" spirit. Already in the *Iliad*, Odysseus marks a transition from the simplicities of the heroic to a life of the mind more skeptical, more nervous, more wary of conviction. Like Odysseus, Homer himself abandoned the stark, rudimentary values inherent in the world of Achilles. When composing the *Odyssey*, he looked back to the *Iliad* across a wide distance of the soul—with nostalgia and smiling doubt.

This view of Homer does, at least, match the few facts available to us. The *Odyssey* is younger than the *Iliad*, but not, I think, by very much. The one poem is intensely alive in the other. The two epics express judgments of man's condition which differ considerably. But a related craftsmanship is at work in both. Behind each lie remote, partially misunderstood legacies from the Mycenaean past; in the *Iliad* they are more obtrusive. In the *Odyssey*, on the other hand, gleam the first dawn lights of the Socratic future. The bridge between Troy and Ithaca could be the personal life of an incomparable editor and poet.

We shall never really know. But the *Iliad* and the *Odyssey* remain as the unassailable fact. And although there are many books by which men have ordered their lives, I wonder whether any can do more than the Homeric poems to make us understand the relationship of man to time and to the necessary outrage of the death we carry within us.

THE BOOK

The long, intricate communion between the English language and the Bible continues. It began a thousand years ago. About 950, the priest Aldred wrote an Anglo-Saxon paraphrase, in Northumbrian dialect, between the lines of the Latin text of the great Lindisfarne Gospels—a sumptuous manuscript written about 700. This is the first fragment of English translation to have come down to us. In the late tenth century, there appeared in Wessex the first independent version of the Gospels in English. One hears, in this rough assay, something of the cadence that was to mold the language: "Nu ic asende mine aengel beforan thinre ansyne." By the year 1000, Aelfric, Archbishop of Canterbury, had translated a considerable part of the Old Testament.

The Norman Conquest brought further progress to a sharp halt. Not until about 1250 does the story take up again, and then only with the Psalter. But in the first half of the fourteenth century, in a prose Psalter attributed to one Richard Rolle, we take a leap forward: "Have mercy of me, God, for man trad me; al day the fyghtygne troublede me . . . In God I schal prevse my wordes, in God I hopede." The language was now at the threshold of the necessary eloquence.

In 1382–1383, John Wyclif completed his rendering of the Bible into English. The text used was, by modern standards, corrupt, being a late unscholarly version of the Vulgate. Moreover, there were glaring discrepancies in style between the work of Wyclif and that of his collaborators. But the revised Wyclif Bible of 1400 is the first of the major English Scriptures. For all its archaicism, we can turn to it with a sense of recognition. Here is a passage from Isaiah (35:5–6):

188

"Thanne the iyen of blynde men schulen be openyd, and the eeris of deef men schulen be opyn. Thanne a crokid man schal skippe as an hert, and the tunge of doumbe men schal be openyd; for whi watris ben brokun out in desert, and stremes in wildirnesse." The Authorized Version will make one superb improvement: "and the tongue of the dumb *sing*." But when it replaces a crooked man skipping by a lame man leaping, the advantage seems to lie with Wyclif.

Between Wyclif and the Bible of 1611 come the invention of printing and the genius of one man who, more than any other, put his mark on the development of English. Between 1454 and 1500, some 125 editions of the Latin Vulgate were issued from diverse presses. A century after Wyclif had set down his text, much of it was available in print in Caxton's *Golden Legend* (1483). And in 1516, Erasmus of Rotterdam called for the right of private individuals to read Scripture in their own common language: "I wish that the plowman might sing parts of them at his plow and the weaver at his shuttle, and that the traveler might beguile with their narration the weariness of his way." For those who spoke English, William Tyndale was to make this possible. Working under extreme peril and the harassment of Catholic agents, Tyndale translated some books of the Old Testament and the whole of the New. Thus the first printed English New Testament appeared in Worms in 1525. Eleven years later, Tyndale paid with his life; he was burned at the stake after having been betrayed by one of his intimates into the hands of the Spaniards. But his work was done, and it altered enduringly the sensibility of the English mind and the cadence of the language.

Tyndale's Bible is the first of our scholarly texts: the old Testament is founded on the Hebrew, and the New Testament is a translation from the Greek, as edited by Erasmus in 1516 and 1522. But it is more. Even beyond Shakespeare, Tyndale molded the governing forms of English style. The modern English Bible is, to a great extent, a mere modification of his work. Sixty percent of the text of the Authorized Version had reached its final shape in Tyndale. Of the 287 words in the Sermon on the Mount in the King James (or Authorized) Version, 242 are from Tyndale. And how lasting has been their splendor:

No man can serve two masters. For either he shall hate the one and love the other: or else he shall lean to the one and despise the other: ye cannot serve God and mammon. Therefore, I say unto you, be not careful for your life, what ye shall eat, or what ye shall drink, nor yet for your body, what ye shall put on. Is not the life more worth than meat, and the body more of value than raiment? Behold the fowls of the air: for they sow not, neither reap, nor yet carry into the barns: and yet your heavenly father feedeth them.

Tyndale's style is more spare and sinewy than was that of his contemporaries. Where the King James alters Tyndale, it usually adds: "Come unto me all ye that labour and are laden," writes Tyndale, "and I will ease you." The AV reads: "Come unto me all ye that are heavy laden, and I will give you rest." The rhythm is more stately, but the sequence is less exact: "easing" follows more justly on "laden."

Tyndale set down the basic usages of English biblical translation. He varies the English where Hebrew or Greek uses a single, repeated formula. Luke, for example, always says something that Tyndale closely rendered as "it came to pass." But Tyndale also translated this narrative formula by "it happened," "it fortuned," "it chanced," "it followed." In Matthew 18:33, the Greek uses a single word (the verb *ele-eo*). Tyndale uses two: "Thou shouldest have had *compassion* on thy fellow, even as I had *pity* on thee." Tyndale's liking for awkward inversion—"brought they," "went Jesus"—probably reflects the influence of Luther's German. But elsewhere he draws richly on words of Latin and French origin, a famous example being the use of *to minister*, where *to serve* would do as well. In fact, it may have been from Tyndale that Shakespeare derived his tactic of sharp juxtapositions between Anglo-Saxon monosyllabic words and Latinate leviathans ("the multitudinous seas incarnadine, making the green one red").

It is with Tyndale that the English Bible attains the rather paradoxical glory of being more eloquent than some of the Hebrew and most of the Greek original. Where translation diminishes a text, it traduces; where it surmounts the original while yet being loyal to it, it transfigures.

In 1535–1536, Miles Coverdale issued an English Bible based mainly on Tyndale, with additional readings from the Vulgate and the German. As Tyndale had not completed the Old Testament, Coverdale's is, strictly regarded, the first complete English Bible in print. Though it leans heavily on Tyndale's genius, Coverdale's version is less radical in its theology. Scholars agree, moreover, that Coverdale's ease and fluency of manner gave to the King James many of its ample rhythms. Coverdale acts as a bridge between the austere beat of Tyndale and the plenitude of the Authorized Version. In Hebrews 1:8 (an example which I owe, like much of this summary, to Sir Frederic Kenyon's *Our Bible and the Ancient Manuscripts*), Tyndale renders: "But unto the sonne he sayth: God thy seate shall be for ever and ever. The cepter of thy kyngdom is a right cepter." Coverdale reads "*endureth* for ever and ever" and keeps the whole one sentence. At once, the shape seems to broaden and grow more ceremonious.

Between Coverdale and the King James occurred several short but notable steps: the Great Bible of 1539–1541 (essentially Coverdale using a better Vulgate text); the famous Geneva Bible, issued by English Calvinists in 1560 and 1576, extracts from which served Cromwell's soldiers as a pocket Bible; the Bishops' Bible, an official revision of the Great Bible, published in 1568; and the Douai Bible, which English Catholics issued in France in 1582 and 1609 (and on which President Kennedy took his oath of office). Of these, the Geneva and the Douai contributed most to the AV. In the passage from Hebrews, for instance, it is the Geneva Bible that replaces *seat* by *throne* and makes of the *right cepter* a *sceptre of righteousness*. From the exaggerated Latinity of the Douai Bible, the King James derived some of its sonorous technical and ecclesiastic terms. But the Bible of 1611 is essentially Tyndale and Coverdale revised. By 1535, the major work had been done.

We must bear this in mind when approaching the AV. Its language is not really that of the Jacobean scholars and churchmen who compiled it. It is slightly archaic, as if the editors had wished to give to Scripture a lofty strangeness. Yet at the same time, it was produced at that moment in which the English language lived in singular excellence and vitality. Where the editors of 1604–1611 chose to improve on their predecessors, they did so with the instrument of Spenser, Hooker, Sidney, Florio, Shakespeare, Jonson, Bacon, and Donne.

The King James is the only great thing in this world ever done by a committee. Divided into six panels—two at Westminster and two each at Oxford and Cambridge—some fifty linguists and divines collaborated on the final text. There were notables among them:

Lancelot Andrewes, Richard Thomson (renowned both as linguist and drunkard), Thomas Holland, and Richard Brett, reputed to know Arabic, Hebrew, and Aramaic. There are many reasons for the supremacy of the AV: progress in the interpretation of the Hebrew and Greek meanings; the plurality of judgment brought to bear on every word; the tradition of previous English texts. Yet there is much about the King James that still seems wondrous. Countless times, one marvels at the felicity of phrase and the evenness of tone—the more striking in view of the number of editors involved. It is truly as if tongues of fire had spoken.

No other work has played a comparable role in determining the habits of feeling and imagination of the English-speaking world. None has done as much to ingrain in the English sensibility uses of speech which we feel to be, in some central way, native to the language. Wherever English prose has a natural excellence, whether in Swift or George Eliot or Lincoln, there sounds inside it the regal simplicity, the alternance of Anglo-Saxon and Latin, the graphic imagery and narrative pace of the King James. If only the Bible of 1611 and a dictionary survived, the English language would stand in no mortal danger.

But we must remember two facts. Philologically, the text on which the AV is based is primitive. Only sixteen years after the publication of the King James, the Codex Alexandrinus reached England. Soon the limits of historical awareness moved back to the fourth century. The discovery of the Codex Vaticanus and the Codex Sinaiticus made possible the establishment of a Bible text greatly superior to anything the Jacobeans could have envisaged. Secondly, the poetic, deliberately archaic language of the AV meant that the work would, by force of time, grow increasingly remote from current speech. Thus the need for future revision was implicit in the very genius of the King James. The surprising fact is not that such revisions should have been made but that none has challenged the pre-eminence of the Authorized Version.

Two new translations appeared in England in 1729 and 1768. An American version by Rodolphus Dickinson was published in Boston in 1833. It is remembered, somewhat uncharitably, for its rendering of Luke 1:41: "And it happened, that when Elizabeth heard the salutation of Mary, the embryo was joyfully agitated." Noah Webster's Bible, issued the same year, was sounder and a number of its readings have been retained by modern scholars.

192

But the real history of modern biblical translation begins with the Revised New Testament of 1881, followed by the American Standard Version in 1901. In nearly six thousand readings, the Greek text underlying these revisions differs from that available to the Jacobean divines. Roughly a quarter of these differences imply a change of meaning. After the turn of the century, three further translations require mention: James Moffatt's (1913), Msgr. Ronald Knox's Bible (1945), and the Revised Standard Version of 1946. But the last had scarcely been issued when the discovery of the Dead Sea scrolls gave dramatic proof that new textual problems and opportunities will continue to face the biblical scholar.

The latest response to these problems now lies before us. It is the New Testament of the New English Bible (NEB). It is the work of an eminent body of English and Scottish ecclesiastics and scholars who have met in common labor since January 1948. Undertaken in a Protestant but nonsectarian vein and published under the joint imprint of the Oxford and Cambridge University Presses, the NEB sets out to provide "a faithful rendering of the best available Greek text into the current speech of our own time, and a rendering which should harvest the gains of recent biblical scholarship." This is not "another revision of the Authorized Version but a genuinely new translation" using the idioms of contemporary English. In contrast to the revisers of 1881, the present translators, like their Jacobean forebears, make no effort to render the same Greek word everywhere in the same way. Their constant aim is fluency, clarity, and accuracy of interpretation. How far has it been achieved?

There is only one way of finding out: one must set certain passages of the NEB beside previous translations, particularly the AV, and compare. It is a pedestrian method, but there is no other. I shall look first at three passages illustrative for their familiar power of poetic beauty, then at two in which there are difficulties of comprehension.

Here is the King James version of Matthew 26:38–41:

Then saith he unto them, My soul is exceeding sorrowful, even unto death: tarry ye here, and watch with me.

And he went a little further, and fell on his face, and prayed, saying, O my Father, if it be possible, let this cup pass from me: nevertheless not as I will, but as thou wilt.

And he cometh unto the disciples, and findeth them

193

asleep, and saith unto Peter, What, could ye not watch with me one hour?

Watch and pray, that ye enter not into temptation: the spirit indeed is willing, but the flesh is weak.

Knox alters to conform more closely with the Vulgate and to stress the Catholic values. The *cup* becomes a *chalice*, and the grammar of Christ—"only as thy will is, not as mine is"—is severely Latin (*non sicut ego volo, sed sicut tu*).

Now here is the NEB:

"My heart is ready to break with grief. Stop here, and stay awake with me." He went on a little, fell on his face in prayer, and said, "My Father, if it is possible, let this cup pass me by. Yet not as I will, but as thou wilt." He came to the disciples and found them asleep; and he said to Peter, "What! Could none of you stay awake with me one hour? Stay awake, and pray that you may be spared the test. The spirit is willing, but the flesh is weak."

In this instance, the King James carries the day. The soul sorrowful "even unto death" is much superior to the modern version both in weight and meaning. *Stop* and *pass me by* are flat colloquialisms. *Stay awake* is somewhat closer to the original text, but *watch* has the more intense connotation of vigilance in the hour of supreme danger. And surely *temptation* is a finer rendering than *test* (the Greek, *peirasmos*, allows either translation).

Let us consider next Luke 21:25–28; first in the Authorized Version:

And there shall be signs in the sun, and in the moon, and in the stars; and upon the earth distress of nations, with perplexity; the sea and the waves roaring;

Men's hearts failing them for fear, and for looking after those things which are coming on the earth: for the powers of heaven shall be shaken.

And then shall they see the Son of man coming in a cloud with power and great glory.

And when these things begin to come to pass, then look up, and lift up your heads, for your redemption draweth nigh.

Knox differs perceptibly: "men's hearts will be dried up with fear . . . the very powers of heaven will rock . . . lift up your heads; it means that the time draws near for your deliverance."

And now the NEB:

> Portents will appear in sun, moon, and stars. On earth nations will stand helpless, not knowing which way to turn from the roar and surge of the sea; men will faint with terror at the thought of all that is coming upon the world; for the celestial powers will be shaken. And then they will see the Son of Man coming on a cloud with great power and glory. When all this begins to happen, stand upright and hold your heads high, because your liberation is near.

Here the new version has distinct advantages. Like Knox, it makes Christ's prophecy assured rather than conditional (*will* instead of *shall*), and it has an appropriate swift pace, as if expectation were bringing the event to the very horizon. "Faint with terror," on the other hand, is mildly Victorian, and I think Knox's "the very powers of heaven will rock" (*virtutes caelorum movebuntur*) the most graphic of the three. But the real problem lies in the last phrase. Three translations are proposed: *redemption*, *deliverance*, *liberation*. Which shall it be? The Greek (*apolutroo*) can signify any or each. The Vulgate chooses *redemptio*. Does Jesus mean deliverance from Roman power, spiritual redemption, or both? I am not scholar or theologian enough to judge; but *deliverance* seems to me best, as it allows more aptly than *liberation* for either a secular or transcendental emphasis.

Revelation is a text notorious for its demands on imaginative translation. Here is how the Jacobeans read Revelation 6:12–13:

> . . . and, lo, there was a great earthquake; and the sun became black as sackcloth of hair, and the moon became as blood;
>
> And the stars of heaven fell unto the earth, even as a fig tree casteth her untimely figs, when she is shaken of a mighty wind.

Moffatt simplifies to a plain *sackcloth* and the stars drop like *unripe figs* when the tree is shaken by a *gale*. But he makes the red moon *full* (following the Vulgate). The NEB contracts yet further:

195

And there was a violent earthquake; the sun turned black as a funeral pall and the moon all red as blood; the stars in the sky fell to the earth, like figs shaken down by a gale.

I can see that this is a clearer version; but it loses the precise vision of the original. The Apocalypse was seen through the eyes of a man familiar with desert sandstorms, with sackcloth woven thickly of hair, and familiar also with the loss of unripened figs when the desert wind strikes. The essential quality of Revelation is its down-to-earth approach to the transcendent. In this passage, the NEB seems to miss the flavor.

Let me conclude by looking at two examples which offer some crux of meaning. In I Corinthians 7:39, Paul declares that a widow is "at liberty to be married to whom she will; only in the Lord" (AV). Just what does that mean? Knox is no help: "so long as she marries in the Lord." Moffatt proceeds boldly: "only, it must be a Christian." His support, presumably, is II Corinthians 6:14: "Be ye not unequally yoked together with unbelievers." The NEB reads: "provided the marriage is within the Lord's fellowship." This seems to me most ingenious: it communicates the spirit of the injunction without betraying the letter.

Finally, let us look at the close of Philippians 3 in the King James:

> for our conversation is in heaven; from whence also we look for the Saviour, the Lord Jesus Christ;
> Who shall change our vile body, that it may be fashioned like unto his glorious body, according to the working whereby he is able even to subdue all things unto himself.

The archaic language (*conversation*) and the gnarled syntax make for heavy going. Knox simplifies to "our true home in heaven" and renders *configuratum corpori claritatis* as "the image of his glorified body." Now the NEB:

> We, by contrast, are citizens of heaven, and from heaven we expect our deliverer to come, the Lord Jesus Christ. He will transfigure the body belonging to our humble state, and give it a form like that of his own resplen-

dent body, by the very power which enables him to make all things subject to himself.

This is, perhaps, a little too brisk, and one regrets the loss of *vile body*. But *transfigure* is beautifully to the point and the crux of *politeuma* is resolved: it does imply *citizenship*. Neither Knox's *home* nor Moffatt's quaint *colony of heaven* is as close.

For a tentative judgment, I would say that the New Testament of the *New English Bible* is generally preferable to Moffatt, many of whose readings are idiosyncratic. It lacks much of the stylistic felicity of Knox, but is, of course, far more reliable, since it can go beyond the often dubious sanction of the Vulgate. So far as study of the Greek text and of its linguistic nuances is concerned, the NEB is now the most authoritative version available. Moreover, its fluency, colloquialism, and willingness to enlarge by paraphrase make for a most lucid narrative. This, as the Preface states, is truly a translation for those not previously familiar with the Bible.

At the same time, it is doubtful whether the NEB will win for itself anything of the place still held commandingly by the AV. Being founded wholly on current speech, the NEB is often flat. It uses too many words that have present meaning but will not, I think, acquire future resonance. Often their shallow modernity jars: "liberal-minded," "my friends" (for brethren), "loophole," "frustration" (in the current psychological sense), "environment" (with a psycho-sociological nuance), "pack our baggage," "affairs" (for deeds or acts). It happens that English, as now spoken in England, is in a rather flat and diminished state. There is much propriety but little savor. Yet the translators of the NEB have been unwilling to draw on the richness and zest of American English, where they would often have found modern but spirited equivalents of Jacobean usage. The result is that the style of the NEB suffers from an irritating mixture of coyness and colloquialism.

But taken as a whole, this new translation is a fine achievement. I can think of none better to keep next to one's King James to check the sense of the Greek or resolve obscurities created by the archaic speech and convoluted syntax of the Jacobean divines. The NEB is a lucid, erudite page boy, carrying the train of its majestic ancestor and, by an occasional discreet tug, showing the right road.

SHAKESPEARE—
FOUR HUNDREDTH

The words with which we seek to do him homage are his. We look for new celebration and find echo. Shakespeare has his mastering grip on the marrow of our speech. The shapes of life which he created give voice to our inward needs. We catch ourselves crooning desire like street-corner Romeos; we fall to jealousy in the cadence of Othello; we make Hamlets of our enigmas; old men rage and dodder like Lear. Shakespeare is the common house of our feelings. He has seen so exactly, so variously for us; he has struck the note of consciousness over so wide a range of human experience; he found for what he saw and felt such authority of statement—making his words not only a mirror of truth, but its vital, inexhaustible form—that we meet his voice around every corner of our sensibility. Even our cry and our laughter are only partly ours; we find them where he left them, and they bear his stamp.

Thus whoever tries to add something worth saying to the din of commemoration and affirm "how noble he was in reason, how infinite in faculty, in form and moving how express and admirable," is only quoting.

The hint of a power beyond rational account tempts our thought of him. We seek Shakespeare's measure and come short of breath. A leap of invention, a technical resource which comprehend the moon-bright garden at Belmont and Lear on the convulsed rotundity of earth, the crow of the Danish cock at purgatorial dawn and sea-changes five fathoms five off the coast of Bohemia, challenge our scale of human gift. An instrument which can render, with equal truth and timbre, the acid needlings of Iago and the silences of Cordelia, Falstaff's belly-talk or the high jingles of Ariel, seems to set a limit only to itself. Critics who are honest know what Cassius speaks for them:

> Why, man, he doth bestride the narrow world
> Like a Colossus, and we petty men
> Walk under his huge legs and peep about
> To find ourselves dishonorable graves.

It was not always so. Ben Jonson, in whom justice strove with rivalry, spoke the first, enduring epitaph: "He was not for an age, but for all time!" Yet he asserted with no less conviction that "Shakespeare wanted art," and that it had been better had he blotted a thousand of his lines. Dryden revered Shakespeare's "comprehensive soul," but did not regard him as incomparable; in signal respects, he preferred Jonson or Beaumont and Fletcher. To Milton, Shakespeare's was a wild, untutored talent; he scorned to set it beside Sophocles. In editing Shakespeare, Pope found great virtues, but defects "almost as great."

This sense of poise between genius and infirmity, between beauty and blemish, gives Samuel Johnson's judgment its circumscribed but confident strength: "Shakespeare with his excellencies had likewise faults sufficient to obscure and overwhelm any other merit. I shall shew them in the proportion in which they appear to me, without envious malignity or superstitious veneration." To Johnson, Shakespeare was a very great writer, at moments unsurpassed. But his achievement was not, in essence, different from that of other poets; it posed no unique riddle of glory. Critic and playwright could meet on level ground.

The notion of transcendence, of a genius so apart that it solicits metaphors of supernatural power, is Romantic. It animates the impatient ecstasy of the Shakespearean criticism of Lamb and Coleridge: "but combine all—wit, subtlety and fancy, with profundity, imagination, and moral and physical susceptibility of the pleasurable—and let the object of action be man universal; and we shall have—O, rash prophecy! say, rather, we have—a Shakespeare!" Keats asked whether one could conceive of a superior being looking on Shakespeare, and finding in him weakness or nullity, and answered No. He added, echoing Hazlitt, that "Shakespeare is enough," that his insight is sufficient to man's day and labor.

The modern tone is more astringent. It rebukes mere rapture.

But our essential stance is heir to that of Coleridge. We do not imagine that we look on Shakespeare as equal to equal; textual scholar and literary critic, actor and producer are as moths to his great flame. Those who would challenge Shakespeare's stature do so with a betraying nervousness. There was a streak of uneasy clowning in Shaw's subversions of Shakespeare, in his claim to match or improve on Shakespearean drama. T. S. Eliot has austere reservations; *Hamlet* is an artistic failure, and Shakespeare lacked a sustaining metaphysic. But the argument closes in homage: Shakespeare and Dante divide Western literature between them. There is no third. The only modern attack that discards the very premise of Shakespeare's greatness, that sees his work as persistently and blindly overrated, is Tolstoy's. And it is an attack mounted not from literature, but from an exterior ground of anarchic moralism.

This universality of homage makes it difficult to "see new." An incessant tide of commentary and edition—it requires a fair-sized library to house what has been written and spoken about Shakespeare in 1964—bars us from the risks and privileges of novel impression. We no longer share the serene innocence of George III when he confided to Fanny Burney that he had read Shakespeare and found in him "a lot of twaddle." We start from a legacy of reverence, from the assumption that the work before us is of unique grandeur and fascination.

What philology and criticism *have* done since the fireworks and choral odes of 1864, is to make our admiration more exact. We know a little more of the source and nature of Shakespeare's pre-eminence, of the general means that went into the particular devices of his art. If our judgment still moves in frequent doubt (and more is now known of Shakespeare than of many an Elizabethan figure), it moves more surely.

Shakespeare was marvelously lucky in his times. In England, the period from 1580 to 1640 represented a special constellation of emotional and intellectual energies. Though the new mercantile society and centralized state followed hard on the decay of feudalism, the old, close-woven patterns of medieval feeling, with its habits of imagery and allegoric statement, with its profound, subtle imaginings of a world-anatomy, was still vital. The scholarship of E. K. Chambers, of Tillyard, of Hardin Craig has taught us how much of the dynamism of Elizabethan drama derived from the survivance of medieval, popular values; how it was to a medieval precedent that the Elizabethan theater owed its characteristic yoking of farce with high tragedy, and its assumption that the natural world of tempest and heath, of blazing comet and portentous star, gives expressive attendance to the lives of men.

When Lorenzo tells Jessica, in *The Merchant of Venice*, that there is not an orb in heaven "But in his motion like an angel sings," the precise doctrine of the music of the spheres, and the larger inference of animate, cosmic harmony, go back to their antique source through the Middle Ages, and through medieval legends of Pythagoras. When the branch and leaf-clad forces of redemption advance on Dunsinane, the castle of evil in a blighted land, we apprehend behind the action of *Macbeth*, though at far remove, an older pattern of ritual, of annual combat between winter's barren dark and the coming of the Green Man. In the Morris dance or the dance of the horned maskers in the Elizabethan village, such patterns had their afterlife. A traditional coherence related the whole of the Elizabethan world-image, from insensate stone to burning star. It gave firm pivot to the individualism and passionate turbulence of the Elizabethan play.

Yet at the same time, the "new Americas" of mathematics and astronomy, of Galilean physics and global navigation, were transforming the contours of life and feeling at a fantastic pace. The heroic bias of Elizabethan tragedy, the representation of will and ambition at full stretch, dramatize the pressure of intellectual conquest. The Elizabethan spirit is dizzy with new horizons. And following on Marlowe, the playwrights sensed what was electric in the air.

As early as *The Comedy of Errors*, with its reference to "Lapland sorcerers," Shakespeare was alert to material such as Giles Fletcher's travels to the Russian arctic. If "poor Tom," in *King Lear*, feeds on "Mice and rats and such small deer," it may well be because that was the diet of Hawkins' mariners after their disastrous repulse from the West Indies. Ulysses' speech on order in *Troilus and Cressida* makes provisional use of the Copernican-Galilean design of planetary motion:

> And therefore is the glorious planet Sol
> In noble eminence enthroned and sphered
> Amidst the other.

201

Thus Shakespeare could draw at will on medieval and modern, on the intricate weave of tradition and the forward motion of intellect. Many of his primary devices and conventions rely on this simultaneity of impulse. He could conjure the Ghost of Hamlet's father and the Weird Sisters out of a reality of witchcraft and supernatural presence that were still urgent in Jacobean England. But such presences were, in Hamlet's profound, ambiguous phrase, "questionable." Shakespeare could play the speculative instincts of Baconian empiricism against the archaic authority of a daemonic world. His assent to the supernatural is, therefore, tentative—and the richness of the dramatic treatment springs from uncertitude.

It was a brief spell of creative imbalance between two worlds, between two modes of consciousness. After 1640, the achievements of Bacon, Descartes, and Newton made the old order unrecapturable. "The mischief," wrote Yeats, "began at the end of the seventeenth century when man became passive before a mechanized nature."

Shakespeare was lucky also in the quality of his playhouse and audience. Despite the important work of modern social historians and Alfred Harbage, we still do not know as much as we should like about the precise character of that audience. Marx's challenge that one cannot account for the brilliance and profusion of Elizabethan drama without analyzing the economic and class structure of stage and public, has been admitted but only partially met. Unquestionably, Shakespeare's genius, and the relationship of that genius to a large audience, are part of the history of pre-inflation. All but the destitute were able, now and again, to pay a penny to stand in the pit of the Globe; it was no more than the cost of a pint of ale. By the time modern mercantilism had been fully established in the eighteenth century, the price of a novel would feed a family for up to a fortnight. Thus Shakespeare's playhouse embodied an exceptional range of economic and social interests. Aristocrat and tradesman, gentry and apprentice, lawyer and mercenary, stood side by side, or in crowded proximity, under the open sky. No other theater that we know of could command so wide a context of social response.

To hold such an audience against the distractions of bear-baiting or downpour, the Elizabethan play had to move at various levels of meaning and delight. It could not, as does the art of Racine, define a single, rigid code of statement. In the very same scene in *Hamlet* or *Othello*, the arcane flash of meditation or word-play, rousing the wit of the few, of the courtier or scholar, is borne on a current of intrigue and raw action broad enough to rivet the excitement of the un-schooled. The humane largesse of Shakespearean drama, its essential commitment to a tragi-comic view of life, reflect the multiple instincts and demands of this wide audience. As soon as the playhouses moved indoors, into a medium of candlelight and courtly entertainment, as soon as the gathering strength of Puritanism made the urban middle class shy of the stage, drama lost its superb breadth. It left what Coleridge called "the high road of life" to play upon more special nerves. G. E. Bentley has shown how significantly the later Jacobean and Caroline theater differ from the popular genius of the Eliza-bethan. Shakespeare's own late plays show this sophistication of art. He came just in time.

This is true, above all, of the condition of the language. Even as Elizabethan sensibility drew its tone from the conflict and weld of medieval and renaissance values, so English in the late sixteenth and seventeenth centuries realized a unique coherence of inheritance and innovation. The radical cadence of the language, its sinew of verb and strong solemnities, had come down from the Middle Ages and Cax-ton. The Authorized Version of the Bible, with its deliberate recourse to John Wyclif and fourteenth-century turns of speech, characterizes the Elizabethan and Jacobean awareness of the old lineage; but it also exhibits the resolve to enrich that lineage, to make it more pliant by the import of classic and European resources. It is these which tide into the Elizabethan vocabulary giving it its fantastic wealth of ex-pression.

The Elizabethans ransacked Greek and Latin, the European vulgate, and the speech of the new worlds, as they did Spanish harbors. They took the Spanish *brisa* to make *breeze;* they borrowed *indigo* from Portugal, and *gong* from Malay. When an Elizabethan tragic personage confesses to *forlorn hope*, he is distorting the Dutch *verloren hoop* (a routed military unit) which men such as Sidney and Ben Jonson had heard during their battles in the Low Countries. But it was from Greek and Latin that the Renaissance took most avidly; here was ancient gold out of which to forge the very *mettle* of free minds (and as it enters the language in the 1580's the word carries its fine ambiguity and echo). It is at this point, using Greek and Latin forms, that much of the vocabulary of our politics and science, of our art and metaphysics, first came into play.

The ear of Spenser and Marlowe made of English verse an ideal medium of linguistic congruence. It was they who adopted the great trick of music and unity whereby the Anglo-Saxon and the Latin conjoin. That trick, with its formidable means of tension and resonance, is one of the keys to Shakespeare's style. He hammered it out gradually. By the time of *Henry IV*, he has it perfect:

> Wilt thou upon the high and giddy mast
> Seal up the ship-boy's eyes and rock his brains
> In cradle of the rude imperious surge,
> And in the visitation of the winds. . . .

But language is far more than a currency of rational and emotional exchange. It stands in a vital, reciprocal relationship to the contours of society. Elizabethan England was still in close, natural contact with rural life; and even in the cities the technical modes of production and trade were still of an essentially personal, local character. A man knew whence his bread came and how it was baked; how his boots were shod and his cloth woven. In a day's walk he could span the entire vista of the *body politic* (itself a metaphor of organic cohesion), from palace and law-court to open field. This meant that the words he used had immediacy and concreteness. He knew whereof he spoke by personal experience, and the names of things retained the subtle liveliness of that which we have held in hand.

In Shakespeare's English the vocabularies of wheelwright and mariner, of soldier and apothecary, of law-clerk and midwife, have their specific weight and precision. Each embodies a closely observed and felt reality. It has often been noted that Shakespeare used more words than any other poet, and used them with more sensuous accuracy. But what matters is that the twenty thousand words at his reach give an all but total rendering of the Elizabethan world. Scarcely any sphere of action or thought is left out; scarcely anything was too remote or specialized for concrete, dramatic use. And it was a concreteness which, time and again, directs the mind to rural life and manual labor. Thus, as Dover Wilson has pointed out, the fierce harrowings of Hamlet and his mother in the bedroom scene—

> Nay, but to live
> In the rank sweat of an enseamèd bed
> Stewed in corruption, honeying, and making love
> Over the nasty sty—

are based on a set of technical yet banal terms taken from wool-dyeing. Himself the son of a wool merchant, Shakespeare had seen wool greased (*enseamèd*) with hog's lard. Hence the pig-sty, and the characteristic awareness, an awareness central to the meaning of the play, that trough and honey-comb are only a step apart.

Today, the more than half a million words available to current English fall increasingly short of the needs of a splintered, technological society. Where it is not mere commonplace, our usage grows more and more specialized. The mass jargon of the modern city is stranger to the names of stones and flowers, as it is stranger to the making of its bread. We communicate; but being second-hand and abstract, the modes of our communication do not achieve community.

This vivid immediacy of idiom, and the capacity of the individual to be in natural contact with the whole of the social condition, are crucial to Shakespearean drama. As Newton and Leibniz were among the last to apprehend the entire spectrum of the natural sciences, to experience knowledge as a complex unity, so Shakespeare appears to have been the last to enclose in poetic speech a total view of human action, a *summa mundi*. After 1640 the old unities break. Here again, the hour met the man.

But once we acknowledge the vital coincidence between the individual talent of the Elizabethan playwrights and the opportunities opened by economic, psychological, and linguistic circumstance, the fact of Shakespeare's supremacy remains. He is greater than Marlowe or Jonson; much greater than Webster, Ford, or Tourneur. In what way?

It is in its attempt to answer this question that the modern reading, the quality of our present admiration, differ most from the Romantics and Victorians. Hazlitt focused his insight on Shakespeare's "men and women," on his creation of "living beings"; the Victorians anthologized Shakespeare's "mastery of human wisdom," they harvested his plays for intellectual guidance and precepts of feeling. By contrast, it is Shakespeare the organizer of language who is the pivot of modern criticism. L. C. Knights's well-known essay *How Many Children Had Lady Macbeth?* (1933) summarized and argued the new approach.

The plays of Shakespeare consist of words chosen and arranged toward specific poetic and dramatic ends. These words are our sole evidence. To speak of Hamlet before the play, to evoke Falstaff in the lean sundown of his days, is mere verbiage. No character is "real" in any exterior sense. It exists within the statement of the play, and that statement is a particular marshaling of words. A different arrangement—a different order of image or rhetoric—would create a different personage and dramatic meaning. A true reading of Shakespeare, therefore (and producers and actors are, in fact, readers out loud), signifies a response of the utmost delicacy, of the utmost comprehension, to the text before us.

What emerges from such reading?

More than any other human intellect of which we have adequate record, Shakespeare used language in a condition of total possibility. What I mean is this: the great majority of men use language in an essentially unreflective, utilitarian way; they take words to have a fixed, single meaning. They regard speech as if its potential could be set down in a primer, in a pocket dictionary of basic usage. With education and the complication of our emotional needs through literature, we are made aware of the polyphonic structure of language, of the multiplicity of intents and implications, at times contradictory, latent in individual terms, in their placing and stress. We grow alert to the fact that none but the most formal or rudimentary of linguistic propositions has a single equivalence.

In Shakespeare, this alertness, this mastering response to the sum of all potential meanings and values, reached an intensity far beyond the norm. (One may, at least, raise the question whether Shakespeare was not harnessing more fully, more economically than other men, areas of the cortex in which speech functions are thought to be localized.) When using a word, or set of words, Shakespeare brings into controlled activity not only the range of definitions and current modes noted in the dictionary; he seems to hear around the core of every word the totality of its overtones and undertones; of its connotations and echoes. The analogy would be certain extreme subtleties and acuities of the musical ear. To Shakespeare, more than to any other poet, the individual word was a nucleus surrounded by a field of complex energies.

These reach back to the subconscious, to the obscure primary zone where human language emerges from a "pre-vocabulary" of biological and somatic stimulus or recognition. In Shakespeare, words often come to the surface with their full charge of pre-conscious association; their roots go unbroken to the dark. But the

Shakespearean sense of total possibility also extends forward. Many of his words do not come to rest in any single meaning. They move like a pendulum sweeping a wide terrain of partial synonyms and analogues. Often, a word will shade, by pun or suggestion of sound, into an area of new definitions. In part, this vibrant action is due to Shakespeare's ready use of the instabilities of the Elizabethan vocabulary, to the fact that before Dryden and before Johnson's *Dictionary* definitions and syntax remain fluid.

To read Shakespeare is to be in contact with a verbal medium of unequaled richness and exactitude; with a mode of statement which does not, as in ordinary men, limit itself to a conventional, fixed pattern of significance, but persistently conveys a multiple, creative energy of thought and feeling. We speak as if words were a piano score; Shakespeare's is the full orchestration.

The proof lies in the study of the plays and poems as a whole. I need give only one or two examples.

In Act I of *Hamlet*, a number of key words derive their power to rouse and control our attention from the fact that Shakespeare has made explicit the buried strength of their etymologies. Behind the primary meaning a larger resonance is brought into play. In Horatio's narrative, *disasters* implies the literal chaos or ruin of the stars, an implication that prepares Hamlet's confession that to him the star-studded heavens have grown "a foul and pestilent congregation of vapors." In Horatio's reference to *extravagant* spirits, the etymology —far-wandering—modulates into overtones of waste and tragic excess which were imminent in the usage of the 1590's. Together, the root and the overtones organize Horatio's graphic use of *confine* in the following verse. *Confine* is both boundary and prison-house (and various intermediary nuances of restriction are active in the image); the Ghost has strayed from desperate captivity, all the extravagance of sensual life upon his soul. Or observe the self-betrayal in Claudius' deference to *obsequious sorrow*, where *obsequious* carries the concrete force of its Latin etymology (funeral *obsequies*), together with the more modern hint of falsehood, of hollow gesture. Note too, how the phrase cuts back in irony to what we know of the hasty bestowal of Hamlet's father.

There is a superb instance of how a single word shapes an entire complex of emotion and intelligence in the first speech of the Ghost. The "fretful porpentine," Shakespeare's simile of hair-raising fright, suggests an heraldic beast, the crest of a coat of arms, a suggestion faintly announced in Horatio's earlier description of the Ghost, "Armèd at point exactly, cap-a-pe." From it springs the Ghost's admonition to Hamlet that the hideous truths of Purgatory must not be *blazoned* forth. Originally, *blazon* means a painted shield; by derivation, it comes to mean the action of disclosure which is the aim of heraldry. But in the very sound of the word, by an echo deeper than a mere pun, Shakespeare makes us hear the *blaze*, the purging fires in which the Ghost is doomed for a certain time to dwell. Did Shakespeare know—or need to know—that modern philology believes the two words to have a very remote, common origin? Hardly; but when he did so, he used a word with its totality of relevance.

Shakespeare's plays have been described as the unfolding of certain primary metaphors. Because the words he chose for stress and deepening have an enormous potential, they give to the action of the plays their close-knit order. The entirety of *King Lear*, with its dramatic realization of a world in primal chaos, may be seen to develop from the Fool's prophecy that Lear shall be used *kindly* by Regan. In that small word, terrible queries and subversions lurk. Is there *kindness* in our human *kind;* if each man deal after his *kind*, what then? Did Shakespeare, with his final sensitivity to linguistic values, implicate the common root which makes of *kind* the German word for *child?* Similarly, the intricate argument of *Macbeth* on unnatural proceedings in nature, politics, and private conduct, is concentrated in the opening tag: "Fair is foul, and foul is fair."

Shakespeare's discernment of human motive, his fantastic divinations of historical atmosphere, his seeming foresight into modern psychology (the Freudian impact in the Clown's farewell to Cleopatra: "I wish you well of the worm")—all arise, in the final analysis, from an exhaustive realization of linguistic possibility. His plays are patterns of words used with a totality of ordered meaning. Through that completeness is achieved a medium, in Ben Jonson's superb phrase—

so ramm'd with life
That it shall gather strength of life, with being.

Will that medium, and our understanding of it, endure? Can we imagine Shakespeare, as Carlyle did in 1840, "radiant aloft over all nations . . . a thousand years hence"? Will the Shakespeare anniversary of 2064 find laser beams carrying the sight and rejoicing of Stratford bells to all stations in space, or will it have diminished to an observance of textual scholars and antiquarians?

Each age has had its particular vision of Shakespeare. Each selects from the compass of his performance that which speaks most cogently to its own temper. As it moves through time, a work of art becomes barnacled with successive bearings and revaluations. The recent landscape of politics has lent to the image of unnatural hatreds and racked humanity in *Lear* a novel and specific reference. The contemporary bias toward psychological ambiguity gives such plays as *Measure for Measure* and *Troilus and Cressida* a prestige, a fascination, they never enjoyed before. By contrast, we set *Romeo and Juliet* or *A Midsummer Night's Dream* much lower in the canon than did the nineteenth century. Our present concept of Shakespeare the poet, the master-builder of intricate verbal structures (a criterion which puts *Coriolanus* near the summit), may alter and lose authority.

Any prophecy is rash. But certain possibilities of change and detraction are discernible. Mass-education has immensely widened Shakespeare's audience. Never before have so many human beings had some measure of acquaintance with the plays. There is hardly a language or organized community, with access to mass-media, in which an occasional bit of Shakespeare is not read or acted. But what has been produced by popular education since the latter part of the industrial revolution is a special kind of semi-literacy, an ability to read and perceive in a very limited, utilitarian range. It is a literacy drastically out of touch with the verbal consciousness, with the habits of feeling and reference implicit in an Elizabethan text. The core of primary knowledge which Shakespeare shared with his audience, and with humanistic Europe—a familiarity with Scripture and classic myths, with the common trove of Christian symbolism and renaissance allegory—is receding into the confine of the scholar.

In Act II of *Cymbeline*, Iachimo climbs out of a trunk to spy on the sleeping Imogen. He compares himself to Tarquin "softly pressing the rushes ere he wakened/The chastity he wounded." The young woman is "Cytherea"; the bracelet he steals off her arm is "slippery as the Gordian knot was hard." Before falling asleep, Imogen has been reading

> The tale of Tereus; here's the leaf turned down
> Where Philomel gave up.

Each of these classic allusions was natural to the literacy of an Elizabethan schoolboy; it was part of the rudiments of European bourgeois education until the early twentieth century. How many present readers can, without special help, follow the careful plotting of Iachimo's intent? For the issue here is not one of critical refinement. These five references, and the order in which they are made, constitute the essential dramatic form. If one does not grasp, with an immediate sense of terror, the pointer to Ovid's tale of rape and silence, the whole of Iachimo's stance, of his shallow, embarrassed malignity, is made insignificant. Shakespeare is using an alphabet which we have largely lost.

The complete Shakespeare in inexpensive paperbacks, now being issued by the New American Library, is a triumph of editorial scruple and democratic hope. But it may mark one of the last historic moments in which a genuine text, supported by only a reasonable scaffold of explanations and gloss, will reach a mass audience; in fact, I wonder how many of those who buy these remarkable volumes actually *read* the plays. With each semi-literate generation, the distance between Shakespeare and reader will grow. So will the temptation to "modernize," to prepare versions in digest form or colloquial paraphrase. Even as Shakespeare is translated into languages ever more remote from the world, from the conventions of meaning he knew, so he may come to be "translated" into an Anglo-American ever more unlike Elizabethan speech.

Indeed, the authority of the written text may yield increasingly to visual presentment. Three-dimensional television and the graphic transmission of the most realistic performances to every habitation may reduce awareness of the book to a minor role. The plays could become once more what they were before the innovation of the Folio: pure theater. And as is already the case with much classical music, a numerous public would follow in action works whose score they cannot read or genuinely judge. Shakespeare himself might not flinch at such a prospect. He was a man of the playhouse, mysteriously indifferent, if our evidence is right, to the survival of the written text.

Is there any set of circumstances, outside nuclear catastrophe, which could bring *Hamlet* or *Othello* into partial oblivion, which could reduce Shakespeare's work to the concern of a few specialists?

What is involved here is the retreat from the primacy of the word, of linguistic authority. It is by no means evident that civilization will produce in future those constructs of verbal, syntactic representation, or *mimesis*, which we find in Dante, Shakespeare, and Joyce. Simenon may be among the last to have taken an entire culture for his verbal canvas. If language, as we use it, were to lose part of its function and universality, the works of Shakespeare would become comprehensible only to a specialized caste of "interpreters." They would preserve their secret radiance; but the ordinary man might find them as difficult to decipher, as mute, as are the cavern paintings of Altamira.

But this is mere conjecture. Only one thing seems strangely certain: that no other writer will surpass Shakespeare. To say that Shakespeare is not only the greatest writer who has ever lived, but who will ever live, is a perfectly rational statement. But it is, in the deepest sense, a shocking statement. It outrages the instinctive forward motion of human expectation. It sets a defiant limit to the hopes of any poet, of any man who seeks to master and render life on the written page. It insinuates into the study and criticism of literature a constant backward glance. There is a mustard-seed of truth in the slogan of the surrealists that if poetry is to be made new, if we are to grow innocent again before the magic of speech, the works of Shakespeare must be burned. We do him honor, also, if we recognize how heavy is the burden of his glory.

TWO TRANSLATIONS

No, no, my friend, we're off! Six months have passed
since Father heard the ocean howl and cast
his galley on the Aegean's skull-white froth.
Listen! The blank sea calls us—off, off, off!
I'll follow Father to the fountainhead
and marsh of hell. We're off. Alive or dead,
I'll find him.

Robert Lowell, of course. The lines carry the stamp of his vivid rhetoric. The howling ocean, the skull-white froth, the marsh of hell declare that oratory of sea and Gothic landscape distinctive of Lowell. Yet these lines purport some scrupulous relation to the opening couplets of Racine's *Phèdre*. "My version is *free*," says Lowell, "nevertheless I have used every speech in the original, and almost every line is either translated or paraphrased." We must be reading from different editions:

> *Le dessein en est pris, je pars, cher Théramène,*
> *Et quitte le séjour de l'aimable Trézène.*
> *Dans le doute mortel où je suis agité,*
> *Je commence à rougir de mon oisiveté.*
> *Depuis plus de six mois éloigné de mon père,*
> *J'ignore le destin d'une tête si chère;*
> *J'ignore jusqu'aux lieux qui le peuvent cacher.*

Not only has Lowell made no attempt to render the general meaning, but the whole thrust of his version goes wrong. Racine opens on a muted, dubious note. The long vowel endings, the repetition of *j'ignore*, the dark, delicate premonition in *doute mortel*, define Hippolyte.

Rougir tells us of his easy blushing. The lines "place" him accurately in the complex tangle of the drama. They bespeak his candid but shy and bending virtue. Nothing of all this is even hinted at in the robust eloquence of Lowell. Let us try elsewhere.

The crux of the play occurs in Act II, scene v. Maddened by her incestuous love, Phèdre seeks out Hippolyte. Through hint and oblique metaphor she tries to enforce upon his chaste, naïve spirit an awareness of her own ardent and dread condition. At first the young prince shows no apprehension of what she is trying to get across. Suddenly a terrible light flashes through his incredulous mind. Stunned, he asks the Queen whether she has forgotten that his father, Theseus, is her husband. In a final surge of reason and self-command, Phèdre seeks to deny her own revelation:

> *Et sur quoi jugez-vous que j'en perds la mémoire,*
> *Prince? Aurais-je perdu tout le soin de ma gloire?*

Hippolyte stammers his apology and turns to flight. But now the doors of chaos spring open. Phèdre drops all pretense and yields to the rush of her roused blood (blood and fire is the dominant trope of the whole play). She proclaims her love in wild, self-accusing accents. All the horrors that have gathered beneath the mask of decorum stand naked:

> *Ah! cruel, tu m'as trop entendue.*
> *Je t'en ai dit assez pour te tirer d'erreur.*
> *Hé bien! connais donc Phèdre et toute sa fureur.*
> *J'aime.*

Yet this ultimate crisis is conveyed essentially through a change of syntax. It is the brusque passage from the formal, customary *vous* to the intimate *tu* which proclaims the catastrophe. Repeated four times in three lines (once in the verb *connais donc*), this *tu* signifies the total collapse of Phèdre's governance over her own soul. Only an art as formal and economic as that of Racine can provoke so great a shock by so sparse a means. In the taut stylistic conventions of French neo-classicism, a change of grammatical person can stand for an entirety of moral ruin. Music knows such reversals in a change of key. Any translation of Racine must grapple with them. Lowell does not even attempt to do so:

> You monster! You understood me too well!
> Why do you hang there, speechless, petrified,

213

polite! My mind whirls. What have I to hide?
Phaedra in all her madness stands before you.
I love you! Fool, I love you, I adore you!

Clearly, *you* and *thou* cannot reproduce the formidable shock of *vous* and *tu*. What is required is some equivalent change in tonality, a veering away from contained pressure to wild, agonized avowal. But having pitched the whole preceding play in a key of uniform vehemence, Lowell can no longer modulate. The crucial sense of inward collapse is lost. Moreover, "I love you! Fool, I love you, I adore you!" is a betrayal of Racine's superb strategy. What Phèdre says is "*j'aime*," meaning simply "I am in love." Then comes a momentous caesura. The actual designation of her love—"*je t'aime*"—is hurried over in a burst of self-revilement. Even in her hour of unreason, Phèdre retains that fineness of spirit which makes her a tragic and not a melodramatic heroine. "Speechless," "petrified," "polite" are gratuitous inventions by Mr. Lowell. Racine knew there was no need of waste motion; Hippolyte's posture is implicit in the discourse. All Phèdre says, with a delicate ambiguity on *entendre*, is: "Ah! cruel man, you have heard [understood] me all too clearly./I have said enough to dispel your confusion."

One more example: at the close of Act IV, Phèdre spurns her accomplice and confidante, Oenone. Loathing has taken her by the throat. She knows that what has come to pass is monstrous and heaps her own sense of guilt on the pliant, wretched nurse:

> *Qu'entends-je? Quels conseils ose-t-on me donner?*
> *Ainsi donc jusqu'au bout tu veux m'empoisonner,*
> *Malheureuse! Voilà comme tu m'as perdue.*
> *Au jour, que je fuyais, c'est toi qui m'as rendue.*
> *Tes prières m'ont fait oublier mon devoir.*
>
> . . . . . .
>
> *Et puisse ton supplice à jamais effrayer*
> *Tout ceux qui, comme toi, par de lâches adresses.*
> *Des princes malheureux nourrissent les faiblesses,*
> *Les poussent au penchant où leur coeur est enclin,*
> *Et leur osent du crime aplanir le chemin. . . .*

Now Lowell's text:

> Must I still listen and drink your poisoned breath?
> My death's redoubled on the edge of death.
> I'd fled Hippolytus and I was free

214

till your entreaties stabbed and blinded me,
and dragged me howling to the pit of lust.

. . . .

may your punishment be to terrify
all those who ruin princes by their lies,
hints, acquiescence, filth, and blasphemies—
panders who grease the grooves of inclination
and lure our willing bodies from salvation.

The tone could hardly be more remote from Racine. Marlowe, Tourneur, and Webster glow behind Lowell's diction. At the outset there
is a plain error: it was not from Hippolytus that Phèdre had escaped,
but from the sight of the sun (*le jour*). She was about to kill herself
when Oenone persuaded her to live and enact her passion. What is
more serious: the whole context of Lowell's version is Christian-
baroque. There is nothing in Racine's lines, or in his lyric, Euripi-
dean mode, of "the pit of lust," of "blasphemies," of "panders who
grease the grooves of inclination," or of bodies "lured from salvation."

Let me be clear: I yield to no one in my admiration of Lowell's
poetry or in my awareness of his stature as a poet. I rejoice in the
rhetorical flourish and pace of his *Phaedra*. As an exercise in verse
drama it is often brilliant. More than anyone else now writing iambic
pentameter, Lowell can instill into an English cadence the weight and
noble violence of Latinity. But I submit that *Phaedra* has an unsteady
and capricious bearing on the matter of Racine. Far too often, it
strives against the grain of Racine's style and aga nst the conventions
of feeling on which the miraculous concision of that style depends.
Lowell's play is much closer to Seneca's *Hippolytus*. It has the same
grim rhetoric and extravagance:

> *Expelle facinus mente castifica horridum,*
> *Memorque matris, metue concubitus novos.*
> *Miscere thalamos patris et gnati apparas,*
> *Uteroque prolem capere confusam impio!*
> *Perge, et nefandis verte naturam ignibus.*
> *Cur monstra cessant?*

In short: what Lowell has produced is a variation on the theme of
Phaedra, in the manner of Seneca and the Elizabethan classicists. To
link this version with Racine implies a certain abeyance of modesty.
But modesty is the very essence of translation. The greater the poet,
the more loyal should be his servitude to the original; Rilke is servant

to Louise Labé, Roy Campbell to Baudelaire. Without modesty translation will traduce; where modesty is constant, it can, sometimes against its own intent of deference, transfigure.

By contrast, Robert Fitzgerald's *Odyssey* is freely submissive to the voice and aims of the Homeric text. Fitzgerald is taking his place beside Chapman and Pope in the unbroken lineage of English Homeric translations. In many respects he excels them.

Fitzgerald's supreme virtue is to have solved the dilemma of adequate language. Avoiding the obtrusive singularities of Chapman's approach and the mannered archness of T. E. Lawrence, he has developed a mode which is at once neutral and modern, lyric yet full of technical resource. It has many of the qualities of very good prose, being at all times in forward motion and responsive to the claims of precision. But it has the economy and soar of the poet. Written in a flexible blank verse, Fitzgerald's narrative moves with such ease of tread that we often forget the sheer virtuosity of the artisan. And throughout, we have the impression of an idiom that is both our own, yet more stable and refined than the colloquial parlance which mars the Homeric versions of Rieu and Robert Graves:

> Laërtês' son, whose home is Ithaka.
> I saw him weeping, weeping on an island.
> The nymph Kalypso has him, in her hall.
> No means of faring home are left him now;
> no ship with oars, and no ship's company
> to pull him on the broad back of the sea.
> As to your own destiny, Prince Meneláos,
> you shall not die in the bluegrass land of Argos;
> rather the gods intend you for Elysion
> with golden Rhadamanthos at the world's end,
> where all existence is a dream of ease.
> Snowfall is never known there, neither long
> frost of winter, nor torrential rain,
> but only mild and lulling airs from Ocean
> bearing refreshment for the souls of men—
> the West Wind always blowing.

"Bluegrass land" is characteristic. It is not, of course, a precise equivalent to the Homeric epithet; Lawrence's "Argos of the fair horse-pastures" is closer. But Fitzgerald's term, being anchored in our own present terms of reference, is translation in the full rare sense. It re-defines and makes native to our own ground the Homeric vision. Equally deft is Fitzgerald's conveyance of the pastoral close. Chapman is no mean precedent:

> A never-troubled life, where snow, nor showres,
> Nor irksome Winter spends his fruitless powres,
> But from the Ocean Zephyr still resumes
> A constant breath, that all the fields perfumes.

Lawrence comes nearest the actual sound of the Homeric wind; it "sings soft and thrillingly." Yet Fitzgerald alone manages to combine the sensuous with the mythological; in the Greek, *Okeanos* and the West Wind have exactly that embodied presence which Fitzgerald gives them.

No poem is more pervious than the *Odyssey* to the lives of the sea. The roil and hiss of water, the storm rising, and the drowsy calm of the night-swell salt its every line. The diverse tempests which assail Odysseus are a test of the translator's skill, of his practical grasp of what the poem is about. One of the worst storms is recounted in Book XII. Fitzgerald does it full justice:

> We held our course, but briefly. Then the squall
> struck whining from the west, with gale force, breaking
> both forestays, and the mast came toppling aft
> along the ship's length, so the running rigging
> showered into the bilge.
>
> > On the after deck
> the mast had hit the steersman a slant blow
> bashing the skull in, knocking him overside,
> as the brave soul fled the body, like a diver.
> With crack on crack of thunder, Zeus let fly
> a bolt against the ship, a direct hit,
> so that she bucked, in reeking fumes of sulphur,
> and all the men were flung into the sea.
> They came up 'round the wreck, bobbing a while
> like petrels on the waves.
>
> > No more seafaring
> homeward for these, no sweet day of return;
> the god had turned his face from them.

There are details one might argue about. I wonder why Fitzgerald inverts the natural direction of the narrative, "knocking him overside, / as the brave soul fled the body, like a diver." Lawrence is both more obvious and true to Homer: "He dropped from his high platform in one headlong dive, and the brave spirit left his bones." Chapman's dire close is unmatched: "And there the date of their return was out." But taken as a whole, Fitzgerald's is the most vivid and circumstantial of available versions. It has the breathless terror of Odysseus' narrative. It has none of the spurious associations brought in by Lawrence's "brimstone smoke." The terms are beautifully exact without being precious.

Sometimes Fitzgerald adds. In the *Nekuia*, Odysseus' conjuration of the mighty dead in Book XI, occurs a renowned episode. The wraith of Achilles has receded:

> for he had gone off striding the field of asphodel,
> the ghost of our great runner, Akhilleus Aiákidês,
> glorying in what I told him of his son.

Among the thronging shadows one stands aloof, implacable. It is Ajax who went mad after Odysseus bested him in the contest for the arms of the slain Achilles. He cannot forgive:

> but one
> remained alone, apart: the son of Télamon,
> Aîas it was—the great shade burning still. . . .

Nowhere in either Homer or previous translation do we find that sumptuous image. The Greek is perfectly plain: Ajax stands apart because he is still angry, or as Chapman puts it in his gnarled manner: "Only the spirit Telamonian / Kept farre off, angrie for the victorie / I wonne from him." "Burning still" is transfiguration, justified by the implicit metaphor of anger, but fusing with Homer's meaning a new poetry. Dante seems to hover within resonance. But in strong contrast with Lowell's practice, Fitzgerald's addition does not distort or "improve" the original; it augments while remaining strictly concordant with the inward motion and tone of the Greek.

There are many other felicities and solutions one would want to examine in this superb achievement. Fitzgerald's book is a primer in the vexed craft of translation. Teiresias prophesies to Odysseus that he will suffer a gentle, mysterious end. Here is how Fitzgerald renders this famous passage:

> Then a seaborne death
> soft as this hand of mist will come upon you
> when you are wearied out with rich old age.

"Soft as this hand of mist" is not a bad motto for translators.

MASTERS

F. R. LEAVIS

No ceremony. Only a don, spare of voice and stature, but unforgettable in his intensity, leaving a lectern in a Cambridge hall and brushing out the door with a step characteristically lithe and unheeding.

Yet when Dr. Leavis quits Mill Lane for the last time, an era will have ended in the history of English sensibility. No less, perhaps, than that of Wittgenstein or R. H. Tawney, Leavis' retirement, the cessation of his teaching at Cambridge, marks an intricate, controversial chapter in the history of feeling.

That a literary critic should have done so much to reshape the tenor of spirit in his time, that he should have enforced on the development of literary taste much of his own unrelenting, abstract gait—the man walks in the outward guise of his thought—is, of itself, an arresting fact. In the vulgate sense literary criticism is not that important. Most critics feed upon the substance of literature; they are outriders, hangers-on, or shadows to lions. Writers write books; critics write about books in an eternity of second-hand. The distinction is immense. Where criticism endures, it does so either because it is a counterpart to creation, because the poetic force of a Coleridge and a T. S. Eliot gives to their judgment the authority of private experience, or because it marks a signal moment in the history of ideas. The vitalizing power of the *Poetics* is normative; it depends only in minor part on our awareness of the works Aristotle is actually citing. The great mass of criticism is ephemeral, bordering on journalism or straightforward literary history, on a spurt of personal impression scarcely sustained, or on the drab caution of traditional, erudite assent. Very few critics survive in their own right. Those that do—and how many can one add to Dr. Johnson, Lessing, Sainte-Beuve, and Belinsky?—make of criticism an act of pivotal social intelligence. They work outward from the particular literary instance to the far reaches of moral and political argument.

This has been radically the case with Leavis. Writing of *Ulysses*, Ezra Pound declared: "We are governed by words, the laws are graven in words, and literature is the sole means of keeping these words living and accurate." Leavis would add that only criticism can see to it that literature does the job. Behind this vision of criticism as "the central humanity," as the exhibitor and guardian of values which are no less moral and social than they are technical, lies a complex, articulate theory of the critical process.

To Leavis, the critic is the complete reader: "the ideal critic is the ideal reader." He realizes to the full the experience given in the words of the poet or the novelist. He aims at complete responsiveness, at a kind of poised vulnerability of consciousness in the encounter with the text. He proceeds with an attention which is close and stringent, yet also provisional, and at all times susceptible to revaluation. Judgment arises from response; it does not initiate it:

> The critic's aim is, first, to realise as sensitively and completely as possible this or that which claims his attention; and a certain valuing is implicit in the realising. As he matures in experience of the new thing he asks, explicitly and implicitly: "Where does this come? How does it stand in relation to . . . ? How relatively important does it seem?" And the organisation into which it settles as a constituent in becoming "placed" is an organisation of similarly "placed" things, things that have found their bearings with regard to one another, and not a theoretical system or a system determined by abstract considerations.

The critical judgment (the "placing") is put forward with an attendant query: "This is so, isn't it?" And what the critic hopes for is qualified assent, a "Yes, but . . ." which will compel him to re-examine or refine his own response and lead to fruitful dialogue. This notion of dialogue is central to Leavis. No less than the artist—indeed, more so—the critic is in need of a public. Without it the act of ideal reading, the attempt to re-create the work of art in the critical sensibility is doomed to becoming arbitrary impression or mere dictate. There must exist or be trained within the community a body of readers seeking to achieve in vital concert a mature response to literature. Only then can the critic work with that measure of consent which makes disagreement creative. Language itself is a supreme act of community. The poem has its particular existence in a "third realm," at a complex, unstable distance between the poet's private use of words and the shape of these same words in current speech. To be realized critically the work of literature must find its complete reader; but that reader (the critic) can only quicken and verify his response if a comparable effort at insight is occurring somewhere around him.

Such effort bears directly on the fortunes of society. The commanding axiom in Leavis' life-work is the conviction that there is a close relation between a man's capacity to respond to art and his general fitness for humane existence. That capacity can be woken and richened by the critic. Literacy of feeling is a pre-condition to sane judgment in human affairs: "thinking about political and social matters ought to be done by minds of some real literary education, and done in an intellectual climate informed by a vital literary culture." Where a society does not have within it a significant contemporary literature and the parallel exercise of critical challenge, "the 'mind' (and mind includes memory) is not fully alive." In short, Leavis' conception of literary criticism is, above all else, a plea for a live, humane social order.

Hence the tremendous importance he ascribes to the idea of a university. Like Newman (who is one of the really distinctive influences on his style and manner), Leavis regards the ideal university as the root and mold of those energies of spirit which can keep the body-politic functioning in a sane, creative way. All his criticism has sprung from the context of teaching. The words which come at the close of the preface to *Revaluation* are meant literally:

> The debt that I wish to acknowledge is to those with whom I have, during the past dozen years, discussed literature as a "teacher": if I have learnt anything about the methods of profitable discussion I have learnt it in collaboration with them.

If he execrates the "academic mind," losing no occasion to pour upon it the vials of his prophetic scorn, it is because Leavis believes that Oxford and Cambridge, in their present guise, have largely betrayed the true, indispensable functions of teaching. But he has dwelt inside their walls in angry devotion.

Much of the finest in Leavis' performance is unrecapturable, being the sum of a generation of actual teaching, of unstinting commitment to the art of broken discourse between tutor and pupil. Yet his impact extends formidably beyond Downing. He has made a banal academic title inseparably a part of his own name; the Muses have conferred only two doctorates, his and Dr. Johnson's. Like certain writers of narrow, characteristic force, Leavis has set aside from the currency of language a number of words and turns of phrase for his singular purpose. Strong use has made these words nearly his property; *ils portent la griffe du maître:*

> discrimination ... centrality ... poise ... responsibility ... tactics ... enforcement ... realisation ... presentment ... vitalising ... performance ... assent ... robustness ....

"Close, delicate wholeness"; "pressure of intelligence"; "concrete realisation"; "achieved actuality"—are phrases which carry Leavis" signature as indelibly as "high seriousness" bears that of Matthew Arnold.

The list is worth examining. It does not rely on jargon, on the shimmering technical obscurities which mar so much of American New Criticism. It is a spiky, gray, abstract parlance, heavy with exact intent. A style which tells us that Tennyson's verse "doesn't offer, characteristically, any very interesting local life for inspection," or that "Shakespeare's marvelous faculty of intense local realisation is a faculty of realising the whole locally" can be parodied with fearful ease. But what matters is to understand why Leavis "writes badly," why he insists on presenting his case in a grim suet of prose.

His refusal of elegance is the expression of a deep, underlying Puritanism. Leavis detests the kind of "fine" writing which by flash of phrase or lyric surge of argument obscures thinness of meaning or unsoundness of logic. He distrusts as spurious frivolity all that would embroider on the naked march of thought. His manner is easy to parody precisely because there lies behind it so unswerving a preoccupation with the matter in hand, so constant a refusal to be distracted by grace of touch. It has a kind of noble ugliness and points a finger of Puritan scorn at the false glitter of Pater.

But the source of Leavis' style, of that bleak, hectoring, yet ultimately hypnotizing tone, may lie even deeper. One striking fact distinguishes him from all other major critics. So far as I am aware, he has never wished or striven to be a writer—a poet, novelist, or playwright. In the criticism of Dryden, Coleridge, and Arnold, there is an immediate neighborhood of art. In Edmund Wilson there lurks a disappointed novelist. Sainte-Beuve yielded to his critical genius with rage in heart, having failed to match the fiction and lyric verse of his Romantic peers. John Crowe Ransom, R. P. Blackmur, Allen Tate are poets who turned to criticism either in defense or elaboration of their own view of poetry, or when the vein of invention had run dry. In most great critics (perhaps even in Johnson) there is a writer manqué.*

This has two effects. It can make of criticism a minor art, an attempt to achieve, by force of style, something like the novel or drama which the critic has failed to produce successfully. Dryden's *Essay of Dramatic Poesy*, Sainte-Beuve's critical portraits, Edmund Wilson's *To the Finland Station*, have in them strong relics of poetic form. Blackmur's critical essays are often poems arrested. This can produce a grace of persuasion to which Leavis hardly comes near. But he would not wish to. For it can also entail a subtle disloyalty to the critical purpose. Where it becomes a substitute for "creative writing," where it shows the scars of lost dreams, criticism tends towards rhetoric, self-revelation, shapely aphorism. It loses its grip on the objects before it and turns to an unsteady mirror held up by the critic to his own ambitions or humility.

Leavis conveys persistently the absolute conviction that criticism is a central, life-giving pursuit. It need offer no apology for not being something else. Though in a manner radically different from that of the poet, it creates possibilities of apprehension and a consensus of perceived values without which poetry could not be sustained. To see Dr. Leavis at his lectern, compact and indrawn as if wary of some inner challenge, yet richly communicative to his listeners, is to observe a man doing precisely the job he wishes to do. And it is a job he regards as immensely important.

[* This is very obviously true of the past. It may no longer be so. As I try to suggest in other essays in this collection, distinctions between literary *genres* are losing their relevance. Increasingly, the "act of writing" supersedes, in its problematic, self-conscious character, the particular form chosen. The role of the essay and of fact/fiction in present literature suggests that the whole distinction between creation and criticism, between analytic statement and poetic invention, needs rethinking. Both may be, as Roland Barthes says, part of a linguistic totality more significant, more comprehensive, than either.]

What has he made of it?

Unlike Coleridge or Hegel, Leavis has not initiated a formal theory of art; he has not sought to re-define the epistemology of aesthetic judgment. He regards the generalizing, abstract mode of philosophy as sharply distinct from the specific re-creative perception which is the job of the literary critic; philosophic training might lead to

> blunting of edge, blurring of focus and muddled misdirection of attention: consequences of queering one discipline with the habits of another. The business of the literary critic is to attain a peculiar completeness of response and to observe a peculiarly strict relevance in developing his response into commentary; he must be on his guard against abstracting improperly from what is in front of him and against any premature or irrelevant generalizing—of it or from it. . . . There is, I hope, a chance that I may in this way have advanced theory, even if I haven't done the theorizing. I know that the cogency and precision I have aimed at are limited; but I believe that any approach involves limitations, and that it is by recognizing them and working within them that one may hope to get something done.

The "general ideas" behind Leavis' criticism are derived, in large part, from T. S. Eliot, D. H. Lawrence, I. A. Richards, and William Empson. By the time he began his own revaluation of the history of English poetry, Eliot, Ezra Pound, and Robert Graves had already proclaimed the quality of the new. The attitudes which inspired *The Oxford Book of English Verse* to give Donne only as much space as Bulwer Lytton and less than a third as much as Herrick, or which made of Bridges a major figure who had, in munificence of heart, been patron to the eccentric thwarted talent of Hopkins, were already under critical fire. After *Prufrock* and the first Pound and Eliot essays, it was becoming increasingly difficult to regard Tennyson or Swinburne as the sole or pre-eminent forces directing English poetry. A colder air was blowing.

Leavis' reorientation of critical focus—his stress on that lineage of intelligence and realized form which goes from Shakespeare and the Metaphysicals to Pope, Blake, Hopkins, and Eliot—is rooted in the change of sensibility occurring in the 1920's and early '30's.

What he has done is to give that change its most precise and cogent critical justification. His mastery lies not in the general devising, but in the particular instance.

Here there is much that will live among the classic pages of criticism. Wherever one turns in the impressive array of Leavis' writings, one is arrested by the exhilarating presence of an intelligence superbly exact, and having within reach formidable resources of historical and textual knowledge. That intelligence is brought into close, subtle commerce with the poem in an act of total awareness which is, in the best instances, near to art. Leavis is difficult to quote from because the progress of response is so continuous and dense-woven. Yet certain moments do stand out for sheer brilliance and propriety of gathered insight.

The reading of Hopkins' *Spelt from Sibyl's Leaves* (from *New Bearings in English Poetry*) is unusual in that it shows Leavis re-creating the sense and impact of the poem not only by responsive judgment, but by a kind of lyric counterpart:

> The trees are no longer the beautiful refreshing things of daylight; they have turned fantastically strange, hard and cruel, "beak-leaved" suggesting the cold, hard light, steely like the gleam of polished tools, against which they appear as a kind of damascene-work ("damask") on a blade. Then follows the anguished surrender to the realisation:

> . . . Oúr tale, O oúr oracle! | Let life, wáned, ah lét life wind
> Off hér one skéined stained véined varíety | upon áll on twó spools; párt, pen, páck
> Now her áll in twó flocks, twó folds—black, white; | right, wrong . . .

> The run of alliterations, rimes and assonances suggests the irresistible poignancy of the realisation. The poem ends with a terrible effect as of unsheathed nerves grinding upon one another. The grinding might at first be taken to be merely that of "right" against "wrong," the inner conflict of spirit and flesh, and the pain that which the believer knows he must face, the simple pain of renunciation. Yet we are aware of a more subtle anguish and a more desperate plight.

Criticism is, necessarily, comparison. But only a great critic is able to make of the act of preference, of the "placing" of one writer above another, an exercise of equal illumination. The sustained, gradually deepening comparison of Pope and Dryden in *Revaluation* is one of Leavis' master strokes. Setting the *Dunciad* beside *Mac Flecknoe*, Leavis notes that

> above every line of Pope we can imagine a tensely flexible and complex curve, representing the modulation, emphasis, and changing tone and tempo of the voice in reading; the curve varying from line to line and the lines playing subtly against one another. The verse of *Mac Flecknoe*, in the comparison, is both slack and monotonous; again and again there are awkward runs and turns, unconvinced and unconvincing, requiring the injected rhetorical conviction of the declaimer to carry them off.

Yet at once, the qualifying mechanism of Leavis' approach intrudes. The comparison "*is* unfair: Dryden's effects are all for the public ear." Read in a spirit appropriate to their intent, Dryden's satiric poems were "magnificently effective." But the spirit which Pope demands is something different; behind his immediate effects lies an organization finer, more inward than that required or exhibited by Dryden. Indeed, it is his limitations which make of Dryden the "great representative poet of the later seventeenth century." He belongs entirely to the community of reigning taste. There is between him and the sensibility of the time none of the distance, critical or nostalgic, that forces upon Marvell or Pope a greater delicacy of organization: "Dryden is the voice of his age." The whole analysis is masterly; it shows how Leavis reads with what Klee would have called "the thinking eye."

That eye is at work again, though narrowed, in Leavis' examination of Milton's style: "He exhibits a feeling *for* words rather than a capacity for feeling *through* words . . . habituation could not sensitise a medium so cut off from speech—speech that belongs to the emotional and sensory texture of actual living and is in resonance with the nervous system." I believe that Leavis is wrong, that Milton (like Joyce) built of language a realness no less coherent or filled with the roughage of experience than is common speech—but the cogency and challenge of Leavis' case are obvious.

228

No single passage illustrates more compactly the peculiar genius of Leavis' criticism than the close of his essay on Swift:

> It is not merely that he had an Augustan contempt for metaphysics; he shared the shallowest complacencies of Augustan common sense: his irony might destroy these, but there is no conscious criticism.
>
> He was, in various ways, curiously unaware—the reverse of clairvoyant. He is distinguished by the intensity of his feelings, not by insight into them, and he certainly does not impress us as a mind in possession of its experience.
>
> We shall not find Swift remarkable for intelligence if we think of Blake.

The judgment is formidable for comprehensiveness, for coolness and finality of tone, for sheer implication of evidence marshaled and weighed. The "mind in possession of its experience"—here a purely critical note—takes on pertinent, somber precision if we recall that Swift's intellect fell into the literal possession of madness. But there is more: the power of the verdict is gathered in the final touch, in the evocation of Blake, placed so designedly as the last word. The *rapprochement* of Blake and Swift is of itself superb criticism. Here it sets a seal of relative dimension, of comparable but unequal greatness. Only those who have themselves wrestled with the task of trying to say something fresh or perceptive about established classics will fully realize how much there is of preliminary response, of close, unbroken thought, behind Leavis' concise assurance.

Undoubtedly, Leavis' principal achievement is his critique of the English novel. *The Great Tradition* is one of those very rare books of literary comment (one thinks of Johnson's *Lives of the Poets* or Arnold's *Essays in Criticism*) that have re-shaped the inner landscape of taste. Anyone dealing seriously with the development of English fiction must start, even if in disagreement, from Leavis' proposals. Whereas much of what Leavis argued about poetry, moreover, was already being said around him, his treatment of the novel has only one precedent—the essays and prefaces of Henry James. Like James, but with a more deliberate intent of order and completeness, Leavis has brought to bear on the novel that closeness of reading and expectation of form reserved previously for the study of poetry or poetic drama.

229

Now every book reviewer or undergraduate is able to mouth insights about the "stature" of Jane Austen, the "mature art" of George Eliot, or the "creative wealth" of intelligence in *The Portrait of a Lady*. Today it would seem ludicrous or wilfully eccentric to deny that *The Secret Sharer* or *Women in Love* are works of consummate art and classics of imagined life. But the very triumph of it should not make us forget the novelty, the unflinching audacity of Leavis' revaluation. Even where we challenge his list for ranking or omission, our sense of the novel as form, of its responsibility to moral perception and "vivid essential record," is that defined by Leavis' treatment. The assertion that after the decline of the epic and of verse drama the prose novel has concentrated the major energies in Western literature—an assertion put forward provisionally by Flaubert, Turgenev, and James—is now a commonplace. It was not so when Leavis first focused on a chapter in *Middlemarch* or a paragraph in *Nostromo* the same kind of total apprehension exhibited in relation to Shakespeare or Donne. The mere suggestion (at present nearly a cliché) that there is in *Heart of Darkness* a realization of evil comparable to the study of diminishing moral awareness in, say, *Macbeth*, has behind it a revolution in criticism. More than any man except James, Leavis has caused that revolution.

Only in part by his actual writings; the impact has been that of a *persona*. Like Péguy, Leavis has stood out against the climate of the age in a stance of harried isolation, partially real, partially strategic. I remember waiting for those gray, austerely wrapped numbers of *Scrutiny* as one waits for a bottle flung into the sea. Inevitably, by their gray garb, by the angular tightness of print and page, they conveyed the image of a prophet, surrounded by a tiny, imperiled guard of the elect, expounding and disseminating his acrid truths by bent of will and privation. As a schoolboy, I sent in my subscription with a feeling of embarrassed awe, with a sense of conspiratorial urgency, as if there was food and fuel to be bought so as to keep going an enterprise of eminent danger. In a time of fantastic intellectual cheapness, of unctuous pseudo-culture and sheer indifference to values—in the century of the book club, the digest, and the hundred great ideas on the instalment plan—Leavis' "necessary attitude of absolute intransigence" has had an exemplary, moving force. But he has sustained that attitude at a cruel psychological cost.

He has had to define and, in significant measure, create for himself "the Enemy." Like a fabled, heraldic monster, the Enemy

230

has many heads. They include the Sunday papers and *The Guardian* and all dons who write for them; the *Times Literary Supplement*, Mr. Pryce-Jones and his father (who enters the myth of vituperation in an obscure, recurrent fashion); the Third Programme "intellectuals" and the *entourage* of the *New Statesman;* the British Council and *Encounter;* Mr. John Hayward, Professor C. S. Lewis, Lord David Cecil, and all who divide the study and teaching of literature with the pursuit of elegance or science fiction; and, of late, pre-eminent among hydra-heads, C. P. Snow. The Enemy represents cosiness, frivolity, mundane cliques, the uses of culture for mutual adulation or warmth. He incarnates "the currency values of Metropolitan literary society and the associated University milieux." The Enemy creates philosophic giants such as Mr. Colin Wilson in a Sunday morning only to trample on them when the wind turns. He propagates the notion that Virginia Woolf was a major intellect or that the life-blood of English thought pulses in the Athenaeum, in the still waters of All Souls, or in Printing House Square. The Enemy is the Establishment of the mind. His brow is middle and his tone is suave.

Behind this contrived dragon there *is* a certain complex reality. Being geographically compact, English intellectual life is sharply susceptible to the pressures of club and cabal; the artifice of renown can be swiftly conjured or revoked. In small ponds sharks can be made to pass for momentary leviathans. It is also true that there is between the universities and the world of press, magazine, and radio an alliance of brisk vulgarization. An unusual number of academics have a flair for showmanship; too often, ideas which are, in fact, intricate, provisional, and raw to the throat are thrown to the public as if they were bouquets. Watching some of the more brilliant performers at work, one would scarcely suppose that thought and scholarship are a rare, lonely, often self-consuming exercise of the spirit when it is at full, painful stretch. Above all, there is in the English intellectual and artistic establishment a dangerous bias toward personal charm, toward understatement and amateur grace. The judgments of critics and Fellowship electors are too often shadowed by the complex, hardly indefinable yet deep-rooted criteria of social acceptance. The "good chap," the man one would care to dine with, glides smoothly to the top. The awkward, spiky, passionate genius— whether he be a great historian of politics, the inventor of the jet, or the author of *The Rainbow*—fits ill into the soft grooves of the great common room. The corridors of power or official sponsorship are

231

closed to his obtrusive, tactless intensity.

Unquestionably, Leavis has suffered under the bland claw of coterie culture. And he may be right in his fierce, noncomformist belief that the possibilities of a genuinely educated community—a community able to judge and echo what is radical and serious in art— are being constantly eroded by the "near-culture" of the Brains Trust and the Sunday review. At a time when he was already being widely recognized (particularly in America) as the most compelling voice in the teaching of literature, Leavis found among his own university colleagues little but hostility or amused distaste. Like Péguy's *Cahiers de la quinzaine*, which alone match it in sustained integrity and wealth of provocation, *Scrutiny* was made possible by an utter expense of private energy. Unable to pay its contributors, receiving no official support, it was passed under silence by those (*i.e.*, the British Council) who were seeking to define to the world what was most vital in English culture. The first, and so far the only, gathering from its pages was made in America, on a purely private basis, by Eric Bentley.

Yet between these facts and the legend of self and society in which Leavis has encased his spirit there is a wide, tragic gap. As if out of some essential solitude, he has conjured up a detailed melodrama of persecution and neglect, of conspiracy and betrayal. Though surrounded by disciples who ape even what is most ephemeral in his mannerisms, though approached from many lands by those who hear and acclaim him, Leavis clings tenaciously to the mask of the pariah. He alludes to his endurance at Cambridge as a stroke of occult good fortune, as an oversight by the Enemy. He has in the past refused invitations from America lest dark malignity achieve its ends during his absence. Though a number of distinguished critics have been among his students and sought to carry on his own vision (M. Turnell, D. A. Traversi, Marius Bewley, L. C. Knights), there is hardly one with whom Leavis has not broken. Though he claims that he invites no more than qualified, challenging assent, Leavis has come to demand, perhaps unconsciously, complete loyalty to his creed. The merest doubt or deviation is heresy, and is soon followed by excommunication from the kirk. Thus, although he is one of the greatest teachers of the age, he leaves behind few representatives of what is most vital in his manner. There are those who can mimic his lashing tone, his outward austerities and turns of phrase. But like the rows of students who snicker, in drilled fidelity, at every rasping mention of

"Sunday papers," Leavis' immediate followers do him little honor. They merely bark and fang on the heels of his greatness.

But it is not the personal commitment to artificial or obsolete polemics, it is not the charring expense of nerve or intellect that matter. These are sad, demeaning aspects; but they are, in the last analysis, private to Dr. Leavis. What needs alertness is the measure in which Leavis' melodramatic image of his own life and role has bent or corroded his critical judgment. It is this which gives his assault on C. P. Snow what relevance it has.

The Richmond Lecture was an ignoble performance.* In it, Leavis yielded entirely to a streak of obsessed cruelty. Over and over, he proclaimed to his audience that Snow was ignorant, that he knew nothing of literature or history and not much, one gathered, of science. Such attempt to prove by mere repetition is characteristically totalitarian. Though he is personally ignorant of America, Leavis threw out shop-worn clichés about the "emptiness" of American life, about the inhumanity of technological values. One realized, with a painful start, how much of Leavis' arsenal of insight dates back to the mythologies and tactics of the 1930's. Whereas Snow is immensely of the present, responsive in every way to what is new and jarring in our novel condition, Leavis has sought to bring time to a halt in a pastoral, Augustan dream of order.

Leavis accused Snow of using clichés; his own performance was nothing else. Banality followed on banality in dull virulence. He did not even attempt to engage seriously what is crucial in Snow's argument—the sense of a re-alignment in international affairs, the re-definition of literacy to include the syntax of number. Snow is, indeed, trying to be a "new kind of man," if only in that he wishes to be

[* Looking back, one is struck by the underlying political, social significance of the affair. The controversy between Leavis and Snow is, essentially, a controversy over the future shape of life in England. It sets the vision or reactionary utopia of a small, economically reduced but autonomous and humanistically literate England against that of a nation renewed, energized, rationalized according to technological and mass-consumer principles. It is, thus, a debate over the relationship of England both to its own past and to the essentially American present. England's future, the kind of society in which Leavis' and Snow's children will grow up and live—or from which they will emigrate—hinges on the alternative chosen. *Can* England, a small, crowded island, blessed neither by climate nor natural elbow-room for waste, "go modern" without sacrificing irreplaceable amenities of tolerance and humane leisure? But can any of the latter survive effectively if it diminishes too sharply, if it folds inward into a kind of "post-Habsburg" provincialism? These are, I think, the questions underlying the Leavis/Snow debate, and they give to it a dignity far exceeding the obsessive, injurious form of the Richmond Lecture.]

equally and vitally at home in England, Russia, or the United States. Now it could be argued, in a close, discriminating way, that this "new ubiquity" of the imagination jeopardizes those values of narrow, rooted inwardness for which Leavis stands. Though a rearguard action, such counter-statement to Snow would be stimulating. But none was forthcoming; instead of argument came stale insult. On the one hand was "Snow," on the other side were a set of approved clichés—"life," "humane values," "vital intelligence." What had been advertised as a responsible examination of the concept of "the two cultures" dissolved—as so much else in Leavis' recent work has done—into a ceremonial dance before the dark god, D. H. Lawrence.

Leavis' relation to Lawrence has become obsessive. It has passed from rational exposition into a weird self-identification. Lawrence is not only the "greatest English writer of the twentieth century," but a master of life, a prophet by whose teaching alone our society may recapture humane poise and creative fire. That there is much in Lawrence which is monotonous and hysterical, that very few of his works are unflawed by hectoring idiosyncrasies, that there was little in his genius either of laughter or tolerance—these are considerations Leavis can scarcely allow. In a dualistic image, as artificial and shallow as all Manicheism, Leavis opposes Lawrence to all that is inhuman, frivolous, insensitive, or modish in our culture. To query Lawrence, or to propose as Snow has done by his work and example that there are crises of spirit and political fact more actual or different than those dreamt of in *Women in Love*, is to query "life." Yet nothing could be less humane or more devoid of the tact of living encounter than was Leavis' harangue. Hearing it, one was brought up against the stubborn fact that a critic, however great, is barred from certain generosities of imagination to which an artist has title.

The Richmond Lecture and much else that is indefensible in Leavis' late pronouncements may soon be forgotten. But even at its prime, Leavis' criticism exhibits certain grave limitations and quirks. If the scope of his radical accomplishments is to be defined, these too must be noted.

There are the overestimates (particularly in Leavis' early criticism) of such minor talents as Ronald Bottrall or the novelist L. H. Myers. There is the lack of any confrontation, large or sustained, with the poetry of Yeats, a body of work, one would have thought, no less in need of close valuation than that of Eliot or Pound. Like the Augustan critics, Leavis has been most at ease with the poetry in which the pulse of argument and systematic intelligence beats strong. Hence his decisive reading of *Mauberley* but his disinclination to allow for the occasions of pure lyric force, of articulate image, in the parched chaos of Pound's *Cantos*.

With respect to the novel, one's sense of omission is more acute. The case of Dickens is notorious:

> the genius was that of a great entertainer, and he had for the most part no profounder responsibility as a creative artist than this description suggests. . . . The adult mind doesn't as a rule find in Dickens a challenge to an unusual and sustained seriousness. I can think of only one of his books in which his distinctive creative genius is controlled throughout to a unifying and organising significance, and that is *Hard Times*. . . .

The limitation proposed here has always seemed to me restrictive of Leavis, not of Dickens. And the preference of *Hard Times* over such manifestly ampler achievements as *Bleak House* or *Great Expectations* is illuminating. In the main, Dickens is working outside the criteria of organizing awareness and "significance" exhibited in *The Wings of the Dove* or *Nostromo*. But there is another vein of utter seriousness, of seriousness of committed feeling, of vehement imaginative enactment. It is this which Dickens possesses and that makes of him, after Shakespeare, the principal creator of remembered life in English literature.*

Equally suggestive of a limitation in allowed criteria has been Leavis' neglect of Joyce. He has observed in *Ulysses* set pieces of sensuous realization, but has nowhere done justice either to the architectural genius of the book, or to its enrichening and renovation of the language. Leavis has taken over D. H. Lawrence's scorn and misapprehension of Joyce's achievement. By Leavis' own requirements of seriousness and vitalizing moral poise, much in *Dubliners* and *The Portrait of the Artist* should rank high in the tradition. But he has read in the obscuring light of a false distinction. The choice is not Lawrence *or* Joyce. Both are indispensable; and it is Joyce who has

---

[* Dr. Leavis is, reportedly, at work on a full-scale critical study of Dickens' major novels. A number of essays which may be part of this study have already appeared in print. Such a book will not only be of very great interest in itself, but as constituting one of the rare instances in which Dr. Leavis has "revalued" one of his own, and most influential, dismissals.]

done as much as any writer in our age to keep English confident and creative.

Closely related to this imperception of Joyce is Leavis' failure to extend the reach of his criticism to two other novelists, both of them masters of poetic structure and vision. The one is Melville; a lineage of the English novel which can find a central place for James and an important preliminary role for Hawthorne, but which tells us nothing of *Moby Dick* or *Benito Cereno* (a tale to match the finest in Conrad), is necessarily incomplete. Only a full response to Dickens, Melville, and Joyce, moreover, makes possible a just approach to the novelist whom I take to be, after Hardy and Lawrence, the eminent master of modern English fiction—John Cowper Powys. If neither *The Glastonbury Romance* nor *Wolf Solent* (the only book in the language to rival Tolstoy) can find a place in the Great Tradition, it is precisely because their distinctive virtues—lyric, philosophical, stylistic, religious—lie outside the central but narrowing grasp of Leavis' sensibility.

One other great domain lies outside it. Leavis has refused to concern himself, on any but a perfunctory scale, with foreign literature. There is in this refusal a proud scruple. If criticism presumes complete response to a text, complete possession, how can a critic hope to deal maturely with anything but his own language? There is, unquestionably, a stringent honesty in this position. But it can be carried too far. How, for example, could most critics refer to landmarks as dominant, as unavoidable as the Bible, Homer, Dante, or Goethe, if they did not rely, in one or the other instance, on the crutch of translation? And is it not the duty of a critic to avail himself, in some imperfect measure at least, of another language—if only to experience the defining contours of his own?

Leavis' austere concentration may, indeed, have a deeper root. The vision of a nonconformist, morally literate England, of an England in the style of Bunyan, Cobbett, and D. H. Lawrence, informs his critical thought. "Englishness" is in Leavis' interior vocabulary a notion of tremendous positive force; it connotes a specific tone and natural excellence: "in *Rasselas* we have something deeply English that relates Johnson and Jane Austen to Crabbe." Much of the argument against Joyce is conducted in terms of the native as against the eccentric and uprooted. Joyce's experiments with language reflect a "cosmopolitan" sophistication. The veritable genius of English lies nearer home:

236

> This strength of English belongs to the very spirit of
> the language—the spirit that was formed when the Eng-
> lish people who formed it were predominantly rural. . . .
> And how much richer the *life* was in the old, predomi-
> nantly rural order than in the modern suburban world.
> . . . When one adds that speech in the old order was a
> popularly cultivated art, that people talked (so making
> Shakespeare possible) instead of reading or listening to the
> wireless, it becomes plain that the promise of regeneration
> by American slang, popular city-idiom, or the invention of
> *transition*-cosmopolitans is a flimsy consolation for our
> loss.

Written in 1933, this passage has a curious ring; it belongs to that
complex of agrarian autonomism, of *la terre et ses morts*, which
ranges from Péguy and Barrès to Allen Tate and the southern Fugitives in America. Behind it shimmers an historical vision (largely
fanciful) of an older order, rural, customary, moralistic. It is the
vision of men who fought the first World War—as Leavis did, a
Milton in his pocket—only to observe what had been striven for at
inhuman cost decline into the cheap chaos of the 1920's.

Leavis' "critical nationalism," which contrasts so sharply with
the far-ranging humanism of an Edmund Wilson, is an instrument of
great discrimination and power. But it has limiting consequences.
The wide, subtle plurality of modern culture, the interplay of languages and national styles, may be regrettable—but it is a fact. To
"place" Henry James without close reference to Flaubert and Turgenev; to exalt the treatment of politics in *Nostromo* and *Middlemarch* without an attendant awareness of *The Possessed;* to discern
the realization of social nuance in Jane Austen without allowing the
presence in the critical context of Proust—all this is to proceed in an
artifice of isolation. Is it possible to discuss comprehensively the
nature of prose fiction without introducing, at signal stages of the
argument, the realization that Kafka has altered, lastingly, the relations between observed and imagined truth? Could Leavis advance as
far as he does in support of Lawrence, of Lawrence's treatment of
social feeling, if he set *Women in Love* next to *The Brothers Karamazov?*

This resolute provincialism has its counterpart in Leavis' treatment of time. There is scarcely anything written during the past

twenty years that he has found worthy of serious examination. He has abdicated from one of the commanding functions of criticism, which is to apprehend and welcome the new. One has the impression that he cannot forgive Auden for the fact that English verse should have a history after Eliot even as he cannot forgive Snow for suggesting that the English novel should have a future beyond Lawrence. To use an epithet which he himself applies to Johnson, Leavis' criticism has, since 1945, rarely been "life-giving." Dealing with contemporary literature it has pleaded not from love but from scorn.

These are, obviously, major reservations. They accumulate toward the image of a career divided midway by some essential constriction of mood and purpose. Much in the late Leavis exhibits a quality of inhumane unreality (the Richmond Lecture being merely a flagrant instance). The depth of insight is increasingly marred by waspish contempt. There has been no criticism since Rymer's less magnanimous.

It is this which makes any "placing" of Leavis' work difficult and premature. Great critics are rarer than great poets or novelists (though their gift is more distant from the springs of life). In English, Johnson and Coleridge and Matthew Arnold are of the first order. In the excellence of both Dryden and Saintsbury there is an unsteadiness of focus, a touch of the amateur. Among moderns, T. S. Eliot and Edmund Wilson are of this rare company. What of Leavis? One's instinct calls for immediate assent. There is in the sum of his labors a power, a cogency that looms large above what has been polemic and harshly arrogant in the circumstance. If some doubt persists, it is simply because criticism must be, by Leavis' own definition, both central and humane. In his achievement the centrality is manifest; the humanity has often been tragically absent.

ORPHEUS WITH HIS MYTHS: CLAUDE LÉVI-STRAUSS

There can be no doubt of Monsieur Lévi-Strauss's influence on the life of ideas in France. It is, perhaps, second only to that of Sartre. But the exact nature of that influence is not easy to define. Much of Lévi-Strauss's work is highly technical. In their manner of expression and in the range of reference they assume, his more recent writings are exceedingly intricate, almost hermetic. How many among those who invoke Lévi-Strauss's name and what they take to be the method of his thought have, in fact, read *La Pensée sauvage*, the whole of the *Anthropologie structurale*, let alone *Le Cru et le cuit?* The difficulty itself may be part of the spell. As did Bergson, Lévi-Strauss has been able to project a certain tone, a presence nearly dramatic, in a culture which has traditionally seen ideas as highly individualized and which, unlike England, gives to philosophic discussion a public, emotionally sharpened context.

A page of Lévi-Strauss is unmistakable (the two opening sentences of *Tristes tropiques* have passed into the mythology of the French language). The prose of Lévi-Strauss is a very special instrument, and one which many are trying to imitate. It has an austere, dry detachment, at times reminiscent of La Bruyère and Gide. It uses a careful alternance of long sentences, usually organized in ascending rhythm, and of abrupt Latinate phrases. While seeming to observe the conventions of neutral, learned presentation, it allows for brusque personal interventions and asides. Momentarily, Lévi-Strauss appears to be taking the reader into his confidence, *derrière les coulisses*, making him accomplice to some deep, subtle merriment at the expense of the subject or of other men's pretensions in it. Then he

239

withdraws behind a barrier of technical analysis and erudition so exacting that it excludes all but the initiate.

But through his aloof rhetoric, with its tricks of irony and occasional bursts of lyric élan, Lévi-Strauss has achieved a fascinating, sharp-etched individuality. Rejecting the Sartrian view of ordered, dialectical history as yet another myth, as merely another conventional or arbitrary grouping of reality, Lévi-Strauss adds: "*Cette perspective n'a rien d'alarmant pour une pensée que n'angoisse nulle transcendance, fût-ce sous forme larvée.*" The sentence is characteristic in several ways: by its mannered Pascalian concision and syntax; by the implicit identification which Lévi-Strauss makes between his own person and the "abstract concretion" of *une pensée;* but principally by its note of stoic condescension. It is that note, the cool inward and downward look, the arrogance of disenchanted insight, which fascinates Lévi-Strauss's disciples and opponents. As the young once sought to mime the nervous passion of Malraux, so they now seek to imitate the *hauteur* and gnomic voice of the Professor of Social Anthropology at the Collège de France.

In making of anthropology the foundation of a generalized critique of values, Lévi-Strauss follows in a distinctive French tradition. It leads from Montaigne's subversive meditation on cannibals to Montesquieu's *Lettres persanes* and to his use of a comparative study of cultures and mores as a critique of ethical, political absolutism. It includes the large use made by Diderot, Rousseau, and the *philosophes* of travel literature and ethnography, and extends to the moral polemic so carefully plotted in Gide's narratives of his African journeys. The *moraliste* uses "primitive" cultures, personally experienced or gathered at second hand, as a tuning-fork against which to test the discord of his own milieu. Lévi-Strauss is a *moraliste*, conscious in style and outlook of his affinities with Montesquieu and Diderot's *Supplément au Voyage de Bougainville*. The concept does not translate readily into "moralist." It carries a literary, almost journalistic stress which has no immediate analogy with, say, the Cambridge Platonists. The *moraliste* can use fiction, journalism, drama, as did Camus. Or he may, like Lévi-Strauss, work outward from what is, in its origin and technical form, a highly specialized field of interest.

Only the comparative anthropologist and ethnographer are equipped to pass judgment on the solutions which Lévi-Strauss puts forward to complex problems of kinship and totemism, of cultural diffusion and "primitive" psychology. The technical literature which has grown up around the work of Lévi-Strauss is already large. But the bearing of that work on the notion of culture, on our understanding of language and mental process, on our interpretation of history is so direct and novel that an awareness of Lévi-Strauss's thought is a part of current literacy. "Like Freud," remarks Raphaël Pividal, "Claude Lévi-Strauss, while solving special questions, has opened a new road to the science of man."

That road begins with the classic achievement in sociology and social anthropology of Durkheim, Hertz, and Mauss. In the latter's "Essay on Certain Primitive Forms of Classification" (1901–2) we see outlined important aspects of the study of taxonomy and "concrete logic" in *La Pensée sauvage*. As he makes clear in his own "Introduction à l'oeuvre de Marcel Mauss," it is to Mauss's way of thinking about kinship and language, and above all to Mauss's *Essai sur le don* of 1924, that Lévi-Strauss owes certain assumptions and methodologies which inform his entire work. It is in this essay that Mauss puts forward the proposition that kinship relations, relations of economic and ceremonial exchange, and linguistic relations are fundamentally of the same order.

Beginning with his paper on structural analysis in linguistics and in anthropology (*Word*, 1945) and his first full-scale treatise, *Les Structures élémentaires de la parenté* in 1949, Lévi-Strauss has made this conjecture of essential identity the core of his method and world-view. Examining a specific problem of kinship nomenclature and marital taboos, Lévi-Strauss argues that the evidence can only be sorted out if the women exchanged in marriage are regarded as a *message*, allowing two social groups to communicate with each other and to establish a vital economy of rational experience. Beginning with the particular instance, Lévi-Strauss has elaborated the view that all cultural phenomena are a language. Hence the structure of human thought and the complex totality of social relations can be studied best by adopting the methodology and discoveries of modern linguistics. What political economy is to the Marxist concept of history (the circumstantial, technical basis underlying an essentially metaphysical and teleological argument), the work of Saussure, Jakobson, M. Halle, and the modern school of structural linguistics is to Lévi-Strauss.

As summarized in the chapters on "Language and Kinship" in the *Anthropologie structurale*, Lévi-Strauss's image of culture can be expressed, quite literally, as a syntax. Through our understanding of this syntax particular rites, processes of biological and economic exchange, myths and classifications as they are set forth in native speech may be analyzed into "phonemes" of human behavior. This analysis will disclose the true interrelations of otherwise disparate or even contradictory elements, for like structural linguistics Lévi-Strauss's anthropology regards as axiomatic the belief that each element of social and psychological life has meaning only in relation to the underlying system. If we lack knowledge of that system, the particular signs, however graphic, will remain mute.

Speaking to the Conference of Anthropologists and Linguists held at the University of Indiana in 1952, Lévi-Strauss evoked the ideal of a future "science of man and of the human spirit" in which both disciplines would merge. Since then he has gone farther, and it is hardly an exaggeration to say that he regards all culture as a code of significant communication and all social processes as a grammar. According to Lévi-Strauss, only this approach can deal adequately with the question asked in each of his major works: how do we distinguish between nature and culture, how does man conceive of his identity in respect of the natural world and of the social group?

The actual way in which Lévi-Strauss applies the tools of structural linguistics, or, more precisely, the analogue of linguistics, to deal with problems of kinship, totemism, and ecology among the Indian peoples of North America and the Amazon basin has been much debated. The attack of George C. Homans and David M. Schneider on *Les Structures élémentaires de la parenté* (*Marriage, Authority, and Final Causes*, 1955) has been met in Rodney Needham's *Structure and Sentiment* (1962). A more subtle critique is argued in E. R. Leach's fascinating paper on Lévi-Strauss in the *Annales* for November-December 1964. Dr. Leach shows how strongly Lévi-Strauss's "linguistics of culture" reflect the techniques and logical presuppositions of contemporary information theory and linear programming. Myths and behavior patterns in primitive society store and transmit vital information as does the electronic circuit and magnetic tape in the computer. Lévi-Strauss regards mental and social processes as fundamentally binary, as coded in sets of positive and negative impulses, finally balancing out in an equation of belief or folk custom which is at once harmonious and economic. Hence the binary elements which seem to govern so much of his argument: animality / humanity, nature / culture, wet / dry, noise / silence, raw / cooked. But, as Dr. Leach points out, the binary is not the only or necessary system of relations and information coding. Analogue computers perform tasks which digital computers are not suited for. In particular, says Dr. Leach, the matrices which Lévi-Strauss sets up to tabulate linguistic-ethnic relations, or totemic and mythical conventions, do not allow for gradations of value, for partial choices between alternatives which are not unambiguously positive or negative.

This is a controversy from which the layman would do well to abstain. What is striking are the rich suggestions which Lévi-Strauss's "meta-linguistics" bring to a general theory of culture, to poetics and psychology. In the *Anthropologie structurale*, for example, we find the notion that our civilization treats language with immoderation, wasting words in a persistent recourse to speech. Primitive cultures tend to be parsimonious: "verbal manifestations are often limited to prescribed circumstances, outside which words are used only sparingly." And it is characteristic of Lévi-Strauss's ironic moralism that the discussion of the grammar of marriage in primitive cultures—words and women being set in analogy as media of communication—should end with the aphorism: "*A l'inverse des femmes, les mots ne parlent pas.*"

Increasingly, the thought of Lévi-Strauss can be understood as part of that revaluation of the nature of language and symbolism whose antecedents may be traced to Vico and Liebniz, but whose most radical effects have been modern. No less than Wittgenstein's *Tractatus*, *La Pensée sauvage* and *Le Cru et le cuit* infer that man's place in reality is a matter of syntax, of the ordering of propositions. No less than Jung, Lévi-Strauss's studies of magic and myth, of totemism and *logique concrète*, affirm that symbolic representations, legends, image-patterns, are means of storing and conceptualizing knowledge, that mental processes are collective because they reproduce fundamental structural identities.

Where "domestic" and scientific thought strives toward the economy of a single code, "savage" thought is a semantic system perpetually regrouping itself and rearranging the data of the empirical world without reducing the number of discrete elements. Scientific methodology is obviously different from the "concrete logic" of primitive peoples. But not necessarily better or more advanced. Lévi-Strauss insists that "the science of the concrete" is a second major way of apprehending nature and natural relations. He argues that the great achievements of neolithic man—pottery, the weaving of cloth, agriculture, the domestication of animals—cannot have been the result of hazard or randomly perceived example. These brilliant "conquests" which "remain the substratum of our civilization" are the product of a science different from ours, but continuing a parallel life of its own. If magic had not proved to be a supple and coherent mode of perception, why should science in the experimental-deterministic sense have begun so late in man's history?

Lévi-Strauss does not see history as a case of linear progression (this is the crux of his debate with Hegelianism and Sartre's dialectical historicism). By making of history a transcendental value, a concealed absolute, Sartre excludes a major part of past and contemporary humanity from the pale of significant experience. Our sense of history, with its dates and implicit forward motion, is a very special, arbitrary reading of reality. It is not natural but culturally acquired. Chronology is an ever-changing code. The grid of dates we use for pre-history is based on an entirely different scheme of values and admissible data than the grid we use to conceptualize the period from, say, 1815 to the present. It is of the essence of primitive thought to be *intemporelle* (timeless, untimely), to conceive of experience in simultaneous and partial *imagines mundi*. But as Lévi-Strauss observes, such a mental praxis may not be unrelated to the world-picture of quantum mechanics and relativity.

Since *Tristes tropiques* (1955), if not before, Lévi-Strauss has done little to mask the general philosophic and sociological implications of his technical pursuits. He knows that he is arguing a general theory of history and society, that his specific analyses of tribal customs or linguistic habits carry an exponential factor. Of late, as if by some instinct of inevitable rivalry, he has challenged Sartre and the relevance of the existentialist dialectic. This may, in part, reflect the circumstances of contemporary French intellectual life. More pervasive has been Lévi-Strauss's concern to delimit his own thought from that of the two principal architects of rational mythology, Marx and Freud. His work is in frequent self-conscious dialogue with theirs.

One of the crucial statements occurs in the opening, autobiographical section of *Tristes tropiques* (in their ironic, detached intimacy, these chapters recall *The Education of Henry Adams*, and it is Adams' fastidious agnosticism which Lévi-Strauss's own posture most resembles). Unfortunately, the entire argument is of extreme concision and difficulty. Lévi-Strauss records his initiation to Marxism at about the age of seventeen:

> a whole world was revealed to me. Since which time, my passionate interest has never lapsed; and I rarely concentrate on unravelling a problem of sociology or ethnology without having, beforehand, braced my thought by reading some pages of the *18th Brumaire of Louis Bonaparte* or of the *Critique of Political Economy*.

Marx has taught us

> to build a model, to study its properties and the different ways in which it reacts in the laboratory, in order to apply these observations to the interpretation of empirical data which may be far removed from what one had foreseen.

(This is, one should note, a rather curious gloss on Marx, making of his concrete historicism an almost abstract phenomenology.)

In the *Anthropologie structurale*, Lévi-Strauss cites Marx's well-known remark that the value of gold as repository and medium of wealth is not only a material phenomenon, but that it also has symbolic sources as "solidified light brought up from the nether world," and that Indo-Germanic etymology reveals the links between precious metals and the symbolism of colors. "Thus," says Lévi-Strauss, "it is Marx himself who would have us perceive and define the symbolic systems which simultaneously underlie language and man's relations to the world." But he goes on to suggest, and this is the crux, that Marxism itself is only a partial case of a more general theory of economic and linguistic information and exchange-relations. This theory will be the framework of a truly rational and comprehensive sociology of man. Not surprisingly, the Marxists have challenged the "totalitarian" claims of Lévi-Strauss's "science of man" and have attacked its irrationalist, "anti-historical" aspects (the general issues are carefully set out in Lucien Sebag's *Marxisme et Structuralisme*).

In *Tristes tropiques*, Lévi-Strauss relates Marxism to the two other main impulses in his own intellectual development and conception of ethnography: geology and psychoanalysis. All three pose the same primary question: "that of the relation between the experienced and the rational (*le sensible et le rationnel*), and the aim pursued is identical: a kind of super-rationalism seeking to integrate the former with the latter without sacrificing any of its properties." Which may be a very abstract way of saying that Marxism, geology, and psychoanalysis are aetiologies, attempts to trace the conditions of society, of physical environment, and of human consciousness, to their hidden source. Social relations, terrain, and collective imaginings or linguistic forms are, in turn, the primary coordinates of Lévi-Strauss's *étude de l'homme*.

As Lévi-Strauss advances more deeply into his own theory of symbolism and mental life, the Freudian analogues grow more obtrusive and, probably, irritating. Hence the sporadic but acute critique of psychoanalysis throughout the *Anthropologie structurale*, the argument that Freudian therapy, particularly in its American setting, does not lead to a treatment of neurotic disturbance but to "a reorganization of the universe of the patient in terms of psychoanalytic interpretations." Hence also, one may suppose, Lévi-Strauss's determination to appropriate the Oedipus motif to a much larger context than that put forward by Freud. In Lévi-Strauss's ethnic-linguistic decoding of the legend, and of its many analogues among the North American Indians, the primary meaning points to the immense intellectual and psychological problem faced by a society which professes to believe in the autochthonous creation of man when it has to deal with the recognition of the bisexual nature of human generation. The Oedipus motif does not embody individual neurosis, but a collective attempt to regroup reality in response to fresh and perplexing insights. Again, as in the case of Marxism, the Freudian theory of consciousness emerges as a valuable, but essentially specialized and preliminary chapter in a larger anthropology.

How does *Le Cru et le cuit* fit into this powerful construct? It is a detailed, highly technical analysis of certain motifs in the mythology of the Indians of the Amazon, more exactly, in the creation myths of the Bororo and Ge peoples. The first volume is the start of a projected series and deals with one sub-topic of the larger binary unit: nature/culture. This sub-topic is the discrimination between raw and cooked foods as reflected in Indian myths and practices. Starting with one Bororo "key-myth," Lévi-Strauss analyses significant elements in 187 Amazonian legends and folk-tales; by means of complex geographical, linguistic, and topical matrices, he shows that these myths are ultimately interrelated or congruent. The argument leads to the proposition that the discovery of cooking has profoundly altered man's conception of the relationship between heaven and earth.

Before the mastering of fire, man placed meat on a stone to be warmed by the rays of the sun. This habit brought heaven and earth, man and the sun into intimate juxtaposition. The discovery of cooking literally set back the sphere of the gods and of the sun from the habitat of man. It also separated man from the great world of animals who eat their food raw. It is thus an immensely important step in the metaphysical, ecological, psychic severance of the genus *Homo sapiens* from his cosmic and organic surroundings. That severance (there are definite echoes from Freud's *Beyond the Pleasure Principle* and *Civilization and its Discontents*) leads to the differentiation and strenuous confrontation between the natural and cultural stages of human development.

But the design of the book reaches beyond even this large theme. To what Lévi-Strauss defines as the "primary code" of human language and the "secondary code" of myths, *Le Cru et le cuit* aims to add "a tertiary code, designed to ensure that myths can be reciprocally translated. This is why it would not be erroneous to regard this book itself as a myth: in some manner, the myth of mythology."

The formula is lapidary and obscure, but the idea itself is not new. It crops up in Giordano Bruno, in Bacon's *De Sapientia Veterum* in which myths or "fables" are regarded as a transparent veil occupying "the middle region that separates what has perished from what survives," and in Vico. Lévi-Strauss is seeking a science of mythology, a grammar of symbolic constructs and associations allowing the anthropologist to relate different myths as the structural linguist relates phonemes and language systems. Once the code of myths is deciphered and is seen to have its own logic and translatability, its own grid of values and interchangeable significants, the anthropologist will have a tool of great power with which to attack problems of human ecology, of ethnic and linguistic groupings, of cultural diffusion. Above all, he may gain insight into mental processes and strata of consciousness which preserve indices (the fossils or radioactive elements of the palaeontologist and geologist) of the supreme event in man's history—the transition from a primarily instinctual, perhaps pre-linguistic condition to the life of consciousness and individualized self-awareness. This, and the flowering of human genius and "concrete logic" during the neolithic era are, for Lévi-Strauss, realities of history far more important than the brief adjunct of turmoil and political cannibalism of the past 3000 years.

Proceeding from the linguistic axiom that all elements in a

complex system are related, and that their sense can be derived only from an analysis of their interrelations, of the place which the unit can occupy in the set, Lévi-Strauss weaves a host of apparently disparate Amazonian and North American hunt- and creation-myths into a unified pattern. In the course of the argument, he seeks to demonstrate that successive variants of a myth cannot be discarded as irrelevant, that the sum of related tales is a living aggregate, a code of cultural reinterpretation in which single elements are regrouped but not lost (the analogy being that of mathematical topology which studies those relations that remain constant when configurations change). The result is a kind of moiré pattern which we learn to read as the physicist reads superimposed photographs of cloud-chamber particles.

Philosophically and methodologically, Lévi-Strauss's approach is rigorously deterministic. If there is law in the world of the physical sciences, then there is one in that of mental processes and language. In the *Anthropologie structurale*, Lévi-Strauss presages a time when individual thought and conduct will be seen as momentary modes or enactments "of those universal laws which are the substance of the human unconscious" (*des lois universelles en quoi consiste l'activité inconsciente de l'esprit*). Similarly, *Le Cru et le cuit* concludes with the suggestion of a simultaneous, reciprocal interaction between the genesis of myths in the human mind and the creation by these myths of a world-image already pre-determined (one might say "programmed") by the specific structure of human mentality. If human life is, basically, a highly developed form of cybernetics, the nature of the information processed, of the feedback and of the code, will depend on the particular psychosomatic construct of the mental unit. Digital computers and analogue computers may learn to have different dreams.

Once more, the substance and empirical solidity of Lévi-Strauss's case can be judged only by the qualified anthropologist (is he right about this or that aspect of Bororo life and language?). But the general implications are wide-ranging. This is particularly true of the first thirty pages of *Le Cru et le cuit*, entitled "Ouverture." They constitute the richest, most difficult piece of writing Lévi-Strauss has produced so far. It is not easy to think of any text as tightly meshed, as bristling with suggestion and fine intricacy of argument since the *Tractatus*. At various points, in fact, the themes of the two works come into contact.

248

Some of the difficulty seems gratuitous. There is hardly a proposition in these opening pages which is not qualified or illustrated by reference to mathematics, histology, optics, or molecular chemistry. Often a single simile conjoins several allusions to different scientific concepts. Looked at closely, however, a good many of the scientific notions invoked are elementary or vaguely pretentious. How much mathematics does Lévi-Strauss really know or need to know? But this constant use of mathematical and scientific notations points to a much larger and more urgent motif. In "Ouverture" Lévi-Strauss is articulating a radical distrust of language. A theme which has been latent in much of his work now comes to the fore: set against the pure syntax and tautological efficiencies of mathematics, of symbolic logic, and of scientific formulas, traditional discourse is no longer a predominant or wholly satisfactory medium. By universalizing structural linguistics, Lévi-Strauss is, in fact, diminishing the unique genius and central authority of common speech. As storehouses and conveyors (the vacuum tube and the electronic impulse) of felt life and human conjecture, myths embrace words but go beyond them toward a more supple, inventive, universal syntax.

Yet even they fall short of the "supreme mystery among the sciences of man" which is music. That arresting formula concludes a dazzling rhetorical flight in which Lévi-Strauss contends that "to think mythologically" is to think musically. Wagner has proved the quintessential kinship of myth and musical statement. Among all languages, only music "unites the contrary attributes of being both intelligible and untranslatable." It is, moreover, intelligible to all—a fact which makes "the creator of music a being similar to the gods."

In consequence, *Le Cru et le cuit* is given the formal structure of a piece of music: overture, theme and variations, sonata, fugue, three-part invention, rustic symphony in three movements. The conceit is not new: one finds it in Baudelaire's theory of "correspondance" (to which Lévi-Strauss implicitly refers), in Mallarmé, and in Broch's *Death of Virgil*, a novel divided in analogy with the changes of mood and rhythm in a string quartet. Lévi-Strauss does little, moreover, to enforce the musical mimesis. It remains a rather labored *jeu d'esprit*. But the underlying concept has a deep fascination. The idea that music and myth are akin, that they build shapes of being more universal, more numinous than speech, haunts the Western imagination. It is incarnate, as Elizabeth Sewell has shown, in the figure of Orpheus. He is myth himself and master of life through his power to create harmony amid the inertness of primal silence or the ferocity of discord (the fierce beasts pause and listen). His presence—order and perception as the condition of the mind when that condition is nearest music—is discernible in Pythagorean doctrine and in Bacon's *Magna Instauratio;* it has the energy of living myth in Rilke and Valéry. In its celebration of music and mathematics, in its proud obscurity and claim to be itself a myth unfolding, a song of the mind, *Le Cru et le cuit* is, in the literal sense, an Orphic book. Would that its opening measures were quoted from a stronger source than Emmanuel Chabrier's *À la musique.*

Le Cru et le cuit is work in progress, and it would be fatuous to pass any general judgment on the complex ensemble of Lévi-Strauss's achievement to this date. That it is one of the most original and intellectually exciting of the present age seems undeniable. No one seriously interested in language or literature, in sociology or psychology, can ignore it. At the same time, this newest book exhibits to a disturbing degree characteristics latent in Lévi-Strauss's work, certainly since the early 1950's. It is prolix, often arbitrary, and maddeningly precious (a technical discussion of the relations between Amazonian myths and the zodiac is entitled *"L'Astronomie bien tempérée"*). The argument is decked out with an apparatus of pseudo-mathematical notations which appears to carry more weight and relevance than it actually does. At times, the hard astringent scruple of Lévi-Strauss's best style yields to an odd, post-romantic lyricism (Chabrier after Satie). It is as if the prophet were pausing to draw his mantle close.

Perhaps this is both the genius and the danger of the enterprise. It is not, primarily, as anthropology or ethnography that this fascinating body of work may come to be judged and valued, but as extended poetic metaphor. Like so much in Marx and Freud, the achievement of Lévi-Strauss may endure, to use a term from *La Pensée sauvage*, as part of "the mythology of our time." It is too early to tell; *Le Cru et le cuit* ends with a catalogue of myths, not with a coda.

ON READING MARSHALL
MCLUHAN

This is not an easy thing to do. The writings of Marshall McLuhan are so compounded of novelty, force of suggestion, vulgarity of mind, and sheer carelessness that one is quickly tempted to put them aside. Many aspects of his success represent modern journalism at its most obvious. The McLuhan cult is characteristic of those confidence tricks of "high journalism" which, perhaps more than any other force, deafen and cheapen the life of ideas. Yet all this is part of the point: the question of how to read McLuhan, of whether reading him is in itself an obsolescent mode of contact, is implicit in McLuhan's own work. The crises of relationship between traditional literacy and the hypnotic mendacities of the mass-media are exactly those to which McLuhan himself applies his rhetorical, confused, but often penetrating attention. "Better written," McLuhan's books and essays would be false to their implications. A McLuhan too fastidious or ironic to make use of the advertising powers of the mass-circulation magazines or the television interview would be negating his own principal argument. He sets his readers a perpetual, irritating problem: that of reading any further. But that is his master stroke: by making of his manner a close representation of the anomalies which he observes in the act of reading, in the essential nature of human communication, McLuhan draws us into his argument. To put him down is to let that argument pass unchallenged.

Until now, *The Gutenberg Galaxy* remains his most important statement. *Understanding Media*, a good deal of which gives the impression of having been written, or rather jotted down, earlier is a set of variants on the *Galaxy*. McLuhan's initial, often brilliant study of controlled imagery and messages in the mass-media, *The Mechanical Bride*, can now be seen as a preliminary essay. It is in *The Gutenberg Galaxy* that both the virtues and failures of his method can be fairly judged.

The book bristles with oracular assertions: "China and India are still audile-tactile in the main"; Russia, "where spying is done by ear and not by eye," is still "profoundly oral." The Chinese ideograph "is a complex *Gestalt* involving all the senses at once." The Germans and Japanese, "while far-advanced in literate and analytic technology, retained the core of auditory tribal unity and total togetherness." Numerous pronouncements have a majestic simple-mindedness:

> The miseries of conflict between the Eastern and Roman churches, for example, are a merely obvious instance of the type of opposition between the oral and the visual cultures, having nothing to do with the Faith.

Some statements are slipshod; "the Koreans are reputed to have a phonetic alphabet"; others are false: "the Viennese musician Carl Orff." The bibliography is eccentric. An accurate notion of the Babylonian and Greek treatment of volumes and spatial relations is vital to McLuhan's theory; yet he discloses no awareness of Neugebauer. More disturbing is the nervous cheapness of McLuhan's prose—language being the very matter of his concern. He tells us of woman's "haptic bias, her intuition, her wholeness":

> What a fate, to be integral and whole in a fragmented and visual flatland! But the homogenization of women was finally effected in the twentieth century after the perfection of photo-engraving permitted them to pursue the same course of visual uniformity and repeatability that print had brought to men. I have devoted an entire volume, *The Mechanical Bride*, to this theme.

Referring to Professor Mircea Eliade's *The Sacred and the Profane*, McLuhan questions "the quality of insight that causes a human voice to quaver and resonate with hebdomadal vehemence." Used in this (non)-sense, *hebdomadal* is a real comic find.

It would be easy to anatomize *The Gutenberg Galaxy* in this way: easy and stupid. Many of the irritants, many of the crudities of presentment which exasperate or bewilder, are strategic. *The Gutenberg Galaxy* is an anti-book. It seeks to enforce, physically, the core of its own meaning. Its bearing on traditional modes of philosophic-historical argument is deliberately subversive. It is precisely part of McLuhan's achievement that we should be irked and affronted by the strangeness or inadequacy of his resources. He is saying to us, in a verbal mime which often descends to jugglery but also exhibits an intellectual leap of great power and wit, that books—a linear progression of phonetic units reproduced by movable type—are no longer to be trusted. He is retreating rapidly from the word. And because the classic verbal medium is inimical or irrelevant to McLuhan's purpose, his argument is difficult to follow. But the effort yields reward. Marshall McLuhan posits that Western civilization has entered, or is about to enter, an era of electro-magnetic technology. This technology will radically alter the milieu of human perception, the reality-coordinates within which we apprehend and order sense data. Experience will not present itself serially, in atomized or linear patterns of causal sequence, but in "fields" or simultaneous interaction. To offer a very crude analogy (and the process of analogy may itself be a vestige of an earlier logic), our categories of immediate perception will shift from those at work in an Ingres drawing to those we experience in a Jackson Pollock.

But we are unready to master the new spontaneity, randomness, and "totalization" of the electronic experience-field, because print, and all the habits of feeling and thought print has grafted on the Western mind, have broken the creative, primal unity of the senses. By translating *all* aspects of the world into the code-language of *one* sense only—the reading eye—the printing press has hypnotized and fragmented Western consciousness. We lie rigid in what Blake called "Newton's sleep."

Yet obscure promptings bid us wake. Hence the present malaise, that feeling as sharp-edged in Klee and in Kafka as it is in the ferocities or pointlessness of our politics, that Western man is no longer at home in the world:

> We are today as far into the electric age as the Elizabethans had advanced into the typographical and mechanical age. And we are experiencing the same confusions and indecisions which they had felt when living simultaneously in two contrasted forms of society and experience. Whereas the Elizabethans were poised between medieval corporate experience and modern individualism, we re-

verse their pattern by confronting an electronic technology which would seem to render individualism obsolete and the corporate interdependence mandatory.

McLuhan's reading of ancient and medieval history is related to Nietzsche's indictment of Socrates and Henry Adams' vision of a golden age of unified sensibility. He argues that the phonetic alphabet began the fatal dissociation between the senses, that it splintered individual consciousness from the creative immediacy of collective response:

> Only the phonetic alphabet makes a break between eye and ear, between semantic meaning and visual code; and thus only phonetic writing has the power to translate man from the tribal to the civilized sphere. . . . Nor is this to give any new meaning or value to "civilization" but rather to specify its character. It is quite obvious that most civilized people are crude and numb in their perceptions, compared with the hyperesthesia of oral and auditory cultures. For the eye has none of the delicacy of the ear.

The printing press and the associated development of the conventions of perspective (precisely what *is* the correlation between these two great steps?) have made our apprehension and use of sense data explicitly linear, sequential, discrete. We are imprisoned in the unexamined assumption or unconscious illusion of a homogeneous, forward-flowing space-time continuum. Our notion of the categories of past and future is mechanistic, as if the universe were itself a printed book and we were turning the pages. The vast majority of literate men are unable to cope, sensorily or imaginatively, with the new "vitalistic" space-time concepts of Einsteinian physics and electro-magnetic field theory. Hence the widening gap between the picture of physical reality on which we base our lives, and the mathematical-statistical image proposed by the natural sciences: "The new physics is an auditory domain and long-literate society is not at home in the new physics, nor will it ever be." The fascinating concomitant is the possibility that "primitive" cultures will find it much easier to work with concepts of indeterminacy or with the idea that space is altered by the quality of neighboring events.

Print helped to initiate and formalize the economic ambitions of Renaissance Europe. It gave spur to the new forces of nationalism and cultural arrogance. McLuhan conjectures that movable type "enabled men to *see* their vernacular for the first time, and to visualize national unity and power in terms of the vernacular bounds: 'We must be free or die who speak the tongue that Shakespeare spoke.'" The world-image codified by typography made of Western man a unit at once impersonal and private, unique and repeatable. In that light the modern city, the warren of crowded solitudes, is a product and expression of the Gutenberg galaxy. We move through it scarcely calling on the manifold, subtle functions of ear, nose, or touch; when we die, our name survives for a spell in the typographical pantheon of the telephone directory.

By its exclusive stress on visual order, on Cartesian logic and abstract nomenclature, the Gutenberg mode of perception has divided and sub-divided the categories of action and knowledge. The Baconian dream of a total, rational classification, of a universal taxonomy, in which every art, science, and technology would have its distinct place, is emblematic of a typographic sensibility (Miss Elizabeth Sewell's study of Bacon in *The Orphic Voice*, a profoundly exciting though neglected book, is relevant here). The dissociation of sensibility which T. S. Eliot discerns in post-metaphysical poetry was merely one tactical aspect of that larger intellectual attempt to conquer all knowledge through division.

But already, as McLuhan suggests, we are moving into a phase of creative disorder; everywhere the lines are blurred. Physics and biology have reached outside their classic bounds; the important work is being done within the shifting, undogmatic contours of "middle-fields" such as biochemistry, molecular biology, or physical chemistry. A Calder mobile asks of us, as it might of Aristotle or Lessing, why statues should not move. Novels are presented as loose pages, randomly gathered in a folder; we may, if we choose, arrange the narrative in varying sequence. Elements of improvisation and calculated hazard are being introduced into modern music; an orchestral statement has been described as a "cluster of possible simultaneous tonal occurrences." In the book of modern life (a Gutenberg simile) the hinges are loosening. But where Yeats saw the coming of "mere anarchy," Marshall McLuhan speaks of "the greatest of all human ages" resulting from "this dramatic struggle of unlike modes of human insight and outlook." Beyond the present chaos lies the possibility of "new configurations" of perception; man's dormant senses, his powers of integration, the chthonic, magic fiber of his being, will be liberated from the closed, passive system of Gutenberg literacy. Else a great prince in prison lies.

These are the main lines of McLuhan's case. The obvious objection is a matter of cart before horse. What evidence is there that printing and the typographical world-order were the cause rather than the technically inevitable consequence of the specialization and diminution of sensibility? Can we assert, except by Romantic, utopian convention, that the era of oral and manuscript communication possessed the gift of integrated perception? The Henry Adams-T. S. Eliot myth of a twelfth- or a seventeenth-century organic unity is not much more than a useful metaphor. It sharpens our alertness to some of our own difficulties and limitations; but there is no very solid evidence for it. In many respects the medieval community was as fragmented, as riven by doubt and economic antagonisms as any we have knowledge of. If Dante or Donne could extend their poetic reach to a more comprehensive range of experience, it was because the sum of available matter was smaller and because words could give a more inclusive, adequate map of reality. Today we confront a topography of experience in which the word occupies only a central precarious domain; on each side lie the provinces of number.

Historically it is likely that the phonetic alphabet and the development of movable type (a technical, not a metaphysical innovation) were themselves the end-process of a long evolution. The syntax and structure of the Indo-Germanic languages are strongly disjunctive; the bias toward logical stylization, toward linear progression and analytic delimitation, is rooted in the morphology of our speech-patterns. It obviously antedates not only Gutenberg but also the adoption, by pre-classical Greece, of the Phoenician alphabet. Moreover, it may well be that those forms of aural mass-communication which McLuhan regards as heralding the new age have, in fact, persisted beneath the surface of visual literacy. Where McLuhan assumes a Spenglerian sequence of historical epochs, there is most probably an overlapping simultaneity of mental habits and techniques.

But even if one balks at the general argument, the local insights of *The Gutenberg Galaxy* are rewarding. This book has a Coleridgean breadth. McLuhan points out that the notion of private ownership of ideas and words—the notion of plagiarism and the correlative of acknowledged citation—only evolve with the printed text. His own use of a cluster or mosaic of long quotations is meant to illustrate an earlier attitude, a " collectivity" of truth. He points acutely to the source of the characteristic problems and symbolic proceedings of contemporary philosophy:

> As our age translates itself back into the oral and auditory modes because of the electronic pressure of simultaneity, we become sharply aware of the uncritical acceptance of visual models and metaphors by many past centuries.

An apt quotation from Hopkins' letters leads to a discussion of how much major literature—poetry in particular—was never intended for silent perusal by the private eye, but demands recital and the live friction of voice and ear. Though Mr. McLuhan's reading of *King Lear* is absurdly unconvincing, he has fascinating marginalia on Rabelais, Cervantes, Pope, and Joyce. He describes *Gargantua*, *Don Quixote*, the *Dunciad*, and *Finnegans Wake* as the "four massive myths of the Gutenberg transformation of society." Looked at closely, the idea seems beautifully right. Might one add Swift's *Tale of a Tub* and, as myth of the combat between ideogram and letter, Elias Canetti's *Auto-da-fé*?

Indeed, it is often in the throw-away suggestion, in the local perception, that McLuhan is most interesting. Nothing is more Blakeian in quality of vision than the notion, hinted at in *Understanding Media*, of a world falling silent as electronic means of storage and appropriate selection replace the spendthrift chaos of traditional writing and human speech. Like Ernst Bloch, like Lévi-Strauss, McLuhan has the capacity to materialize his theoretic arguments in sudden myth. He too is one of those shapers of the present mood who seem to mark a transition from the classic forms of Cartesian order to a new, as yet very difficult to define, poetic or syntax of experience. It is quite possible that McLuhan's own sermons will soon be rejected as chaotic and self-contradictory; but the process of rejection will almost certainly be creative of new insight. That, and not any academic canon of definitiveness, is the mark of significant work.

FICTIONS AND
THE PRESENT

MÉRIMÉE

S uch is the strange vitality of fiction that it often overshadows the identity of its inventor. We know next to nothing of Homer, but Agamemnon and Achilles, Circe and Helen, are stable, habitual landmarks by which our culture finds its bearings. The historical fact of Shakespeare is enigmatic, but Lear and Macbeth, Cleopatra and Caliban, Malvolio and Prince Hal, are as distinct and familiar as the air we breathe. We discern our own features in their fictive presence. Who but the scholar can identify the first begetters of Faust and Don Juan? Yet these two names, which signify man's untarrying ascent of the ladder of desire, are household words.

Without these personages our inward past would be a crypt of the speechless dead. From Homer and the Socrates whom Plato dreamed, down to our own time, to the Charlus of Proust or Joyce's Leopold Bloom, it is from fiction that we draw the landmarks of our truth. It is this dialogue between the unquenched shades and the living that gives to our words their echoing power. To have brought off the miracle of persistent life is an artist's supreme achievement. Only then will he have realized *le dur désir de durer*, the harsh desire to endure beyond the shortness of mortality. But though each period produces innumerable characters in art, poetry, or fiction, only a few have in them the spark of grace. Only a few can leap the gulf from momentary substance to lasting shadow. Of that number is Carmen.

Cigar girl, Gypsy, thief, tramp, seducer, victim, Carmen has secured her place in modern mythology. Sung in every opera house the world over, mimed in countless ballets, filmed, decked out in traditional or contemporary garb, as the Sevillian gitana or Carmen Jones, she has passed into the language. The black-haired girl with the rose in her teeth, the castanets clacking over her tossing head, the stiletto in her belt, has slipped across frontiers as easily as past the sentinels of Granada or Málaga. France and Spain claim her for their own; she has had an immense vogue in German letters and on the German stage; she is a familiar demon to millions of Russian readers who think her native to the Caucasus; there is a Chinese version of her tale.

At first glance it is not easy to say why Carmen should have blazed into such profusion of life. The fatal lady, the doomed temptress with the black, riveting eye, was a cliché of romantic fiction. Descended from the vampire women of the Gothic ballad, she had by the 1840's become a shopworn fixture of pulp and pathos. Nor was there anything new in the authentic local color and exotic circumstances of the story. Sir Walter Scott, Victor Hugo, and Delacroix had surfeited the public with outlandish settings and garish plots. By 1845, when *Carmen* was first published, the hot, violent tints, the Gypsies and the heroic brigands of Spain, were commonplace. No— the spell of *Carmen* lies deeper.

Carmen is an addict of freedom. She would rather die than yield a jot of her wanton sovereignty. "Carmen will always be free": that imperious claim to liberty resounds through the novella, again and again, like fire crouching and leaping in the wind. Yet, at the same time, she recognizes the bondage of love. It is not a servitude she herself can long endure. Yielding so little of herself, Carmen glides from man to man with ironic ease. But she knows that in others love can be a lasting venom. She senses that José will kill her. Indeed, she acknowledges his right to do so: "you have the right to kill your *romi*." When he strikes, she accepts the blow as if it were a gust of wind.

It is this lightness of death that gives the story its great force. Though she has read the imminence of doom in her fortune-teller's cards, though she sees murder writ large in star and coffee grounds, Carmen does nothing to evade José's knife. Freedom is stronger than love and stronger than fear. She goes toward death with somber yet amused majesty. She refuses to lie in order to save her life—"I do not wish to take the trouble." Falsehood is a kind of slavery. "Death, where is thy sting?" That is the meaning of the tale, and it plucks at one of the major, hidden chords of human subversion. In each of us there lurks, in some hour, the thought of mocking death, of showing up the summoner for what he is, a mere importunate scarecrow, a beggar at the door of our freedom. Shallow, exotic, frivolous as she may be, Carmen shares with other enduring fictions an essential trait: she speaks something of our own innermost meaning. Like all great characters in art, she is part mirror and part dream.

Yet, ask the common reader who created this superbly vivid being, and he will, if at all, venture the name of Bizet. As opera, *Carmen* is unquestionably a masterpiece. It fulfills the peculiar conditions of its *genre*, being at once meretricious and sublime, full of bright froth and strong motion. And it was in her musical garb that Carmen went to the ends of the earth, from Paris to Carson City, from Rio to Moscow. But Bizet and his shrewd librettists went to work thirty years after Carmen had been invented. What they added —the bleached, redeeming Micaela—merely weakened the plot. In all else the opera owes its sweeping simplicity and strength of feeling to the novella. But as is true in so many instances of classic art, the imagined being glows before us vivid and substantial, whereas the creator has faded.

Not altogether unjustly. For although he was a compact, richly talented, and successful man, Prosper Mérimée cuts a somewhat pallid figure amid the bright concourse of his contemporaries. Born in 1803, Mérimée belongs to the generation that grew up under the brass bands and turbulence of the Napoleonic Wars. Come of age, he and his generation found a world gone gray and nervous. Old men were in power, and the whole of Romanticism was an attempt to recapture in the realm of fancy the tension, the eloquence, and the high feats that had been banished from the realm of fact. Those who entered into adult life in the late 1820's had at their backs a vastness of glory, and before them the pale noon of the industrial and bourgeois age.

Ripeness of art came to Mérimée at one stroke. At twenty-six he published his only full-length novel, *La Chronique du temps de Charles IX*, and a set of tales as concise and arresting as any he produced. By 1846 he had written nearly all that makes his performance memorable. Mérimée never grew: from the start he measured the exact range and tonality of his keyboard and played on it with trim virtuosity. He shared in the boisterous triumph of the Romantic movement; Victor Hugo, George Sand, and Sainte-Beuve were of his circle. But Mérimée's own career, like that of the Goncourts, had a spinsterish and urbane tenor.

Trained as an administrator and a historian, Mérimée pursued a decorous career in the French civil service. After serving in the departments of the navy and of commerce, he was appointed Inspector of Historical Monuments. This made of him an official custodian of the past. Each year, he traveled across France, surveying and reporting on historical sites, buildings, and archives. The ornaments of office came to him with easy grace: he was elected to the French Academy in 1844 and achieved the rank of *Grand Officier* in the Legion of Honor. His long-standing amity with Eugénie de Montijo, who became the wife of Louis Napoleon, assured Mérimée of a privileged place under the Second Empire. A frequent guest of the imperial household, he was appointed to the Senate in 1853. He died in the dread autumn of 1870, seeing the France he knew go down before the Prussian hammer.

This scholarly, officious mode of life has its bearing on Mérimée's art. He was both a master and a servant of history. His imagination leaned heavily on a scaffolding of antiquarian records or local historical circumstance. He used his own times with shrewd deference, expending on the past what wildness or secrecy of spirit he possessed. What is more important: Mérimée wrote, as it were, from a distance. Literature was to him an eminent craft, not an obsession or the whole of life. He looked on it as his mistress; his marriage lay on more solid ground. And it is precisely the virtues of a liaison rather than of a deepening commitment that we find in Mérimée's best work.

Even in his most ardent narratives there is a touch of arrogance, the self-mocking condescension of a gentleman who entertains his guests with an after-dinner tale. Mérimée's characteristic device, the assertion that he is recounting events at second-hand, that the story has been told to him by someone else, is both a literary convention and a piece of snobbery. Amid the tight, professional skein of his art, one comes across the *gaucheries* of an amateur. When he published *Carmen* in book form, Mérimée added a final chapter on the manners and language of Spanish Gypsies. The fierce climax is blighted by this pedantic epilogue. Only an amateur or a writer in whom there is some covert disdain for his own trade would have committed this error.

Mérimée was a close friend and admirer of Stendhal. Together they incarnate the survival in the Romantic era of eighteenth-century ideals of irony, reserve, and nonchalance. There was in them a touch of the dandy. They were neither priests nor servants to literature, but lovers and familiars. But whereas Stendhal made of this attitude a mask for his genius, it became the actual guise of Mérimée's great talent. The wonder is that Mérimée should have achieved so much with so sparse an enlistment of his soul.

Nietzsche, with his flair for the aristocratic and the playful, regarded Mérimée as one of the masters of modern prose. But, having the discretion of complete command, Mérimée's style is not easy to describe. It is hard of surface, swift and sinuous of pace. Like Stendhal, Mérimée is a virtuoso of the short sentence and the full stop. His eloquence consists in the unflagging progress of his narrative and in the bare, nervous immediacy of his dialogue, not in the music of words. Mérimée worked consciously against the Romantic trend, rejecting the poetic glitter and sonority of Chateaubriand and Victor Hugo. He stands in a classic lineage, in the tradition of Voltaire and Laclos. To cite an English counterpart, one would turn most accurately to the urbane, lithe prose of Hume and Chesterfield.

Observe the climax of *The Venus of Ille:* "*Un coq chanta. Alors la statue sortit du lit, laissa tomber le cadavre et sortit. Madame Alphonse se pendit à la sonnette, et vous savez le reste.*" The crow of the rooster proclaims the hellish allegory of the fable. The weight of the bronze visitant is gathered in the implacable tread of the verbs (the repetition of *sortit* being both a piece of carelessness and a fine stroke). No epithet, no pedal-point of oratory, heightens the effect. The end is an urbane gambit. Mérimée appears to be saying: "This is how a gentleman tells a story. If you want anything more garish or clamorous, go to the scribblers."

Yet this cool manner can bring off moments of formidable emotion. Little outside Poe or Dostoevsky rivals the malignity, the tangle of hatred and contempt, rendered in the last scene of *Colomba*. All passion spent, the four principals are traveling in Italy. The mood is nuptial. "Farewell to daggers," says Colomba; her only weapon now is a fan. But hazard sets old Barricini in her path. Robbed of his two sons, the old man is an invalid waiting for death. Having sought to banish the nightmare of recollection, his mind is vacant. Colomba advances toward him "till her shadow took away his sunlight." She stares at him until the ravaged mayor recognizes his relentless foe. In broken tones he pleads for compassion. He asks, "But why did you kill the two of them [my sons]?" Colomba's reply is a piece of sheer, cold horror:

I had to have both. . . . The branches have been hewn away. And if the root had not been rotten, I would have torn it up. Come, don't complain. You haven't long to suffer. I have suffered for two years!

She returns to Colonel Nevil, light of step. In the garden, the old man has withered. "Who the devil are you talking about?" inquires the colonel. Colomba answers with feigned indifference: "Oh, some senile person from my country. . . . From time to time I shall send for news of him." On this note, as inhuman as the purr of a cat, the story ends.

Though nothing else in his work quite matches the incandescence of *Carmen* and *Colomba*, nearly all of Mérimée's tales show a comparable economy and strength. *The Storming of the Redoubt* is a memorable sketch. One does not easily forget the vision of the Russian grenadiers, motionless, arms primed, above the heads of their assailants. The entire account of the chaotic, brutal mauling is a model of clarity. In *The Etruscan Vase*, Mérimée writes in the vein of Pushkin, whom he in fact helped introduce to Western European readers. The story is slight, yet it casts a grim spell. It plays on the nervousness and frivolous heroics of the post-Napoleonic generation. Amid the morass of peace, these dandies and ex-soldiers seek in dueling the lost fervor of battle. *The Game of Backgammon* is a classic in a *genre* characteristic of the nineteenth century—the gambling tale. Again we note the curious mixture of casualness and reserve in Mérimée's style. At the very instant of its pathetic climax, the story is cut short by a trivial interruption.

There is no more stringent test of narrative than violent physical action. Whether it be in the nocturnal brawl of Don Juan, in his account of a naval battle, or in the extraordinary scene of the ambush in *Colomba*, Mérimée's control never falters. He had taken no part in the Napoleonic Wars, but the experience of intense personal danger was part of his immediate inheritance. It gives his stories their particular vision. Mérimée is the poet of "nerve."

The nineteenth century marks the end of the classic status of narrative. Kleist, Poe, Stevenson, Leskov, and Mérimée himself are among the last of the pure storytellers. The revaluation brought on in modern literature through the work of Conrad, Henry James, Kafka, and Joyce has made of plot the agent of more complex intent. The story as such has been demoted and become the carrier of ideological, philosophical, or psychological motives. The narrative, the chain of happenings, is diminished to the thread on which the modern master strings his meaning. Often, as in James and Kafka, the actual fiction vanishes beneath the structure of argument and allegory. Consider the novels most expressive of the modern mode: *The Trial, The Golden Bowl,* Conrad's *Nostromo, The Sound and the Fury.* How much of their persuasion is borne by the story, by the immemorial fascination of "what happens next"?

Today, that fascination is exercised principally by the movies, by cheap fiction, by the slick-magazine romance. Some deep, tacit break has occurred between the novelist and the natural spinner of tales. With certain exceptions—the early Hemingway, Mauriac, Graham Greene—each goes his own way to mutual disadvantage.

Why this should be so is a vast, intractable theme. It is directly related to the decline in our habit of life of silence and private discourse. Hardly any of us read aloud to each other; only children gather to hear stories at nightfall. We spend most of our waking time in a loud vortex. At every moment the avalanche of print, the radio, the flicker of the television screen, solicit our dispersed and shallow attention. We drone from noise to noise, from headline to headline, like bees smoked out of their hive. The ancient craft of the storyteller requires a stillness in the air, even boredom. It relies on the inward drift of expectation as the hours stale toward evening. We are no longer bored in the old mellow sense, only harrowed or blasé. Hurled at us from every quarter, enforced by all the shocks of immediate vision, the day's news steeps us in more drama, more rawness of feeling, than any classic story would dare evoke. Only the writer of lurid pulp or science fiction can compete in the market of excitement. Imagination lags behind the garish extremity of fact.

Above all, the art of the story demands a listener, for even beneath the most sophisticated of classic narrative styles there sounds the antique cadence of the spoken word. A story is something told; it lives in the hearing. But we have lost the art of listening; we no longer delight in the digressions and lapses of the unrehearsed voice. Made lazy by the profusion of brilliant, instantaneous graphic devices —the photograph, the poster, the moving picture, the comic strip— we have grown to be spectators rather than audience. Today the only listeners are the children, and that is why so many of the classics of narrative, from Aesop to Dickens, are in their keeping.

Confronted with this turbulence and cheapening of emotion, the art of fiction has drawn inward. It seeks to rouse our attention by difficulty of technique. What has thus been achieved in richening of language and formal resource is obviously very great. But at a price. I keep thinking that a "natural" novelist is a man capable of telling an impromptu story and holding spellbound the passengers of a second-class railway carriage on a hot day. It is a trial to which I should not want to expose too many of our present masters.

But Mérimée would emerge triumphant. Once that somewhat clipped, elegant voice has begun a tale, it becomes nearly impossible to turn away.

THOMAS MANN'S
FELIX KRULL

The first episodes of *Confessions of Felix Krull* appeared in 1911. But Thomas Mann broke off and turned to *Death in Venice*, one of the most haunted, dark-veined of his inventions. In 1936, when including the picaresque fragment in a collection of tales, Mann noted: "I was not destined to turn back to *Felix Krull*." Yet throughout his life, and in the deliberate unfolding of his art—*The Magic Mountain*, the *Joseph* tetralogy, *Doctor Faustus*—Mann saw by his side, like a gay, secret sharer, the figure of the rogue. He adverted to it, briefly, in 1943. But the hour was too bitter, and there was ripe in Mann the compelling intimation of *Faustus*.

In 1954, the seventy-nine-year-old novelist took up what the man of thirty-six had laid aside. Starting on the actual page left incomplete in 1911, Mann wrote with fantastic ease. He did not alter a word or intonation in the preceding fragment. The coherence is total, the timbre of the voice unchanged. There is no other example in literature of so precise a leap over time and age. *Faust* inheres in Goethe's entire work, from 1772 to the 1830's; but there is between the early *Faust* and the apotheosis of Part II a profound change of intonation. In *Felix Krull*, the sequence is unbroken.

This alone would suggest that the *Confessions* had their special place in Mann's sensibility, that the silhouette of the confidence man lay near its center. Against the gravity of the major novels, against the metaphysical hauteur of Mann's stance—as artist, as exile, as heir to Goethe—*Felix Krull* sets its laughter. The knowledge that the story lay in reserve (the incomplete is the artist's freedom) may have consoled Mann as he strove to impose rational shape on the fierce

269

disorder of German experience. Moreover, it allowed him distance from his own work.

Mann was a writer stiffened by the public solemnity of his performance. The novels exacted from the life rigid, exemplary postures of labor and prophecy. Because they were drawn from the high matter of religious and national myth and because they passed nearly at once from the personal into the domain of the classic (the Germans make their great artists numinous, as they do their political masters), Mann's novels, stories, and essays towered over his person. He came to think of what he had wrought as awesome and signally exterior to himself; he meditated on the authority of his work as might his readers or critics. Hence the strain of oratory, of nervous pomp, in Mann's self-awareness.

But Felix Krull would not stay buried. In his long sleep, the seed of parody and subversion ripened. The *Confessions* guarded in Mann the gift of irreverence. They stepped between the master and the work, and laid upon its monumental façade a garland of laughter.

There are no translations.

Pain is not *bread;* the French word is warm, with a resonance of glebe and famine. *Home* is not *Heim;* the German has covert echoes of refuge, asylum, workhouse, yet it shades into the strong excitement of *Heimat, Heimatland,* the homeplace of national consciousness, the hearth of political exaltation. English has no exact equivalent.

What is true of the single word is truer of the sentence, paragraph, or page. Even the simplest statement does not pass unaltered into another language; each language frames the world uniquely. Furthermore, a writer who matters hammers out his own language from the general quarry. All literary style is language inside language, thus, all that translation can hope to do is recompose something (as much as possible) of what the foreign writer might have put down had he felt and chosen in another language. At the level of normal prose discourse, this is difficult enough; prose has its own very subtle structure, and the syntax of a language codifies complex traditions of behavior and a historical convention of the real. When we deal with poetry, translation is either an honest crib, a crutch to be laid beside the dictionary, or it is an imitation, a re-enactment of parallel gestures in a medium radically transformed.

Great translators—and they are disastrously rare—act as a kind of living mirror. They offer to the original not an equivalence, for there can be none, but a vital counterpoise, an echo, faithful yet autonomous, as we find in the dialogue of human love. An act of translation is an act of love. Where it fails, through immodesty or blurred perception, it traduces. Where it succeeds, it incarnates.

All these difficulties are, in the case of *Felix Krull*, only a starting point for our sense of difficulty because the problem of rendition here has a particular twist, and it takes us to the heart of the book. *Bekenntnisse des Hochstaplers Felix Krull* is a Chinese box, parody encased in parody. Within each section, Thomas Mann's use of style, the singular craft of idiom and grammar, is itself the source of irony and intricate diversion.

The title is parody: imagine something florid, Plutarchian, yet converse to the subject. Fielding struck the same note: *The Life of Mr. Jonathan Wild the Great. Bekenntniss* signifies confession, attestation; it has its distinct legal, moralistic edge. Yet who is inviting us into his solemn confidence? An embezzler, grand larcenist and con man. *Hochstapler* is a sonorously sordid word; it spans a gamut of villainy, from sharping and suave theft to plain forgery. In short, the title is calculated to suggest that abundant seventeenth- and eighteenth-century literature of rogues' memoirs, highwaymen's monitory reminiscences, and cony-catchers' pamphlets and ballads that enter the serious novel via Defoe, Fielding, Smollett, and Lesage. More precisely, Mann refers us to the most famous of German picaresque tales: Grimmelshausen's *Simplicissimus*. In the baroque wildness and buffoonery of the adventurous Simplicissimus, Mann, no less than Brecht, found a counterpart to the modern. There are numerous affinities between Grimmelshausen and *Felix Krull;* at times Mann insinuates a direct quote into his own fiction. Simplex and Felix are brothers under the skin; their very names echo.

The next parody is nearer the center of the box. Splintered by historical crises and the division of Germany into petty states, German literature has a short, uneven record. It has produced or brought to excellence few *genres* entirely its own. But among these one would put the *Erziehungsroman*, or *Bildungsroman* (no other literature has challenged the primacy of the German name). In the *Erziehungsroman*, the novel is conceived as a tale of ripening, a *paideia*. We attend on the history of a man from childhood to ripe self-consciousness. In its classic mode—Goethe's *Wilhelm Meister*, Keller's *Der Grüne Heinrich*—the "novel of education" simulates, in the gradual deepening of stylistic resource and narrative poise and in the widening scope of confronted plot, the parallel unfolding of the hero's own identity. We grow as we read.

Other literatures have produced famous examples: Dickens' *David Copperfield*, Flaubert's *L'Education sentimentale*, Joyce's *Portrait of the Artist*. But the motif of the coming of age, of the soul at school, has a particular grip on the German sensibility. When writing the most characteristic of modern *Bildungsromane*, *Jean-Christophe*, Romain Rolland chose a German protagonist. *Felix Krull* is a beautifully exact, barbed parody of this distinctively national *genre*.

Erziehungsromane begin, inevitably, with a canvas, filial or mutinous, of the hero's family. The storms and pomp of the bourgeois father, the harbor of pardon in the mother's room, the crotchets of aunts and uncles, the revels of the clan (marvelously rendered with all their after-dinner drowsiness in Joyce and Proust), form the necessary overture to the portrait of the artist, magnate, or sensualist as a little boy. So it is in *Felix Krull*, but with an acid difference.

The Krull ménage is bankrupt, bibulous, high as old venison. Under its silver miter and purple cope of wax, *Loreley extra cuvée* is vinegar. Mama measures Olympia's thigh with a tape measure, and the little boy observes the streak of crass lechery "in their unusual intimacy." The dominant note of sanctified corruption is fixed in the name of Felix' godfather, Schimmelpreester. Literally, Mildew-priest. But perhaps the conceit is gayer and more arcane: in certain Moselle vineyards, the mildewed grapes, harvested before sunrise, yield a rare *Eiswein* (the French speak of *pourriture noble*). From the mildewed stock will spring the cold, sparkling vintage of young Krull.

The "novel of ripening" takes its hero on a ritual quest. His voyage (with its dim roots in the chivalric ordeal) leads through successive trials of initiation: school, the choice of profession—itself a word with archaic, sacramental overtones—and eros. *David Copperfield* and *Studs Lonigan* enact the same stylized convention, though the idiom differs. The quest of Felix Krull holds up to the mystery of man's schooling, of his coming to maturity, a mirror of derision. By grace of forgery and feigned illness, Krull plays truant and perches in bed sucking stolen sweets. In a scene of brilliant slapstick (rare in Mann), the young Galahad escapes conscription. Traditionally, the *Bildungsroman* pauses over the hero's discovery of his vocation: he hears the imperative of art, religious faith, or social commitment. He shoulders his pack for the long day's voyage. But no

272

such voice disturbs Krull in his alert reverie of sensual affluence. He is a magpie born. All that glitters is not gold; some of it turns out to be topaz.

Often the sting of parody lies in the small, erudite touch. Consider the road Felix Krull follows when carrying the stolen jewels to Master Jean-Pierre (*pierre*, of course, signifying *stone* and the guardian of heaven). It leads between church and cemetery, then down a little street, *the rue des Vierges Prudentes*. These Wise Virgins are in the Gospel, and we meet them in medieval romances. Here they give access to the *rue de l'Échelle au Ciel*. The impertinent allegory is plain: Felix Krull is ascending heaven's ladder. But it leads to the Ritz.

The growth of spirit through the ache of love is the crucial theme of the *Bildungsroman:* Wilhelm Meister and Mignon; David Copperfield and Dora; Julien Sorel and Madame de Rénal. The adolescent sheds his green bark when first he tastes the salt and anguish of intelligent desire, when he passes from the itch of indiscriminate longing to the lárge narrowness of single passion. In bourgeois civilization, this *rite de passage* is as decisive and stylized as are the puberty-rites of the Papuan or the armored vigil of the medieval knight. From Goethe to Proust, the novel has made of the first realization of mature love its epiphany.

Felix Krull takes a lighter view. Convinced that "with me the satisfaction of love is twice as sweet and twice as penetrating as with the average man," this Don Juan of bellhops flits from housemaid to whore, from lady novelist to queenly Iberian bosom. He takes sex as lesser men eat oysters, with a happy gulp. Though his sensual spasms are, as he tells us, of unusual power, Krull remains esentially neutral. He kindles but does not burn. Eleanor Twentyman and Nectan Lord Stranthbogie yearn for the golden boy with equal, irreconcilable lust. He moves between them, lithe as a dancer. That gives the *Confessions* their grace, their ease of motion. But it is also their radical weakness. We can no more become imaginatively entangled in Krull than we could in a brilliantly dexterous monkey. The tightrope on which he performs his capers is stretched over a void of feeling.

Only once is there an initiation, an education of feeling in the real sense. Professor Kuckuck's lecture on cosmology stands out with edgy grandeur from the quicksilver lightness of the tale. Not even the man's risible name, with its double hint of mental eccentricity and amorous license, can detract from the marvels he invokes:

> This interdependent whirling and circling, this convolution of gases into heavenly bodies, this burning, flaming, freezing, exploding, pulverizing, this plunging and speeding, bred out of Nothingness and awaking Nothingness— which would perhaps have preferred to remain asleep and was waiting to fall asleep again—all this was Being, known also as Nature, and everywhere in everything it was one. I was not to doubt that all Being, Nature itself, constituted a unitary system from the simplest inorganic element to Life at its liveliest, to the woman with the shapely arm and to the figure of Hermes. Our human brain, our flesh and bones, these were mosaics made up of the same elementary particles as stars and star dust and the dark clouds hanging in the frigid waste of interstellar space.

As it stands (and the fact that the novel is unfinished makes our bearings uncertain), Kuckuck's initiation of Krull into the alchemy of science suggests the revelations of Mephistopheles to Faust. There is more than a hint of Satanic clairvoyance in the traveler with the small gray beard and "starlike eyes." But if there is parody here, it is of a yearning kind. Goethe was the titular daemon of Mann's own consciousness as artist and man. No less than *Doctor Faustus*, the one episode of lyric gravity in *Felix Krull* pays homage to the greatest of German poets and to his chosen myth of knowledge and damnation.

Though Goethe stands intact, Mann himself emerges from the *Confessions* delightfully mocked. His place in the lineage of the *Bildungsroman* was eminent. In *Buddenbrooks*, *Tonio Kröger*, *The Magic Mountain*, and the *Joseph* novels, Mann had produced classic studies of education through life, of the flowering of perception in the individual. To Mann, as to Goethe, the fact of crescence, in leaf as in man, was the model and justification of the artist's striving. If there is a contrary to humane education, a ripening through subversion, Felix Krull is a master apprentice. Being a novel of "un-education," the *Confessions* parody the core of Mann's achievement.

One could show in detail how often *Felix Krull* recasts into laughter or shifts subtly out of right focus specific themes and passages from the major fictions. Armand's tumble with Diane Philibert mocks the perils of Joseph in the house of Potiphar. Krull's examination by the medical board parodies one of the moments of highest pathos in *The Magic Mountain:* Joachim Ziemssen's attempt to wrest from the doctor the permission to return to his regiment. It is as if Mann's last novel looked back on the proud but somewhat ponderous array of his work with a glint of doubt. Only a very great artist or one from whom the nearness of death has purged vainglory can so regard his labor.

But parody draws short breath; the Chinese box is a miniature game. *Felix Krull* is weakest where it is most purely a game, a stylistic charade on Grimmelshausen, the *Bildungsroman*, and Mann's own novels. The book is kept vital by a deeper impulse. Below the baroque wit and pastiche of the rogue's chronicle moves a strong theme of social satire.

Satire suggests the other Mann, Heinrich Mann, whose *The Blue Angel* and *Der Untertan* are notorious derisions of bourgeois, imperial Germany. The arcane involutions of Thomas Mann's style, his vision of the artist as reader of omen and myth, contrast with the notion of the satirist. Yet, as Georg Lukács has argued, Thomas Mann is one of the major witnesses to the crisis of the bourgeois order. Mann recorded, with the veracity of intense artistic scruple, the manners, inflections, and values of that mercantile, middle-class regime that spun the fine, tough web of its morals over the harsh facts of industrial profit from 1830 to 1914. Mann is heir to Balzac and Zola. In *Buddenbrooks* and the early novellas, in the image of familial citadels that shimmers behind the fevers of *The Magic Mountain*, the world of nannies and gilt edge, of paternal cigars and little folk in sailor's hats, the ideals of bourgeois law, of station and decorum, which came to utter hideousness on the Marne and the Somme, have their memorial.

But being a great artist, a man in whom truth speaks louder than design, Mann could not but express his premonitions of its ruin. He saw the cracks branching with ghostlike rapidity along the walls of the old house of order; he heard the deathwatch beetle gnawing at the beams. Thus he spoke out, against his own bias as a patrician, against his own adherence to the stability of aesthetic and moral values. It is this that gives the end of *Buddenbrooks*, *Tonio Kröger*, and *The Magic Mountain* their nostalgic yet pitiless irony. *Death in Venice* is epitaph to an age.

When Mann returned to the fragment of *Felix Krull* in 1954, the polity of bourgeois values lay in rubble, as did the actual streets on which Consul Buddenbrook had walked. There was worse: men knew, in a way which only Kierkegaard and Nietzsche had foreseen, that the proud edifice of liberal, humanistic values, the very construct of art and culture, had produced from within—in some mysterious mechanism of self-damnation—the age of the concentration camp and of atomic incineration. How this came to pass and what it bodes for the future of Western consciousness is the theme of *Doctor Faustus*. *Felix Krull* returns to the background of social and moral crisis in the mode of laughter, as a satyr play reverts to the plot of tragedy.

The satiric shafts fall thick, but with concentration of design. The opening mocks the spurious largesse of the Krull household; the absurd tinkle over the door chimes Strauss's "Enjoy Your Life" at the very moment when the establishment is sapped with ruin. When creditors strip the house, its master falls like a stuffed dummy. Following this, the novel embarks on its flyting of wealth, bourgeois snobberies, philistine manners, and high-minded politics. Krull's oration to the King of Portugal is venomous fun. Every cliché of class condescension and paternalism is argued into literal absurdity:

> By his very existence the beggar, huddled in rags, makes as great a contribution to the colorful picture of the world as the proud gentleman who drops alms in his humbly outstretched hand, carefully avoiding, of course, any contact with it. And, Your Majesty, the beggar knows it; he is aware of the special dignity that the order of the world has allotted to him, and in the depths of his heart he does not wish things otherwise. It takes the instigation to rebellion by men of ill will to make him discontented with his picturesque role and to put into his head the contumacious notion that men must be equal.

The satiric trope that underlies the *Confessions* is, of course, disguise. Nothing is what it appears. In Langenschwalbach, Felix poses as an infant Paganini, though he can't play a note on the violin. In his dressing room, Müller-Rosé turns from a lustrous dandy into a grubby, worn-out *cabotin*. By larceny of wit, Krull manages to spout all foreign languages without, in fact, knowing any: he is the quintessence of the Berlitz dream. He slips into the skin of the Marquis de Venosta as into a safecracker's gloves: "Clothes make the man, marquis—or perhaps the other way around: the man makes the clothes." Such is his power of counterfeit that he appropriates not only the marquis' signature, affluence, and turn of phrase, but also that which we can least hand over to another man, the baggage of our private memories.

Hence Krull's constant identification with Hermes. Hermes is both god of thieves and master of mask. One recalls his filching of identity in the myth of Amphitryon. Mann found, in Molière's and Kleist's treatments of that myth, disturbing studies of the mercurial. Like the god, Krull is a virtuoso of disguise; whenever it suits him, he takes a new soul off the hanger:

> ... in each disguise I assumed I looked better and more natural than in the last. I might appear as a Roman flute-player, a wreath of roses twined in my curly locks; as an English page in a snug-fitting satin with lace collar and plumed hat; as a Spanish bullfighter in spangled jacket and broad-brimmed hat; as a youthful abbé at the time of powdered white wigs ... whatever the costume, the mirror assured me that I was born to wear it, and my audience declared that I looked to the life exactly the person whom I aimed to represent.

Everyone is deceived. That is the barb of the satire. The children "of the noble family of Siebenklingen" hurry to acclaim the fake violinist; the King finds in the counterfeit marquis a tone and philosophy "appropriate to your origin." Mann is saying that a social order that had made of cant its holy writ and that has lived by ruthless exploitation and pretended gentility is ready to be plundered. More than ready: in its hysterical blasé frivolity, the bourgeois world welcomed those who came to rob it, whether they were Ivar Kreuger, the match king, or Felix Krull, embezzler.

That is the meaning of the finest scene in the novel. Diane Philibert cries out: "Armand, you shall steal from me. Here under my very eyes. That is, I'll shut my eyes and pretend to both of us that I am asleep. But secretly I'll watch you steal. ... Go on, steal away from my side, prowl, find and take it! It is my dearest wish." And when she begs, "beloved, turn me over and whip me till I bleed!" the satire strikes at the nerve of abasement, of masochism in a decadent society.

Like Balzac, Mann makes of the erotic the principal medium of his critique. It is in the chase and enforcement of desire that the truth will out. With our clothes we shed our assumed morals. Mann paro-

277

dies a characteristic motif in *fin-de-siècle* memoirs—the housemaid's sexual initiation of the young master. Under Krull's complacent narrative obtrudes the unsavory economic and social fact:

> It was different with the son of the house, who may well have won her favour as he developed, and she may have had the feeling that in satisfying him she was not only performing a domestic duty but advancing her social position. Thus it happened that my desires encountered no serious resistance.

Gifted with hermaphroditic charm (love in the arms of larceny), Felix-Armand-Loulou moves among the rich like a catalyst of infatuation. Lords envision him in kilts; American heiresses plead for scandal. There is a fine, harsh sagacity in the double entendre of our slang: *prick* as phallus and needle. Either will burst the gaudy balloons of money or caste. The *Confessions* remind us that whatever its outward elegance, a society is naked twice: in bed and in the grave.

As we have it, *Felix Krull* is a fragment—Part I. How would this picaresque masque have ended? Mann's death makes it impossible to know for certain. But there are hints of a crowning device.

The story moves up a spiral staircase set with mirrors. It is allegoric of that Nietzschean theory of "eternal recurrence" which fascinated Mann. Everything seems to be happening twice, in near facsimile. The two young people, seen as an icon of youth and exotic beauty on the balcony of the Frankfurter Hof, will obviously recur in the guise of the Novaros in Argentina. Ribeiro, the handsome *espada*, is wearing a costume identical with that in which Schimmelpreester decked young Krull; and the bullfighter's features are those of the marquis. Dona Maria Pia (Zouzou) is Zaza reincarnate; in their tense, erotically jealous relationship, she and her mother re-create Olympia and Mrs. Krull. The authentic Venosta and his counterfeit are, of course, twin reflections of a single image. The rest of the novel would have followed their adventures as they receded or drew near in a gallery of facing mirrors. Only Kuckuck seems unique and able to *see through* Felix Krull. There are hints that he will reappear as guide or unmasker.

We know that the fancy-dress party will end in an unsavory dawn, that Krull will be found out. The opening sentence of the

Confessions tells of weariness, leisure, and complete retirement. There are frequent hints of prison. It is vital to the conventions of a rogue's tale that the trickster should be tricked. Is Krull exposed by Kuckuck? Does he overreach in some high blaze of erotic or financial larceny? Does he go to prison in order to clear the name of his twin, the true marquis? Yet there are also intimations of a happy ending. Schimmelpreester "was to intervene in my destiny decisively and providentially." The voice of the *Confessions* is tired, but not broken.

We cannot say more. In *Felix Krull*, Mann relaxed into a sovereign ease of fancy. The details of the story may not have been fixed in his own mind. If they were, the artist bore his secret into death. There, as well, Hermes is guide.

LAWRENCE DURRELL
AND THE BAROQUE NOVEL

With the publication of *Clea*, Lawrence Durrell has completed his quartet of novels set in Alexandria. Few recent works of fiction have provoked fiercer disagreement. There are critics who assert that Durrell is a pompous charlatan; a mere word-spinner and gatherer of flamboyant clichés; a novelist whose angle of vision is grotesquely narrow; a late Victorian decadent and minor disciple of Henry Miller. Elsewhere, and particularly in France, it is held with equal vehemence that the Alexandria Quartet is the most vivid performance in the modern novel since Proust and Joyce, and that Durrell is a talent of the first rank. The main source of controversy is Durrell's style. And that style is, in fact, the vital center of Durrell's art. It meets the reader like a bristling hedge when he first enters the world of *Justine;* and when he has finished *Clea*, he will realize that that style is also the inward place of Durrell's meaning. It is, therefore, with the shape of the syntax and the rare glitter of the words that one must start. Let me cite two examples from *Mountolive:*

> The waters thickened to glue and silver bodies began to leap into the darkness only to fall back, glittering like coinage, into the shallows. The circles of light touched, overlapped, and the whole ceinture was complete, and from all around it there came the smash and crash of dark bodies leaping into the shallows, furling out the long hand-nets which were joined end to end and whose dark loops were already bulging like Christmas stockings with the squirming bodies of fish. The leapers had taken fright too

and their panic-stricken leaps ripped up the whole surface
of the pan, flashing back cold water upon the stuttering
lamps, a shuddering harvest of cold scales and drumming
tails. Their exciting death-struggles were as contagious as
the drumming had been. Laughter shook the air as the nets
closed. Mountolive could see Arabs with their long white
robes tucked up to the waist pressing forward with steady-
ing hands held to the dark prows beside them, pushing
their linked nets slowly forward. The light gleamed upon
their dark thighs. The darkness was full of their barbaric
blitheness.

.   .   .   .   .

He entered the penumbra of the storm slowly, mar-
velling at the light, at the horizon drawn back like a
bow. Odd gleams of sunshine scattered rubies upon the
battleships in the basin (squatting under their guns like
horned toads). It was the ancient city again . . . broken
pavements made of tinfoil, snail-shells, cracked horn, mica;
earth-brick buildings turned to the colour of oxblood; the
lovers wandering in Mohammed Ali Square, disoriented
by the unfamiliar rain, disconsolate as untuned instruments; the clicking of violet trams along the sea-front
among the tatting of palm-fronds. The desuetude of an
ancient city whose streets were plastered with the wet
blown dust of the surrounding desert. He felt it all anew,
letting it extend panoramically in his consciousness—the
moan of a liner edging out towards the sunset bar, or the
trains which flowed like a torrent of diamonds towards the
interior, their wheels chattering among the shingle ravines
and the powder of temples long since abandoned and silted
up. . . .

The style is a mosaic. Each word is set in its precise and
luminous place. Touch by touch, Durrell builds his array of sensuous,
rare expressions into patterns of imagery and tactile suggestion so
subtle and convoluted that the experience of reading becomes one of
total sensual apprehension. Such paragraphs live to the touch of the
reader's hand; they have a complex aural music; and the light seems
to play across the surface of the words in bright tracery. "The
clicking of violet trams" is as complete a sensuous rendition as might

281

be achieved by a *pointilliste* painter, breaking light into minute, precise flecks and reassembling the elements of vision into memorable design. No one else writing in English today has quite the same commitment to the light and music of language.

But this does not mean that this jeweled and coruscated style springs full-armed from Durrell's personal gift. He stands in a firm tradition of baroque prose. In the seventeenth century, Sir Thomas Browne built sentences into lofty arches and made words ring like sonorous bells. Robert Burton, in his *Anatomy of Melancholy*, used the same principal device as Durrell: richness through accumulation, the marshaling of nouns and epithets into great catalogues which the eye pursues in antiquarian delight. The feverish, brass-sounding prose of De Quincey is a direct ancestor to that of *Justine*. And more recently, there is the example of Conrad. In the later parts of *Lord Jim* and throughout *The Rescue*, Conrad uses words with the sumptuous exuberance of a jeweler showing off his rarest stones. Here also, language falls upon the reader's senses like brocade.

This baroque ideal of narrative style is, at present, in disfavor. The modern ear has been trained to the austere, deliberately impoverished cadence and vocabulary of Hemingway. Reacting against the excesses of the Victorian manner, the modern writer has made a cult of simplicity. He refines common speech but preserves its essential drabness. When comparing a page from the Alexandria novels to the practice of Hemingway or Graham Greene, one is setting a gold-spun and jeweled Byzantine mosaic next to a black-and-white photograph. One cannot fairly judge the one by the other. But that does not signify that Durrell is a decadent show-off or that his conception of English prose is erroneous. We may be grateful that Hemingway and his innumerable imitators have made the language colder and more astringent and that they have brought back into fiction the virtues of direct focus. But they have done so at a price. Contemporary English usage is often thin and unimaginative. The style of politics and factual communication verges on the illiterate. Having far fewer words at our reach than had the educated man of the seventeenth and even of the late nineteenth century, we say less or say it with a blurred vagueness. Whether in its advertisements, its comic books, or its television, our culture lives by the picture rather than the word. Hence a writer like Durrell, with his Shakespearean and Joycean delight in the sheer abundance and sensuous variety of speech, may strike one as mannered and precious. But the objection arises in part from our impoverished sensibility.

Who is to say, moreover, that the Alexandria Quartet will not lead to a new pleasure in narrative prose? A number of contemporary writers are beginning to return to the reserves of language. The enchantment of *Lolita* lies precisely in Nabokov's rediscovery of the resources of style, of stylization as a mode of ironic perception. And the lineage, Conrad-Nabokov-Durrell, is suggestive. All three approach English from a certain distance. Conrad and Nabokov as foreigners who learned the language, Durrell as an Irishman born in India and steeped in the Greek and French legacy of the eastern Mediterranean. Their prose has the quality of marvel and surprise which comes with personal discovery. Unlike most current novelists, they use words as if they had lain buried in some treasure-trove.

But Durrell's style is more than a formal instrument; it carries the heart of his meaning. *Justine, Balthazar, Mountolive,* and *Clea* are founded on the axiom that the ultimate truths of conduct and the world cannot be penetrated by force of reason. Where truth can be apprehended at all, in brief spells of total illumination, the process of insight is one of total sensuous absorption. In a conceit which is the very crux of his argument, Durrell instructs us that the soul enters truth as man enters woman, in a possession at once sexual and spiritual. Again, this is a view which has existed before Durrell. It plays a vital role in oriental and medieval mysticism; it is at work in Dante and in the erotic metaphors of the seventeenth-century metaphysical poets. Moreover, it is crucial in the theories of Gnosticism and the citadel of Gnosticism was Alexandria. And it is here that the example of D. H. Lawrence is relevant. The presence of Lawrence is felt through the four novels and one of the main characters is in personal touch with him. Like Lawrence, Durrell believes in a wisdom of the senses truer and subtler than that of the predatory mind. Both men see in the act of love the crucial affirmation of human identity and the only true bridge for the soul. Durrell's personages pursue each other in an elaborate cross-weaving of sexual encounter, for only thus can the ghostliness of the human spirit be given the substance of life.

This mystique of sensual recognition encompasses more than individual identity. Our entire perception of reality depends on similar illuminations (Joyce called them "epiphanies"). It is by accumulating these moments of vision, touch by exact touch, that we arrive at a grasp of the surrounding world—in this instance, at a true image of

Alexandria. The long, glittering arabesques of adjectives with which Durrell surrounds objects are not only exercises in verbal acrobatics. They are successive assaults on the inner mystery of things, attempts, often exasperated and histrionic, to trap reality inside a mesh of precise words. Being equipped with a superb apparatus of sensual receptivity, Durrell is aware of the myriad movements of light, scent, and sound. He sees the world reflected in waters which are never still and tries to capture the essence of a city from the kaleidoscope of changing seasons, colors, and moods. So far as Alexandria goes, he has succeeded magnificently. Durrell's Alexandria (not, of course, the Egyptian harbor-city of our ordinary acquaintance) is one of the true monuments in the architecture of imagination. It compares in manifold coherence with the Paris of Proust and the Dublin of Joyce.

The technique of accumulated nuance, the painter returning constantly to the same scene in the changes of the light, applies not only to the portrayal of the city but also the entire plot. As in the Japanese fable of *Rashomon* and in the plays of Pirandello, identical events are recounted from successive points of view. The narrator's first impression of Justine, of the Coptic magnates in whose secretive life she becomes involved, of Melissa the golden tramp, and of the relations between Justine and Pursewarden, is submitted in *Balthazar* to ironic revision. The four volumes should be printed in the manner of loose-leaf notebooks allowing one to close earlier gaps with later disclosure. Nowhere in the Quartet are things what they seem to be. In *Clea*, the principal narrator is himself drawn into the vortex of action. Nothing is ever wholly explained; neither the murder of Narouz—one of the great set pieces of writing in recent fiction—nor Justine's odd flight into Palestine, nor the true nature of the conspiratorial web which surrounds Nessim and Mountolive, keeping them entangled yet divided. To complicate matters further, there are three writers in the novel who are themselves characters, and even those personages who are not professional artisans of language, share something of their creator's dazzling virtuosity of style and feeling. The novel closes in mid-course, on a series of tantalizing notations of what might be further developments. This too is essential to Durrell's meaning. The true poet (and Durrell is a minor poet before being a novelist) knows that time and action flow like the Nile. He can show us the depth and rush of the water and throw stones into it to break the images of the moon; but he cannot arrest the river in his sieve of words.

Durrell says that "the central topic of the book is an investigation of modern love." The reach of his inquiry is large; it draws on Sade and psychology at its most liberal. We find in this labyrinthine city not only the love of man and woman, but the more oblique byways of desire; no less than *L'Astrée*, the Quartet is a geography of eros. *Clea* contains, in miniature, as gross a tragedy of homosexual passion as any in Proust. Mountolive is lured into a house of wizened child-prostitutes who swarm at him like bats. Memlik, the police chief, is a delicate sadist. We encounter fetishists and transvestites, phallic rituals and private lubricities. The gravest love story in the entire novel, the unendurably intense love of Pursewarden and Liza, is a story of incest. Critics have seen in this profusion and variety of sexual concern a mark of decadence. Durrell has been accused of being a follower of Swinburne and Beardsley, a purveyor of ornate morsels of erotic lore. There are one or two instances in which such a charge can be sustained. But on the whole, it is wide of the mark. Durrell must explore the ambiguities and covertness of sensual lust precisely because he believes that it is only in the lambent or desperate contact of the flesh that we can gain access to the truth of life. In his treatment, moreover, there is little of prurience or the snigger of the eroticist. Love in Durrell has an ashen taste. When Liza burns her brother's "immortal" letters (there is here a muffled echo of the Byron legend), she illustrates Durrell's feeling that the extremity of passion brings with it utter ruin. And our last vision of Justine, standing naked beside Darley's bed, soliciting the empty gestures of spent ardor, is one of total defeat. As in so many dandies able to experience the fullness of sensuous life, there is in Durrell a touch of the Puritan.

But although its range of material and emotion is great, the Alexandria Quartet leaves one, at the last, with a suspicion of triviality. There lies the real problem for the critic. Why should there be at the center of this superbly contrived fable of life an undeniable hollowness? There are, I think, two reasons.

Durrell dramatizes a wide spectrum of sensibility; but his cast of characters is of an exceedingly special kind. All these fascinating and exotic beings share a high degree of nervous intelligence; they articulate their emotions with lyric power and unfailing subtlety; they live life at a constant pitch of awareness, more searching and vulnerable than that of ordinary men. They are cut from the same fragile and luminous stone and so they reflect each other like mirrors disposed in cunning perspectives. Mirrors play a crucial symbolic role throughout the action (as they do in Sade). And it is a dangerous role; for although they multiply vision and drive it inward, they also shut it off from the outside. In Durrell even the sea is a pool for Narcissus.

The angle of vision, moreover, is rigorously private. The gusts of social and political life blow across the scene, but they are not accorded much importance. Nessim and his clan are involved in a tenebrous conspiracy to further Coptic independence and they run guns to Palestine. But we are given no clear account of what they are really up to. Between *Mountolive* and *Clea* falls the shadow of world war, and at the start of *Clea* there is an account of an air-raid on Alexandria. It is a memorable patch of writing; rockets empty on the sky "their brilliant clusters of stars and diamonds and smashed pearl snuff-boxes"; the German planes are like "silver moths" moving with "fatal languor" among the "strings of hot diamonds" which spout from the batteries below. But neither the terror nor the real meaning of the action comes through. It is merely one more jeweled miniature to treasure in the vault of style. All that Durrell touches is somehow diminished to the scale of goldsmith's work.*

Now no one would be so absurd as to demand from him a novel of "social consciousness." But by severing his imagined world from the intrusions of political and social fact he makes it even narrower and more fragile than it need be. Behind the intimacies and stylistic experiments of Joyce lies the stabilizing structure of the Homeric epic. Proust buttressed his singular and even perverse view of human conduct with a close, technical awareness of social, political, and military affairs. Charlus is no less eccentric than Nessim or Baltha-zar. But the Zeppelins which cruise above Paris during his nocturnal prowlings are grimly real and carry with them the weight of histori-cal crisis. Similarly, D. H. Lawrence gave to his accounts of private experience a firm anchorage in social reality. The legend of Lady Chatterley is as narrow and private as that of Darley and Melissa; but *Lady Chatterley's Lover* is a profoundly intelligent study of class relations.

Because of its enclosedness and utter privacy, the Alexandria

[* It is surprising that Durrell has not been claimed as a predecessor or example by the proponents of Camp. Many of his stylistic attitudes and the tone of his personages have affinities with the insouciance, edgy elegance, bitchy camaraderie, verbal sophistication, and erotic coolness of the Camp world. Seen in this way, moreover, the Quartet suggests the links between Camp and the dandyism of the Edwardians.]

Quartet is more convincing in its details than in its broad design. It is the marginal characters who spring most completely to life: Scobie, one of the finest examples of the grotesque in English fiction since Uncle Toby; and Narouz, in whom massive silence becomes a kind of rhetoric. It is not so much the main plot which sticks in one's memory, as it is the digressions and minor episodes: the shadowy account of Mountolive's childhood; the affair between Justine and Arnauti, who never even appears in the Quartet; the exquisite misadventures of Pombal, the French diplomat; Capodistria's recital of his experiments in black magic. As in medieval illuminations, the fringe is often brighter than the center.

But there is also a particular failure. *Clea* marks a drastic falling-off. It is a brittle, self-conscious gloss on the three preceding volumes. The long extracts from Pursewarden's notebooks are not only insufferably tedious, but they act as a parody of Durrell's own style. The episode of Clea's near-drowning is a classic exhibit of how symbolism should not be used. The ravages which time and the death of the heart have caused in Justine and Nessim are thrust before us as stark facts. There is no attempt to render them psychologically plausible. What happened, I imagine, is this: Durrell had completed the first three movements of his quartet and sensed that he had a major achievement in hand. When he turned to the finale, he seems to have been beset with the fear of spoiling the whole. He took no risks and wrote a series of narrow variations on earlier themes. Thus *Clea* represents a distinct failure of nerve.

Yet even when we make such reservations, there can be little question of the fascination of Durrell's novel. Anyone caring about the energies of English prose and the forms of prose fiction will have to come to grips with this strange, irritating work. We are too near the fact to say what place the Alexandria Quartet will hold in future estimates of twentieth-century English literature. I would guess that it will stand somewhere above the range of *Green Mansions*, with the less complete but more central performance of Malcolm Lowry. That Durrell will have his place is almost certain.

BUILDING A MONUMENT

The word "*œuvre*" is hard to translate. It means more than the actual count of a writer's work. It implies a logic of unfolding, of gradually revealed design. In an *œuvre*, different *genres*—fiction, poetry, critical essays—take on a personal unity. The achievement argues as a whole, its sum greater and more coherent than any of the parts. The outward statement of an *œuvre* is that characteristic French and German enterprise, the complete edition in a row of uniform volumes. The contrast with American habits is sharp. Even the classics go ungathered (there is, as yet, no complete edition of Herman Melville). It was in the explicit image of European custom that Henry James built his own sepulcher of print, the great New York Edition in its plum-colored solemnity.

There is here more than a difference of editorial form. The American writer, particularly during the past few decades, has found it difficult to achieve continuity, to make individual acts of invention part of a natural growth and completion. Faulkner is the sovereign exception, and his particular tactics of cunning and patience point up the failure of many of his contemporaries. The history of the writer who produces a stunning first novel, whose second book is either a nervous pastiche of his own success or a botched fling at something new, and whose later work moves erratically between quality and routine, is almost an American cliché. Much of the best of recent American fiction has been won or lost at a roulette of talent; it is not built.

Some of the reasons look obvious. The financial rewards, the critical adulation, the personal celebrity that can be harvested by a very successful first novel are such as to place the writer in a vulnerable position. If his next work fails or defies the format the critics have prepared for it, judgment turns with a vengeance (Mailer, James Jones, William Styron). Under present American conditions, it is not easy for a writer to win that small body of readers, devoted but critical, who will become a sustaining, patient echo to the deepening of his own craft. Room for experiment is hard come by.

In England, circumstances are grayer but they allow breathing space. A book earns far less, even if it is very well received. By American terms, advances against the next are derisively small (many a successful English novelist counts himself lucky if his publisher offers £250). Criticism is more wary, less prone to hosannas. Universities or creative-writing conferences do not pounce on the living writer with their paralyzing scrutiny. It is still possible for a good publisher to nurse an author through a series of novels that sell only moderately, and keep them in print. Thus may be established an invaluable core of readers who have discovered the work for themselves and who will gradually assert its stature (witness the subterranean growth to fame of the *œuvre* of John Cowper Powys or Charles Williams). Above all, English life fosters privacies, a narrow quiet and modesty of material existence, such as encourage a writer's slow development of his own voice and purpose. Hence the striking number of contemporary English novelists who genuinely have "work in progress," in whose writing there is a vital architecture: Anthony Powell, Iris Murdoch, Ivy Compton-Burnett, Evelyn Waugh, C. P. Snow, Lawrence Durrell, Muriel Spark. One may not like what they are doing, but their individual books carry the sense of a whole.

This has been strikingly true of William Golding. His manner of life illustrates the case. He did not publish fiction until he was forty-three. His professional career has been that of a schoolmaster in Salisbury. He has lived in the West Country, away from the literary froth and journalism of London. Despite his fame, Golding's earnings remained modest until recently; his independence is probably based on American lecture fees rather than on English royalties. His style of life and his schoolmastering have allowed (and compelled) him to work slowly. *Lord of the Flies* was published in 1954; *The Inheritors* followed in 1955, but had been written and rewritten earlier. *Pincher Martin*, a very short book, appeared in 1956; *Free Fall* in 1959. Golding's new novel has been impatiently awaited, but he held back and reworked. *The Spire* has been nearly five years in the making. It too is part of an unfolding shape, of a vision in progress.

At present, Golding's place is even higher in America than it is in England. For a time he replaced Camus and Salinger as the idol of the college bookstore. *Lord of the Flies* has been a password among the young. Theses are starting to grind the living flesh to fine, dead powder. He has touched a particular American nerve.

This is no accident. He represents, nearly too neatly, the classic contrast between the American tradition of the novel as romance, as dark fable and philosophic allegory, and the English norm of social fiction. The natural precedents to *Lord of the Flies* and *Pincher Martin* are the tales of Hawthorne and *Billy Budd*. (This is true even though the plot of *Lord of the Flies* has its source in an English boys' adventure story, and owes something to *A High Wind in Jamaica*.) Golding's peculiar conjunction of moral allegory and sensuous detail, the fantasy, solitude, and violence of his outlook touch at many points on the art of Poe, Hawthorne, and Melville. To find anything like it in the English tradition, one would look to the "outsiders"—to the Brontës, to Stevenson, to John Cowper and T. F. Powys.

Consciously or not, Golding has chosen themes and settings remote from the conventions of the contemporary English novel. Only *Free Fall*, with its possible echoes of Joyce Cary, is located on home ground and amid the props of habitual society—and even here the controlling device is one of violence and extreme situation. *The Inheritors* is set in pre-history, *The Spire* in the Middle Ages. Obvious strands relate the island of *Lord of the Flies* and Pincher Martin's rock fang to a mainland of class, society, and current crisis, but they run through strange, isolating seas.

Golding's novels turn on three major themes or obsessions: barbarism, solitude, and will. One can watch how Golding initiates and explores a motif from book to book, how he mines it from different directions of imagination until he has made it his own. Thus *The Inheritors* and *Lord of the Flies* form a close pair, whereas *Pincher Martin*—sea-girt as is the island fable—maps the study in confinement and solitude carried out in *Free Fall*. By its very title, *Free Fall* proclaims the metaphors of height and vertigo, of free will and imperiled grace, which define the theme of *The Spire*.

There are close interrelations. The fabric of human sanity and rational custom is persistently gnawed by savagery or the break of will. A statement from *The Golden Bough* could stand in epigraph: "We seem to move on a thin crust which may at any moment be rent by the subterranean forces slumbering below. From time to time a hollow murmur underground or a sudden spirt of flame into the air tells of what is going on beneath our feet." And clearly, Frazer's hypothesis of how much of ritual terror and magic has survived in the modern psyche matters to Golding. But the counter-strokes of civilization are ambiguous. The "humane barbarism" of the aboriginals in *The Inheritors* is supplanted by a more rational, efficient savagery. The frenzied pack in *Lord of the Flies*, with its barbed parody of Rousseau's dream of child and noble savage, is reclaimed to order and civilization by an instrument of modern war, by a ferocity more disciplined but ultimately more damned than that of the boys—a point made more insistent in the film than in the book.

Solitude is also two-edged. There is no easy escape from the contagion of the group. Alone on a sliver of rock or in the black broom-closet of *Free Fall* (like Poe, Golding is a master of suffocation and solitary confinement), the human character splinters into raw fragments of fear and hysterical egotism. Together we cry havoc; alone we rend our own flesh. The hazard of grace lies in enormous labors of will: by making of the soul a pure blaze of will, we claw to the top of the rock, we defy the jeering totem of evil, we burst out of the closet. But the price is mortal poise; at its uttermost stretch, the human will makes dizzy and we plummet.

That is the plot of *The Spire*. Jocelin, Dean of the Cathedral Church of Our Lady at Salisbury, is possessed, to the point of near madness, by the vision of a stone arrow, four hundred feet high, in eternal flight to God's heaven. To stonemason and fellow priest, to the Cathedral chapter and the outside world, Jocelin's vision is blasphemous folly. No such spire can be built; the foundations are crumbling beneath its crazy weight; the base pillars of the church sing and bend in intolerable strain; the rising fabric of stone and wood moves sickeningly in the autumn gales.

Jocelin sacrifices every duty, every discrimination, to the shrill fixity of his dream. The money he uses to build is tainted with mockery and corruption. In the stricken nave, open to rubble and the rise of stinking water, the candles go out and the choirs fall silent. There is lechery and murder among the workers; they scurry about like the wolf pack in *Lord of the Flies*. Thrust out of the stripped loins of the church, the steeple infects all who pass under its shadow. But Jocelin lashes himself into a frenzy of will. An angel stands at his back in mysterious affirmation. Is he God's messenger, or Jocelin's will kindled to incarnate flame? The Dean forces himself up the spire in a final lust of soul; he hammers in the crowning nail. Then, in a gesture which is both supreme abasement and a probing of God's purpose, Jocelin drives a spike deep into the southeast pillar. Even as the spire should come crashing down, he himself falls to the stone floor, his body scorched with a fatal burning.

The fable has a rigorous simplicity. Minor characters exist only as they pass in and out of the wild light of Jocelin's obsession. The huddled roofs and the river, the downs and the distant beat of the sea, are viewed solely from the angle of the spire. The wheel of the sky and seasons pivots on the mounting structure of pinnacle and octagon. Every page of the novel bears the stress of mutinous stone.

The writing shows all of Golding's characteristic devices: the very short sentences with their effect of arrested speed; the knit of abstract noun and concrete verb; the omission of the article to give a curious, archaic intensity. The dialogue, as nearly always in Golding, jerks abruptly between normal communication and inward speech. The language is formidably tactile. Even light is made solid to the skin:

> Everywhere, fine dust gave these rods and trunks of light the importance of a dimension. He blinked at them again, seeing, near at hand, how the individual grains of dust turned over each other, or bounced all together, like mayfly in a breath of wind. He saw how further away they drifted cloudily, coiled, or hung in a moment of pause, becoming, in the most distant rods and trunks, nothing but colour, honey-colour slashed across the body of the cathedral.

Clearly, this is a book of great beauty and distinction of style. But it is not, I think, a good novel. The fierce excitement which is its theme grows static and rhetorical. We *know* from the first page on that the spire will be built and that Jocelin shall perish in the charring of his will. The very glitter of the language becomes monotonous. I found myself skipping ahead, hoping for some twist of life or modulation of tone. One has the impression of one of those Indian *ragas*, subtle, formal, beautifully played and controlled, but getting nowhere.

The essential design, and many of the details, moreover, are heavily dated. The novel or drama of obsession, of insane singularity of will and purpose, is a nineteenth-century *genre:* Ahab, Balzac's *La*

Recherche de l'Absolu, Zola's *L'Oeuvre*. A maniac craftsman trafficking with darkness to achieve a perfect object is a stock theme in Hawthorne. The mad will and the mystic church, the tower and vertigo, take us back to Ibsen's *Brand* and *The Master Builder*. The mute stonecarver who acts as guardian of Jocelin's conscience has the unexamined pathos of his forebear in *Notre-Dame de Paris*—a link with Victor Hugo which seems relevant also to *Hans d'Islande* and *Pincher Martin*.

The allegory creaks with labored cliches. The spire is the mast of a storm-battered ship. It is a phallus. It ends, in the instant of Jocelin's death, by being the apple tree of man's knowledge and "free fall." Sexual temptation has red hair. Most of the figures are as graphic and flat as playing cards.

That is becoming the main problem of Golding's art. Allegory generates a surface strength. But it goes hollow unless there is behind it a genuinely complex argument and reading of experience. Golding's allegoric fiction renders an incisive but increasingly narrow view of human possibility. Notably, it excludes a full treatment of the relations between men and women. The only woman who has come fully alive in Golding is Taffy, and all we see of her in *Free Fall* are a few glimpses. Here again, Golding's novels fit the pattern of tense masculinity that prevails in Poe, Hawthorne, and Melville.

In Golding's choice of a medieval setting, in the stark naïveté of his tale, there may be an element of withdrawal, of a refusal to enmesh his creative gift with issues more perplexed and contemporaneous. But final simplicity, as in Kafka, works best where it is paradox; where a deep originality and richness of meaning is implicit. As Jocelin crawls down from the reeling summit, the query that nags is—so what?

I say this with diffidence. When dealing with someone of Golding's stature and integrity of purpose, judgment is provisional. I have been rereading *Free Fall* and the purgatorial intimations in *Pincher Martin*. Obviously, some kind of quest is being pursued, and the next novel may give weight to what seems facile and rhetorical in the passion of Dean Jocelin. This is precisely where the notion of an *œuvre* intervenes. Golding's novels modify each other in mutual response. We are in mid-course, and it would take rashness to assert that one had unraveled the mastering design.

My worry is, simply, that we are heading toward a religiosity, a positive mystique, far less interesting and personal than Golding's considerable powers as an artist. The light beckons, and its present absence or tormenting shimmer is finely rendered, but it may turn out to be no more than a High Church candle. This would account for Golding's prestige on the American campus. Like Camus and Salinger, though in an entirely different vocabulary, he seems to embody and dignify a nervous appetite for revelation. A great novelist, a shaper of new feelings and discomforts, has better to do.

"DYING IS AN ART"

I have not read *The Bell Jar*, a novel that Sylvia Plath published under the name of Victoria Lucas. The rest of her work consists of two volumes of poems: *The Colossus*, first published in England in 1960, and *Ariel*, published in London in the spring of 1965, two years after her death, together with a number of poems first printed in *Encounter*. Some of these have not been included in the posthumous collection.

It is fair to say that no group of poems since Dylan Thomas' *Deaths and Entrances* has had as vivid and disturbing an impact on English critics and readers as has *Ariel*. Sylvia Plath's last poems have already passed into legend as both representative of our present tone of emotional life and unique in their implacable, harsh brilliance. Those among the young who read new poetry will know "Daddy," "Lady Lazarus," and "Death & Co." almost by heart, and reference to Sylvia Plath is constant where poetry and the conditions of its present existence are discussed.

The spell does not lie wholly in the poems themselves. The suicide of Sylvia Plath at the age of thirty-one in 1963, and the personality of this young woman who had come from Massachusetts to study and live in England (where she married Ted Hughes, himself a gifted poet), are vital parts of it. To those who knew her and to the greatly enlarged circle who were electrified by her last poems and sudden death, she had come to signify the specific honesties and risks of the poet's condition. Her personal style, and the price in private harrowing she so obviously paid to achieve the intensity and candor of her principal poems, have taken on their own dramatic authority.

All this makes it difficult to judge the poems. I mean that the vehemence and intimacy of the verse is such as to constitute a very powerful rhetoric of sincerity. The poems play on our nerves with their own proud nakedness, making claims so immediate and sharply urged that the reader flinches, embarrassed by the routine discretions and evasions of his own sensibility. Yet if these poems are to take life among us, if they are to be more than exhibits in the history of modern psychological stress, they must be read with all the intelligence and scruple we can muster. They are too honest, they have cost too much, to be yielded to myth.

One of the most striking poems in *Colossus*, "All the Dead Dears," tells of a skeleton in the Cambridge museum of classical antiquities:

> How they grip us through thin and thick,
> These barnacle dead!
> This lady here's no kin
> Of mine, yet kin she is: she'll suck
> Blood and whistle my marrow clean
> To prove it. As I think now of her head,
>
> From the mercury-backed glass
> Mother, grandmother, greatgrandmother
> Reach hag hands to haul me in,
> And an image looms under the fishpond surface
> Where the daft father went down
> With orange duck-feet winnowing his hair—

On a small scale, the lines illustrate a good deal of Sylvia Plath's tactics and syntax of feeling. The short lines are paced with delicate, seemingly offhand control. The half-rhymes, cross-rhymes, and alliterations give tautness to what might otherwise appear an arbitrary measure. The allusion to *The Duchess of Malfi* ("When I look into the fish-pond in my garden,/Methinks I see a thing armed with a rake") is nicely judged. The motifs touched on are those which organize much of Sylvia Plath's poetry: the generation of women knit by blood and death, the dead reaching out to haul the living into their shadowy vortex, the personage of the father somehow sinister and ineffectual, the poet literally bled and whistled clean by the cruel, intricate quality of felt life.

"Watercolour of Grantchester Meadows" is explicitly conventional in setting and tone. But at the close, this version of pastoral deflects abruptly into darkness and muted hysteria:

> Droll, vegetarian, the water rat
> Saws down a reed and swims from his limber grove,
> While the students stroll or sit,
> Hands laced, in a moony indolence of love—
> Black-gowned, but unaware
> How in such mild air
> The owl shall stoop from his turret, the rat cry out.

The black gowns, which are merely the ordinary garb of the Cambridge undergraduate, are so placed as to alert the reader to mourning; the vegetarian cries out under the sudden beak of the carnivore. One recognizes the props: the moon, the reed-fringed water, the owl and turret. They are a part of that Gothic strain which is so constant beneath the surface of English lyric poetry, and which has been reinforced in modern verse by its consonance with the mortalities and erotic conceits of the Metaphysicals and Jacobeans.

This penchant for the Gothic effect seems to me to weaken much of Sylvia Plath's earlier verse, and it extends into her mature work. She used Gothicism in a particular way, making the formal terrors an equivalent to genuine and complex shocks of feeling, but the modish element is undeniable. Her resources were, however, more diverse. Possessed of a rare intensity and particularity of nervous response—the "disquieting muses" had stood at the left side of her crib "with heads like darning-eggs"—Sylvia Plath tested different symbolic means, different modes of concretion, with which to articulate what rang so queer and clear inside her. It is almost silly to argue "influences" when dealing with a young poet of this honesty and originality. But one can locate the impulses that helped her find her own voice. Wallace Stevens for one:

> Death whitens in the egg and out of it.
> I can see no colour for this whiteness.
> White: it is a complexion of the mind.

Or Emily Dickinson, whose authority gives a poem like "Spinster" its spiky charm:

> And round her house she set
> Such a barricade of barb and check. . . .

The tactile, neutral precision of D. H. Lawrence's observations of animal and vegetable is recognizable in "Medallion" and "Blue Moles." These poets, together with Andrew Marvell and the Jacobean dramatists, seem to have meant a lot. But the final poem in *Colossus*, a seven-part garland "For a Birthday," is unmistakable. In at least three sections, "Dark House," "Maenad," and "The Stones," Sylvia Plath writes in a way that is entirely hers. Had one been shown only the last six lines, one would have known—or should have—that a formidable compulsion was implicit and that a new, mature style had been achieved:

> Love is the bone and sinew of my curse,
> The vase, reconstructed, houses
> The elusive rose.
>
> Ten fingers shape a bowl for shadows.
> My mendings itch. There is nothing to do.
> I shall be good as new.

Undoubtedly, the success of this poem arises from the fact that Sylvia Plath had mastered her essential theme, the situation and emotive counters around which she was henceforth to build much of her verse: the infirm or rent body, and the imperfect, painful resurrection of the psyche, pulled back, unwilling, to the hypocrisies of health. It is a theme already present in *Colossus* ("Two Views of a Cadaver Room"). It dominates, to an obsessive degree, much of *Ariel*. As "Lady Lazarus" proclaims:

> Dying
> Is an art, like everything else.
> I do it exceptionally well.
>
> I do it so it feels like hell.
> I do it so it feels real.
> I guess you could say I've a call.

It requires no biographical impertinence to realize that Sylvia Plath's life was harried by bouts of physical pain, that she sometimes looked on the accumulated exactions of her own nerve and body as "a trash / To annihilate each decade." She was haunted by the piecemeal, strung-together mechanics of the flesh, by what could be so easily broken and then mended with such searing ingenuity. The hospital ward was her exemplary ground:

> My patent leather overnight case like a black pillbox,3ems
> My husband and child smiling out of the family photo;
> Their smiles catch onto my skin, little smiling hooks.

This brokenness, so sharply feminine and contemporary, is, I think, her principal realization. It is by the graphic expression she gave to it that she will be judged and remembered. Sylvia Plath carries forward, in an intensely womanly and aggravated note, from Robert Lowell's *Life Studies*, a book that obviously had a great impact on her. This new frankness of women about the specific hurts and tangles of their nervous-physiological makeup is as vital to the poetry of Sylvia Plath as it is to the tracts of Simone de Beauvoir or to the novels of Edna O'Brien and Brigid Brophy. Women speak out as never before:

> The womb
> Rattles its pod, the moon
> Discharges itself from the tree with nowhere to go.
>> ("Childless Woman")

> They have swabbed me clear of my loving associations.
> Scared and bare on the green plastic-pillowed trolley. . . .
>> ("Tulips")

It is difficult to think of a precedent to the fearful close of "Medusa" (the whole poem is extraordinary):

> I shall take no bite of your body,
> Bottle in which I live,

> Ghastly Vatican.
> I am sick to death of hot salt.
> Green as eunuchs, your wishes
> Hiss at my sin.
> Off, off, eely tentacle!

> There is nothing between us.

The ambiguity and dual flash of insight in this final line are of a richness and obviousness that only a very great poem can carry off.

299

The progress registered between the early and the mature poems is one of concretion. The general Gothic means with which Sylvia Plath was so fluently equipped become singular to herself and therefore fiercely honest. What had been style passes into need. It is the need of a superbly intelligent, highly literate young woman to cry out about her especial being, about the tyrannies of blood and gland, of nervous spasm and sweating skin, the rankness of sex and childbirth in which a woman is still compelled to be wholly of her organic condition. Where Emily Dickinson could—indeed was obliged to—shut the door on the riot and humiliations of the flesh, thus achieving her particular dry lightness, Sylvia Plath "fully assumed her own condition." This alone would assure her of a place in modern literature. But she took one step further, assuming a burden that was not naturally or necessarily hers.

Born in Boston in 1932 of German and Austrian parents, Sylvia Plath had no personal, immediate contact with the world of the concentration camps. I may be mistaken, but so far as I know there was nothing Jewish in her background. But her last, greatest poems culminate in an act of identification, of total communion with those tortured and massacred. The poet sees herself on

> An engine, an engine
> Chuffing me off like a Jew.
> A Jew to Dachau, Auschwitz, Belsen.
> I began to talk like a Jew.
> I think I may well be a Jew.
>
> The snows of the Tyrol, the clear beer of Vienna
> Are not very pure or true.
> With my gypsy ancestress and my weird luck
>
> And my Tarot pack and my Tarot pack
> I may be a bit of a Jew.

Distance is no help; nor the fact that one is "guilty of nothing." The dead men cry out of the yew hedges. The poet becomes the loud cry of their choked silence:

> Herr God, Herr Lucifer
> Beware
> Beware.

300

Out of the ash
I rise with my red hair
And I eat men like air.

Here the almost surrealistic wildness of the gesture is kept in place by the insistent obviousness of the language and beat; a kind of Hieronymus Bosch nursery rhyme.

Sylvia Plath is only one of a number of young contemporary poets, novelists, and playwrights, themselves in no way implicated in the actual holocaust, who have done most to counter the general inclination to forget the death camps. Perhaps it is only those who had no part in the events who *can* focus on them rationally and imaginatively; to those who experienced the thing, it has lost the hard edges of possibility, it has stepped outside the real.

Committing the whole of her poetic and formal authority to the metaphor, to the mask of language, Sylvia Plath *became* a woman being transported to Auschwitz on the death trains. The notorious shards of massacre seemed to enter into her own being:

A cake of soap,
A wedding ring,
A gold filling.

In "Daddy" she wrote one of the very few poems I know of in any language to come near the last horror. It achieves the classic act of generalization, translating a private, obviously intolerable hurt into a code of plain statement, of instantaneously public images which concern us all. It is the "Guernica" of modern poetry. And it is both histrionic and, in some ways, "arty," as is Picasso's outcry.

Are these final poems entirely legitimate? In what sense does anyone, himself uninvolved and long after the event, commit a subtle larceny when he invokes the echoes and trappings of Auschwitz and appropriates an enormity of ready emotion to his own private design? Was there latent in Sylvia Plath's sensibility, as in that of many of us who remember only by fiat of imagination, a fearful envy, a dim resentment at not having been there, of having missed the rendezvous with hell? In "Lady Lazarus" and "Daddy" the realization seems to me so complete, the sheer rawness and control so great, that only irresistible need could have brought it off. These poems take tremendous risks, extending Sylvia Plath's essentially austere manner to the very limit. They are a bitter triumph, proof of the capacity of poetry to give to reality the greater permanence of the imagined. She could not return from them.

Already there are poets writing like Sylvia Plath. Certain of her angular mannerisms, her elisions and monotonies of deepening rhyme, can be caught and will undoubtedly have their fashion. But minor poets even of a great intensity—and that is what she was—tend to prove bad models. Sylvia Plath's tricks of voice can be imitated. Not her desperate integrity.

MARXISM AND
LITERATURE

MARXISM AND
THE LITERARY CRITIC

". . . Difficulties encountered when writing the truth"

At the origins of the Marxist theory of literature there are three celebrated and canonic texts. Two of them are citations from Engels' letters; the third is contained in a short essay by Lenin. Engels wrote to Minna Kautsky in November 1885:

> I am by no means an opponent of tendentious, programmatic poetry (*Tendenzpoesie*) as such. The father of tragedy, Aeschylus, and the father of comedy, Aristophanes, were both strong *Tendenzpoeten* no less than Dante and Cervantes; and it is the finest element in Schiller's *Kabale und Liebe* that it is the first German political *Tendenzdrama*. The modern Russians and Norwegians, who produce excellent novels, are all *Tendenzdichter*. But I believe that the thesis must spring forth from the situation and action itself, without being explicitly displayed. I believe that there is no compulsion for the writer to put into the reader's hands the future historical resolution of the social conflicts which he is depicting.

Writing in English to Margaret Harkness, at the beginning of April 1888, Engels was more emphatic:

> I am far from finding fault with you for not having written a point-blank socialist novel, a "Tendenzroman" as we Germans call it, to glorify the social and political views of the author. That is not at all what I mean. The more the

opinions of the author remain hidden, the better for the work of art.

By virtue of this principle, Engels defends his preference of Shakespeare over Schiller, of Balzac over Zola. The third text, however, is altogether different. In his essay on "Party Organization and Party Literature," published in *Novaia Jizn* in November 1905, Lenin wrote:

> Literature must become Party literature. . . . Down with un-partisan *littérateurs!* Down with the supermen of literature! Literature must become a part of the general cause of the proletariat, "a small cog and a small screw" in the social-democratic mechanism, one and indivisible—a mechanism set in motion by the entire conscious vanguard of the whole working class. Literature must become an integral part of the organised, methodical, and unified labours of the social-democratic Party.

These injunctions were put forward as tactical arguments in the early polemic against aestheticism. But cited out of context, Lenin's call for *Tendenzpoesie* in the most naked sense, has come to be regarded as a general canon of the Marxist interpretation of literature.

Clearly, there is between Engels' pronouncements and the Leninist conception a profound divergence in bias and drift of argument —if not a formal contradiction. The kinds of critical response and sensibility engaged by the literary work are, in the respective instances, wholly different. This disparity has not escaped the awareness of Marxist theoreticians. Georg Lukács has twice attempted to reconcile Engels' defense of the poet's uncommitted integrity with Lenin's demand for total partisanship and aesthetic discipline. In his major essay on Engels as a theoretician and critic of literature (1935), Lukács quotes from the letter to Minna Kautsky and proposes an intricate gloss. He argues that the type of *Tendenz* (Edmund Wilson renders this crucial term by "tendency" but "thesis" and "programmatic bias" are closer) which Engels would find acceptable is, at bottom, "identical with that 'Party element' which materialism, from the time of Lenin on, encloses in itself." According to this analysis, Engels is not objecting to a *littérature engagée* as such but rather to the mixture "of mere empiricism and empty subjectivity" in the bourgeois novel of the period. Obviously dissatisfied with this treatment of the problem, Lukács reverted to it in 1945, in his "Introduction to the Writings on Aesthetics of Marx and Engels." Here he contends that Engels was distinguishing between two forms of *littérature à thèse* (it is significant that the English language and its critical vocabulary have developed no precisely equivalent expression). All great literature, in Lukács' reading has a "fundamental bias." A writer can only achieve a mature and responsible portrayal of life if he is committed to progress and opposed to reaction, if he "loves the good and rejects the bad." When a critic of Lukács' subtlety and rigor descends to such banalities—banalities which directly challenge his own works on Goethe, Balzac, and Tolstoy— we know that something is amiss. The attempt to reconcile the image of literature implicit in Lenin's essay with that put forward by Engels is a rather desperate response to the pressures of orthodoxy and to the Stalinist demand for total internal coherence in Marxist doctrine. Even the most delicate exegesis cannot conceal the plain fact that Engels and Lenin were saying different things, that they were pointing toward contrasting ideals.

This fact is of signal importance in the history of Marxist literature and Marxist literary criticism. Time and again the ideal of a literature in which "the opinions of the author remain hidden" has clashed with the Leninist formula of militant partiality. According to the choice which they were compelled to make, even unconsciously, between Engels' aesthetics and Lenin's, Marxist critics have split into two principal camps: the orthodox group and those whom Michel Crouzet has aptly called the "para-Marxists." Zhdanovism and the First Soviet Writers' Congress of 1934 rigorously proclaimed the orthodox position. In his address to the Congress, Zhdanov deliberately chose Engels' own terms but rejected Engels' meaning in the name of Leninism:

> Our Soviet literature is not afraid of the charge of being "tendentious." Yes, Soviet literature is tendentious, for in an epoch of class struggle there is not and cannot be a literature which is not class literature, not tendentious, allegedly non-political.

Bukharin followed suit and declared that *Tendenzpoesie* and poetry recognized as of the first rank on purely formal grounds would, more often than not, prove to be one and the same. In evidence, he cited names which recur incessantly in Marxist poetics: "Freiligrath and

Heine, Barbier and Béranger."

The orthodox school, orthodoxy being in this case a political rather than an historical notion, has its journals both in Russia and in the West (*Soviet Literature* and *La Nouvelle Critique* are prominent examples). It has its primers such as André Stil's *Vers le réalisme socialiste*, Howard Fast's *Literature and Reality*, and the compendious theoretical pronouncements of Aragon. In England it has found expression in some of the writings of Jack Lindsay and Arnold Kettle. The purest strain of orthodoxy in German Marxism has been embodied in the poems and essays of Johannes Becher. Becher stated in 1954: "Primarily I owe it to Lenin that I gradually learned to see things as they really are." The invocation of Lenin is, indeed, the invariable talisman of the orthodox critic.

In the Soviet Union itself, orthodoxy assumed the dour and turgid guise of Zhdanovism and Stalinist aesthetics. To it we owe the most consequent and tragically successful campaign ever waged by a political régime to enlist or destroy the shaping powers of the literary imagination. Only those impelled by professional interest to wade through the official critical journals and state publications of the Stalinist era can fully realize to what levels of inhumanity and mere verbiage *belles-lettres* and the art of the critic can descend. The pattern is one of desperate monotony: interminable discussions as to whether or not this novel or that poem is in accord with the Party line; strident exercises in self-denunciation by authors who have, through some momentary failure of agility, taken an "incorrect" position on some aspect of socialist realism; incessant demands that fiction, drama, and poetry be forged into "weapons for the proletariat"; glorifications of the "positive hero" and condemnations, at times hysterical in their puritanism, of any hint of eroticism or stylistic ambiguity. The ideal of Zhdanovism was, precisely, the reduction of literature to "a small cog and a small screw" in the mechanism of the totalitarian state. By hazard of genius or partisan anger, such a literature could (though, in fact, it did not) produce something of the order of *Uncle Tom's Cabin*. Any work of more genuine complexity or impartiality constitutes a potential threat to "the organised, methodical, and unified labours" of the Party. Under such circumstances a critic has only two functions: he is an interpreter of Party dogma and a discerner of heresy. This, precisely, was the inglorious and ultimately suicidal role of Fadeyev.

But neither imprimatur nor anathema are the critic's job of

work. What authentic critical impulses did survive went underground into scholarship. Remnants of the liberal imagination took refuge in the craft of the editor and the translator. Thus we find, even during spells of ideological terror, competent translations and discussions of Shakespeare and Dickens, of Molière and Balzac. The war somewhat attenuated the dreariness of the Soviet literary scene. Private anguish and patriotic fervor coalesced with the political necessities of the moment. But there was no evolution in criticism to match the achievements of novelists and poets. The war, in fact, reinforced the Leninist-Zhdanovite thesis that literature is an instrument of battle, that its ultimate values lie in the rhetoric of persuasion and total commitment.

Essentially, therefore, the orthodox wing of Marxist literary criticism and theory, the Leninist espousal of *Tendenzpoesie* as the ideal for both writer and Party, has proved barren. There are very few examples of wholly orthodox, yet valid and creative, applications of Leninist principles to a literary text. Perhaps the most distinguished occur among the critical writings of Brecht. These writings should be considered apart from his plays across which there usually falls the brightening shadow of heresy. Brecht's "Five Difficulties Encountered when Writing the Truth" (1934), has real urgency and conviction. It exemplifies the dictum of another Marxist critic that literary criticism and the study of poetics is the "act of strategy in the literature-battle (*im Literaturkampf.*)" Brecht's most fascinating exercise in critical orthodoxy, however, came much later, in 1953. It is a dialectical examination (presented in the guise of a discussion between producer and actors) of Act I of Shakespeare's *Coriolanus*. The problem is posed in Leninist terms: how should the scene of the plebeians be interpreted and acted so as to yield the fullest measure of political insight—of insight compatible with a dialectical interpretation of history? In the course of discussion, a high degree of critical intelligence and an acute awareness of theatrical means are brought to bear on the Shakespearean text. The final exchanges are particularly illuminating:

> *R.* Do you believe that all this and more may be "read out" of the play?
> *B.* Read out of and read into.
> *P.* Do we propose to perform the play because of these insights?

B. Not for that reason alone. We want to have the pleasure and convey the pleasure of dealing with a piece of illumined (*durchleuchteter*) history. We wish to experience, to live, a piece of dialectic.

P. Is that not a somewhat esoteric notion, reserved to the initiate?

B. By no means. Even at the panoramas shown at public fairs and when hearing popular ballads, simple folk, who are in so few respects simple, enjoy stories of the rise and fall of the mighty, of the cunning of the oppressed, of the potentialities of men. And they seek out the truth, that which "lies behind it all."

But this "living of the dialectic" and the free play of irony and sensibility over the literary text are exceedingly rare among those Marxists who have adopted Lenin's response to literature, as set forth in *Novaia Jizn*, rather than Engels'. (The restriction is necessary, for elsewhere—in the two short essays on Tolstoy and in remarks made to Gorky—Lenin took a subtler and more tolerant view of poetic freedom.)

I I

Of far greater importance, both with respect to past accomplishment and future influence, is the work of the para-Marxist school of criticism and aesthetic theory. It embraces a wide range of attitudes and values—from those of the early Edmund Wilson, whose Marxism was in essence an extension of Taine's historical and social determinism, to those of Theodor Adorno, a critic at times on the verge of orthodoxy. What do the para-Marxists (or we might call them, the "Engelians") share in common? The belief that literature is centrally conditioned by historical, social, and economic forces; the conviction that ideological content and the articulate world-view of a writer are crucially engaged in the act of literary judgment; a suspicion of any aesthetic doctrine which places major stress on the irrational elements in poetic creation and on the demands of "pure form." Finally, they share a bias toward dialectical proceedings in argument. But however committed they may be to dialectical materialism, para-Marxists approach a work of art with respect for its integrity and for the vital center of its being. They are at one with Engels in regarding as inferior the kinds of literature which, in Keats's phrase, have a palpable design upon us. Above all—and it is this which distinguishes them from the orthodox—para-Marxists practice the arts of criticism, not those of censorship.

For evident reasons, these critics have flourished principally outside the immediate orbit of Soviet power. The one exception is, however, decisive. Georg Lukács stands as a lone and splendid tower amidst the gray landscape of eastern European and Communist intellectual life. His stature as a critic and theoretician of aesthetics is no longer in question. In capaciousness of intellect and breadth of performance, he ranks with the master-critics of our age. No contemporary Western critic, with the possible exception of Croce, has brought to bear on literary problems a philosophic equipment of comparable authority. In no one since Sainte-Beuve has the sense of history, the feeling for the rootedness of the imagination in time and in place, been as solid and acute. Lukács' writings on Goethe and Balzac, on Schiller and Hegelianism, on the rise of the historical novel and the dark upsurge of irrationalism in German poetry, are classics. Few have spoken with finer discrimination of Tolstoy and Thomas Mann. The very massiveness of his labors —a collected edition would run to more than twenty volumes— constitutes something of a miracle: the growth and endurance under Communist rule of an independent aesthetics, of a large body of practical criticism which diverges time and again from Leninist and Stalinist orthodoxy. The end of Lukács' personal Odyssey is, at present, in tragic doubt.* But his accomplishments lie beyond the reach of political attainder. They demonstrate that Marxism can yield a poetics and a metaphysic of the highest order.

Any consideration of the "Engelian" strain in Marxist literary criticism leads inevitably to Lukács. Much of his work may indeed be regarded as a broadening of the famous distinction between Balzac and Zola which Engels proposed to Miss Harkness. But I want to consider Lukács' complex and voluminous criticism in another essay, and draw attention here to a number of lesser-known critics all of whom are Marxists in substance and methodology, yet none of

[* This is, fortunately, no longer the case. Lukács survived the aftermath of the Hungarian rising and has lived to see eastern Europe assume new and complex shapes of national feeling. Whether this resurgence of energies founded, essentially, in the nationalistic, agrarian past brings him comfort is, of course, another matter.]

whom would subscribe to the Leninist image of literature as a cog and screw in the Juggernaut of the proletariat.

Around the hard core of French Stalinism, a harsh and disciplined *cadre* oddly untouched by the "thaw" of 1953–54, there has always flourished a large and animated world of intellectual Marxism. Its leading figures, such as Merleau-Ponty and Sartre, have often inclined toward the vortex of total adherence. But they draw back in the final moment, seeking to establish an ideological position which will be outside the Party—but not hostile to it. From both the dialectical and the practical point of view, such an attempt is doomed to ambivalence and failure. But the making of it charges French intellectual life with rare intensity and gives to abstract argument the strong pertinence of conflict. In France, even old men are angry.

There are significant elements of the para-Marxist position in Sartre's writings on literature. But the work of Lucien Goldmann offers a purer and more stringent example of dialectical criticism. His massive treatise *Le Dieu caché* (1955) has led to a major revaluation of the role of Jansenism in seventeenth-century literature. If there has, during the past three years, been an *affaire Racine* in French criticism and scholarship, Goldmann is in part responsible. His gnarled and intricate argument—the aura of Hegelianism having fallen across the directness of a French style—seeks to relate the "tragic vision" of Pascal's *Pensées* and Racine's dramas to an extremist faction in the Jansenist movement. Goldmann's view of religion, theology, and literature is that of a classical Marxist. He sees in a philosophy or a poem an ideological edifice—what Marx called *ein Ueberbau*—whose foundations are economic, political, and social. He demonstrates, with a wealth of textual erudition, how elements of class strategy entered into even the most subtle and unworldly of seventeenth-century theological conflicts. But like Engels, and Marx himself, Goldmann insists on the radical complexity of the ideological structure, on the fact that relationships between economic forces and philosophic or poetic systems are never automatic and unilinear. This gives to his treatment of Racine's career a persuasive subtlety. The Racine who emerges from *Le Dieu caché* is a poet anchored in history. It is no longer possible, for example, to ignore the relations between the darkening of his world-view and the period of disillusion which seized on French Jansenism after 1675. Frequently, moreover, Goldmann arrives, through a process of dialectical analysis, at conclusions sanctioned by scholars of a wholly different conviction. Thus he sees in the problem of the chorus in neo-classical tragedy a direct reflection of the fragmentation of post-feudal society, the metamorphosis of a unified community into an aggregate of *monades sans portes ni fenêtres*. This accords precisely with the views of Tillyard and Francis Fergusson. At his finest, Goldmann is simply a critic responding with mature admiration to a great text. Commenting on Phèdre's decision to rise from her chair (Act I, scene iii), he observes: "One approaches the universe of tragedy on one's feet." Quite so, and Bradley might have said it.

At times, however, Goldmann's Marxism or, more strictly speaking, his materialist left-Hegelianism, does obtrude on the integrity of his judgment. He oversimplifies the structure of Racinian drama by seeking to impose on it a constant pattern—the triad of hero, society, and "hidden God":

> The *solitaires* and nuns of Port-Royal, in effect, conceived of life as a spectacle enacted before God; the theatre was in France, until Racine's arrival, a spectacle enacted before men; it sufficed to achieve a synthesis, to write for the stage the spectacle performed before God and to add to the habitual human audience the mute and hidden spectator who devalues and replaces that audience, for Racinian tragedy to be born.

It is fascinating to note that Goldmann's orthodox opponents have rejected his treatment of Racine as excessively schematic. Writing in *La Nouvelle Critique* (November 1956), Crouzet points out that Goldmann has neglected the question of *genre* and poetic diction in neo-classicism. In so doing, he has reduced complex poetry to the bare bones of prose content. "Form and content constitute a unity, but a unity of contradictions," said Bukharin in a notable aphorism. Authentic Marxist criticism, says Crouzet, "could not lead to such a dessication of art." He goes on to claim that in para-Marxism two vices necessarily coalesce: subjectivism and a mechanistic view of literature. Yet even in making these charges, Crouzet and his Leninist colleagues are ill at ease. They ask, with genuine worry—where is the true Marxist interpretation of Racine? Why has critical orthodoxy produced so little of value? Constantly, the Party intellectuals, of whom H. Lefebvre is easily the most eminent,[1] have to admit to their

---

[1] On June 22, 1958, Lefebvre was "temporarily" expelled from the Party. He was accused of "revisionism" and he is now an independent Marxist.

own failings. Outside Lefebvre's works on Pascal and Diderot, official French Marxism has produced little of critical substance. Pierre Albouy's *Victor Hugo, essai de critique marxiste* (*La Nouvelle Critique*, June–August 1951), is tedious and inferior work. Though they deplore its heresies, French Communists recognize in *Le Dieu caché* one of the most distinguished attempts yet made to apply dialectical materialism to the high noon of French literature.

Nothing in Goldmann's book caused greater concern among orthodox Marxists than an entry on the *errata et addenda* page. In it, Goldmann declares that when referring to Lukács (which he does constantly), he has in mind Lukács' *History and Class Consciousness*, a famous essay published in 1923 but long since condemned as erroneous by the Communist Party of the U.S.S.R. and by the author himself. It is to this very same essay, however, that Walter Benjamin, the most gifted of the German "Engelians," owed his conversion to Marxism in 1924.

Both as a stylist and thinker, Benjamin is difficult to characterize. In him, more perhaps than in any other Marxist, the texture of language precedes and determines the contours of argument. His prose is close-knit and allusive; it lies in ambush, seizing on its subject by indirection. Walter Benjamin is the R. P. Blackmur of Marxism—but of a Marxism which is private and oblique. Like Rilke and Kafka, Benjamin was possessed by a sense of the brutality of industrial life, by a haunted, apocalyptic vision of the modern metropolis (the *Grosstadt* of Rilke's *Malte Laurids Brigge*). He found his feelings verified and documented by Marx's theory of "dehumanization" and Engels' account of the working class. Thus, Benjamin's essay "On Certain Motifs in Baudelaire" (1939) is, essentially, a lyric meditation on the brooding immensity of nineteenth-century Paris and the concordant solitude of the poet. The same impulse underlies his admiration of Proust—an admiration obviously suspect from the point of view of the Party. Benjamin's two principal essays, "Goethe's *Elective Affinities*" (1924–1925) and "The Origin of German Tragedy" (1928), are among the most difficult and closely argued in modern European criticism. But if there is in them anything dialectical, it pertains to what Adorno, Benjamin's friend and editor, has called "the dialectics of fantasy."

Only once did he approach a problem from a thoroughly Marxist bias. The result is of extreme interest. In a paper entitled "The Work of Art in the Era of its Technical Reproducibility" (1936),

Benjamin proposed to consider neither proletarian art nor art in a classless society, but rather the evolution of art "under prevailing modes of production." The ambiguity in the word "production"—the industrial process in general and the "reproduction" of art works in particular—is relevant to his theme. Benjamin clearly preceded Malraux in recognizing the "materiality" of art, the dependence of aesthetic sensibility on changes in the setting and reproduction of painting and sculpture. He wonders, as did Schiller, whether the history of technology might not be matched by a corresponding "history of perception." The essay contains yet another seminal idea. Benjamin refers to the strident support which Marinetti and Italian Futurism gave to the invasion of Ethiopia. He suggests that it is of the essence of Fascism to beautify the outward trappings and actual inhumanities of political life. But all efforts toward the "beautification of politics" (*die Aesthetisierung der Politik*) lead fatally to the image of "glorious war." Communism, on the other hand, does not render politics artistic. It makes art political. That way, according to Benjamin, lie sanity and peace.

This is a complex notion, either to apprehend or to refute. Benjamin did not live to clarify it further. Like Christopher Caudwell, whose work does by comparison strike one as rather drab, he fell victim to Fascism. Theodor Adorno has observed that Benjamin injected dialectical materialism into his own system as a necessary poison; around this foreign body and creative irritant his sensibility crystallized. So far as literature goes, Adorno himself presents a case of lesser interest. His importance lies in the application of Marxist principles to the history and aesthetics of music.

Sidney Finkelstein, one of a small yet interesting group of American Marxists, is also primarily a critic and sociologist of music. "The forms of music," he writes, "are a product of society.... The validity of a musical form does not rest upon its 'purity,' but upon the easy communication it offers, in its time, for stimulating ideas." In *Art and Society*, however, Finkelstein has ranged more widely, and his book is illustrative of a classical strain in Marxist theory—the alliance between the new culture of the proletariat and ancient folkways. "I have used a philosophic system," he declares:

> It is the body of Marxist thought, which can be described simply as springing from the fact that ideas can only be understood in connection with the material realities of life,

and the realities of life can only be understood in terms of their inner conflicts, movement and change. Karl Marx and Frederick Engels say, "Men, developing their material production and their material intercourse, alter, along with their real existence, their thinking and the products of their thinking. Life is not determined by consciousness but consciousness by life." This is the general approach I have tried to apply to art.

The art forms in which Finkelstein sees the most enduring value are those which are rooted in popular modes. Thus, he argues that Bach's fugal style derived its strength and clarity from the fact that it was based on the division into voices and contrapuntal parts of current folk song. Correspondingly, much of the best in American literature —Mark Twain, Whitman, Sandburg, Frost—would stem from folk rhetoric and the tradition of the popular ballad. Finkelstein discerns in the abstraction and "difficulty" of modern art a direct consequence of the estrangement between the individual artist and the masses. He concurs with Engels in believing that this estrangement was brought on by the commercial aesthetics of the bourgeoisie. Revolted by the "tawdry cheapness" (Ezra Pound's phrase) of bourgeois taste, artists of the late nineteenth and early twentieth centuries lifted anchor and put out to sea. There they dwell in a world increasingly private and increasingly divorced from the maturing energies of communal life.

But in stubborn dissent from Zhdanovite orthodoxy, Finkelstein persists in admiring such lone voyagers as Schoenberg, Proust, and Joyce. He regards *Ulysses* not as Radek did at the Writers' Congress in 1934—"A heap of dung, crawling with worms, photographed by a cinema apparatus through a microscope"—but as a tragic, perhaps self-defeating protest against the "shallowness and dishonesty of the tons of verbiage" disgorged by the commercial literature of the day. One of Finkelstein's most original notions bears on the nature of Romanticism. He seeks to distinguish between negative and positive strains in Romantic sensibility. With the former he associates Dostoevsky. This is a point of some importance. The problem of how to approach Dostoevsky is the moment of truth in all Marxist criticism. Not even Lukács has been able to disengage himself from the Leninist and Stalinist condemnation of the Dostoevskyan world-view as one implacably hostile to dialectical materialism. A Marxist critic who dealt with the works of Dostoevsky, prior to 1954, was by that mere action giving proof of real courage and independence. In reference to *The Brothers Karamazov*, Finkelstein says of Dostoevsky that

> by emphasising the irrational over the rational, hinting at subconscious drives which could be neither understood nor controlled, he led to the climax of romanticism in which the artist and human being cuts himself off completely from the world as unreal.

In the poetry of Aragon, on the other hand, he sees the "positive value of romanticism," its kinship with the liberal instincts and sensuous vitality of the masses.

One could examine a host of other figures among critics and historians of literature to illustrate varying strategies within the larger context of the Marxist tradition. But the essential point can be made quite simply: outside the rigid bounds of Party ideology, there are numerous critics and philosophers of art whose work is either centrally or in substantial measure conditioned by the dialectical method and historical mythology of Marxism. Among them there are theoreticians and practical critics whom anyone seriously concerned with literature would be wrong to ignore.

III

The struggle between Leninist orthodoxy and para-Marxism is bitter and incessant. It has compelled Soviet publicists to query the writings of Engels himself. They cannot accept his distinction between Balzac and Zola and yet adhere, at the same time, to Lenin's axiom that the supreme virtue of art lies in its explicit revolutionary bias. Hence Boris Reizov's curious and tormented book, *Balzac the Writer*. Once again, it takes up the vexed problem of the Harkness letter concerning which, as Fadeyev ruefully conceded in his "Notes on Literature" (February 1956), "some confusion reigns." It will be recalled that Engels judged Balzac "a far greater master of realism than all the Zolas, *passés, présents et à venir*." He did so despite the fact that Balzac was a Legitimist and a Catholic of a somber and reactionary cast:

> That Balzac thus was compelled to go against his own class sympathies and political prejudices, that he *saw* the

necessity of the downfall of his favourite nobles, and described them as people deserving no better fate; and that he *saw* the real men of the future where, for the time being, they alone were to be found—that I consider one of the greatest triumphs of Realism, and one of the grandest features in old Balzac.

Out of this famous passage has arisen the theory of dissociation between ideology and poetic vision. "The history of literature," remarks Lucien Goldmann, "is full of writers whose thought was rigorously contrary to the sense and structure of their work (among many examples, Balzac, Goethe, etc.)." But at the same time, this pronouncement by Engels and its corollary—"The more the opinions of the author remain hidden, the better for the work of art"—pose a drastic challenge to the Leninist ideal of Party literature. If a reactionary novelist, in fact, achieves greater realism than one whose views were explicitly "progressive," the entire conception of the ideological commitment of art is put in doubt. To resolve this dilemma, Reizov is compelled to infer that Engels may have been mistaken; one need hardly comment on the weight of anxiety behind such a supposition. He perceives in Balzac's world-view

> direct links with the revolutionary philosophy of the French Encyclopædists. . . . Balzac remains a true successor of the French revolutionary philosophers—whatever his own political declarations.

Historically, of course, this is nonsense. But it does constitute a desperate attempt to reconcile Engels' views and, *a fortiori*, those of Lukács, with Leninist orthodoxy. For as Valentin Asmus wrote, in an important paper on "Realism and Naturalism" (*Soviet Literature*, March 1948), Lenin, in contrast to Engels, saw in a "direct and frank assertion" of tendentiousness "the chief difference between the proletarian writer and the bourgeois apologist of capitalism."

That the "proletarian writer" has, until now, produced little of enduring value, is a fact of which Soviet critics are recurrently aware. In his notorious intervention at the second Congress of Soviet Writers in 1955, Sholokhov ventured to assert that it was the principal task of contemporary Russian literature to escape from official mediocrity and render itself worthy of its inheritance. This has also been Lukács' persistent contention. Hence his unwillingness to deal, at any length,

with Russian fiction and poetry of the Stalinist era. But to an orthodox critic such an attitude verges on treason. If Lenin is right, even
the most mediocre of post-revolutionary literature is intrinsically
more useful to the modern reader than are classics written under
feudalism or the rule of the bourgeoisie. As Zhdanov categorically
proclaimed: Soviet literature is, by definition, "the richest in ideas,
the most advanced, and the most revolutionary." A critic who devotes
the vast majority of his writings to the works of Schiller, Goethe,
Balzac, Pushkin, and Tolstoy is obviously yielding to counter-revolutionary temptations.

This is the crux of the long-muffled but now open and murderous campaign waged against Lukács by the Communist hierarchies of
eastern Europe. Lukács' brief role in the Hungarian insurrection
merely dramatized or, to use a Marxist term, "objectified" the inevitable conflict between an orthodox and a para-Marxist interpretation
of history. Joseph Revai, the Hungarian Zhdanov, launched the assault on Lukács in 1950. In a pamphlet entitled *Literature and
Popular Democracy*, he asks:

> What could Hungarian literature gain from the pass-word
> given it by Lukács in 1954: "Zola? No, Balzac!"? And
> what could it gain from the slogan put forward by Lukács
> in 1948: "Neither Pirandello nor Priestley, but Shake-
> speare and Molière"? In both instances—nothing.

Lukács' concentration on Balzac and Goethe, suggests Revai, is dangerously obsolete. The dissociation between a writer's ideology and
his actual works is no longer admissible. If a novelist seeks to convey
an adequate image of reality, he must, indeed he can only, do so
within the tenets of Marxist-Leninism. Revai hints that, in the final
reckoning, Lukács places "pure" or "formalistic" literary canons
above Party and class interests. From this would logically follow his
inability to recognize the pre-eminence of Soviet literature.

On the surface, this might appear as a debate between a Zhdanovite hack and a great critic. But the real conflict lies deeper. It is,
once again, a confrontation between the "Engelian" and the Leninist
conceptions of art and the role of the artist in a revolutionary society.
Lefebvre saw this as early as 1953. Taking issue with Lukács, he
went on to state in his *Contribution à l'esthétique* that Engels had not
yet grasped the problem of Party literature. The whole debate has

319

been further clarified in the aftermath of the Hungarian uprising. In a recent pronouncement, Revai charges Lukács with being one of those who "under the guise of the struggle against Zhdanovism," a struggle rendered semi-respectable by the "thaw" in the Soviet Union, "in fact are trying to destroy Leninism." If we understand by "Leninism" the theory of literature outlined in 1905, Revai is undeniably right. For that is a theory which neither Lukács, nor any other responsible critic, can accept.

In only one domain has there been a *rapprochement* between orthodox and para-Marxist criticism. During the period of "de-Stalinization," the forbidden ground of Dostoevskyan studies was reopened to Marxist scrutiny. We owe to this fact a distinguished essay by Vladimir Yermilov (*Soviet Literature*, February 1956). Its critical assumptions are plainly derived from Engels. Yermilov observes a radical dissociation between Dostoevsky's sense of human suffering and his hostility "to any attempt to find effective ways of struggling for the liberation of man from that injury and insult." He seeks to substantiate this general interpretation by a close reading of *The Idiot*. Acutely, he sees in that novel a parable on the cruel majesty of money and a "right-wing critique of capitalism." In points of detail, Yermilov is often indiscriminate. One leaves his essay with the odd feeling that *The Idiot* is a posthumous work by Balzac. But there is no doubt that Yermilov's conclusion represents a notable change in the tone of Soviet criticism:

> Mankind cannot overlook a writer who, in spite of the official lies of his time and reactionary tendencies in his own outlook, found in himself the strength to protest against humiliation and insult.

To find a comparable acknowledgment, one must go back to Lunacharsky and the Dostoevsky centennial of 1920–1921.

A few months after the appearance of Yermilov's essay, French orthodox criticism followed suit. G. Fridlander's discussion of *The Idiot* (*La Nouvelle Critique*, May 1956) contains little of importance. He too believes that the "progressive reader" will know how to distinguish between Dostoevsky's accurate depiction of social and psychological conflicts in bourgeois society and his erroneous, reactionary point of view. The startling element in the piece comes at the outset. Here, Fridlander finds it necessary to inform his Communist reader that Dostoevsky was born in such and such a year, that he spent some time in Siberia, and that he wrote a number of novels among which *Crime and Punishment*, *The Idiot*, and so on. Such candor speaks volumes.

IV

The problems we have touched upon so far are internal; they engage Party doctrine and varying modes of dissent. Let us now ask the larger question: what have Marxism, as a philosophy, and dialectical materialism, as a strategy of insight, contributed to the resources of the literary critic? To what aspects of the Marxist performance will a future Saintsbury address himself when writing a history of modern criticism?

First, there is the concept of dissociation—the image of the poet as Balaam speaking truth against his knowledge or avowed philosophy. "There is nothing absurd," argues Goldmann, "in the notion of a writer or poet who does not apprehend the *objective* significance of his own works." Between his explicit ideology and the representation of life which he in fact conveys, there may be a contradiction. Engels put forward this idea with reference to Goethe and Balzac. It throws light also on Cervantes and Tolstoy—whether we approach the latter via Lukács or Isaiah Berlin. Thus, in both *Don Quixote* and *Anna Karenina* the rhetoric of prior intent goes against the grain of the actual narrative. In a good deal of major literature, we are made aware of the latent paradox and tension generated by such internal contrariety. Hence the curious, but suggestive, affinities between a Marxist reading of Balzac and William Empson's recent revaluation of *Tom Jones*. Where Empson perceives the complex play of irony, the Marxist would observe a dialectical conflict between a poet's thesis and his actual vision of things.

Secondly, there is the intricate, yet ultimately persuasive, distinction which Marxist theory draws between "realism" and "naturalism." It goes back to Hegel's reflections on the *Iliad* and the *Odyssey*. Hegel found that in the Homeric epics the depiction of physical objects, however detailed and stylized, did not intrude upon the rhythm and vitality of the poem. Descriptive writing in modern literature, on the other hand, struck him as contingent and lifeless. He

321

threw out the illuminating hint that the industrial revolution and the correlative division of labor had estranged men from the material world. Homer's account of the forging of Achilles' armor or the making of Odysseus' raft presupposes an immediacy of relationship between artisan and product which modern industrial processes no longer allow. Compared to Homeric or even to medieval times, modern man inhabits the physical world like a rapacious stranger. This idea greatly influenced Marx and Engels. It contributed to their own theory of the "alienation" of the individual under capitalist modes of production. In the course of their debate with Lassalle and of their study of Balzac, Marx and Engels came to believe that this problem of estrangement was directly germane to the problem of realism in art. The poets of antiquity and the "classical realists" (Cervantes, Shakespeare, Goethe, Balzac) had achieved an organic relationship between objective reality and the life of the imagination. The "naturalist," on the other hand, looks on the world as on a warehouse of whose contents he must make a feverish inventory. "A sense of reality," says a contemporary Marxist critic, "is created not by a reproduction of all the features of an object but by a depiction of those features that form the essence . . . while in naturalistic art—because of a striving to achieve an elusive fullness—the image, also incomplete, places both the *essential* and the *secondary*, the unimportant, on the same plane."

This distinction is far-reaching. It bears on the decline of French realism after Balzac and Stendhal, and tells us something of Zola's obsessive attempt to make of the novel an index for the world. By virtue of it, we may discriminate between the "realism" of Chekhov and the "naturalism" of, say, Maupassant. Through it, also, we may ascertain that *Madame Bovary*, for all its virtues, is a slighter thing than *Anna Karenina*. In naturalism there is accumulation; in realism what Henry James called the "deep-breathing economy" of organic form.

Thirdly, Marxism has sharpened the critic's sense of time and place. In so doing, it has carried forward ideas initiated by Sainte-Beuve and Taine. We now see the work of art as rooted in temporal and material circumstance. Beneath the complex structure of the lyric impulse lie specific historical and social foundations. The Marxist sensibility has contributed a sociological awareness to the best of modern criticism. It is the kind of awareness realized, for example, in

Lionel Trilling's observation that Dostoevskyan plots originate in crises in monetary or class relationships. Through the perspective implicit in Marxism, moreover, historians and critics of literature have been led to a study of the audience. What can be said, historically and sociologically, of the Elizabethan spectator? In what respect was the Dickensian novel a calculated response to the evolution of a new reading public? Without the presence of the Marxist element in the "spirit of the age," such critics as L. C. Knights, Q. D. Leavis, and Richard Hoggart might not have arrived at their own understanding of the social dynamics of art.

The final point is the most difficult to make. It may give rise to misunderstanding however cautiously I put it. But it is simply this: Marxist-Leninism and the political régimes enacted in its name take literature *seriously*, indeed desperately so. At the very height of the Soviet revolution's battle for physical survival, Trotsky found occasion to assert that "the development of art is the highest test of the vitality and significance of each epoch." Stalin himself deemed it essential to add to his voluminous strategic and economic pronouncements a treatise on philology and the problems of language in literature. In a Communist society the poet is regarded as a figure central to the health of the body politic. Such regard is cruelly manifest in the very urgency with which the heretical artist is silenced or hounded to destruction. This constant preoccupation with the life of the mind would alone serve to distinguish Marxist autocracy from other species of totalitarianism. To shoot a man because one disagrees with his interpretation of Darwin or Hegel is a sinister tribute to the supremacy of ideas in human affairs—but a tribute nevertheless.

Let us, moreover, distinguish Marxism and the philosophy of art of Marx and Engels from the concrete actualities of Stalinist rule. If we do so, the dread gravity of the Marxist view of literature should remind us of certain truths which few Western critics, with the exception of Ezra Pound and Dr. Leavis, seem willing to affirm. The health of language *is* essential to the preservation of a living society. It is in literature that language is most truly challenged and guarded. A vital critical tradition, vital even in its polemics, is not a luxury but a rigorous need. The abandonment of values under the pressures of commercialism, the failure of the journalist-critic to discriminate between art and *kitsch*, does contribute to a larger decay. For all its obscurantism and inhumanity, the Marxist conception of literature is neither academic, in the manner of some of the "New Criticism" practiced in America, nor provincial, as is so much of current English criticism. Above all, it is not frivolous. The genuine Marxist critic— as distinct from the Zhdanovite censor—cannot look upon literature in the light of that French idiom, proverbial of frivolity, *ce n'est que de la littérature*.

GEORG LUKÁCS
AND HIS DEVIL'S PACT

In the twentieth century it is not easy for an honest man to be a literary critic. There are so many more urgent things to be done. Criticism is an adjunct. For the art of the critic consists in bringing works of literature to the attention of precisely those readers who may least require such help; does a man read critiques of poetry or drama or fiction unless he is already highly literate on his own? On either hand, moreover, stand two tempters. To the right, Literary History, with its solid air and academic credentials. To the left, Book Reviewing—not really an art, but rather a technique committed to the implausible theory that something worth reading is published each morning in the year. Even the best of criticism may succumb to either temptation. Anxious to achieve intellectual respectability, the firm stance of the scholar, the critic may, like Sainte-Beuve, almost become a literary historian. Or he may yield to the claims of the novel and the immediate; a significant part of Henry James's critical pronouncements have not survived the trivia on which they were lavished. Good reviews are even more ephemeral than bad books.

But there is yet another major reason why it is difficult for a serious mind, born into this troubled and perilous century, to devote its main strength to literary criticism. Ours is, pre-eminently, the season of the natural sciences. Ninety percent of all scientists are alive. The rate of conquest in the sciences, the retreat of the horizon before the inquiring spirit, is no longer in any recognizable proportion to the past. New Americas are found each day. Hence the temper of the age is penetrated with scientific values. These extend their influence and fascination far beyond the bounds of science in the classical sense. History and economics hold that they are, in some central measure, sciences; so do logic and sociology. The art historian refines instruments and techniques which he regards as scientific. The twelve-tone composer refers his austere practices to those of mathematics. Durrell has prefaced his Quartet by saying that he endeavors to translate into language and into the manner of his narrative the perspective of Relativity. He sees the city of Alexandria in four dimensions.

This ubiquity of science has brought with it new modesties and new ambitions. Distrustful of mere impulse, science demands a mythology of rigor and proof. In splendid exchange it offers the mirage of certitude, of assured knowledge, of intellectual possession guarded against doubt. The very great scientist will reject this prospect; he will persevere in doubt even at the heart of discovery. But the hope of objective, demonstrable truth is always there and it has drawn to itself the most powerful minds of our time.

In literary criticism there is no promised land of established fact, no utopia of certainty. By its very nature, criticism is personal. It is susceptible neither of demonstration nor of coherent proof. It disposes of no instrument more exact than Housman's beard bristling as the great line of poetry flashed across his mind. Throughout history, critics have sought to show that their *métier* was a science after all, that it had objective canons and means of attaining absolute truths. Coleridge harnessed his intensely personal, often unsteady genius to the yoke of a metaphysical system. In a famous manifesto, Taine proclaimed that the study of literature was no less exact than that of the natural sciences. Dr. I. A. Richards has underwritten the hope that there is an objective psychological foundation to the act of aesthetic judgment. His most distinguished disciple, Professor Empson, has brought to the arts of literary criticism the modalities and gestures of mathematics.

But the fact remains: a literary critic is an individual man judging a given text according to the present bent of his own spirit, according to his mood or the fabric of his beliefs. His judgment may be of more value than yours or mine solely because it is grounded on a wider range of knowledge or because it is presented with more persuasive clarity. It cannot be demonstrated in a scientific manner, nor can it lay claim to permanence. The winds of taste and fashion are inconstant and each generation of critics judges anew. Opinions

326

on the merits of a work of art, moreover, are irrefutable. Balzac thought Mrs. Radcliffe to be as great a writer as Stendhal. Nietzsche, one of the acutest minds ever to concern itself with music, came to argue that Bizet was a more genuine composer than Wagner. We may feel in our bones that such views are perverse and erroneous. But we cannot refute them as a scientist can refute a false theory. And who knows but that some future age will concur in judgments which today seem untenable? The history of taste is rather like a spiral. Ideas which are at first considered outrageous or *avant-garde* become the reactionary and sanctified beliefs of the succeeding generation.

Thus a modern critic finds himself in double jeopardy. Criticism has about it something of a more leisured age. It is difficult, on moral grounds, to resist the fierce solicitations of economic, social, and political issues. If some mode of barbarism and political self-destruction is threatening, writing essays on *belles-lettres* seems a rather marginal pursuit. The second dilemma is intellectual. However distinguished, a critic cannot share in the principal adventure of the contemporary mind—in the acquisition of positive knowledge, in the mastery of scientific fact or the exploration of demonstrable truth. And if he is honest with himself, the literary critic knows that his judgments have no lasting validity, that they may be reversed tomorrow. Only one thing can give his work a measure of permanence: the strength or beauty of his actual style. By virtue of style, criticism may, in turn, become literature.

The masters of contemporary criticism have tried to resolve these dilemmas in different ways. T. S. Eliot, Ezra Pound, and Thomas Mann, for example, have made of criticism an adjunct to creation. Their critical writings are commentaries on their own poetic works; mirrors which the intellect holds up to the creative imagination. In D. H. Lawrence, criticism is self-defense; though ostensibly discussing other writers, Lawrence was in fact arguing for his own conception of the art of the novel. Dr. Leavis has met the challenge head-on. He has placed his critical powers at the service of an impassioned moral vision. He is intent upon establishing standards of maturity and order in literature so that society as a whole may proceed in a more mature and orderly manner.

But no one has brought to the moral and intellectual dilemmas besetting literary criticism a more radical solution than Georg Lukács. In his works two beliefs are incarnate. First, that literary criticism is not a luxury, that it is not what the subtlest of American critics has called "a discourse for amateurs." But that it is, on the contrary, a central and militant force toward shaping men's lives. Secondly, Lukács affirms that the work of the critic is neither subjective nor uncertain. Criticism is a science with its own rigor and precision. The truth of judgment can be verified. Georg Lukács is, of course, a Marxist. Indeed, he is the one major critical talent to have emerged from the gray servitude of the Marxist world.

II

In an essay, dated 1948, Lukács put forward a significant analogy. He said that Newtonian physics gave to the consciousness of the eighteenth century its foremost liberating impulse, teaching the mind to live the great adventure of reason. According to Lukács, this role should be performed in our own time by political economy. It is around political economy, in the Marxist sense, that we should order our understanding of human affairs. Lukács himself came to literature via economics, as we may say that Aristotle approached drama via a systematic inquiry into morals.

Dialectical materialism holds that literature, as all other forms of art, is an "ideological superstructure," an edifice of the spirit built upon foundations of economic, social, and political fact. In style and content the work of art precisely reflects its material, historical basis. The *Iliad* was no less conditioned by social circumstance (a feudal aristocracy splintered into small rival kingdoms) than were the novels of Dickens which so strongly reflect the economics of serialization and the growth of a new mass-audience. Therefore, argues the Marxist, the progress of art is subject to laws of historical necessity. We cannot conceive of *Robinson Crusoe* prior to the rise of the mercantile ideal. In the decline of the French novel after Stendhal we observe the image of the larger decline of the French bourgeoisie.

But where there is law there is science. And thus the Marxist critic cherishes the conviction that he is engaged not in matters of opinion but in determinations of objective reality. Without this conviction, Lukács could not have turned to literature. He came of intellectual age amid the chaotic ferocity of war and revolution in central Europe. He reached Marxism over the winding road of Hegelian metaphysics. In his early writings two strains are dominant: the search for a key to the apparent turmoil of history and the endeavor of an intellectual to justify to himself the contemplative life. Like Simone Weil, of whom he often reminds me, Lukács has the soul of a Calvinist. One can imagine how he must have striven to discipline within himself his native bent toward literature and the aesthetic side of things. Marxism afforded him the crucial possibility of remaining a literary critic without feeling that he had committed his energies to a somewhat frivolous and imprecise pursuit. In 1918 Lukács joined the Hungarian Communist Party. During the first brief spell of Communist rule in Budapest, he served as political and cultural commissar with the Fifth Red Army. After the fall of Belá-Kun, Lukács went into exile. He remained in Berlin until 1933 and then took refuge in Moscow. There he stayed and worked for twelve years, returning to Hungary only in 1945.

This is a fact of obvious importance. German is Lukács' principal language, but his use of it has grown brittle and forbidding. His style is that of exile; it has lost the habits of living speech. More essentially: Lukács' entire tone, the fervent, at times narrow tenor of his vision, mirror the fact of banishment. From Moscow, surrounded by a small coterie of fellow-exiles, Lukács observed the advance of crisis over western Europe. His writings on French and German literature became an impassioned plea against the lies and barbarism of the Nazi period. This accounts for a major paradox in Lukács' performance. A Communist by conviction, a dialectical materialist by virtue of his critical method, he has nevertheless kept his eyes resolutely on the past. Thomas Mann saw in Lukács' works an eminent sense of tradition. Despite pressure from his Russian hosts, Lukács gave only perfunctory notice to the much-heralded achievements of "Soviet realism." Instead, he dwelt on the great lineage of eighteenth- and nineteenth-century European poetry and fiction, on Goethe and Balzac, on Sir Walter Scott and Flaubert, on Stendhal and Heine. Where he writes of Russian literature, Lukács deals with Pushkin or Tolstoy, not with the poetasters of Stalinism. The critical perspective is rigorously Marxist, but the choice of themes is "central European" and conservative.

In the midst of the apparent triumph of Fascism, Lukács maintained a passionate serenity. He strove to discover the tragic flaw, the seed of chaos, whence had sprung the madness of Hitler. One of his works, in itself a strident, often mendacious book, is entitled *The Destruction of Reason* (1955). It is a philosopher's attempt to resolve the mystery which Thomas Mann dramatized in *Doctor Faustus*.

How was the tide of darkness loosed on the German soul? Lukács traces the origins of disaster back to the irrationalism of Schelling. But at the same time he insisted on the integrity and life-force of humane values. Being a Communist, Lukács had no doubt that socialism would ultimately prevail. He regarded it as his particular task to marshal toward the moment of liberation the spiritual resources inherent in European literature and philosophy. When Heine's poems were once again read in Germany, there was available an essay by Lukács building a bridge between the future and the scarce-remembered world of liberalism to which Heine had belonged.

Thus Lukács has put forward a solution to the two-fold dilemma of the modern critic. As a Marxist, he discerns in literature the action of economic, social, and political forces. This action follows on certain laws of historical necessity. To Lukács criticism is a science even before it is an art. His preference of Balzac over Flaubert is not a matter of personal taste or fiat. It is an objective determination arrived at through an analysis of material fact. Secondly, he has given his writing an intense immediacy. It is rooted in the political struggles and social circumstances of the time. His writings on literature, like those of Trotsky, are instruments of combat. By understanding the dialectic of Goethe's *Faust*, says Lukács, a man is better equipped to read the sanguinary riddles of the present. The fall of France in 1940 is writ large in the *Comédie humaine*. Lukács' arguments are relevant to issues that are central in our lives. His critiques are not a mere echo to literature. Even where it is sectarian and polemic, a book by Lukács has a curious nobility. It possesses what Matthew Arnold called "high seriousness."

III

But in practice, what are Lukács' major achievements as a critic and historian of ideas?

Ironically, one of his most influential works dates from a period in which his Communism was tainted with heresy. *History and Class Consciousness* (1923) is a rather legendary affair. It is a *livre maudit*, a burnt book, of which relatively few copies have survived.* We find

[* *History and Class Consciousness* is now available in French. It is also being re-published in the West German edition of Lukács' collected writings, together with other early works. These are among his finest philosophic achievements and show him to be the true predecessor to Walter Benjamin. The cultural authorities in the East allow such Western publication of heretical but prestigious Marxist books; a characteristic touch of "Byzantine" policy.]

in it a fundamental analysis of the "reification" of man (*Verdingli-chung*), the degradation of the human person to a statistical object through industrial and political processes. The work was condemned by the Party and withdrawn by the author. But it has led a tenacious underground life and certain writers, such as Sartre and Thomas Mann, have always regarded it as Lukács' masterpiece.

To my mind, however, his pre-eminence lies elsewhere: in the essays and monographs which he wrote during the 1930's and 1940's and which began appearing in a row of imposing volumes after the end of the war. The essential Lukács is contained in the study of *Goethe and His Time* (1947), in the essays on *Russian Realism in World Literature* (1949), in the volume entitled *German Realists of the Nineteenth Century* (1951), in the book on Balzac, Stendhal, and Zola (1952), and in the great work on *The Historical Novel* (1955). To this should be added a number of massive works of a more strictly philosophic character, such as the *Contributions to a History of Aesthetics* (1954), and what is perhaps Lukács' *magnum opus*, the study of Hegel (the first volume of which appeared in 1948).

It is impossible to give a brief yet adequate account of so great a range of material. But a number of motifs do stand out as classic enrichments of our understanding of literature.

There is Lukács' analysis of the decline of the French novel. He is the foremost living student of Balzac and sees in the *Comédie humaine* the master edifice of realism. His reading of *Les Illusions perdues* is exemplary of the manner in which the vision of the historian is brought to bear on the fabric of a work of art. It is this vision which leads directly to Lukács' condemnation of Flaubert. Between Balzac and Flaubert falls the defeat of 1848. The brightness of liberal hopes has faded and France is moving toward the tragedy of the Commune. Balzac looks on the world with the primitive ardor of conquest. The *Comédie humaine* built an empire in language as Napoleon did in fact. Flaubert looks on the world as through a glass contemptuously. In *Madame Bovary* the glitter and artifice of words has become an end in itself. When Balzac describes a hat, he does so because a man is wearing it. The account of Charles Bovary's cap, on the other hand, is a piece of technical bravado; it exhibits Flaubert's command of the French sartorial vocabulary. But the thing is dead. And behind this contrast in the art of the novel, Lukács discerns the transformation of society through mature capitalism. In a pre-industrial society, or where industrialism remains on a small scale, man's relationship to the physical objects that surround him has a natural immediacy. The latter is destroyed by mass-production. The furnishings of our lives are consequent on processes too complex and impersonal for anyone to master. Isolated from sensuous reality, repelled by the inhumane drabness of the factory world, the writer seeks refuge in satire or in romantic visions of the past. Both retreats are exemplified in Flaubert: *Bouvard et Pécuchet* is an encyclopaedia of contempt, whereas *Salammbô* can be characterized as the reverie of a somewhat sadistic antiquarian.

Out of this dilemma arose what Lukács defines as the illusion of naturalism, the belief that an artist can recapture a sense of reality by mere force of accumulation. Where the realist selects, the naturalist enumerates. Like the schoolmaster in Dickens' *Hard Times*, he demands facts and more facts. Zola had an inexhaustible appetite for circumstantial detail, a passion for time-tables and inventories (one recalls the catalogue of cheeses in *Le Ventre de Paris*). He had the gusto to breathe life into a stockmarket quotation. But his theory of the novel, argues Lukács, was radically false. It leads to the death of the imagination and to reportage.

Lukács does not compromise with his critical vision. He exalts Balzac, a man of royalist and clerical principles. He condemns Zola, a progressive in the political sense, and a forerunner of "socialist realism."

Even more original and authoritative is Lukács treatment of the historical novel. This is a literary *genre* to which Western criticism has given only cursory attention. It is difficult to get the range of historical fiction into proper focus. At times, its head is in the mythological stars, but more often the bulk of the thing is to be found in the good earth of commercial trash. The very notion brings to mind improbable gallants pursuing terrified yet rather lightly clad young ladies across flamboyant dust-wrappers. Only very rarely, when a writer such as Robert Graves intervenes, do we realize that the historical novel has distinct virtues and a noble tradition. It is to these that Lukács addresses himself in a major study, *The Historical Novel*.

The form arose out of a crisis in European sensibility. The French Revolution and the Napoleonic era penetrated the consciousness of ordinary men with a sense of the historical. Whereas Frederick the Great had asked that wars be conducted so as not to disturb the normal flow of events, Napoleon's armies marched across Europe and back reshaping the world in their path. History was no longer a matter for archives and princes; it had become the fabric of daily life. To this change the *Waverley* novels gave a direct and prophetic response. Here again, Lukács is on fresh ground. We do not take Sir Walter Scott altogether seriously. That is most probably an injustice. If we care to learn how deliberate an artist Scott was, and how penetrating a sense of history is at work in *Quentin Durward* or *The Heart of Midlothian*, we do best to read a book written in Moscow by a Hungarian critic.

Lukács goes on to explore the development of historical fiction in the art of Manzoni, Pushkin, and Victor Hugo. His reading of Thackeray is particularly suggestive. He argues that the antiquarian elements in *Henry Esmond* and *The Virginians* convey Thackeray's critique of contemporary social and political conditions. By taking the periwig off the eighteenth century, the novelist is satirizing the falsehood of Victorian conventions (what a Marxist calls *zeitgenössische Apologetik*). I happen to believe that Lukács is misreading Thackeray. But his error is fruitful, as the errors of good criticism usually are, and it leads to a most original idea. Lukács observes that archaic speech, however deftly handled, does not in fact bring the past closer to our imaginings. The classic masters of historical fiction write narrative and dialogue in the language of their own day. They create the illusion of the historical present through force of realized imagination and because they themselves experience the relationship between past history and their own time as one of live continuity. The historical novel falters when this sense of continuity no longer prevails, when the writer feels that the forces of history are beyond his rational comprehension. He will turn to an increasingly remote or exotic past in protest against contemporaneous life. Instead of historical fiction, we find laborious archaeology. Compare the poetics of history implicit in *The Charterhouse of Parma* with the erudite artifice of *Salammbô*. Amid lesser craftsmen than Flaubert this sense of artifice is reinforced by the use of archaic language. The novelist endeavors to make his vision of the past authentic by writing dialogue in what he supposes to have been the syntax and style of the relevant period. This is a feeble device. Would Shakespeare have done better to let Richard II speak in Chaucerian English?

Now as Lukács points out, this decline from the classical conception of the historical novel coincides precisely with the change from realism to naturalism. In both instances, the vision of the artist loses its spontaneity; he is, in some manner, alien to his material. As a result, matters of technique become pre-eminent at the expense of substance. The image of Glasgow in *Rob Roy* is historically perceptive, but more significantly it arises out of the social and personal conflicts of the narrative. It is not a piece of antiquarian restoration. But that is exactly what the image of Carthage in *Salammbô* is. Flaubert has built a sumptuous hollow shell around an autonomous action; as Sainte-Beuve noted, it is difficult to reconcile the psychological motivations of the characters with the alleged historical setting. Sir Walter Scott believed in the rational, progressive unfolding of English history. He saw in the events of his own time a natural consequence of energies released during the seventeenth and eighteenth centuries. Flaubert, on the contrary, turned to antique Carthage or Alexandria because he found his own epoch intolerable. Being out of touch with the present—he saw in the Commune a delayed spasm of the Middle Ages—he failed to achieve an imaginative realization of the past.

Whether or not one agrees with this analysis, its originality and breadth of implication are obvious. It illustrates Lukács' essential practice: the close study of a literary text in the light of far-reaching philosophic and political questions. The writer or particular work is the point of departure. From it Lukács' argument moves outward traversing complex ground. But the central idea or theme is kept constantly in view. Finally, the dialectic closes in, marshaling its examples and persuasions.

Thus the essay on the Goethe-Schiller correspondence deals primarily with the vexed topic of the nature of literary forms. The discussion of Hölderlin's *Hyperion* gives rise to a study of the crucial yet ambiguous role of the Hellenic ideal in the history of the German spirit. In his several considerations of Thomas Mann, Lukács is concerned with what he takes to be the paradox of the bourgeois artist in a Marxist century. Lukács argues that Mann chose to stay outside the stream of history while being aware of the tragic nature of his choice. The essay on Gottfried Keller is an attempt to clarify the very difficult problem of the arrested development in German literature after the death of Goethe. In all these instances, we cannot dissociate the particular critical judgment from the larger philosophic and social context.

Because the argument is so close and tightly woven, it is difficult to give representative quotations from Lukács' works. Perhaps a short passage from a paper on Kleist can convey the dominant tone:

> Kleist's conception of passion brings drama close to the art of the short story. A heightened singularity is presented in a manner underlining *its accidental uniqueness*. In the short story this is entirely legitimate. For that is a literary genre specifically designed to make real the immense role of coincidence and contingency in human life. But if the action represented remains on the level of coincidence ... and is given the dignity of tragic drama without any proof of its objective necessity, the effect will inevitably be one of contradiction and dissonance. Therefore, Kleist's plays do not point to the high road of modern drama. That road leads from Shakespeare, via the experiments of Goethe and Schiller to Pushkin's *Boris Godunow*. Due to the ideological decline of the bourgeoisie, it had no adequate continuation. Kleist's plays represent an irrational byway. Isolated individual passion destroys the organic relationship between the fate of the individual person and social-historical necessity. With the dissolution of that relationship, the poetic and philosophic foundations of genuine dramatic conflict are also destroyed. The basis of drama becomes thin and narrow, purely personal and private. ... To be sure Kleistian passions are representative of a bourgeois society. Their inner dialectic mirrors typical conflicts of individuals who have become "windowless monads" in a bourgeois milieu.

The reference to Leibniz is characteristic. The quality of Lukács' mind is philosophic, in the technical sense. Literature concentrates and gives concretion to those mysteries of meaning with which the philosopher is eminently concerned. In this respect, Lukács belongs to a notable tradition. The *Poetics* are philosophic criticism (drama seen as the theoretic model of spiritual action); so are the critical writings of Coleridge, Schiller, and Croce. If the going is heavy, it is because the matter of the argument is persistently complex. Like other philosopher-critics, Lukács engages questions that have bedeviled inquiry since Plato. What are the primary distinctions between epic and drama? What is "reality" in a work of art, the ancient riddle of shadow outweighing substance? What is the relationship between poetic imagination and ordinary perception? Lukács raises the problem of the "typical" personage. Why do certain characters in literature—Falstaff, Faust, Emma Bovary—possess a force of life greater than that of a multitude of other imagined beings and, indeed, of most living creatures? Is it because they are archetypes in whom universal traits are gathered and given memorable shape?

Lukács' inquiries draw on an extraordinary range of evidence. He appears to have mastered nearly the whole of modern European and Russian literature. This yields a rare association of tough, philosophic exactitude with largeness of vision. By contrast, Dr. Leavis, who is no less of a moralist and close reader than Lukács, is deliberately provincial. In point of universality, Lukács' peer would be Edmund Wilson.

But there is an obverse to the medal. Lukács' criticism has its part of blindness and injustice. At times, he writes with acrimonious obscurity as if to declare that the study of literature should be no pleasure, but a discipline and science, thorny of approach as are other sciences. This has made him insensible to the great musicians of language. Lukács lacks ear; he does not possess that inner tuning-fork which enables Ezra Pound to choose unerringly the instant of glory in a long poem or forgotten romance. In Lukács' omissions of Rilke there is an obscure protest against the marvel of the poet's language. Somehow, he writes too wondrously well. Though he would deny it, moreover, Lukács does incline toward the arch-error of Victorian criticism: the narrative content, the quality of the fable, influence his judgment. Its failure to include Proust, for example, casts doubt on Lukács' entire view of the French novel. But the actual plot of the *Recherche du temps perdu*, the luxuriance and perversities which Proust recounts, obviously outrage Lukács' austere morality. Marxism is a puritanical creed.

Like all critics, he has his particular displeasures. Lukács detests Nietzsche and is insensitive to the genius of Dostoevsky. But being a consequent Marxist, he makes a virtue of blindness and gives to his condemnations an objective, systematic value. Dr. Leavis is evidently ill at ease with the works of Melville. T.S. Eliot has conducted a lengthy and subtle quarrel with the poetics of Milton. But in it, the essential courtesies are observed. Lukács' arguments go *ad hominem*. Infuriated by the world-view of Nietzsche and Kierkegaard, he consigns their persons and their labors to the spiritual inferno of pre-Fascism. This is, of course, a grotesque misreading of the facts.

Of late, these defects of vision have become more drastic. They mar *The Destruction of Reason* and the essays on aesthetics which have appeared since that time. Doubtless, there is a question of age. Lukács was seventy in 1955 and his hatreds have stiffened. In part, there is the fact that Lukács is haunted by the ruin of German and western European civilization. He is searching for culprits to hand over to the Last Judgment of history. But above all, there is, I think, an intense personal drama. At the outset of his brilliant career, Lukács made a Devil's pact with historical necessity. The daemon promised him the secret of objective truth. He gave him the power to confer blessing or pronounce anathema in the name of revolution and "the laws of history." But since Lukács' return from exile, the Devil has been lurking about, asking for his fee. In October 1956, he knocked loudly at the door.

IV

We touch here on matters of a personal nature. Lukács' role in the Hungarian uprising and the subsequent monasticism of his personal life are of obvious historical interest. But they contain an element of private agony to which an outsider has little access. A man who loses his religion loses his beliefs. A Communist for whom history turns somersaults is in danger of losing his reason. Presumably, that is worse. Those who have not experienced it, however, can hardly realize what such a collapse of values is like. Moreover, the motives of action in the Lukács case are obscure.

He accepted the post of Minister of Culture in the Nagy government. Not, I think, to be among the leaders of an anti-Soviet movement, but rather to preserve the Marxist character of Hungarian intellectual life and to guard its radical inheritance against the reviving forces of the Catholic-agrarian right. More essentially, perhaps, because a Lukács cannot stand to one side of history even when the latter assumes absurd forms. He cannot be a spectator. But on November 3, one day before the Red Army re-conquered Budapest, Lukács resigned from the cabinet. Why? Had he decided that a Marxist should not oppose the will of the Soviet Union in which, for

337

better or worse, the future of dialectical materialism is incarnate? Was he persuaded to withdraw from a doomed cause by friends anxious for his life? We do not know.

After a period of exile in Rumania, Lukács was allowed to return to his home. But he was no longer permitted to teach and his past work became the object of derisive and increasingly fierce attack. This attack actually pre-dates the October rising. Hungary had its miniature version of Zhdanov, a ferocious little man called Joseph Revai. Originally a pupil of Lukács, but later jealous of the master's eminence, he published a pamphlet on *Literature and Popular Democracy* in 1954. In it, he drew up a Stalinist indictment of Lukács' life-work. He accused Lukács of having consistently neglected contemporary Soviet literature. He charged that Lukács' concentration on Goethe and Balzac was dangerously obsolete. Even a mediocre novel by a Communist, declares Revai, is infinitely preferable to a great novel by a reactionary or pre-Marxist. Lukács places "formalistic" literary ideals above class and Party interests. His style is inaccessible to a proletarian reader.

After October, these accusations became more strident. Hungarian and East German publicists revived the old charges of heresy made against Lukács' early writings. They recalled his youthful admiration for Stefan George and hunted down traces of "bourgeois idealism" in his mature works. Yet the old man was not touched and through one of those odd, Kafkaesque judgments sometimes passed by Communist regimes, he was even allowed to publish a small volume of essays with a West German press (*Wider den missverstandenen Realismus*, Hamburg, 1958).

Lukács' relative immunity may have been due to the interest which socialist intellectuals outside the iron curtain have taken in the case. But surely, the more important question is this: how did Lukács himself regard his beliefs and achievements in the light of the October tragedy? Was he drawn toward the great limbo of disillusion? Did his gods fail him at the last?

Such questions cannot be urged very far without impertinence; they involve that inward place of vital illusion which preserves the religious or revolutionary conscience. Lukács' judgment of the Hungarian revolution is contained in a preface which he wrote in April 1957: "Important events have occurred in Hungary and elsewhere, compelling us to re-think many problems connected with Stalin's life-work. The reaction to the latter, both in the bourgeois world and in socialist countries, is taking the guise of a revision of the teachings of Marx and Lenin. This certainly constitutes the principal threat to Marxism-Leninism." The words seem desperately beside the point. But let us keep one thing firmly in mind: to men such as Koestler or Malraux, Communism was a temporary expedient of passion. Lukács' Communism is the root-fiber of his intelligence. Whatever interpretation he puts on the crisis of October 1956 will have been arrived at within the framework of a dialectical vision of history. A man who has lost his sight continues to view his surroundings in terms of remembered images. In order to survive intellectually, Lukács must have hammered out some kind of inner compromise; such punitive forays into one's own consciousness are characteristic of the Marxist condition. His comment about the threat of revisionism gives us a lead. If I interpret him at all accurately, he is saying that the Hungarian episode is a final extension, a *reductio ad absurdum* of Stalinist policy. But that policy was a false departure from Marxist-Leninist doctrine and the violence of its enactment merely proves its bankruptcy. Therefore, the proper response to the Hungarian disaster does not imply an abandonment of Marxist first principles. On the contrary, we must return to those principles in their authentic formulation. Or as one of the insurrectionist leaders put it: "Let us oppose the Red army in the name of the Leningrad workers' Soviet of 1917." Perhaps there is in this idea that old and most deceptive dream: Communism divorced from the particular ambitions and obscurantism of Russian domination.

Lukács has always held himself responsible to history. This has enabled him to produce a body of critical and philosophic work intensely expressive of the cruel and serious spirit of the age. Whether or not we share his beliefs, there can be no doubt that he has given to the minor Muse of criticism a notable dignity. His late years of solitude and recurrent danger only emphasize what I observed at the outset: in the twentieth century it is not easy for an honest man to be a literary critic. But then, it never was.

AN AESTHETIC MANIFESTO

M any charges can and have been pressed against Georg Lukács. But parochialism is not among them. The geography of his spirit is large. He is one of the last of the "central Europeans" with their passionate distinctive knowledge of classical culture and European languages and literature. He has kept faith with the original Marxist commitment to an international vision, and to the legacy of the classic, radical past. Like Marx himself, Lukács is steeped in post-Kantian philosophy, in Hegel and Feuerbach. His sphere of immediate reference extends from the pre-Socratics and Aristotle to Vico, Spinoza, and Lessing. It includes the *philosophes*, the French novel from Lesage to Zola, the historical sensibility of European romanticism—Scott, Manzoni, Pushkin—Russian fiction of the nineteenth century. Above all, he is intimate with Goethe, with Goethe's rational lyricism and perception of organic energy.

In Lukács' career, as in that of Brecht, there are stretches of dogmatic intolerance; there are moments of fear and indignity. The destruction of Weimar and the utter defeat of the German Communist Party—a defeat in which the cynical follies of Stalinism played a large part—drove Lukács into long exile. But it was precisely in Moscow, isolated and under constant suspicion, that he wrote on Shakespeare and Balzac rather than on Fadeyev. It was there that he reasserted the essentially European, humanistic origins and structure of Marxist thought.

In that thought there has long been an acknowledged gap. Though he intended to do so, Marx never wrote a formal aesthetic. The numerous theoretic and practical observations he and Engels made on art and literature have been gathered by Mikhail Lifschitz in

340

a standard compendium. They amount to an engaging miscellany of dialectical argument and personal taste. In the writings of Mehring, Plekhanov, and Kautsky there is further material toward a philosophy of art. Through the individual, often heretical, speculations of Caudwell, Adorno, and Walter Benjamin, Marxist aesthetics have been related to anthropology, psychology, and certain elements in modern linguistics.

But as a whole—and this is true of much of Lukács' best work—the Marxist critic has operated with the tools of nineteenth-century historicism. Where he has not been mouthing party propaganda or merely dividing art into progressive and decadent in a parody of last judgment, he has applied, with more or less talent and finesse, those criteria of historical condition and cause already implicit in Herder, Sainte-Beuve, and Taine. In so far as it locates the artist and his achievement in a material setting of economic and social forces, in so far as it insists on the essentially social and historically determined character of artistic perception and public response (an insistence vital also to the argument of such historians of art as Panofsky and Gombrich), Marxist criticism is part of a larger *Historismus*.

To this tradition it has brought important refinements: Lukács' discrimination between realism and naturalism; Benjamin's insight into the influence of technology and mass-reproduction on the individual work of art; the application of the concepts of alienation and dehumanization to twentieth-century literature and painting. But in essence Marxism has contributed to aesthetics a disciplined historical awareness and a general radical optimism—witness Trotsky's *Literature and Revolution*—rather than a coherent epistemology. There has been no Marxist Longinus, no *Laokoon* setting out a complete theory of aesthetic form in the framework of dialectical materialism.

The difficulties are obvious. Concepts of spontaneity, of irrational or subconscious formulation, of despair and "reaction," which are relevant to art, fit awkwardly into "scientific materialism." There is the puzzle of anachronism with which Marx wrestled: why is it that some of the most mature, definitive art forms spring from societies whose economic and class structure is archaic or morally inadmissible? How does Sophocles, whose *Antigone* meant to Marx something of what it had meant to Hegel, accord with slavery? Like Einsteinian physics, moreover, modern literature, art, and music have proved intractable to Marxist assumptions of humanistic realism. A vocabulary of feeling developed in relation to Rembrandt and Balzac, a canon in which reciprocities between ordinary sensory perception and artistic realization are explicit, will find it difficult to deal, except by abuse, with the world of Klee or Beckett.

Lukács is aware of this, though he may not grasp the full contradiction between the commitment of Marxism to an historical mode of judgment and the inability of the Marxists to come to terms with the modern. *Die Eigenart des Ästhetischen*, whose 1,700 closely printed pages are only the first part of an intended *summa*, seeks to establish a comprehensive philosophy of art, an epistemology of art forms and artistic creation on a rigorous basis of dialectical materialism and Hegelian phenomenology. In effect, this means the foundation of a coherent aesthetic in accord with Marxist historicism, with Pavlovian psychology, and with Marxist-Leninist theories of language and society. It is Lukács' merit that he has set out to do the whole job. He fully realizes that a Marxist aesthetic must be a cogent, integral part of a total Marxist world-view and analysis of human behavior. Otherwise Marxist criticism will remain an aggregate of partisan or ideological polemic, local insights, and borrowed jargon.

The aim of achieving a systematic *Ästhetik* has been discernible in nearly all Lukács' work. There are hints of it as early as 1911 in *Die Seele und die Formen*. It is treated from a comparative, historical point of view in the papers collected in 1956 as *Beiträge zur Geschichte der Ästhetik*. Lukács' *Prolegòmeni a un'estetica marxista* appeared in Rome in 1957. In fact, the initial design of the present enterprise goes back to Florence and the winter of 1911–12; Lukács' argument retains distant echoes of visual impressions gathered at that time. He himself would say that the large corpus of his practical criticism, and the incomplete but major study of Hegel, have been logical preliminaries to a formal, systematic statement of values.

It is not easy to give a summary of these two volumes. The underlying program is analytic: Lukács proposes to discriminate and thus define the specific category of the aesthetic from the totality of human functions, and more particularly from other modes of perception and mental action such as religion and the historical and natural sciences. Starting from the primary Marxist law that being determines consciousness—*die Priorität des Seins*—and from the materialist axiom that all human understanding mirrors objective reality, Lukács seeks to define the peculiar "objective-subjective" nature of artistic creation and response. Art is a "mirroring" of objective realities, but there is in it a vital, irreducible subjective component.

Beneath the epistemological arguments runs the assertion that religion "from Tertullian to Kierkegaard" is fundamentally and necessarily anti-aesthetic. The religious sensibility has recognized in art a mortal enemy. "From Epicurus through Goethe, until Marx and Lenin" art presents a radical, humanistic alternative to the claims of revelation.

Lukács' method is primarily historical. Arguing along lines established by Marx, Lévy-Bruhl, and Gordon Childe, he seeks to demonstrate the historical genesis of the aesthetic function. He agrees with Ernst Fischer (*Kunst und Menschheit*) that the subject-object relationship is itself the result of long historical processes, that our sense of personal identity and "outside" reality is a gradual resultant of the need to labor, to use tools, to recognize and perfect divisions of skill in our senses and, finally, in the social group. The perception and uses of reality in the particular focus of art are, in turn, the product of a long process of specialization and sophistication of consciousness. It is this process and, more particularly, the severance of aesthetic realization from anthropomorphic religious imaginings on the one hand, and from "objective science" on the other, which Lukács analyzes in much of the first volume. Both religion and science make demands of positive assent, which art does not.

Five chapters are devoted to a study of the origins and evolution of mimesis. Proceeding from evidence offered by Aristotle's *Poetics*, by Frazer, and by Gordon Childe's *Man Makes Himself*, a book by which he has been heavily influenced, Lukács seeks to show how the gradual dissociation of mimetic representation from an immediate utilitarian purpose (magic) led to the development of a specific art condition and art sense. At the same time he emphasizes the extent to which the space-time conventions of even the "purest" art are linked to material needs and possibilities, to the social and economic *données* of human evolution.

The first volume concludes with an intricate examination of the subject-object relationship in the particular light of catharsis, of the effects and after-effects of the work of art on the "receiver." Here Lukács is at his finest. He traces the notion of catharsis from Aristotle to Goethe and Lessing, and argues the universal relevance of the "cathartic process" to the very definition of art, of how it shapes our feelings and thoughts. The argument ends in a frankly Arnoldian formula of art as enacted criticism of life. Indeed, there are frequent points of contact between Marx and Matthew Arnold in this closing section, a reminder that they, like Lukács himself, are in many respects Victorian moralists and common heirs to classical humanism.

The second volume sets out to modify and enrich Pavlovian psychology with particular reference to artistic invention and response. Lukács rejects Pavlov's tendency to identify the artist with a purely sentient organism. He puts forward the hypothesis of a mode of linguistic and plastic communication located between the world of objective data and that of determined mental reflexes. This middle language or "signal of signals" (*das Signalsystem*), with its subjective, non-utilitarian character, is the particular matrix of art. Between the conditioned reflex and the associated verbal abstraction lies a special zone of spontaneity and recreation. Man's recognition and exploitation of this aesthetic domain is the result of a lengthy process of division of mental and emotional labor. A notable excursus in this section deals with the breakdown of logic and control in Hölderlin's late poems. The history of the case suggests that plastic mimesis survives longer than linguistic mimesis when the more complex centers of conditioned reflex are impaired.

After an analysis of the work of art as *Fürsichseiendes*—an integral activity directed wholly to the world of man and not to that of natural phenomena (a distinction first drawn by Vico and taken over by Marx)—Lukács examines several "border areas" of mimesis. The chapter on music is indebted to Adorno and contains a number of stimulating ideas. Musical mimesis would be an imitation of our interior kinetics of consciousness by analogy of rhythm, key, and change of tonality. The discussion of film reasserts a distinction vital to Lukács' entire critical theory, that between realism, with its creative ordering and selection of values, and naturalism, with its inert, serial accumulation of detail. The argument follows on the brilliant pioneer work of Benjamin. The volume concludes with a set of all but impenetrable post-Kantian considerations on natural beauty and its role in aesthetic canons.

There is a fascinating epilogue on art and the liberation of the human spirit from anthropomorphic religiosity. Here Lukács takes up the problem of Stalinism which has engaged his principal moral energies since 1956. By compelling art to be programmatic and ideologically didactic, Stalin made impossible the cathartic effect— the impulse toward a deepening and clarification of consciousness which will free the mind from irrational religious hopes and bonds. Through the cathartic shock, man comes to discern in life the complex struggle for higher values. He comes to see reality as a process of dynamic crisis, a notion close to Ernst Bloch's utopian dialectic, *Das Prinzip Hoffnung*. By simplifying reality and imposing on it a fiat of accomplished truth, Stalinism made man's place in history static and, literally, without need of hope. In Stalinist art man was not a concrete being endowed with contradictory impulses and possibilities, but a cipher in an equation with a single right solution. In short, the Stalinist regime was an ultimately irrational attempt to arrest the Hegelian, dynamic process of human experience. Nevertheless, and characteristically, the book ends with the observation that the Stalinist period resulted in "the greater strength and security of Socialism." History is mightier than those who would violate its laws.

Such a summary does inadequate justice to the centrality and range of Lukács' argument. In a style of vision which recalls that of Auguste Comte, Lukács is attempting to record the liberation of the human psyche from religious fantasies, from the intellectual and moral servitude that comes of vain reliance on a "transcendent void." In that record art and the evolution of creative objectivity play a dominant part. But there are few areas of metaphysics, epistemology, social history, and psychology not pertinent to the general brief. The breadth of exact reference is formidable. Lukács draws on Wagner and Tolstoy, on Strindberg and Tertullian. He has taken for his province a major part of classical European and Russian thought. As nearly always in his work, the essential bias is one of subversive, radical conservatism. He solicits the revolutionary future in the name of classic humanistic ideals many of which belong to the leisured civilization and generosities of the bourgeois past. These ideals imply a range of literacy which makes much of Western criticism after Taine and Saintsbury look parochial.

But *Die Eigenart des Ästhetischen* is an uneven work. Long stretches are turgid to the point of being almost unreadable. The book is monstrous in prolixity. It suffers from a compulsive outpouring of words. Attention drowns in a gray deluge of print. The Germanic tradition of philosophic amplitude, of the exhaustive, crowning *Werk*, has left its mark. Moreover, the deepening solitude of Lukács' life, its long isolation from the living current of German speech, seems to have provoked an immense monologue. The printed word has become his sole action and companionship.

As a Marxist, Lukács is committed to historicism, to the location of consciousness in a setting of concrete temporal fact. Yet hardly anywhere, in this great scaffolding of generalization and axiomatic proposal, is there a contour of specific reality. Where actual historical considerations appear, as in the chapters on magic and primitive mimesis, the evidence is often vague and second-hand. Lukács scarcely ever allows himself reference to a particular site or work of art. He would say that this is not the job in hand, that he is trying to give inclusive, systematic guise to the ideas and sensibility implicit or scattered throughout his performance as a practical critic. But the result is an uneasy compromise between detailed abstraction and generalized proof. Paradoxically, this austere, colorless array of philosophic arguments comes to resemble the fireworks of Malraux's *Les Voix du silence*. Lukács blurs with generality, Malraux with rapturous singularity. Neither persuades. There is often more of general substance, scrupulously focused, in a short essay by E. H. Gombrich than in this vast torso.

Lukács' remarks on literature carry the weight of obvious, renewed intimacy. But his vision of art, of architecture, of modern music is indistinct and lifeless, as if it drew, almost wholly, on distant memories and second-hand witness. When, one wonders, has Professor Lukács last seen a movie? Until very recently, the eye and imagination of eastern Europe were rigorously cut off from the tradition of the new. Some of the necessary names appear in Lukács' index, but most—Klee, Webern, Frank Lloyd Wright—do not. The equipment of emotional awareness and response with which Lukács approaches the visual arts hardly goes beyond 1935. There is in him, as in other rear-guardsmen of European philosophic Marxism, an exile from the present.

Can one embark on a vast compendium of abstract propositions about language, art, and consciousness as if Wittgenstein had not existed (he is one of Lukács' darkest aversions)? As if no challenges had been issued to the authority and verifiability of linguistic description? Is it possible, in 1964, to dismiss Freud in a curt aside—which, absurdly, equates his work with that of Jung—and to ask that one's own psychologizing be taken seriously? Is the design of a formal *Ästhetik* not itself an anachronism, a charnel house of metaphysical bones?

These are unpleasant questions to ask of a man who has accomplished a tremendous intellectual labor under political and private circumstances of acute difficulty, and who has done so at an age when most men rest. But as one compares the hollow immensities of the

Ästhetik with the bite and vitality of Lukács' actual criticism, a feeling of waste is inescapable. The very audience for which this leviathan is conceived, the young artists and intellectuals of eastern Europe who are asking whether there is anything left of life and incitement in the Marxist legacy, will close Lukács' book bewildered. There is hardly anything in it that fits the landscape of their needs. It belongs to the world of Richard Hamann, the embodiment of academic aesthetics in the 1920's, and the countless, forgotten treatises on *le vrai et le beau;* not to that of Kafka and Jackson Pollock. Nor, indeed, to that of Brecht.

OUT OF CENTRAL EUROPE

H ans Mayer's decision not to return to his chair at Leipzig means
that the last humanist of European stature has abandoned
East Germany. One by one, the lights have gone out in that gray
land.

This is no cause for rejoicing. The reduction of East Germany
to brutal parochialism and servility leaves a dangerous gap. The
D.D.R. stands, in denial of humane contact, between the vulnerable
energies of independent intellectual life in eastern Europe and the
efforts of the West to "get through" on a basis of argument and
response. Moreover, by virtue of history and language, East Germany is intensely a part of Europe, and the diminution of any such
part to barbarism is a threat to the vitality of the whole. In cities in
which Goethe wrote and Wagner composed, generations are coming
of age in a miasma of lies and controlled hatreds. Already, under the
pressure of different truths, of "un-facts" and history rewritten, the
East German language is developing its own jargon and dialect. This
divorce, across the wall of silence or vituperation, has direct bearing
on West Germany. On balance, the East Germans have dealt more
drastically and honestly with the Nazi past than have the West
Germans. But precisely because the truth and summons of conscience
have so often come barbed with Ulbricht propaganda, the West
Germans have found it easy not to listen. Many a West German,
furthermore, has felt that the evils of Nazi rule, and his own share in
them, were somehow made good or canceled by the miseries of his
eastern neighbors.

The linguistic and cultural separation between the two Germa-
nies, their isolation from each other, bodes ill for any rational prospect

of reunification. The process of insulation of consciousness—of the way in which totalitarian schooling can falsify the entire world-image and reflex system of a nation or generation—is one which is grimly characteristic of our time and which we do not yet fully understand. But obviously it makes the resumption of dialogue immensely difficult. The words no longer refer to the same underlying experiences; they may continue to sound alike, but have contrary definitions. A young East German might come to be more at home, in the syntax of his politics and feelings, in Peking or Albania than in Cologne.

This divorcement of East Germany from European life signifies the defeat of a specific historical possibility. Marxism is a reading of history and a utopia of human conduct profoundly rooted in European civilization. Marx is as much an heir to Vico, Lessing, and Diderot as he is to Hegel. The impulse of rational doctrine and utopian idealism behind the Russian revolution is part of the genius and legacy of European enlightenment. And it is on this common heritage of Western liberalism and Eastern revolution—a heritage to which Bolshevism pays tribute, often naïvely, in its claim of kinship with 1776 and 1789—that the chances of effective coexistence and intellectual encounter ultimately depend. East Germany represented the possibility of a bridge, of the re-inclusion of the Marxist presence in a flexible, widened compass of European sensibility. Even granted the brutishness and ineptitudes of the Pankow regime, there seemed to be a chance to relate Marxism to its true and primary roots in western European history and culture.

That is why Ernst Bloch hung on grimly until 1961. That is why Hans Mayer was persuaded to leave Frankfurt in 1948 and go to Leipzig University. Now they are gone, and the best of their students are silent or in prison. It is in East Germany that the major achievements of European Marxist thought of the past decades are banned. It is here that the alliance between classical humanism and the dialectics of Hegel and Marx—as represented in the works of Lukács, Bloch, Adorno, Walter Benjamin—is regarded as treason.

The literacy of Hans Mayer, the repertoire of awareness and tradition on which his criticism draws, is wide but of a specific historical type. It derives from the tastes and habits of reference of the more progressive elements of the German and Central European bourgeoisie (often Jewish) of the period from 1880 to 1914. It has its markers: a sound knowledge of Goethe, and the realization that Goethe is one of the few genuine examples of a human being for whom civilization was a homeland. An uneasy, yet profound admiration of Wagner. Intimacy with Heine and Stendhal, with Lessing, Voltaire, and Ibsen. Men of that background tend to use Greek poetry, and particularly Homer, as a tuning-fork of the ideal. They regard Shakespeare as, in some essential way, a European, nearly a continental possession. They read Karl Kraus.

The type is recognizable. It is at home, or at least a familiar guest, in several languages. It has its distinctive note of wide, passionate allusion. But also its solitude. Nazism and the Stalinist terror in east Europe have all but destroyed this particular "Central European Humanism." It survives in exile or uneasy return: in Erich Kahler's library in Princeton, in the book-crammed study of Georg Lukács, high over the river in Budapest. It has its active life when Ernst Bloch is lecturing at Tübingen or Friedrich Torberg is at the Café Raimund in Vienna. It can be found in England, when Elias Canetti is in the room. A central humanism, classical in background, radical of bias. It gives to the writings of Hans Mayer their essential idiom.

Much of Mayer's most solid work deals with German literature of the late eighteenth and nineteenth centuries. It is gathered in two volumes: *Von Lessing bis Thomas Mann* (1959), and *Zur Deutschen Klassik und Romantik* (1963). Being historically compact and salient in its main problems and crises, German literature confronts the critic and literary historian with certain clearly defined challenges. There is scarcely an essay by Hans Mayer which does not have its counterpart in the critical writings of Lukács, Adorno, Thomas Mann, Emil Staiger, or Benno von Wiese. This makes it possible to define Mayer's quality, the tone which he adds to a traditionally established process of critical discussion.

It is against the dominant fact of Goethe that a German critic tests the reach of his awareness. First published in 1960, the ample preface to Goethe's *Italienische Reise* shows Mayer at his best. Without seeking to break novel ground, he admirably defines the nervous and moral crisis which drove Goethe to leave Weimar, with such covert abruptness, in September 1786. He deals lucidly with the delicate interaction between Goethe's botanical, morphological studies—his quest for the "primal plant"—and the resurgence of his unifying and inventive powers under the Italian sky. Without ideological rancor, and in an argument which corrects the dogmatism of Franz Mehring, Mayer shows *why* Goethe remained innocent of any specific awareness of the nearing political upheaval. The essay closes with an acute comparison of the limitations and insights of Stendhal's *Histoire de la peinture en Italie*. Though written at different times (Stendhal cheerfully plagiarized Goethe), both works mark the transition from a primarily classic to a modern focus. For closeness and modesty of perception, Mayer's preface compares interestingly with W. H. Auden's. The parallel reminds one of how much Auden is, among Anglo-Saxons, the nearest to "Central European" values and tones.

In a long essay on Heinrich von Kleist, first published as a monograph in 1962, Mayer argues that the neurotic stress and complications of Kleist's brief, self-destructive career recapitulate the ambiguities and crises of the German urban middle class between the time of Kant and the rise of militant nationalism. I translate "urban middle class" because, significantly, Mayer prefers to use *bürgerlich* rather than *bourgeois*. He is persuasive in his rebuke to Lukács' thesis of an irrationalist Kleist, and illuminating when he affirms that the *Prinz von Homburg* is a precedent to that characteristic nineteenth-century motif, the artist as tragic hero.

The paper on Heine implicitly refutes any facile appropriation of the poet by a Marxist or pre-Marxist pantheon. Mayer underlines the ambivalence of Heine's position, his fastidious recoil before populist forces and ideologies whose triumph he foresaw and, in a certain measure, hoped for. To Mayer, Heine is the great exception, *die Ausnahme*, the Jew freed from a Ghetto he did not know at first hand but not yet at home in German culture, "The unique instance of a human being entirely without tradition, but also, to start with, nearly without resentment." Mayer notes with admiring reproof how often this unhoused genius made of literary style his sole loyalty, how often he wounded others because he himself had learned to move without ties.

Lessing: Mitwelt und Nachwelt is among the best introductions available to this fascinating, deeply attractive, yet so little-read figure. In it, Mayer touches on one of his primary themes: the failure of German culture to take stable root in the rational, skeptical consciousness of eighteenth-century Europe. He shows how alone Lessing stood amid the surge of Romantic chauvinism, how little in German literature can be said to derive directly from Lessing's example and achievement. Lessing's ideal of a coherent, reciprocal relation between poet and society was not realized. Out of this failure, says

Mayer, sprang the fierce subjectivity, the edgy, often pathological isolation of the German artist.

Where, in all this, is Mayer's commitment to dialectical materialism and Marxist aesthetics?

There are obvious Marxist tenets in Mayer's historicism, in his placing of the literary work or personage in a context of specific social background and political moment. But if this tactic points to Marx, it points no less to Taine and Sainte-Beuve. Marx's postulate of the involvement of the work of art in the political, social milieu is itself representative of that alliance between history and poetics which colors so much of nineteenth-century thought from Herder to Comte.

A Marxist flavor is also apparent in Mayer's internationalism, in his refusal—finely demonstrated in his essay, *Aussenwelt und Innenwelt*—to assign to German literature or German culture an exemplary merit. On the contrary: like Lukács, Mayer sees in German history a crucial failure of responsible communication between artist and society, an inability of the poet to translate inward values into effective social attitudes. Here, indeed, he touches on that most pressing and complex riddle: the recurrent coexistence in German life of political barbarism and high art. But this anti-chauvinism, this capacity to judge "from outside" are not exclusively or primarily Marxist. They belong to what I have tried to describe as a particular "European centrality." The two overlap; they are conjoined in the hatred lavished by Nazism and Stalinism on the "rootless cosmopolitan."

Perhaps the only distinctive Marxist bias in these essays on classic and Romantic literature is Mayer's insistence on the implication of the individual writer in the pervasive, historically determined crisis of the European bourgeoisie.

To see his actual use of Marxist canons, to note the ways in which the pressures and exactions of East German cultural life have shaped his critical discernments, one must look elsewhere—to Mayer's articles on contemporary literature, *Ansichten: Zur Literatur der Zeit*.

This is not an easy book to judge. Writing from the safety of the West, one finds it difficult even to imagine, concretely, the net of dangers and insinuations, of blackmail and soft menace, under which a civilized mind has to work in an East German university. Noting some of Hans Mayer's most dubious arguments, one asks oneself: does he *really* believe this, or did he have to say it in order to continue saying anything at all? Does he really believe, or want us to believe, that Anna Seghers' *Der Ausflug der toten Mädchen* has a finer moral insight, a more valid criticism of life, than Proust, whose work Mayer knows and loves so well? Does he honestly fail to observe the treasons and servilities in the talent of Louis Aragon, or believe that the weakness of Sartre's fiction derives from Sartre's attempt to modify and complicate dialectical materialism with elements of American sociology and post-Freudian psychology? Or take the essay on Durrell. Very possibly, my initial response to the *Quartet*, with which Mayer takes issue, represents an overestimate. But of what rational use is it when Mayer applies to Durrell—as he does to half a dozen figures ranging from Richard Strauss and Hofmannsthal to Karl Kraus—the cliché of "decadence," when he dismisses Durrell's success as a sign of "anachronism, decay, and regression"?

In such a context, queries about intellectual honesty are facile rhetoric. What presumably takes place is a continuous and precarious adjustment of the mind to an unstable equilibrium, a tight-rope act of conscience over an abyss of personal danger. It is, I think, in the essays on Pasternak and Kafka that the virtues and limitations of Mayer's ideological position—the braveries and concessions of the humane sensibility in a context of totalitarian dogma—can most fairly be seen.

It must have taken real courage to write this poised, calm critique of *Doctor Zhivago*. Mayer observes in Pasternak's "un-hero" a total avoidance of human commitment, an abdication from the claims and realities of history. He is neither, as the more crass of Soviet critics proclaimed, a symbol of reaction and subtle treason, nor, as was sometimes argued in the West, a champion of liberalism and aesthetic freedom. Mayer sees Zhivago as a complex *anachronism;* he is, in both senses of the word, impertinent to the time. In one cardinal point, moreover, Mayer agrees with the official critics who refused to publish the novel in *Novy Mir*. By making Zhivago the alleged author of some of his own most perfect and characteristic poems, Pasternak pulls a sleight of hand; he enforces the claim for Zhivago's stature and depth of perception (a claim which the novel itself does not support), and he all but compels identification between himself and his principal character. Is this proceeding entirely honest? One of the answers would, of course, be to suggest to Mayer that Paskernak was working under conditions comparable in danger and indirection to those under which he himself was writing.

Kafka und kein Edne? is a well-known paper which Mayer read in Paris in February 1960. Surveying the mass of one-sided or polemic studies—Kafka the religious allegorist, Kafka the satirist of decaying imperial bureaucracy, Kafka the existentialist—Mayer calls for an ordering and reassessment of the texts themselves. He says very rightly that too little has yet been done to discriminate the successive psychological and stylistic phases in Kafka's development, and that too little heed has been given to Kafka's own division between fragmentary work and work ready or intended for publication. Above all, Mayer proposes to remove Kafka's achievement from a place of mysterious singularity; he seeks to localize it in the current of the general post-romantic theme of the malaise of the artist in society. He concludes by suggesting two analogues to Kafka's art: Gustav Mahler and Proust. In all three, Mayer discerns a similar apprehension of a society innerly torn and splintered (*die Zerrisenheit einer ganzen Zeit und Gesellschaft*), and a consequent pessimism about the means and validity of art. In each, he notes aspects of the Jewish problem and a strategy of retreat into childhood and dreams.

This grouping seems to me, in certain respects, bizarre. But Mayer is surely right when he seeks to relate Kafka to surrounding literature and formal experiment. It has recently, for example, become clear that *The Castle* may owe more than one of its secrets and devices to an earlier Czech classic, Božena Němcová's *Granny*.

The general point is clear: by method and tone, Hans Mayer's criticism tries to define a *via media*. It is equally opposed to party dogma and anarchic impressionism. It is Marxist in its trained awareness of material context, in its refusal to isolate literature from the totality of social fact, and in its general pattern of necessary historical phase and decline. It is humanistic in its respect for the autonomy of aesthetic forms and in its rejection of any facile identification between philosophic and political content and artist value. In voice and ideological bias, it is very near the earlier criticism of Edmund Wilson.

But not in originality or depth. This is the difficulty. There is a gray, flat reasonableness about a good deal of Mayer's work. As if the constant effort toward mediation and equilibrium between dialectical pressures had blunted the edge of feeling.

Mayer's essay on Kleist is lucid; but it lacks the sheer inwardness of Thomas Mann's. Nothing he says of Heine is banal or insensitive, but Adorno's grip on the same theme—the poet not wholly housed in any language—is more forceful. The essay on Kafka, for all its justice, gives less purchase than the haughty reflections of Walter Muschg in *The Destruction of German Literature*. Walter Benjamin is much deeper on Goethe. Topic for topic, and comparison is inevitable, Erich Heller's is often the more trenchant, the more illuminating reading.

This blurring at the edges, the sense of argument muted, is obviously part of Mayer's survival. That he should have accomplished so much under conditions so abrasive is itself a very high achievement. His style, moreover, has precisely those virtues of scruple and modesty which sometimes diminish the bite of his criticism. It has remained delightfully intact from the somber jargon which mars so much of present German prose, Marxist or academic.

It will be exciting to see what a mind so orderly and wide-ranging will produce now that certain pressures are off.

THE WRITER
AND COMMUNISM

One of the striking differences between Fascism and Communism is this: Fascism has inspired no great work of art. With the possible exception of Montherlant, it has drawn into its orbit no writer of the first rank. (Ezra Pound was no Fascist; he used the occasions and trappings of Fascism for his own quirky economics.) Communism, on the contrary, has been a central force in much of the finest of modern literature; and personal encounter with Communism has marked the consciousness and career of many of the major writers of the age.

Why this difference? No doubt, Fascism is too vile and scurrilous an ideology to produce those charities of the imagination which are essential to literate art. Communism, even where it has gone venomous, is a mythology of the human future, a vision of human possibility rich in moral demand. Fascism is the ultimate code of the hoodlum; Communism fails because it would seek to impose upon the fragile plurality of human nature and conduct an artificial ideal of self-denial and historic purpose. Fascism tyrannizes through contempt of man; Communism tyrannizes by exalting man above that sphere of private error, private ambition, and private love which we call freedom.

There is also a more specific difference. Hitler and Goebbels were cunning manipulators of language; but they had scant respect for the life of the mind. Communism, by contrast, is a creed penetrated from the very moment of its historical origin by a sense of the values of intellect and art. In Marx and Engels this sense is explicit. They were intellectuals to the core. Lenin paid to art the supreme tribute of fear; he shied away from it, acknowledging the obscure, entrancing powers of plastic and musical form over the rational intellect. Trotsky was a *littérateur* in the most flamboyant sense of the word. Even under Stalin, the writer and the literary work played a vital role in Communist strategy. Writers were persecuted and killed precisely because literature was recognized as an important and potentially dangerous force. This is a crucial point. Literature was being honored, in however cruel or perverted a way, by the very fact of Stalin's distrust. And when the partial thaw came, the position of the writer in Soviet society grew once again complex and problematic. One cannot conceive of a Fascist state being shaken by a mere book; but *Doctor Zhivago* was one of the major crises in the recent life of the intelligentsia in Communist Russia.

Whether by instinct or meditation, writers have always been aware of their special position in Communist ideology. They have taken Communism seriously because *it* has taken them seriously. Thus a history of the relations between Communism and modern literature is, in certain vital respects, a history of both.

Mr. Jürgen Rühle is one of the host of writers and intellectuals who have experienced the spell of Communism and then broken with Stalinist reality. Since taking refuge in Western Germany, he has established himself as an expert historian and observer of Communist literary and theatrical life. In his book *Literatur und Revolution* he has set out to write a history of "the writer and Communism" throughout the world in the period from 1917 to 1960. It is a massive, wide-reaching enterprise: it spans the course of Russian literature from Blok to *Zhivago;* it deals with the poetry of Pablo Neruda and the fiction of Erskine Caldwell; it passes from a discussion of the politics of Thomas Mann to a critique of Lu Hsun. Furnished with a chronological table and bibliography, *Literatur und Revolution* is both a critical essay and a work of reference. And a mere glance at the index and illustrations shows that there is hardly a major writer in our time (Proust, Joyce, and Faulkner are notable exceptions) who has not been touched at some stage in his life and art by Communism.

The first section of the book deals with the destiny of Russian literature under Lenin, Zhdanov, and Khrushchev. It covers familiar but momentous ground. We observe once again the genius and bitter end of the revolutionary triad: Blok, Yessenin, Mayakovsky. Rühle is particularly interesting on the subject of that unwieldy, much neglected novel of Gorky, *Klim Samgin*. He argues persuasively that Gorky was unable to finish the work because he already discerned that conflict between individual life and Communist organization which was to drive so many Soviet writers into silence or death. Rühle goes on to discuss the chroniclers of the civil war, Isaac Babel and Sholokhov. Here again, his reading is acute: he shows that Sholokhov has always been a regionalist of an archaic anti-intellectual stamp, who has succeeded in being at the same time the voice of nationalist and Stalinist sentiment. He gives a plausible account of the Byzantine evasions and audacities that have kept Ehrenburg alive through winter and thaw. And beneath the crowded narrative of individual careers and works sounds the relentless motif of banishment, execution, or suicide.

Finally, Rühle comes to Pasternak. He sees in Pasternak the true voice of Russia, the vision that will prevail beyond the tyrannies of the moment. He agrees with Edmund Wilson in finding in Lara and Zhivago an unanswerable challenge to the historicism and life-denying determinism of the Communist ideology. The bare fact that Pasternak could conceive of their private rebellious love while remaining inside the Soviet Union proves that the Russian spirit is alive beneath the ice-crust of party discipline. Pasternak was among the first to read the farewell poem which Yessenin wrote with his own blood. He knew the famous suicide note of Mayakovsky. But by virtue of courage and discretion he survived. And in *Doctor Zhivago* he drew up that indictment against Soviet disregard for individual life which his fellow poets had hinted at in the tragic manner of their deaths.

There is much truth in this, and Rühle expresses it well. But not having been in the Soviet Union recently, he fails to realize how remote the world of Lara and Zhivago is from the imaginings and feelings of the present younger generation. It is the rulers, the old men, who are afraid of the book and who have sought to silence it. I wonder whether the young see in *Doctor Zhivago* anything but a deeply moving fairy tale, or a piece of historical fiction as distant as *Anna Karenina*.

The second part of *Literatur und Revolution* is by far the most valuable. It deals authoritatively with the tangled relations between Communism and German literature. It is no exaggeration to say that there is scarcely a single German writer of note since 1919 who has not taken a declared stance, either positive or antagonistic, toward

Communism. There is some deep affinity between the historicism and systematic idealism of the Marxist ideology and the German spirit from which it sprang. Often, as Rühle shows, extreme right and extreme left meet in Germany on a common ground of totalitarian bias. The Hitler-Stalin pact, however deceitful and short-lived, was like an allegory of a genuine relationship.

Rühle excels in his account of Johannes Becher, the Orpheus of Stalinism, and of Egon Erwin Kisch, the most gifted journalist ever to serve the Marxist cause. He offers a sensitive reading of the works of Anna Seghers, showing how her recent novels betray the contortions of a genuine artist trying to come to terms with the gray half-truths of "socialist realism." He illuminates the role of Marxist ideas in the historical fiction of Heinrich Mann and Lion Feuchtwanger. He suggests, in a carefully documented chapter, that the disagreements between Heinrich and Thomas Mann stand for a larger dialectic: the confrontation of the German mind with the opposite but related seductions of right-wing nationalism on the one hand and radical internationalism on the other.

As in the section dealing with Soviet literature, there runs beneath the narrative of individual lives the constant theme of violent death. One after another, the voices of German poetry and drama and criticism were stifled by exile, murder, or suicide. Reading this calendar of destruction—Ossietzky, Mühsam, Kornfeld, Theodor Wolff, Friedell, Toller, Hasenclever, Ernst Weiss, Stefan Zweig—one realizes that literature is indeed the most dangerous of trades.

After this masterful treatment of German letters, *Literatur und Revolution* goes on to survey the rest of the literate world. The pace becomes somewhat dizzying. In only thirty pages, Rühle discusses the manifold impact of Communism on Camus, Sartre, Gide, Malraux, Eluard, Céline, and Aragon. A further twenty pages sum up the Italian writers—Silone, Pavese, Malaparte, Moravia, Carlo Levi. Less than forty pages are taken up by the complex flirtations with Marxism and Communist dreams of such American writers as Dos Passos, Upton Sinclair, Steinbeck, Hemingway, and James T. Farrell. Brief chapters whirl the reader across Latin America and Asia. Inevitably, this latter half of the book tends to become a register of names, dates, and titles—useful for quick reference, but inadequate to the variousness and complexity of the subject.

In the two closing chapters, Rühle deals with the principal apostates and rebels within the camp of Marxist literature. He discusses Koestler's *Darkness at Noon*, Orwell's *1984*, and the rueful memoirs of Gide and Stephen Spender. Finally, he records the rebellion against Stalinism of the young Polish and Hungarian writers of 1956. During the subsequent period of repression in Hungary, Tibor Dery was condemned for having led "an organization hostile to the state." A grim joke was made of this in Budapest: what might that organization have been? Answer: the Hungarian people. And as his compendious survey closes, Rühle reminds us of the many writers still in Soviet, satellite, or Chinese prisons. The alliance between literature and Communism remains both intimate and tragic.

As a brisk chronicle presenting voluminous and scattered material in lucid order, this book has great virtues. But there is in *Literatur und Revolution* much superficiality. Often the problem is one of sheer brevity (there is not much new or revealing that can be said of an important writer in two or three pages). But often, also, it is Rühle's underlying assumptions that lead to oversimplification. Throughout the book, he seeks to establish a pattern of initial idealistic attraction followed by clear-sighted revulsion. The writer is drawn to the ideals of Communism; he discovers the realities of party bureaucracy and Stalinist oppression; he breaks away. The Red gods have failed him. But in reality, this pattern is applicable only to a limited number of writers, and not to the most important. By insisting on it, Rühle tends to distort the evidence. Let me give only a few examples.

The case of Malraux is a test of a critic's insight into the temptations which totalitarianism offers to poetic genius. Rühle's account of Malraux's turn toward and away from Communism is wholly inadequate. Though he has fought successively in alliance with the left and with the right, moving from the International Brigade to de Gaulle's cabinet, Malraux has never adopted a consistent political program. Whatever the area to which he turned, he has always pursued what there is in politics of heroism, violence, and conspiratorial loyalty. In short, his politics are aesthetic; it is the formal shape of political action that draws Malraux, not the content. The clue to Malraux's entire career may be found in Walter Benjamin's observation that those who make of politics a fine art will always end in an elitist or totalitarian posture—whether on the left or on the right. Rühle fails to see this and does not even refer to Benjamin, who was the most original and profound of all Marxist critics.

360

Or take the case of Orwell. *1984* is not, as Rühle flatly asserts, a parable of the totalitarian rule of Stalin, Hitler, and Mao Tse-tung. The polemic of the fable is not unilinear. Orwell's critique bears simultaneously on the police state and on capitalist consumer society, with its illiteracy of values and its conformities. "Newspeak," the language of Orwell's nightmare, is both the jargon of dialectical materialism and the verbiage of commercial advertisement and mass-media. The tragic strength of *1984* derives precisely from Orwell's refusal to see things in black and white. Our own acquisitive society appalled him. He noted in it germs of inhumanity comparable to those endemic in Stalinism. Orwell came back from Catalonia with a kind of bleak, stoic faith in a humane socialism which neither East nor West is prepared to adopt on any but the most limited scale. To make of *1984* a pamphlet in the intellectual cold war is to misread and diminish the book. The true allegory of Soviet society in Orwell's work is *Animal Farm*.

The same reluctance to allow for the complications of truth influences Rühle's account of Lorca. Despite Rühle's confident statement, the circumstances of Lorca's death still remain puzzling. There may have been in them as large an element of private vengeance as of political terror. Or to give one more example, the intriguing thing about the young Polish writer Hlasko is not the fact that he found Communist Poland stifling and sought freedom in the West, but that he then found the "free world" almost equally intolerable. Literature is a complex, ambiguous pursuit; it does not fall naturally into the confines of Communism or anti-Communism which Rühle seeks to impose on it.

But these are cavils. A more essential flaw in *Literatur und Revolution* is Rühle's refusal to distinguish between Marxism and Communism or, more exactly, between Communism as a moral vision and Communism as a bureaucratic and political reality. In Stalinist Russia and the satellite countries, this distinction was eroded. But elsewhere, and with respect to Western writers who fell under Marxist influence, it is crucial. Constantly, Rühle lumps together writers who may fairly be regarded as Communists and those who drew from the Marxist theory of history and the Marxist account of social conduct substance for their own art. One cannot talk in one breath of Howard Fast and Romain Rolland. The difference is too great.

Strictly speaking, there are few notable writers outside the

Soviet Union who have put their art at the deliberate service of the Communist Party or of Soviet policy. Becher, Aragon, Anna Seghers, Fast—the list is not long. It certainly does not include most of the important poets, novelists, and playwrights whom Rühle is concerned with. What Feuchtwanger and Heinrich Mann gained from Marxism was a sense of the material pressures and density of historical fact. Sartre has drawn from Marxism both support and creative contradiction for his own highly personal vision of crisis and history. In Sean O'Casey, Communism has never been more than the quixotic, essentially anarchic outcry of an Irish sensibility against social injustice. In Malaparte, Communism was a kind of private joke, the mask of a brutal but exacerbated Romantic. To Pablo Nerunda, the Communist ideology is a promise of vengeful utopia. Each case is different.

Moreover, there is a sharp distinction between those who have been disillusioned with Marxism and those who have actually broken with the Communist Party. In most instances, a break with the Party leads either to silence or to Hollywood. A withdrawal from Marxism, on the other hand, appears to be vitalizing process, leaving the imagination of the writer bruised but alive. Thus, in the lives of such writers as Camus, Steinbeck, or Silone, Marxism has played a liberating role. Even when they have turned away from it, they retain in their talent certain characteristic precisions of insight and habits of moral protest.

And because Rühle refuses to distinguish between Hegelian-Marxist precepts and Communist practice, he fails to note the deep influence of Marxist ideas on Western aesthetics and literary theory. Whether explicitly or unconsciously, our whole contemporary view of art is penetrated with a Marxist awareness of social context and historical dynamism. Even the most Alexandrine of "new critics" owes to the Marxist tradition some realization of the economic or social *milieu* that lies behind poetic style. Indeed, it may well be in aesthetics, rather than in actual literature, that Marxism has made its most solid contribution. Yet Rühle scarcely mentions the three critics who, together with Lukács, have brought to the West what is most fruitful in the Marxist view of art: Walter Benjamin, Lucien Goldmann, and Edmund Wilson.

As one puts down this informative but one-sided book, a larger question springs inevitably to mind. Where have Marxism and Communism been essential to the realization of individual talent? Where have they been accidental? Do we owe to the confrontation of literature and Communism any masterpieces that might otherwise not have been conceived? Even if we set aside Russian poetry of the period 1917–1925, there are, I think, several.

Two of the most representative of modern novels, Malraux's *Man's Fate* and Koestler's *Darkness at Noon*, stem directly from the impact of the Communist movement on the life and imagination of the writer. They remain valid, moreover, because they recognize in militant Communism the coexistence of nobility and evil. If, in the proceedings of the Party, one finds cruelty, cunning, and the ruthless suppression of private values, one also finds sacrifice, courage, and a fierce conviction of the capacity of men to live and die for ideas. Without Marxism and an eccentric but steadfast adherence to Party ideology, the foremost dramatist of the age, Bertolt Brecht, might not have found his voice and style. The *Three-Penny Opera*, *Mahagonny*, and *Mother Courage* are classics of the modern tone. They have passed into the repertoire of common feeling; but they are rooted in Brecht's personal Communism and in the historical setting of the defeat of the German Communist movement. East Berlin is the city toward which Brecht was heading, however warily, his whole life long.

Similarly, some of the finest poetry of Aragon is inseparable from the world-view and vocabulary of Communism. And the same, in a paradoxical yet decisive sense, is true of *Doctor Zhivago*. One cannot get that diffuse, meditative, often self-contradictory work into focus without realizing how deeply Pasternak was involved in the griefs and aspirations of the Russian Revolution. In many regards, the novel is a plea for a revolution even more total and inward than that which created Soviet society.

Elsewhere, the Marxist or Communist element in the work of art is often a superficial varnish or a convenient code to express a personal radicalism. That is certainly the case with the plays of O'Casey and the poems of Eluard. Often the attempt of the artist to serve the present needs of Party ideology ends in subversive misunderstanding: one recalls how Picasso, seeking to honor the death of Stalin, produced a portrait of a dreamy, vague young man with a Victorian moustache.

Finally, there is that most difficult question of the relationship between art and totalitarianism as such. History instructs us that autocracy, whether in Augustan Rome, in Renaissance Florence, or at the court of Louis XIV, can engender great art and literature. Tyrants and poets have often got along quite well (even in Stalin, there were bizarre traces of this relation—witness his treatment of Bulgakov and Pasternak). But how far can absolutism go before art falls servile or silent? Where do we cross the line between the artist as conveyor of the ideals of his society and the artist as maker of mere propaganda? Just where is the difference between Andrew Marvell's ode to Cromwell and Becher's rhapsodies to Stalin and Ulbricht? If Rühle's book does not provide an answer, it at least sheds much valuable light on the nature of the problem. But this fascinating, urgent subject remains to be dealt with.

TROTSKY AND THE TRAGIC
IMAGINATION

Isaac Deutscher's biography of Trotsky, as large in scale as it is in imaginative and intellectual commitment, makes one ask again: why did Trotsky fall? What brought to ruin the virtuoso tactician of the Bolshevik revolution, a man equaling, at moments excelling, Lenin in foresight and brilliance of device?

The causes are complex, and their roots lie in the time of victory. In December 1919, Trotsky was at the summit of his political and military achievement. Along a circumference of some five thousand miles, the White armies had been broken and flung back. Yudenich and his British tanks were halted at the doors of Petrograd. On the southern front, White Guards were retreating in disorder from Kiev and Poltava. In Siberia, Admiral Kolchak's myth of an anti-Soviet Russia was nearing its macabre end. At the Seventh Congress of the Soviets, Trotsky, newly awarded the Order of the Red Banner, seemed to personify the inventiveness, the cold daring, the ruthlessness of hope which had made victory possible. To the world at large, his name was legend.

Yet only four years later he left the Commissariat of War, and on January 16, 1928, he was a man stripped of power, on his way to exile in Central Asia. How did Stalin, moving feline and tenacious out of the shadow of Party bureaucracy, isolate and overcome the greatest of his potential rivals?

The contour of classic tragedy lies near at hand. Trotsky stumbled at the very moment of triumph. He who had argued and fought for proletarian democracy in the full sense, for the right of worker and peasant to express and organize their views in a process of continued revolutionary debate, now adopted the theory and practice of total Party control. It was the Party, uniquely informed by authentic historical insight and underwritten by victory, that was to be the voice and executor of society. Acutely aware of the social, economic chaos left by revolution and civil war—no individual mind could visualize, let alone master, the sum of local ruin—inspired by his own success in shaping and directing the Red Army, Trotsky in December 1919 proposed that the mechanics of military mobilization be adapted to the mobilization of civilian labor (a notion which Saint-Just examined during the French Revolution). During what Lenin termed the "fever" and "mortal illness" of the Party in the winter of 1920–21, Trotsky led the faction which wanted the trade unions to be deprived of their autonomy and absorbed into the fabric of the state. He railed against those who "have made a fetish of democratic principles" and urged, with abrasive eloquence, that "the Party is obliged to maintain its dictatorship, regardless of temporary waverings in the spontaneous moods of the masses, regardless of the temporary vacillations even in the working class."

It was Trotsky who took the salute after the suppression of the Kronstadt rising, that first chapter in the long, grim duel of the Soviet revolution with its anarchic or radical past; it was Trotsky who hailed as a necessary victory the decimation of the sailors whom he had himself kindled to mutiny in 1917 and led during the civil war. The irony of his new situation was profound and suicidal. Having proclaimed that the Party must substitute itself for the will of society—must incarnate that will as a monistic instrument—Trotsky foresaw that the Central Committee would one day substitute itself for the Party as a whole, and that, finally and inevitably, a single dictator would unite in his own person the functions and processes of decision of the Central Committee. Yet, precisely like a personage in classical tragedy, Trotsky did not act to arrest, to defeat, the dangers he foresaw. Clairvoyance and policy drew apart, as if doom, seen as a historical process, had its irresistible fascination. He stumbled on, majestic. One thinks of Eteocles going clear-sighted to the death gate in the *Seven Against Thebes*, refusing the plea of the chorus for evasion or liberty of action:

> We are already past the care of gods.
> For them our death is the admirable offering.
> Why then delay, fawning upon our doom.

The crisis of interregnum in 1923–24 defined Trotsky's isolation. Here E. H. Carr's study of the internal history of Soviet Russia and of the Party is indispensable. The plight of the Soviet economy and the conflicting claims of industry and agriculture provoked bitter divisions. But precisely because of his earlier negative attitude toward the trade unions, Trotsky could not become the natural leader of an "industrial opposition" (such as was to emerge many decades later against the inefficiencies and archaic savageries of Stalinist rule). Increasingly, Trotsky had to play a lone, impatient hand. This was plainly visible during the dissensions in Moscow over the proper course of action to be followed by the German Communist Party. As Carr puts it: for Trotsky "the destinies of the Russian and German revolutions were irrevocably linked: for him it was an emotional, as much as a rational, belief." In August 1923 Trotsky was confident that the hour was at hand, that proletarian revolution was imminent in the homeland of Marx. The failure of the K.P.D. in October, followed a few days later by Hitler's Munich *putsch*, further weakened Trotsky's emotional and tactical resources. Already Stalin, whose seeming indifference to the German question was compounded of ignorance and instinctive cunning, began to emerge as the dominant partner in the Kamenev-Zinoviev-Stalin triumvirate.

Moreover, there can be no doubt that Lenin's illness and death left Trotsky off balance and curiously vulnerable. The relationship between these two elemental figures of the Russian revolution was intricate and vital, as only a great novelist might have conceived it. It had begun in polemic. In 1904 Trotsky, who had not yet broken with the Mensheviks, wrote of Lenin as a man "hideous" and "dissolute," as a Russian Robespierre drawing a line of blood between his Party and the world (had Trotsky already cast himself in the role of Danton?). They again opposed each other over the formulation of the Zimmerwald program in 1915, and in 1917 Trotsky did not respond immediately when Lenin asked him and his friends to join the Bolsheviks. Their alliance was only forged by the needs and triumphs of October. Deutscher writes of the "discord in temperament and habit" between the two giants; one imagines rock and lava.

But during the six short years of their partnership—years that altered the contour of the century and of a large part of the earth—they developed a profound mutual respect. Lenin, notes Deutscher, "made not a single allusion to their past controversies, except to say privately that in some respects Trotsky had been right and to warn the

Party, in his will, that it ought not to hold his non-Bolshevik past against Trotsky." In that famous document, Lenin, while qualifying Trotsky's genius as too far-reaching in its self-confidence, stated that Trotsky was, "to be sure, the most able man in the present Central Committee."

Trotsky acknowledged Lenin's primacy and uncanny political acumen. He did not renounce his own independence but was distinctly remorseful about his past assaults on Lenin's integrity and leadership. So long as Lenin was in essential control, Trotsky acted with magnificent dash and spontaneity of tactical resource. It was as if Lenin was the firm pivot against which he could exercise, without fear of political disaster, the freedom and irreverence of his own temper. So long as Lenin was there to listen and judge, Trotsky felt immune from the cancerous workings of Party intrigue and old-guard reprisal. His own isolation from Party cadres seemed as nothing when set against the potential strength of a Lenin-Trotsky *entente*.

With Lenin's death, Trotsky's political flair, his buoyant demon of sarcasm and ruse, seemed to desert him. One cannot help wondering whether his failure to enlist Lenin's personal prestige in the nascent struggle against Stalin, whether his failure to invoke the full force of Lenin's testament, with its warnings of Stalin's abuses of bureaucratic power, do not point to a deeply entrenched feeling of guilt. As if Trotsky had never forgiven himself for his initial attacks on Lenin, as if, perhaps at some subconscious level, he did not feel justified in using his collaboration with Lenin to combat those old Bolsheviks who treated him as an opportunist and latecomer. Fatally —though Stalin may have had a hand in the imbroglio—Trotsky was absent from Moscow at the time of Lenin's funeral. It was precisely on this occasion that Stalin struck the new ominous note of the cult of personality, of the Byzantine homage to the leader.

Deutscher summarizes the situation thus:

Slowly but inexorably the circumstances which led to Trotsky's defeat began to unfold and agglomerate. He missed the opportunity of confounding the triumvirs and discrediting Stalin. He let down his allies. He failed to act as Lenin's mouthpiece with the resolution Lenin had expected of him. He failed to support before the entire Party the Georgians and the Ukrainians for whom he had stood up in the Politbureau. He kept silent when the cry for inner-party democracy rose from the floor. He expounded economic ideas the historic portent of which escaped his audience but which his adversaries could easily twist so as to impress presently upon workers, peasants, and bureaucrats alike that Trotsky was not their well-wisher, and that every social class and group ought to tremble at the mere thought that he might become Lenin's successor.

What lay behind the procrastination, behind the refusal to appeal to the Party at large, to the army he had called into being, to the international Communist movement in whose eyes his glory stood undimmed? Was Trotsky, as Stalin hinted, too proud to fight? Probably the causes lay deeper. Marxism can effect a dissociation from personal identity very like that experienced by the protagonist in tragic drama. Having entrusted his imagination, his center of reality, to the historical process, the Marxist revolutionary trains himself to accept a diminished range and validity of private regard. The logic, the emotional authority of the historical fact, even where it entails destruction and humiliation to his own person, surpasses the claims, the intensity, of the self. Doom is accepted, almost acquiesced in, as being part of that historical truth and forward motion in which individual existence anchors its meaning. It is the note sounded by those high, stiff personages waiting on death in Yeats's *Deirdre:*

> They knew that there was nothing that could save them,
> And so played chess as they had any night
> For years and waited for the stroke of sword.
> I never heard a death so out of reach
> Of common hearts, a high and comely end.
> What need have I, that gave up all for love,
> To die like an old king out of a fable,
> Fighting and passionate? What need is there
> For all that ostentation at my setting?
> I have loved truly and betrayed no man.
> I need no lightning at the end, no beating
> In a vain fury at the cage's door.

More obviously, Trotsky was caught in a web of physical illness and nervous exhaustion. It kept him away from Moscow at crucial moments and barred him from that day-to-day exaction of organizational intrigue and factional maneuvering at which Stalin excelled. Victory had left Trotsky strangely tired, strangely unbent. When his temper returned to its full pitch of resolution, when he realized that it was only "fighting and passionate" that he could live, that there would be necessary "lightning at the end," it was too late.

This is the theme of *The Prophet Outcast*, perhaps the finest volume of Deutscher's biography. The events take the shape of a Niobe play. Not much in the chronicle of Stalin's sinuous cruelty surpasses the extermination of Trotsky's children and grandchildren. Deprived of Soviet nationality, Trotsky's daughter Zina was unable to rejoin her husband or children. Her restless mind broke under the strain and she committed suicide in Berlin, where the Nazis would, a few weeks later, have closed in on her. Leon (or Lyova), Trotsky's eldest son, was the untiring companion of exile, his father's courier, publicist, and advocate. Though Trotsky demanded fantastic labor of him under circumstances increasingly hopeless, though he often treated him with impatience, Lyova's courage and fidelity held. It was he who kept alive the harried remnants of the Trotskyite movement in western Europe. It was through his efforts that the wavering dream of a Fourth International retained some substance. But the G.P.U. hunted him incessantly. He died in Paris in February 1938, at the age of thirty-two, sick of heart, short of sleep and food. Deutscher concludes that "much of the circumstantial evidence" points to murder.

Trotsky's youngest son, Sergei, sought to remain wholly outside the contagious glory of his father's convictions and political fortunes. In vain. Despite Trotsky's appeal to world opinion, Sergei was deported to a Siberian concentration camp, then tortured in the hope that he would denounce his father. He was probably done to death sometime in 1938, though there are those who thought they saw him alive later. Experiencing the fate of his children, knowing he had brought it on and could do nothing to prevent it, Trotsky passed inchwise through damnation. He wrote of Lyova:

> His mother, who was closer to him than anyone in the world, and I, as we are living through these terrible hours, recall his image feature by feature; we refuse to believe that he is no more and we weep because it is impossible not to believe. . . . Your mother and I never thought, never expected, that fate would lay this task on us . . . that we

should have to write your obituary. . . . But we have not been able to save you.

As Ovid says of Niobe: *dumque rogat, pro qua rogat, occidit* (even as she prayed, the child for whom she prayed fell dead).

But it was Trotsky himself, of course, whom Stalin was determined to destroy. The long pursuit led from Turkey to France, from France to Norway, from Norway to Mexico. It is not only the hunters who appall, but those who refused asylum or hedged it with conditions so abject that Trotsky had to seek elsewhere. Unlike Herzen, Ogarev, or Marx, Trotsky was not allowed sanctuary in England. Deutscher suggests that Trotsky and Churchill bear a significant resemblance, as masters of rhetoric, as historians, as amateurs of genius in war. But toward Trotsky, Churchill showed no magnanimity. He rejoiced to see "the Ogre of Europe" now a "bundle of old rags" sitting disconsolate on the shores of the Black Sea, or being hounded from place to place. But then it was Trotsky's levies that had routed Churchill's hopes of allied and counter-revolutionary intervention.

The end was in character: "His skull smashed, his face gored, Trotsky jumped up, hurled at the murderer whatever object was at hand, books, inkpots, even the dictaphone, and then threw himself at him. It had all taken only three or four minutes. . . . Trotsky's last struggle. He fought it like a tiger. He grappled with the murderer, bit his hand, and wrenched the ice axe from him."

It was this formidable resurgence of will after his defeat in Moscow which enabled Trotsky to achieve, during eleven years of flight and exile, much of what is permanent in his legacy. Trotsky's presence during these years, the leap of energy out of the single life take on the particularized universality of legend. His writings become of absorbing fascination to the student of literature (books, inkpots, and the dictaphone are the writer's arsenal).

On the island of Prinkipo, in the Sea of Marmara, Trotsky wrote his autobiography, *My Life*, and his *History of the Russian Revolution*. Both are superb books and have stood the test of time. The autobiography was written in limbo, in a tense breathing spell between the momentous historical past and an uncertain future. In it Trotsky achieves a peculiar detachment, seeing much of his life as already in the grasp of history. He has the eye for detail of the natural writer and tactician. In the late summer of 1902, Trotsky escaped from Siberian exile "together with E.G., a woman translator of Marx":

> The driver sped on in the Siberian fashion, making as much as twenty versts an hour. I counted all the bumps with my back, to the accompaniment of the groans of my companion. During the trip the horses were changed twice. Before we reached the railway, my companion and I went our separate ways, so that each of us would not have to suffer the mis-haps and risks incurred by the other. I got into the railway carriage in safety. There my friends from Irkutsk provided me with a traveling-case filled with starched shirts, neckties and other attributes of civilization. In my hands, I had a copy of the "Iliad" in the Russian hexameter of Gnyeditch; in my pocket, a passport made out in the name of Trotsky, which I wrote in it at random, without even imagining that it would become my name for the rest of my life. . . . Throughout the journey, the entire car full of passengers drank tea and ate cheap Siberian buns. I read the hexameters and dreamed of the life abroad. The escape proved to be quite without romantic glamour; it dissolved into nothing but an endless drinking of tea.

The *History* is a very great piece of work, "unique in world literature," says Deutscher, "as an account of a revolution, given by one of its chief actors." The book has that measure of tremendous occasion achieved also by Carlyle; it conveys the human mass in motion—the sum greatly and menacingly exceeding the vision of the individual parts—as little other historical narrative does. At the same time, the *History* abounds in individual portraits (Kerensky, Lieber, Chernov, Tseretelli) as perceptive and acid as Saint-Simon's. The vignettes are unforgettable in their harsh, gay finality of judgment:

> As a writer, Miliukov is heavy, prolix and wearisome. He has the same quality as an orator. Decorativeness is unnatural to him. That might have been an advantage, if the niggardly policies of Miliukov had not so obviously needed a disguise—or if they had had, at least, an objective disguise in the shape of a great tradition. There was not even a little tradition. The official policy in France—quint-

372

essence of bourgeois perfidy and egotism—has two mighty
allies: tradition and rhetoric. Each promoting the other,
they surround with a defensive covering any bourgeois poli-
tician, even such a prosaic clerk of the big proprietors as
Poincaré. It is not Miliukov's fault if he had no glorious
ancestors, and if he was compelled to conduct a policy of
bourgeois egotism on the borders of Europe and Asia.

Principally, the *History* tries to place the tumult and graphic
drama of local incident within a framework of Marxist analysis.
Trotsky's "scenes, portraits, and dialogues, sensuous in their reality,
are inwardly illumined by his conception of the historical process."
The theoretic control is imperfectly achieved. The events were too
near the historian's skin, and much in his own defeat and in Stalin's
seizure of power lay outside any natural Marxist contour. Nevertheless, the *History* moves under pressure of close argument and with a
constant aim of ideological and sociological analysis. Resembling
Churchill's historical narratives in their scenic grandeur and quality
of personal involvement, Trotsky's works are more adult, more resist-
ant to eloquence.

Hardly less impressive was Trotsky's accomplishment as prophet
and interpreter of the catastrophe of the 1930's. Earlier even than
Churchill he tried to rouse the civilized imagination to the reality
of Hitler, and he saw more deeply than Churchill into the sources and
mechanism of the Nazi movement. Because the fate of the German
working class had seemed to him indivisible from that of the Russian
revolution, Trotsky was nearly the first to gauge the consequences of
Hitler's rise to power, of the failure of the proletariat in Germany and
western Europe to halt the onrush of *petit-bourgeois* totalitarianism.
Trotsky saw National Socialism as "the party of counter-revolutionary despair," as the movement and ideology of the "small bourgeois
run amok." Mussolini and Hitler embodied counter-revolution from
below, they "expressed the urge of the lower middle class to assert
itself against the rest of society." National defeat in 1918, arbitrarily
and incompletely brought home, together with the slump of 1929—
which, as Canetti has noted, weakened the inmost fabric of social
coherence by making currency ephemeral and ridiculous—opened the
trap door. Pathological energies of inferiority and vengeance stepped
into the emptiness left by the collapse of national pride and normal
economic self-respect. With uncanny clairvoyance Trotsky recog-

nized, even prior to 1933, that there is a touch of Hitler present in every frustrated *Kleinbürger*. Deutscher summarizes what he terms Trotsky's principal political deed in exile:

> Like no one else, and much earlier than anyone, he grasped the destructive delirium with which National Socialism was to burst upon the world. . . . What underlines even further the political insanity of the times is with what utter unconcern about the future and venomous hostility the men responsible for the fate of German communism and socialism reacted to the alarm which Trotsky sounded . . . . An historical narrative can hardly convey the full blast of slander and derision with which he was met. . . . He had to watch the capitulation of the Third International before Hitler as a father watches the suicide of a prodigal and absent-minded child, with fear, shame, and anger.

Here again the archetype is that of the tragic theater: foresight barred from effective action. Yoked together with political helplessness, Trotsky's lucidity was a curse. He too stood powerless in a place of blood prophesying to those who would not believe him or believed too late:

> Now once again the pain of grim, true prophecy
> shivers my whirling brain in a storm of things foreseen.
> Why do I wear these mockeries upon my body,
> this staff of prophecy, these flowers at my throat?
> At least I will spoil you before I die. Out, down,
> break, damn you! This for all that you have done to me.
> Make someone else, not me, luxurious in disaster. . . .
> Lo now, this is Apollo who has stripped me here
> of my prophetic robes. He watched me all the time
> wearing this glory, mocked of all, my dearest ones
> who hated me with all their hearts, so vain, so wrong;
> called like some gypsy wandering from door to door
> beggar, corrupt, half-starved, and I endured it all.
> And now the seer has done with me, his prophetess,
> and led me into such a place as this, to die.

Like Cassandra, Trotsky saw not only his own peril (the axe and shivered skull waiting for both behind the bloodstained door) but the harrowing unfolding of events in the *polis*. He knew, in a torment of ineffectual insight, that the refusal of the German Communist Party to build a common anti-Nazi front, to marshal its large potential reserves in a common movement to the left, would cause not merely its own doom but that of Germany as a whole. Yet that refusal was the direct expression of Stalin's will and policy. By insisting that the socialists were the real and mortal foe, that one could dispose of Hitler later and indeed make common cause with Nazism in the tactics of the fight against socialists and "plutocrats," Stalin ensured the annihilation of German Communism and did much to facilitate the triumph of Nazism.

Trotsky cried out in vain against this cynical folly and foretold the reaping of the whirlwind: "It is an infamy to promise that the workers will sweep away Hitler once he has seized power. This prepares the way for Hitler's domination. . . . The wiseacres who claim that they see no difference between Brüning and Hitler are in fact saying: it makes no difference whether our organizations exist or whether they are already destroyed. Beneath this pseudo-radical verbiage hides the most sordid passivity." But the Stalinists merely denounced Trotsky as an hysterical saboteur ("beggar, corrupt, half-starved") and went on digging the grave of German democracy. Shortly before Hitler became Chancellor, Thaelmann, the leader of the German Communists, branded Trotsky's warnings as "the theory of an utterly bankrupt Fascist and counter-revolutionary" ("mocked of all, my dearest ones / who hated me with all their hearts, so vain, so wrong"). Only half a year later, behind the barbed wire of the newly established concentration camps, German Communists were to remember the voice of the seer mocked.

Yet as one thinks back on the apparent lunacy of the Stalinist line, a suspicion nags. Was Stalin no less farseeing than Trotsky, though in a cynical, inhuman perspective? Might it have been that he was prepared to see the K.P.D. destroyed and Hitler victorious in groping, instinctive anticipation of a crisis that would ultimately ruin Germany and give the Soviet Union dominance over eastern and Balkan Europe? Or was it that he feared the survival and possible ripening of a competitive, rival version of Communism in the privileged heartland of industrial Europe (as Peter Nettl's important study of Rosa Luxemburg shows, such ambiguities of strategy complicated the relations between German and Russian Marxism from the start)?

There is no certain way of knowing. But one thing is clear. When Trotsky cried out in 1932—"There are hundreds of thousands, there are millions of you. . . . If Fascism comes to power it will ride like a terrific tank over your skulls and spines. . . . Only a fighting unity with social democratic workers can bring victory"—reason and what was left of political decency were on his side. But they stood as alone as in the courtyard of the house of Atreus.

A biography on this scale, and dealing with a life whose resonance deepens and multiplies with the echo of history, stands in as complex a relationship to time as does a work of art. When Deutscher began the first volume, in late 1949, Stalin's seventieth birthday was being celebrated in Moscow with oriental pomp and abjection. When *The Prophet Outcast* was published in 1963, Stalin's body was no longer in the Lenin mausoleum, and there were many who believed that the empty place would be taken, before too long, by Trotsky restored. It appeared as if the process of anti-Stalinist revision initiated at the 20th Party Congress would lead, necessarily, to Trotsky's rehabilitation in Bolshevik history and in the mythology of Communism. Today—1966—that possibility seems remote. The 23rd Party Congress has reverted to the Stalinist terminology of General Secretary and Politbureau, and it looks as if it is precisely the Stalinist legacy, and the encompassing of Stalin's role in an acceptable reading of history, which pose the most urgent, intricate challenges to Soviet society.

Both Stalin and Trotsky have moved into the penumbra of "variable truth." Of all the differences in habits of intelligence that divide Western, post-Cartesian culture from Russian and oriental sensibility, this denial or re-formulation of the historical event is perhaps the most serious. A political system capable of obliterating, by decree, the name of its most heroic city and feat of war (Stalingrad altered to Volgograd) will retreat before no mendacity toward its own past. Soviet totalitarianism is most extreme not in the claims it makes on the utopian future, but in the violence it would do to the past, to the vital integrity of human remembrance. Where is dialogue to begin if a young historian, acting as one's courteous guide to the Winter Palace, states as an assured fact "established by Soviet research" that Trotsky was away from Petrograd at the time of the October assault "intriguing with the Germans"?

It cannot begin with fresh lies. Vilifications of Stalin, attempts to minimize or distort his role in the war, may flatter one's sense of just retribution; but truth is victim again. Lukács, the keeper of the Marxist conscience (and characteristically a Westerner) was one of

376

the first to recognize this aspect of de-Stalinization. To replace myth by myth is to gain nothing, it is to leave the past in servitude to present tactics. The legend of a liberal, pro-Western Trotsky under whose rule the Soviet Union would have evolved along consultative lines, of a great revolution gone wrong through the sinister accident of Stalin's presence, will not hold. It disregards not only the realities of Bolshevik doctrine and the Russian situation, but Trotsky's own character and the totalitarian line he took in 1920–21. Whatever his anti-Stalinism and fervent hopes in a "gradualist" evolution of Soviet society, Deutscher gives such a myth the lie.

This is perhaps the signal achievement of Deutscher's book. It strikes a balance of imaginative justice between Trotsky and Stalin, showing their conflict to be, like the Hegelian paradigm of tragic drama, one of complicated, ironic division of merit. Deutscher, who was himself engaged in the dreams of the Fourth International and whose bias of spirit lies plainly with Trotsky (like many a great biographer possessed of his subject, he has come to look remarkably like Trotsky), nevertheless does complete justice to the cruel magnitude of Stalin's achievement. Similarly to Trotsky himself, who strove for an objective estimate of Stalinist policies even at the worst moments of his personal suffering, Deutscher does not allow us to forget where Stalin was right. This striving for the technical view is the essence of Marxist training and integrity.

In the 1920's the Trotskyite vision of continued revolution and of proletarian insurrection in western Europe did not match the facts. Stalin's concentration on Communism in one country was wholly realistic. Though the methods he used to break the independence of the *kulaks* were appalling and left a society bled and shaken to the core, Stalin's instinct was, by Trotsky's own acknowledgment, accurate. At that point in Soviet history large-scale collectivization or establishment of central economic control over agriculture was a rigorous necessity. No doubt a Trotskyite regime would have had a different flavor from Stalin's, a greater candor of emotional and rhetorical life. But it might well have been no less authoritarian and, at need, no less ruthless. As Deutscher notes: the charge "that Trotsky could have leveled against Stalin was that he instituted a reign of terror like Robespierre's, and that he had monstrously outdone Robespierre. However, Trotsky's own past and the Bolshevik tradition did not allow him to say this." It is as if Deutscher's earlier biography of Stalin had been an exercise in purgation, making possible the emotional, intellectual poise of his portrayal of Trotsky.

In choosing the path of industrial and technological priorities inside the Soviet Union, in their readiness to relinquish overt aims of international incitement in favor of empirical arrangements with capitalism, Khrushchev and his successors are, in fact, developing along Stalinist lines. It is in the Chinese case that strong elements of Trotskyism are present. When the Chinese argue that the process of Communist revolution cannot be limited to one country or power bloc, when they urge that the prevalence of hunger, racial tension, and economic exploitation throughout the underdeveloped world is an immediate challenge and opportunity for militant action, when they hint at the superiority of mass armies over any sophisticated military establishment, they often seem to speak in the great shadow voice of Trotsky. It is a language that commends itself neither to Moscow nor the West.

This axiom of revolution as necessarily international points to one aspect of Trotsky's genius and defeat which Deutscher has, partially on grounds of Marxist methodology, underplayed. It is true that Trotsky was specifically involved with Jewish questions only in 1903 —during the controversy over the *Bund* at the Brussels congress—but the Judaic quality of his vision and sensibility are difficult to deny. Like Marx, he was Jewish in his instinctive commitment to internationalism, in his strategic and personal disregard of national barriers and antagonisms. In Stalin's hatred of Trotsky, in his power to isolate Lev Davidovich Bronstein and make him seem alien to the Party *cadres*, there ran not only the dark, perennial thread of Russian anti-Semitism (as pronounced in Stalin the Georgian as in Khrushchev the Ukrainian), but also the insecurity, the sour fear which the chauvinist, the man rooted in his own ground, feels in the presence of the cosmopolitan, of the wanderer at home in the world. It is precisely that moment at which the Bolshevik revolution abandoned its international hopes and became a matter of Russian circumstance that marks the start of Trotsky's ruin.

If one forgets Trotsky's Jewishness, moreover, it is not easy to get into right focus his passionate concern with survival through the word, his sense of the written book as weapon and watchman's cry, or that fantastic legalism which inspired one of the most moving, bizarre episodes in his career. Under the presidency of the American philosopher John Dewey, a commission of inquiry met in Trotsky's house in Mexico in April 1937. It examined the charges of treason and sabotage hurled at Trotsky during the course of the Moscow purge trials. For thirteen lengthy sessions Trotsky was questioned and cross-questioned on his political record, beliefs, and responsibilities. He argued and defended himself with the same superb sweep, with the same virtuosity of contempt and passion for detail he would have displayed in an actual Moscow court. "He stood where he stood like truth itself, unkempt and unadorned, unarmoured and unshielded, yet magnificent and invincible." Though it altered nothing in his material position and did hardly anything to arrest the murderous reach of Stalinist lies, Trotsky was jubilant at the verdict of acquittal. The entire affair has the abstract pathos of a Talmudic parable. Like Marx, Trotsky was one of the great Jewish seers and exiles of the modern age. And he was, perhaps, the first of his heritage, since Joshua, to show military genius.

There is much in Trotsky's life and in Isaac Deutscher's presentation of it to match the symbolic forms and ironies of tragic art. There are many scenes which rivet the imagination: Trotsky during his first Siberian exile, writing literary and philosophic essays as vermin dropped from the walls of the hut onto the paper; Trotsky haranguing his guards on matters of revolutionary theory during his brief internment in England in 1917; Trotsky on horseback, spectacles flashing, as he rallied stricken soldiers and militia to stop the White advance on Petrograd. The account of a *kulak* orgy in the 1930's sticks in the mind: "as they guzzled and gulped, the *kulaks* illuminated the villages with bonfires they made of their own barns and stables. People suffocated with the stench of rotting meat, with the vapors of vodka, with the smoke of their blazing possessions, and with their own despair." And at the close there is the image of three hundred thousand men and women filing past the dead body, the streets of Mexico resounding with their lament, the *Gran corrido de Leon Trotsky*.

It is in a biography of this order that the specific energies of tragic drama are today most vital. It is here we find the qualities of representative, public action, of heroic dimension, of prophetic irony and divided justice which characterize the form of the tragic play, and which are so markedly absent from the primarily introspective, middle-class values of modern prose fiction. Heroism and the monumental stance are suspect to the contemporary imagination; they have their strong life in Deutscher's triptych or, in a more stoic vein, the hero bound yet victorious through sheer intensity of being, in Ernest

Jones's *Life of Freud*. These books (one thinks as well of Leon Edel's *Henry James*, of George Painter's *Proust*, of Michael Foot's study of Bevan) suggest a renascence of biography on the major, Victorian scale. But with the difference that the modern biographer works with the means and expectations of post-Freudian psychology, of current scholarship, and that he has behind him the stylistic habits and achievements of the novel.

The appetite for splendor, for the gesture that implicates more than private life, for ceremony and pathos, is still with us, though often suppressed. The charge made against tragedy in Anouilh's *Antigone* is damaging; it corresponds to much of our present idiom:

> *Et puis, surtout, c'est reposant, la tragédie, parce qu'on sait qu'il n'y a plus d'espoir, le sale espoir . . . et qu'on n'a plus qu'à crier,—pas à gémir, non, pas à se plaindre,—à geuler à pleine voix ce qu'on avait à dire. . . . Et pour rien: pour se le dire à soi, pour l'apprendre soi. Dans le drame, on se débat parce qu'on espère en sortir. C'est ignoble, c'est utilitaire. Là, c'est gratuit. C'est pour les rois.*

Nevertheless, the world of kings and of nemesis persists as a necessary possibility for our imaginations, as a need, deeper and more tenacious than democratic theory allows, for decisive form. The medieval and Elizabethan convention, embodying the very spirit of tragedy, that the heavens are hung with black, that day yields to night, that "comets, importing change of times and states" flash in the sky when the hero falls, has not lost its meaning. A whole city marches past Trotsky's bier: the great die differently from the small.

LITERATURE
AND POST-HISTORY

In Honor of Georg Lukács

The utopias which are built into revolutions necessarily have an ideal, indistinct contour. It is of the essence of a revolutionary situation that the now must pre-empt the tomorrow, that the imagination, when in the grip of the future tense, should concentrate on the short range. Dreams must be disciplined to cover the ground of the possible.

There is in Marxism a whole set of conjectures and utopian possibilities left vague as being "on the other side of history." The question as to the nature and dynamics of life in the classless society, in true Communism, has been posed from the start. But most answers have, by virtue of logic and necessity, been perfunctory or gruffly humorous. The road ahead is too hard, too beset with concrete potentialities of crisis and reversal. Historical man, engaged in the stress and fragmentary vision of economic and political conflict, knows that in the conjugation of the verb *to be* there is a future perfect. That knowledge, which Ernst Bloch calls the *Prinzip Hoffnung*, is at the core of his endeavor. But he has little time, nor the habits of imagination needed to detail the ideal. We will only be able to formulate precise questions about the condition of liberated, humanized man when and if that condition is historically proximate, when the horizon will have stopped receding—a situation so new, so radical as to require a complete reorientation of our consciousness and of the linear metaphors around which we organize our sense of time.

Marxism is not alone in leaving its ultimate goal vague. Most major religions and mythologies of hope have done likewise. It may be one of the weaknesses of Islam that it has made its paradise too exact. Even perfection stales when it is rendered homely to the imagination. As Dante knew, the mind dreams forward into a light so sharp that it effaces all details.

Nevertheless, it may be possible to ask certain questions about "post-history." Any theory of post-historical society—our sense of being "in history" is largely determined by the pressure of political and social conflicts—will have to consider the dilemma of human motivations in the just city. What would replace the primordial mechanism of thwarted hope? In what way would the energies of forward motion, which seem integral to the human personality, be incited and maintained (or, in terms of the Freudian paradox, how is there to be civilization without discontent)? The prospect of an economy of necessary leisure, on a mass scale, is beginning to give to such questions a stubborn reality.

In this area of future uncertainties, the circumstance of literature poses a specific problem. In so far as literature is dramatized expectation, in so far as it is a critique of the actual in the light of the possible, will there be need of it? Is literature rooted in the imperfection of historical being? Will men consent to commit their imaginings to fiction, when the real satisfies and invites the full capacities of insight and action?

At the rhapsodic close of *Literature and Revolution*, Trotsky affirms that art will last beyond victory, that "the poet of the new epoch will re-think in a new way the thoughts of mankind, and re-feel its feelings." He prophesies that the "wall will fall between art and nature." These are journalistic slogans, and necessarily so. Trotsky's aim was ambiguous: he wished to prove that there would be no such thing as proletarian art once Communism had freed the proletariat from its particular class-consciousness and psychological boundaries. But at the same time, he sought to harness attention to the immediate social, didactic tasks, and away from reveries about the utopian future.

Ernst Fischer finds the notion that art might or *should* become obsolete and unnecessary intolerable (in the tradition of revolutionary thought, Pisarev stands almost alone in his puritanical nihilism). Art will endure even in a classless society because it is the prime mode by which man identifies with nature and his fellow men. The argument looks firmer than it is. Will there be need of such identification—will it be recognized as a vital process—once the various modes of aliena-

382

tion are resolved? Fischer proclaims the enduring validity of Goethe, Stendhal, Pushkin, "and above all Mozart, always and always Mozart." But will *new* art be produced, or will art exist, principally, as a particular discipline of remembrance, as a series of treasures in a museum of feeling?

These are difficult questions. All I would offer here is a brief note about certain elements in the present that may contain hints of future reality.

Our present concept of literary form is, in several respects, related to privacy. The practice of reading a book to oneself, in silence, is a specific, late historical development. It implies a number of economic and social pre-conditions: a room of one's own (Virginia Woolf's significant phrase) or, at least, a home spacious enough to allow areas of quiet; the private possession of books, with the concomitant right to keep a rare book from the use of other men; means of artificial light during the evening hours. What is implicit is the style of life of the bourgeoisie in an industrial, largely urban, complex of values and privileges. That complex crystallized later than is often supposed. It was still customary in the Victorian middle class to read out loud, one member of the family being "reader" to the rest, or the book being passed from "voice to voice." It is hardly necessary to stress the immense changes which the printed book, with its essentially visual code of meaning, brought to older forms of collective, aural literacy. Marshall McLuhan has explored the "Gutenberg revolution" in Western consciousness. What is less generally understood is how much of literature—and how much of *modern* literature—was not conceived to be read in private silence; how it was directed toward recitation, the mimesis of the raised voice and the response of the ear. Dickens, Hopkins, Kipling are examples of modern writers whose root sensibility was oral, and who tried to adapt essentially oral means to the silences of print.

The old, natural impulse survives in the process of learning to read: the child and the less literate adult read "half-aloud," forming words with their lips and, at times, re-enacting the imaginary event on the printed page by sympathetic bodily motion. The man who reads alone in a room with his mouth closed, from a volume which he owns, is a special product of Western bourgeois literacy and leisure. Will he persist in his present guise?

There are distinct indications that contemporary mass-culture and the electronic media of communication—with their radical assault on the available reserves of silence—may alter the character of literacy, that "non-private" forms will carry the day. In the sub-cultures and *kitsch*-languages of modern urban literacy (what is true of the West now will be true of the East and of the underdeveloped areas tomorrow), the authority of vital content has passed from the syntactical, logical patterns of the written word. Increasingly, meanings and attitudes are transmitted and made memorable by aural association— the jingles, the oohs and ahs of modern advertisement—and by the pictorial means of billboard and television. The read sentence is in retreat before the photograph, the television shot, the picture-alphabets of comic books and training manuals. More and more, the average man reads *captions* to various *genres* of graphic material. The word is mere servant to the sensory shock. This, as McLuhan has pointed out, will modify essential habits of human perception. Three-dimensional color television, able to communicate happenings from one part of the earth to any other with instantaneous drama, will not only erode further what is left of private silence, but educate the imagination to an avid passiveness. Our powers of nervous absorption may increase, our tolerance to visual and auditive impact may grow; but the re-creative potential which enables us to construct a coherent image of setting and action from the mere signal of the noiseless word will diminish, like a muscle unused. How are novels or poems, which demand work of us and precise echo, to compete with the sensory "totalization" and realness of the new codes—with technical media that can lower our arm-chair to the bottom of the seas, or place us in a rocket during the blazing rush of its launching? One remembers Goethe's prophetic intimation in the Prologue to *Faust:* how could a spectator fresh *vom Lesen der Journale*, from the turbulent, chaotic claims of news, find the calm, the readiness of imagination required for literature?

But there are positive, liberating aspects to the crisis of privacy and literate comprehension. Unquestionably, nothing is more important to an understanding of the future forms of artistic communication than the simple, immense fact that hundreds of millions of human beings are now, for the first time, entering the world of reading and writing. By comparison with this fact, examinations of literary schools or fashions, of the *nouveau roman* or the theater of the absurd, look trivial. There is a profound logic in the historical coincidence between the emergence of the hitherto illiterate peoples and the simultaneous development of graphic mass-media. To the new literates, with their native traditions of oral and pictorial communication, the patterns of meaning and emotion conveyed by radio, television, comic strip, or film will carry far more immediacy and significance than the silent book. The middle-class Western reader, reading books without pictures—the very badge of the adult literate—is remote from the needs, talents, and cultural legacy of the new Asian and African audience (*audire* = to hear). He is as remote, or more so, than is the modern picture-magazine and paperback from the chained, leather-bound folio of the late medieval scholar.

What may lie ahead are situations of collective consciousness, of communal apprehension and response more genuine than any we have known since pre-literate art and the survivance of certain elements of that art in the Greek *polis*. This would mean that dominant art-forms would be "open" to the sustaining or rebuking interventions of the audience, that the listener and spectator would, at times, be agents in the process of formal creation (a possibility explored by Brecht in his didactic plays). This would signify also that works of art would not have a single, arrested form, that they would not, at each representation, be realized in essentially the same manner. The notion of a binding, invariable original—of the faithful repetition of a piece of music, of a play, of a dance over long periods of time—is a highly specialized development. It is crucially related to the fact that print codifies and preserves the model of the past. It also reflects a profound severance between the professional performer and his amateur public. It is by no means an inherent human mode. The spontaneous, indeterminate, and therefore un-repeatable "happenings" staged by certain *avant-garde* painters and theatrical directors, the attempts to shape music around the free improvisations of the player (jazz and aleatory music), are much nearer to the instinctive bases of art. They express the long-buried recognition that a work of art should be a unique event, a design of energy and mimesis that cannot be exactly reproduced at another time or place, and in whose completion the audience plays a significant role. The group of dancers or singers from which one individual springs forth, momentarily, to incite a movement or theme, is archetypal of art. The dialogue between identities invisible and mute to each other—the printed poem or novel—is a very particular, possibly transient medium. It may represent a style of consciousness analogous to chamber-music. As Adorno has pointed out, chamber-music, with its specific assumptions in terms of leisure (the expert amateur), of space (the small room large enough to accommodate chosen guests), and of economic patronage, is already a *genre* of the past.

Perhaps I might hazard a wilder thought. A major part of Western literature pivots on a sense of irreplaceable personal identity. It derives its vision and principal metaphors from the uniqueness and inevitability of personal death, from the presumption that we carry within us, like a ripening seed, our own particular mortality and passing. But even this sense, which we assume to be so unalterable, so universal, has its psycho-somatic conditions and historical roots. It is an established fact that a number of our vital organs are by no means exhausted at the time of our personal demise, that they can continue to serve for long periods if transplanted into another organic environment. Such transplantation is already possible in the case of eyes, kidneys, muscle tissue. Already, it is plausible to conceive of storage places or "banks" in which vital parts can be preserved for replacement and later use, as blood plasma is preserved now. In which case our root consciousness of a personal, final death might come to alter.

We would know that primary elements of our own body and psychic self-awareness (the brains of monkeys have been kept functional in virtual isolation from the surrounding body) would "live on" in another member of the species. We would come to accept that notion of life-continuance or somatic immortality which, since the work of Weisman in the late nineteenth century, we already ascribe to human germ-cells. Such acceptance would, gradually, cease to be abstract and purely intellectual; it would bring on modifications of our entire sensibility. The concepts of human interrelation, of organic community which we now use superficially or as moral clichés, would come to express concrete realities and felt experience. Man would then pass, for the first time, from the closed sphere of private being into that of collectivity.

Perhaps not for the first time. Our present notion of autonomous identity may be the result of a long, painful process of psychic individuation, of withdrawal from the collective group (the myth of Jacob wrestling with the Angel may be read as a metaphor of the agonizing struggle through which individual members of the species achieved a sense of self, a name). History might then be defined as an episode of personal self-definition, of *egoism* in the proper sense, between much longer pre- and post-historical eras of collective being. Such collectivity would obviously and fundamentally change the nature of art and literature. The voice of man would again be choral.

This, of course, is mere conjecture and play of mind. But if we look nearer than post-history, to the present crisis of values, a number of changes are discernible. And behind the technical change lies the metaphysical shift.

No doubt, good novels are being written and will continue to be so. But individual instances of a literary *genre* appear long after the energies of belief and poetic form which led to its development have grown obsolete or become imitative routine. Milton and Klopstock wrote long after the religious-heroic epic had lost all authority of spontaneous life, long after the conventions of myth, symbolic world-history, and public rhetoric on which the epic is founded had lost their relevance. Where they succeed, they do so in part as avowed renovators of an antique form.

The novel is a *genre* with evident and concrete foundations in history and society. It carries within it the world-view associated with its origins in European mercantile life of the late seventeenth and early eighteenth centuries. With its customary disclaimer of the supernatural or transcendent (the Gothic novel, the novel of religious feeling, and the ghostly tale are eccentric to the main current), classic prose fiction deals with the world of here and now, with man in the condition of social and, more often than not, urban existence. When Robinson Crusoe saw a footprint on the sand, he took it to be the mark of a man, not the spoor of a phantom or the flame-point of an angel. Going back to his stockade, he surveyed his larder and his goods. Even on a solitary island, the world of the novel is as solid with material furnishings as are the houses of Balzac and Dickens. Moreover, there is money on this spur of rock in the Pacific; the main tradition of the novel is intimately inwoven with the monetary values and relations of a mercantile or industrial society.

Being committed to secular reality, the novel made factual information one of its principal devices. George Eliot and Trollope are charged with social, economic, and intellectual history. The art of Balzac is a *summa mundi*, an inventory of contemporaneous life. A man can learn half a dozen professions by reading Zola. Even where it breaks its classic bounds to enter the domain of the epic, with its characteristic daemonology and supernatural forces, a novel such as *Moby Dick* carries a vast and explicit load of fact. In the major lineage of fiction, from Defoe to Dos Passos, history is made private.

387

The guns of Waterloo sound to the ears of Fabrice and Amelia Sedley. But they are the same guns as those of the historian or writer on strategy.

This equivalence gave to the novel its strong grip on life. And for long periods, reality was such that fiction could master it and give it expressive form. It became a commonplace of criticism to assert that historical and social events as mirrored in the plots of Stendhal, Dickens, or Tolstoy had a realness, an authenticity deeper than that conveyed by the journalist or professional historian (a distinction which echoes Aristotle's famous comparison of poet and historian). But is this still the case? Is prose fiction able to match or surpass the claims made on the life of the imagination by the new media of direct knowledge and graphic reproduction? The world is at our breakfast table, its ceremonies and disasters rendered with fantastic completion and intensity. Why turn to fiction—unless it be to escape? But that is the crux. By its very nature and vision, the art of the novel is realistic. Where it abandons its responsibility to the real, the novel betrays itself. The strident absurdities of horror and science fiction, the license of present erotic fantasy are an attempt, ultimately self-negating, to "outbid" reality, to bribe sensibilities numbed by the power of the audio-visual truth.

One need only compare the literature of the two world wars to observe the diminution of the reality-function in the novel. 1914–1918 led to such classic work as Ford Madox Ford's *No More Parades*, Barbusse's *Le Feu*, Cummings' *Enormous Room*, Hemingway's *Farewell to Arms*, the resonance of battle and civilian attitude in the last volume of Proust. The major works to come of the second cataclysm are reportage and immediate witness: *Vol de Nuit*, Hersey's *Hiroshima*, the *Diary* of Anne Frank, Emmanuel Ringleblum's *Notes from the Warsaw Ghetto*. No poet, no novelist has, until now, been able to give to the reality of the concentration camps that discipline of insight, of shaped experience, which we find in Bruno Bettelheim's sociological study, *The Informed Heart*. Fiction falls silent before the enormity of the fact, and before the vivid authority with which that fact can be rendered by unadorned report.

We are, it would seem, in a transitional stage of poetic documentation, a period in which the techniques and conventions of the novel are used for the presentment of psychological, social, and scientific material. Even as eighteenth-century fiction adapted the levels of dialogue and social-sexual conflict mapped out in Restoration comedy, so reportage and factual exposition are now heir to the liberties of the novel. For sheer distinction of style and force of suggestion, few better examples could be found in the past decade of English prose than Rachel Carson's *The Sea Around Us*, Lewis Mumford's *The City in History*, or Oscar Lewis' socio-poetic record of life in a Mexican tenement, *The Children of Sanchez*. The latter is a fascinating instance of the way in which even the most "naked" of reportage —a series of tape recordings—is implicitly shaped by the conventions and possibilities of the novel. What is Doris Lessing's *Golden Notebook*, that acute portrayal of woman and urban society: a novel or an autobiography, a political essay or a psychiatric case-book? It is not in the majority of current novels that the language is being used at its full pitch of invention, but in these *argumenti*, in this poetic of fact and rational discourse. And we can now discern its origins in the psychological and political crises of the 1930's—in the philosophic reportage of Edmund Wilson, in the semi-novels of Orwell and Malraux, in Rebecca West's poetic treatise of travel and history, *Black Lamb and Grey Falcon*. That was the time in which the pressure of the world grew implacable on the imagination.

Following on the epic and on verse-drama, the novel has been the third principal *genre* of Western literature. It expressed and, in part, shaped the habits of feeling and language of the Western bourgeoisie from Richardson to Thomas Mann. In it, the dreams and nightmares of the mercantile ethic, of middle-class privacy, and of the monetary-sexual conflicts and delights of industrial society have their monument. With the decline of these ideals and habits into a phase of crisis and partial rout, the *genre* is losing much of its vital bearing.

While most of the energies and inheritance of prose fiction are being assimilated by documentary forms, there is a small group of experimental works from which the poetics of tomorrow may emerge. These are the most exciting, least understood of modern books; in them, the classic divisions between poetry, drama, prose fiction, and philosophic argument are deliberately broken down. These works admit of no single definition; they declare their own forms of being.

I have in mind metaphysical fantasies or mock heroics of logic such as Valéry's *Monsieur Teste* and Elias Canetti's *Auto-da-fé*. Hermann Broch is one of the masters of free form. His novels conjoin poetry with prose narrative and the art of the philosophic essay. *The Death of Virgil*, one of the major works of our age, attempts to vitalize language with the contrapuntal logic and dynamic simultaneities of music. More radically than Joyce, it subverts the time-structure and linear progressions on which prose fiction is normally built. Broch's style has an uncanny spell, because tangential to it are intimations of entirely different codes of statement, such as the use of silence (as Calder uses space), or the projection into language of the grammar of mathematics. Contemporary writing has scarcely begun to avail itself of Broch's instigations.

Among prolegomena to future forms, one would also want to include Péguy's experiments in circular argument and incantation, and the work of David Jones. Above all, perhaps, Karl Kraus's *Die letzten Tage der Menschheit*.

It is no accident that several of these revolutionary designs should originate in German; for it was in the German language and sensibility after Nietzsche that the crisis and dissolution of values first took clear shape. But there is an earlier precedent. We can locate in Kierkegaard the foreshadowings of a future poetics (more precisely than in Blake whose magnificent singularities often employed conventional modes, and whose influence remained small). Kierkegaard's *Either/Or*—part metaphysics, part memoir, part reverie when language is in a state of total energy—is the antecedent to our tomorrow. We cannot describe it adequately with our present vocabulary of *genres*. It is part of a tremendously important, but difficult to pin down, evolution from a static, discontinuous reading of reality to a live perception of organic process, of change and plurality within forms. In William Burroughs' childish conceit of a loose-leaf book— to be put together at random or at the reader's will—there lurks a Kierkegaardian insight into the unforeseeable, anarchic potential of literary form. More than books, the "happenings" of Kierkegaard, Kraus's *Gesamtdrama*, and the fugues of Broch are new orderings of vision, rule changes in the ancient, intricate game which language plays with the world.

The last point I want to raise has its context in both Christian eschatology and Marxist aesthetics. It is the paradox of tragic drama, of a theater of unresolved conflict, inside a dogma of hope and in the just city of man. Lunacharsky posited that a truly Communist society would regard tragedy as an archaic *genre*, that it would recognize in the underlying metaphors of tragic drama the vestiges of an obsolete, servile religiosity. With his discovery that necessity is not blind, that there are no daemonic, transcendent forces interfering in human affairs, the citizen of the socialist state would come to see tragedy as a noble ruin, a proud torso in the museum of pre-rational imaginings.

Trotsky was less certain. While underlining the critical-creative function of comedy in a revolutionary epoch and calling for a Soviet Gogol, he was too steeped in European literary traditions, too personally committed to a sense of life as bitter, ironic conflict, to renounce tragedy. Hence the dictum: "One cannot tell whether revolutionary art will succeed in producing 'high' revolutionary tragedy. But Socialist art will revive tragedy. Without God, of course." Ernst Fischer adds a Freudian note: "Tragedy will doubtless continue to exist, because the development of any society—even a classless one—is inconceivable without contradiction and conflict, and perhaps because man's dark desire for blood and death is ineradicable."

But no less than a tragedy *with* God, with a compensating mechanism of final justice and retribution (the paradox of Corneille's *Polyeucte*), a tragedy *without* God, a tragedy of pure immanence, is a self-contradiction. Genuine tragedy is inseparable from the mystery of injustice, from the conviction that man is a precarious guest in a world where forces of unreason have dark governance. Lacking this belief, a drama of conflict will hardly be distinguishable from serious comedy, with its pattern of intrigue and mundane resolution (the equations of tragedy cannot be resolved, there are in them too many unknowns). Conflict will persist. But its dramatic treatment will be an "acting-out" of argument, a realization of dialectic in word and gesture, not wholly dissimilar from the drama of a Platonic dialogue.

This is the order of conflict Trotsky seems to have in mind when he says that in the new society men will divide into "parties" over questions of social planning, over scientific hypotheses or "a best system of sports." There will be ideological antagonisms of a local, strategic kind; but they will not impair the consensus of the society over its final aims. The format is that given by the Prologue to Brecht's *Caucasian Chalk-Circle*—the presentation of a play to articulate, explore, and thus resolve a case of social conflict. Such "acting-out" and exploration by patients is already used in certain modes of psychotherapy. Seen in the light of teaching, of healing, of the trial and development of new attitudes and proceedings of action, the future of drama is immense. A dramatic plot—be it *The Suppliants* of Aeschylus or *The Good Woman of Setzuan*—can be a lucid shorthand for a whole complex of social or psychological antagonisms and alternatives. Even as a computer gives rational organization and "visibility" to complicated sets of elements, so a Brechtian play can serve as "program" for the exploration of moral and political decisions. As we noted, moreover, the technical forms of the theater correspond more than those of any other *genre* to the needs and means of the emergent mass-societies. The theater can subvert the barriers of estrangement which divide the writer from the audience, from the community at large. In the playhouse, man is both himself and his neighbor.

But it is doubtful whether the relevant modes will be those of tragedy. If future society assumes the contours foretold by Marxism, if the jungle of our cities turns to the *polis* of man and the dreams of anger are made real, the representative art will be high comedy. Art will be the laughter of intelligence, as it is in Plato, in Mozart, in Stendhal.

INDEX

INDEX

Abel, Niels Henrik, 14
Absalom and Achitophel (Dryden),
62
*"Abstammungsnachweis" zum "Zucht-
wart," Vom* (Berning), 95 *n*
Act Without Words (Beckett), 52
Adamov, Arthur, 139; quoted, 51–52
Adams, Henry, 244, 254, 256; *The
Education of Henry Adams*, 244
Adenauer, Konrad, 114, 115
Adorno, Theodor W., 147, 149, 344,
350; on Auschwitz, 53; on Ben-
jamin, 314; on chamber music,
385–86; on Heine, 125, 151,
354–55; Marxism and, 310, 315,
341, 349; on Schoenberg, 127 *n*,
129, 132, 139; *Quasi una fanta-
sia*, 127 *n*; *"Sakrales Fragment:
Ueber Schoenberg's Moses und
Aron,"* 127 *n*
Advertising, 26, 77, 251, 361, 384
Aegean Sea, 174–75
Aelfric, Archbishop of Canterbury,
188
Aeschylus, 6, 134, 305, 391; *The
Libation Bearers*, 134; *Seven
Against Thebes*, 366; *The Suppliants*, 391
Aesop, 268
Aesthetics: art reproducibility and,
314–15, 341, 385; dehumanization and, 9–10, 61, 166, 202;
ideology and, 305–06, 307, 308,
310, 311, 315, 317–18, 319,
323, 328–29, 337, 352, 356–57,
360, 362, 363, 382; improvisation and, 385; Leavis and, 223,
226; linear perception and, 253–
55, 382; Lukács on, 340–47;
musical dominance in, 29–30,
43–46; new forms and, 86–91,
103, 131–32, 136–37, 173, 253,
383, 385, 387, 390, 391–92;
personal death and, 386; science
and, 16, 18, 21–24, 25, 68,
253, 326–27; silence and, 12,

Aesthetics (*continued*)
22–24, 34, 48–49; of tragedy,
390–91, 392. *See also* Criticism
Africa, 47, 181, 182, 240, 385; anti-
Semitism in, 140, 143, 145;
English of, 60; nationalism in,
152
Aïda (Verdi), 137
Alamein, El, 101
Albouy, Pierre, *Victor Hugo*, 314
Alchemy, 15
Aldred, 188
Alexandria, Egypt, 70, 283, 284
Alexandria Quartet (Durrell), 280–
87, 326, 353
Algebra, 14, 21
Alice in Wonderland (Carroll), 71
"All the Dead Dears" (Plath), 296
Amazon basin, Indians of, 242, 246,
248, 250
American Dream, An (Mailer), 74
*American Standard Version of the
Bible*, 193
Amerika (Kafka), 119
Amphitryon, myth of, 277
Anatomy of Melancholy (Burton),
282
Andrewes, Lancelot, 192
Animal Farm (Orwell), 361
Animals, 36–37, 244, 247
Anna Karenina (Tolstoy), 10, 75,
321, 322, 358
Annales (periodical), 242
Anouilh, Jean, *Antigone*, 380
Ansichten: Zur Literatur der Zeit
(Mayer), 352
Anthropologie structurale (Lévi-
Strauss), 89, 239, 241, 243,
245, 246, 248
Anthropology, 239–50, 341
Antigone (Anouilh), 380
Antigone (Sophocles), 341
Anti-Semitism, *see* Jews; Nazism
Apollinaire, Guillaume, 70
Apollo, 35, 38, 39
Après-midi d'un faune, L'(Debussy),
29

395

Aquinas, Thomas, 14, 19
Arabic, 192
Aragon, Louis, 308, 317, 362; Marxism of, 359, 363; Mayer on, 353; Romanticism and, 317
Aramaic, 192
Archeology, 333; Homer and, 171, 172, 174–76, 178, 180
Arendt, Hannah, 110, 149, 164, 167
Argentina, 64, 143
Ariadne auf Naxos (R. Strauss), 43
Ariel (Plath), 295, 298
Arion, 42
Aristophanes, 305
Aristotle, 19, 36, 221, 255, 388; Lukács and, 328, 335, 340, 343, 345; *Poetics*, 221, 335, 343
Arnold, Matthew: critical style of, 224, 225, 238; Marx and, 343; values of, 4, 5, 56–57, 58, 61, 229, 330; *Culture and Anarchy*, 56; *Essays in Criticism*, 229
Arp, Hans, 23
Art and Society (Finkelstein), 315–16
Asia Minor, 181; Troy and, 174, 175
Asmus, Valentin, "Realism and Naturalism," quoted, 318
Astrée, L' (d'Urfé), 285
"Astronomie bien tempérée, L' " (Lévi-Strauss), 250
Astronomy, 15, 34, 42, 201
Athene, in the *Odyssey*, 182–83
Attica, 175, 184
Auden, Wystan Hugh, 44, 238; quoted, 66, 118; on Kafka, 118, 120; Mayer and, 351
Aus dem Notizbuch eines Philologen (Klemperer), 95 *n*
Aus dem Wörterbuch des Unmenschen (Sternberger, Storz and Süskind), 95 *n*
Auschwitz concentration camp, 107, 123, 145, 163; insurrection, 166; knowledge of, 150, 158, 159
Ausflug der toten Mädchen, Der (Seghers), 353
Aussenwelt und Innenwelt (Mayer), 352
Austen, Jane, 83, 230, 236, 237

Austria, 51, 98, 140
Austro-Hungarian empire, 120, 121
Auto-da-fé (Canetti), 257, 389
Av, Ninth of, 161

Babbit, Milton, 127
Babel, Isaac, 148, 358
Babel, Tower of, 36
Babylonia, 181, 252
Bach, Johann Sebastian, 132, 133, 316
Bacon, Francis, 26, 191, 247, 250; *Magna Instauratis*, 250; *De Sapientia Veterum*, 247; Shakespeare and, 172, 202; taxonomy of, 255
Balthazar (Durrell), 283, 284
Balzac, Honoré de, 9, 63, 71, 79, 147, 309; *La Comédie humaine*, 330, 331; critical writing of, 327; Dostoevsky and, 320; Engels and, 306, 317–18, 321, 322; Golding and, 292–93; history and, 82, 387; *Les Illusions perdues*, 331; Lukács on, 307, 311, 319, 329, 330, 331, 332, 338, 340, 341; Mann and, 275, 277; *La Rabouilleuse*, 71; *La Recherche de l'Absolu*, 292–93
Balzac the Writer (Reizov), 317–18
Barbier, Henri Auguste, 308
Barbusse, Henri, *Le Feu*, 388
Barrès, Maurice, 237
Barthes, Roland, 225 *n*
Baudelaire, Charles, 44, 88, 216, 249; *Tableaux de Paris*, 88
Beardsley, Aubrey, 70, 285
Beaumont, Francis, 199
Beauvoir, Simone de, 7, 164, 299
Becher, Johannes, 308, 359, 362, 364
Beckett, Samuel, 7, 48, 52, 72, 342; *Act Without Words*, 52; *Watt*, 72
Beethoven, Ludwig van, 29
Beiträge zur Geschichte der Ästhetik (Lukács), 331, 342
Bekenntnisse des Hochstaplers Felix Krull (Mann), 6, 84, 269–79
Belá-Kun, Hungary, 329

406

Marlowe (*continued*)
Shakespeare and, 171, 172, 203, 205
Marriage of Figaro, The (Mozart), 184
Marshall, Alfred, 19
Marsyas, myth of, 36, 38–39
Marvell, Andrew, 228, 298, 364
Marx, Karl, 18, 74, 146, 147, 367; art and, 340, 343, 344, 356; *Critique of Political Economy*, 245; on dehumanization, 314; East Germany and, 349; *18th Brumaire of Louis Bonaparte*, 245; on Elizabethan drama, 202; exile of, 151, 371, 379; *Das Kapital*, 74; Lévi-Strauss and, 241, 244, 245–46, 250; literature and, 312, 316, 322, 323, 352; nationalism and, 153, 378; Stalinism and, 148, 338–39
Marxism, 347, 356–64; ethnography and, 245–46; German, 102, 103, 314–15, 340, 348–49, 352–53, 358–59, 363, 367, 375; history and, 241, 337, 339, 341, 342, 345–46, 349, 352, 354, 358, 359, 369, 373, 381–82; internationalism and, 153, 339, 340, 352, 378; Jewish culture and, 90, 147–48; literary criticism and, 305–24, 328, 329–31, 334, 338–39, 342, 354; Stalinism and, 338–39, 344–45, 350, 357, 361–62; tragedy and, 390, 392
Marxisme et Structuralisme (Sebag), 245
Mass media, *see* Communications media
Massachusetts Institute of Technology, 65
Massenet, Jules, *Hérodiade*, 137
"*Mass/stäbe der Sprachkritik*" (Sternberger), 95 n
Master Builder, The (Ibsen), 293
Materialism, 322; dialectic, 306, 310, 315–16, 321, 328, 329, 341, 342, 352, 353
Mathematics, 6, 201, 233, 326; harmony concept and, 42; language and, 14–21, 34, 45, 87, 88, 90,

Mathematics (*continued*)
103, 109, 151, 242–43, 248, 249, 250
Matthausen concentration camp, 100
Matthew, 190, 193–94
Maupassant, Guy de, 322
Mauriac, François, 267
Mauss, Marcel, "Essay on Certain Primitive Forms of Classification," 241; *Essai sur le don*, 241
Maxwell, James Clerk, 17
Mayakovsky, Vladimir, 357, 358
Mayer, Hans, 348–55; *Ansichten: Zur Literatur der Zeit*, 352; *Zur Deutschen Klassik und Romantik*, 350; *Kafka kein Edne?* 354–55; *Lessing: Mitwelt und Nachwelt*, 351–52; *Von Lessing bis Thomas Mann*, 350
Meaning: Lévi-Strauss on, 242, 245, 247–48; linear perception and, 253–57, 383–84; literary form and, 86; mathematics and, 14–16, 19, 20, 21, 24, 103; multiplicity of, 206–08; music and, 23–24, 28–29, 44, 104, 138, 206, 207; political language and, 27, 34–35, 52, 95 n, 99–100, 104; privacy and, 28, 49, 53, 383–84; silence and, 12–13, 21, 39–41, 53, 54
Measure for Measure (Shakespeare), 209
Mechanical Bride, The (McLuhan), 252
Mechanistic philosophy, 202, 205
"Medallion" (Plath), 299
"Medusa" (Plath), 299
Mehring, Franz, 155–56, 341, 350
Melos, Zeitschrift für Neue Musik (periodical), 127 n
Melville, Herman, 62, 288, 290, 293, 387; *Benito Cereno*, 236; *Billy Budd*, 290; Leavis and, 236, 336; *Moby Dick*, 236, 387
Mensheviks, 367
Mercantilism, 202, 328, 387, 389
Merchant of Venice, The (Shakespeare), 42, 58–59, 201
Mérimée, Prosper, 261–68; *Carmen*, 261–63, 266; *La Chronique du temps de Charles IX*, 263; *Co-*

Quakers, 160
Quasi una fantasia (Adorno), 127 *n*
Quattrocento, 6
Quentin Durward (Scott), 333
Qu'est-que ce la littérature (Sartre), 65

Rabelais, François, *Gargantua and Pantagruel*, 257
Rabouilleuse, La (Balzac), 71
Racine, Jean, 82, 118, 202; Goldmann on, 312–14; Lowell translation, 212–16; *Phèdre*, 212–16, 313
Radcliffe, Ann, 327
Radek, Karl B., quoted, 316
Radio, 385
Radioactivity, 27
Rainbow, The (Lawrence), 3
Ramsey, F. P., 19
Ranke, Leopold von, 18
Ransom, John Crowe, 225
Rape of the Lock, The (Pope), 62
Rashomon (film), 284
Rasselas (Johnson), 236
Rationalism, 19, 255, 328, 351; Marxism and, 349, 390–91; moral optimism and, 57, 58; music and, 44, 104; mysticism and, 13–14, 283; poetry and, 310, 311; "super-rationalism," 245–46, 248; World War II and, 5, 6
Réage, Pauline, *Story of O*, 73, 74
Realism, 79, 105; naturalism and, 321–22, 332, 334, 341, 344; the novel and, 80, 81, 82, 83–84, 147, 283–84, 331, 387–89; socialist, 308, 318, 319, 329, 332, 341, 359
"Realism and Naturalism" (Asmus), 318
Recherche de l'Absolu, La (Balzac), 292–93
Recherche du temps perdu, À la (Proust), 336
Reinhardt, Max, 147
Reizov, Boris, *Balzac the Writer*, 317–18

Religion, 354; aesthetics and, 342–43, 344–45, 391. *See also* God; *and see specific faiths*
Rembrandt van Rijn, Harmenszoon, 22, 341
Renaissance, 5, 43, 58, 203. *See also specific centuries*
Renan, Ernest, 87; *Vie de Jésus*, 172
Rescue, The (Conrad), 282
Research, 55, 66–67
Revai, Joseph, 319, 320, 338; *Literature and Popular Democracy*, 319, 338
Revaluation (Leavis), 223, 228
Revelation, quoted, 195–96
Revised Standard Version of the Bible (1946), 193
Riccardo, David, 18–19
Richards, I. A., 57, 65, 226, 326; quoted, 67; *Practical Criticism*, 67
Richardson, Samuel, 389
Richmond Lecture (Leavis), 233–34, 238
Rieu, E. V., 216
Rilke, Rainer Maria, 28, 61, 89, 162; quoted, 48–49; Benjamin and, 314; *Duino Elegies*, 28, 97, 98; Lukács and, 336; *Malte Laurids Brigge*, 314; music and, 42, 45, 98, 250; *Sonnets to Orpheus*, 45, 89, 98; translation by, 215–16
Rimbaud, Arthur, 27–28, 47, 48, 62; *Un Saison en enfer*, 47
Ringelblum, Emmanuel, *Notes from the Warsaw Ghetto*, 161, 388
Rob Roy (Scott), 334
Robespierre, Maximilien, 367, 377
Robinson Crusoe (Defoe), 328, 387
Rolland, Romain, 29, 361; *Jean Christophe*, 272
Rolle, Richard, 188
Roman Orgy (Van Heller), 73
Romanticism, 8, 49, 340, 351; escapist, 332, 334; Finkelstein on, 316–17; of Malaparte, 362; Mérimée and, 262, 263, 264–65; music and, 43–46; Shakespearean criticism and, 199, 205
Romeo and Juliet (Shakespeare), 198, 209

419

Rommel, Erwin, 101
Rosbaud, Hans, 130
Rosenberg, Alfred, 110
Rousseau, Jean-Jacques, 240
Rousset, David, 164
Royal (British) Air Force, 150, 158
Rühle, Jürgen, *Literatur und Revolution*, 357–64
Russia, 4, 39, 62, 63, 234; anti-Semitism in, 140, 143, 144, 145, 148, 150, 152, 157, 158, 161, 378; *Carmen* and, 262; Central Committee, 366, 368; China and, 378; communications theory and, 65, 252; de-Stalinization and, 376–77; Fletcher in, 201; Hungarian uprising and, 337–39, 360; Jewish culture and, 147–48; literary criticism in, 305–24; nationalism of, 116, 119, 148, 153, 339, 352, 358, 359; Nazism and, 100, 101, 107, 359, 375–76; Western influence from, 362–64; World War I and, 98
Russian Realism in World Literature (Lukács), 331
Russian Revolution, 363, 365–66, 373; Churchill and, 371.
Rymer, Thomas, 238

S.S.-Staat (Kogon), 166
Sacher-Masoch, Leopold von, 71
Sacred and the Profane, The (Eliade), 252
Sade, Donatien Alphonse, Marquis de, 69, 71, 73, 74, 122; Durrell and, 285, 286; *Justine*, 73; *120 Days of Sodom*, 69
Sadism, 10, 61; anti-Semitic, 140–54, 155–68; eroticism and, 7, 76, 81; political, 4–5, 99–109, 114, 121, 122
Saint-Exupéry, Antoine de, *Vol de Nuit*, 388
Saint-Just, Louis Antoine Léon de, 265
Saint-Saëns, Camille, *Samson et Dalila*, 137
Saint-Simon, Louis de Rouvroy, Duc de, 372

Sainte-Beuve, Charles Augustin, 3, 222, 225, 263, 311, 325; on Flaubert, 334; Marxist criticism and, 322, 341, 352
Saintsbury, George, 57, 238, 345
Saison en enfer, Un (Rimbaud), 47
"*Sakrales Fragment: Ueber Schoenberg's Moses und Aron*" (Adorno), 127 *n*
Salammbô (Flaubert), 332, 333, 334
Salinger, J. P., 10, 290, 294
Salome (R. Strauss), 29, 137
Samson et Dalila (Saint-Saëns), 137
Sand, George, 263
Sandburg, Carl, 316
Sapientia Veterum, De (Bacon), 247
Sappho, 71
Sartre, Jean-Paul, 17–18, 65, 331; Lévi-Strauss and, 239, 240, 244; Marxism of, 312, 353, 359, 362; *Qu'est-que ce la littérature*, 65
Satie, Erik, 250
Saussure, Ferdinand de, 241
Schaff, Adam, 148
Schelling, Friedrich W. J. von, 330
Scherchen, Hermann, 130
Schiller, Friedrich von, 97, 305, 306, 319; *Kabale und Liebe*, 305; Lukács on, 311, 334, 335; on technology, 315
Schneider, David M., 242
Schoenberg, Arnold, 98, 127–39, 146, 316; *Der Biblische Weg*, 129; *Erwartung*, 130; *Four Pieces*, 129; *Die Glückliche Hand*, 130; *Die Jakobsleiter*, 129, 131; *Kol Nidre*, 129; language and, 51, 125, 127, 130–31; *Modern Psalms*, 129; *Moses und Aron*, 51, 127–39; *A Survivor from Warsaw*, 129
Schoenberg's "Moses und Aron" (Wörner), 127 *n*
Schuldlosen, Die (Broch), 88
Schwarz-Bart, André, *The Last of the Just*, 165
Schwierige, Der (Hofmannsthal), 50–51
Science: culture and, 6, 34–35, 64, 66, 76, 83, 233, 243–244, 325–26; Elizabethan, 201, 202; *Felix Krull* and, 274; harmony con-

Science (*continued*)
cept and, 42; industrial processes and, 314–15, 322; linguistics and, 14–16, 17, 31, 64, 242–43, 244, 251–57; literary study and, 57, 326–27, 328, 336; literature of, 84, 85; Lukács on, 342, 343; mathematical dominance of, 14–21; of mythology, 247–49; personal identity and, 386. *See also specific branches of science*

Score, The (periodical), 127 *n*

Scott, Walter, 63, 79, 262; *The Heart of Midlothian*, 333; Lukács on, 329, 333, 334; *Quentin Durward*, 333; *Rob Roy*, 334; *Waverley Novels*, 333

Scroll of Agony: The Warsaw Diary of Chaim Kaplan, 155, 159–64, 167, 168

Scrutiny (periodical), 230, 232

Sculpture, 22–23, 116, 133, 255

Sea Around Us, The (Carson), 389

Sebag, Lucien, *Marxisme et Structuralisme*, 245

Secret Sharer, The (Conrad), 230

Seele und die Formen, Die (Lukács), 342

Seghers, Anna, 353, 359, 362; *Der Ausflug der toten Mädchen*, 353

Seneca, *Hippolytus*, 215

Serge, Victor, 148

Seven Against Thebes (Aeschylus), 366

Sewell, Elizabeth, 249, 255; *The Orphic Voice*, 255

Sex, 10, 68–77; Durrell and, 283, 284–85; Golding and, 293; Mann's *Felix Krull* and, 273, 277–78; Plath and, 299

Sexus (Miller), 74

Shakespeare, William, 5, 6, 10, 56, 67, 118, 198–218, 319, 340; Brecht on, 309–10; *Comedy of Errors*, 201; *Coriolanus*, 209, 309; *Cymbeline*, 209–10; Dickens and, 235; Engels and, 306, 322; *Hamlet*, 10, 198, 202, 204, 207–08; on harmony, 42, 201; *Henry IV*, 204; Homer and, 182; Humanist tradition and,

Shakespeare (*continued*)
17, 66, 350; identity of, 171, 172, 173, 261; *King Lear*, 5, 198, 208, 209; Jewish culture and, 147; language and, 25, 26, 31, 32, 189, 190, 191, 198, 203–11, 255, 282, 333; Leavis on, 224, 226, 230, 237; *Love's Labour's Lost*, 58–59; *Macbeth*, 201, 202, 208, 230; McLuhan on, 257; *Measure for Measure*, 209; *The Merchant of Venice*, 42, 58–59, 201; *A Midsummer Night's Dream*, 209; *Othello*, 6, 198, 202; *Romeo and Juliet*, 198, 209; *Titus Andronicus*, 173; *Troilus and Cressida*, 201, 209

Shaw, George Bernard, 60, 200

Shelley, Percy Bysshe, 56, 62

Sheridan, Richard Brinsley, 83

Sholokhov, Mikhail Aleksandrovich, 318, 358

Siberia, 321, 370, 379

Sicily, 181, 184

Sidgwick, Henry, quoted, 57

Sidney, Philip, 191, 203

Silone, Ignazio, 359, 362

Simenon, Georges, 211

Simplicissimus (Grimmelshausen), 271

Sinclair, Upton, 359

Singer of Tales, The (Lord), 176

Slavonic languages, 125

Sleepwalkers, The (Broch), 88

Smith, Adam, 18

Smollett, Tobias, 271

Snow, C. P., 289; Leavis debate, 231–34, 238; on the two cultures, 16, 17, 233 *n*

Sobivor concentration camp, 166

Socialism, 153. *See also* Marxism; Nazism

Sociology: drama and, 391; linguistics and, 64, 241, 244–46, 250, 254–55; privacy and, 76, 255; Sartre and, 353; scientific method and, 245, 326; style and, 18, 19, 84, 85, 322–23, 328. *See also* Economics

Socrates, 36, 153, 254, 261

Solomon, King, 183

GEORGE STEINER

Born in Paris in 1929, George Steiner was educated in France, the United States, and England. After being a Rhodes Scholar at Oxford, and serving on the editorial staff of the London *Economist*, he became a member of the Institute for Advanced Study in Princeton. There he wrote *Tolstoy or Dostoevsky* and began *The Death of Tragedy*. These books have been translated into French, German, Italian, and other languages. They were followed by *Anno Domini*, a volume of three long stories. Mr. Steiner, who has taught at Princeton, Stanford, and Harvard, and at a number of European universities, is currently Schweitzer Visiting Professor at New York University. He makes his home in England, where he is Fellow and Director of English Studies at Churchill College, Cambridge. He is now engaged on "a very personal book," part fiction and part political essay.

Atheneum Paperbacks

LITERATURE AND THE ARTS

Atheneum Paperbacks

Atheneum Paperbacks

STUDIES IN AMERICAN NEGRO LIFE

Atheneum Paperbacks

Atheneum Paperbacks

Atheneum Paperbacks

Atheneum Paperbacks

POLITICAL SCIENCE